The Sporting News

SELECTS

BASEBALL'S 50 GREATEST GAMES

The Sporting News

SELECTS

BASEBALL'S 50 GREATEST GAMES

Written by
LOWELL REIDENBAUGH

Co-Editors
JOE HOPPEL
MIKE NAHRSTEDT

Design
BILL PERRY

President and Chief Executive Officer
RICHARD WATERS

Editor/The Sporting News
TOM BARNIDGE

Director of Books and Periodicals
RON SMITH

Published in the United States by THE SPORTING NEWS   A Times Mirror
Publishing Co., 1212 North Lindbergh Boulevard,   Company
St. Louis, Missouri 63132.

Library of Congress Catalog Card Number: 86-61256

ISBN: 0-89204-224-9
10 9 8 7 6 5 4 3 2 1

First Edition

Contents

Introduction

The firm but gentle tug that baseball exerts on the American public is unrelated to the game's role as the oldest professional team sport or to its willingness to grant the richest player contracts.

Rather, it is due to the fact that virtually every citizen, regardless of gender, has gripped a shaft of wood at some point in his formative years and attempted to arrest the flight of a thrown missile.

For a precious few, the national pastime affords widespread acclaim and boundless wealth. For the vast majority, though, the early struggles are nothing more than a screening process, a system to determine that a youth's chances for success are infinitely greater elsewhere.

The realization that the young hero worshiper is not qualified for big-league stardom is rarely easy to accept. After all, did he not once collect a game-winning triple in Little League ball, or make a leaping, game-saving catch against the fence while patrolling center field for P.S. No. 84?

Affection for baseball, born in early years, seldom flickers or dies. It endures wherever the boy dreamer sets foot. He may pilot an 18-wheel rig across the nation's interstates or he may deliver profound opinions from the judicial bench. Whatever his lot, the love affair lives on.

Years pass. The truck driver and the judge, too old now for active participation in their favorite game, adopt other means for expressing their affection. From a seat in the bleachers or in a luxury box, they watch proficient major leaguers at play and they recall their own ineptitude.

With their zeal undimmed, they sit in watchful expectancy, waiting for the unexpected. Unpredictability, after all, is one of the charms of this game. Who knows when the home team's .200 hitter, trying to check his swing, might bloop a double to the opposite field and transform imminent defeat into victory. Or when the visiting team's Gold Glove-winning shortstop will kick a crucial routine grounder.

More years slip by, and the designated fan accumulates his own gallery of memorable games. Few others may agree with his choices, but it matters little. The fan need answer only to himself.

Given time to spare and proper inspiration, a fan might attempt to attach a relationship between the memorable games. With nothing at stake except personal enjoyment, the fan may abandon such a project. Who cares, anyway?

But in the grander scope, there are those who care, like the management team at The Sporting News. After 12 decades of major league baseball, it was decided that the time was right to distill "The 50 Greatest Games" out of the tens of thousands that have been played. This was the year to let the world know what some cognoscenti regarded as baseball's most remarkable contests.

This volume was still in its early stages when it was determined that all games could not be lumped together. In fairness to the entries, classifications had to be devised so that games could be judged and rated against their own kind.

It would be grossly unjust, for instance, to compare Bobby Thomson's "Shot Heard 'Round the World" with Carl Hubbell's spectacular strikeout pitching in the second All-Star Game.

Likewise, Bill Wambsganss' unassisted triple play in the 1920 World Series could not be measured against the 26-inning, 1-1 tie pitched by Joe Oeschger and Leon Cadore during the same season. Nor could Jackie Robinson's debut in the majors be judged against Jim Bottomley's 12-RBI performance in a 1924 game.

After all, the Thomson drama unfolded with the National League pennant on the line; the ninth-inning heroics in a contest of such magnitude made the October 3, 1951, Giants-Dodgers clash a truly *memorable game.* On the other hand, Hubbell's performance, as astonishing as it was, did not decide a pennant or a World Series; in fact, it didn't even decide the outcome of the 1934 midsummer classic, as King Carl's National League teammates frittered away a 4-0 lead and ended up losing. Clearly, though, Hubbell's feat of striking out five of the other league's greatest stars in succession is a *single-game performance* that ranks among the best of baseball's glorious moments.

Game 5 of the 1920 World Series was not devoid of feats beyond Wambsganss' defensive gem, but the fact remains that the play—and not the game—is what rates a special niche in baseball history. In contrast, the game was the thing—all 26 grueling innings of it, all the ebbs and flows therein—when Oeschger and Cadore battled and battled and battled.

Bottomley, of course, drew raves for a sensational one-man effort against the Dodgers. But the game in which the Cardinals' Sunny Jim excelled wasn't exactly a classic struggle—the Cards frolicked, 17-3. But from the moment Robinson stepped on the Ebbets Field turf on April 15, 1947, and cracked the majors' modern racial barrier, the contest was instantly meaningful. Unquestionably, it was a *significant game.*

Accordingly, three categories were devised for this book. One was titled "The 20 Most Memorable Games." Here, Thomson's heart-stopping home run in the '51 National League playoffs could be rated alongside Don Larsen's perfect game in the 1956 World Series and Harvey Haddix's 12 perfect innings of pitching in 1959.

A second division, labeled "The Top 20 Performances," was created. Into this bin were tossed the 1974 game in which Henry Aaron clouted his record 715th home run, Roger Maris' 61st-homer game in 1961 and Babe Ruth's two Series games in which he slammed three home runs.

The third classification pertained to "The 10 Most Significant Games." Here, Robinson's breaking of the color line could be rated with the first night game and the initial contests in the modern World Series and All-Star Game. As might expected, the significant-game list reflects baseball's breakthrough achievements, events that unalterably changed the sport's direction.

After the numerous nominations for the three departments were submitted, they were referred to a 10-man electorate from the editorial staff of The Sporting News. To those "experts" went the chore of not only reducing the games to the prescribed number in each classification, but to rank them in the order of importance as well.

The panel was not confined to a single generation. Some members recalled in minute detail Carlton Fisk's past-midnight home run that won a World Series game for the Red Sox in 1975.

Others remembered clearly Bill Mazeroski's dramatic homer that clinched a World Series championship for the Pirates in 1960.

There were those who recalled with equal clarity Cookie Lavagetto's pinch double in the ninth inning that shattered a no-hit bid and won a pulsating World Series decision for the Dodgers at Ebbets Field in 1947.

And then there were voters with elongated memories. They recalled all too well how four Cub pitchers—Charlie Root, Art Nehf, Sheriff Blake and Pat Malone—tried to stem the tide of a Philadelphia A's assault that produced 10 runs in the seventh

inning of a World Series game in 1929.

The results of the poll are not expected to meet with unchallenged acceptance. Controversy is certain to arise, loud and heated. The Sporting News would not wish it otherwise. Disputes existed in these offices before "The 50 Greatest Games" were determined. Dissension is a healthful sign, an indication that all continues well in the baseball community.

In the months that this volume was in preparation, a number of historic gems were unearthed. What, for example, happened to Mrs. Ray Chapman and the child she was carrying after the Cleveland infielder was beaned fatally in 1920?

And why was it that five umpires worked the final game at Ebbets Field, Brooklyn, in 1957? Why was it such an unlikely number, and not the more conventional four or six arbiters?

After the 50 top games were selected and rated in order of importance, composition on this work proceeded smoothly, sometimes even snappily. The first two sections were researched, written and edited. Text and photographs were assembled in page forms, and there appeared to be no possibility of a delay or revision in plans. Meeting the deadline would be the proverbial piece of pastry.

Or so it seemed until a night in late April.

At that time, a young righthander wearing the colors of the Boston Red Sox established a major league record for a nine-inning game by striking out 20 Seattle batters. Unquestionably, this achievement by Roger Clemens represented one of "The Top 20 Performances" of all time. It had to be included in this anthology.

That being the case, should the book's title be changed to "The 51 Greatest Games"? Never, counseled the marketing department. It wouldn't fly. One individual feat had to go to support the original title and to meet the physical specifications of the book as originally determined.

Very well, one chapter would be expurgated. Which one? Who would wield the knife? Volunteers, step up.

Utter silence permeated the office. Nobody was so daring, or foolish.

Ultimately, one in authority accepted the challenge. He deleted the surplus chapter. Work was resumed, and the deadline was met with days to spare.

Which monumental achievement wound up on the composing-room floor? Whose singular accomplishment would have been thoroughly documented here? Who would have been recognized on these pages if just one more Mariner had popped out or grounded to an infielder? Whose feat was relegated to No. 21 in the second category because of Roger Clemens' superlative effort at Fenway Park?

That's our secret.

BASEBALL'S

20

MOST MEMORABLE GAMES

The Miracle
At Coogan's Bluff

A boisterous euphoria engulfed Ebbets Field in the late afternoon of August 11, 1951. Dem Bums, more formally known as the Brooklyn Dodgers, had just split a doubleheader with the Boston Braves, while across the river at the Polo Grounds, the Giants had suffered a 4-0 shutout at the hands of Robin Roberts and the Philadelphia Phillies.

The Dodgers' lead in the National League pennant race was a comfortable 13 games. And among the 22,308 fans filing out of Ebbets Field, who could forget the confident tone in Chuck Dressen's voice a few weeks earlier when, following the Dodgers' three-game sweep of the second-place Giants, the chipper little skipper had declared: "We knocked 'em out. They won't bother us anymore."

The Dodgers were all but assured of the flag, a flag they had been deprived of the preceding year when, in this very park, Dick Sisler had hit a dramatic 10th-inning home run to give the Phillies the pennant on the last day of the season. Optimism was rampant in Flatbush and few, if any, were alarmed in the days that followed when the Dodgers visited the Polo Grounds and were whipped by scores of 4-2, 3-1 and 2-1. The Giants had narrowed the Dodgers' lead to 9½ games, but few could envision Dem Bums squandering that kind of an edge, even with 6½ weeks of the season remaining.

But sinister influences were at work. While the Dodgers won 10 of their next 16 games, the Giants completed a stretch in which they won 16 consecutive games, all but three at home. That streak brought the Giants to within five lengths of the Dodgers.

Brooklyn subsequently widened the gap to seven games on September 1, the date the Dodgers invaded the Polo Grounds for the start of a two-game series. Ralph Branca and Don Newcombe were primed and ready to pitch for the Dodgers, Sal Maglie and Jim Hearn for the Giants. But it was no contest on either day. Maglie, supported by outfielder Don Mueller's three home runs and five runs batted in, won the first game, 8-1, and Hearn, boosted by another five RBIs and two homers from

Brooklyn's Andy Pafko watches Bobby Thomson's pennant-winning drive disappear into the crowd.

Instant hero Bobby Thomson is mobbed at home plate by jubilant members of the New York Giants.

Mueller, turned in an 11-2 victory the next day. The margin once again was trimmed to five games.

When the contenders launched their final western trips on September 11, Brooklyn enjoyed a 5½-game edge over New York. By going 6-3 in nine games against St. Louis, Chicago, Pittsburgh and Cincinnati (while the Dodgers went 5-4 against the same opponents), the Giants shaved another game from their deficit. The pursuers were drawing ever closer to the pursued, but the calendar favored Brooklyn. As of September 20, the Dodgers (92-52) had lost six fewer games than the Giants (89-58) and had 10 games remaining, New York only seven. With a 4½-game lead, the Dodgers clearly had all the odds in their favor. A miracle was the Giants' only hope, but it was taking form.

Over the next four days, the Dodgers lost two of three games to the Phillies at Ebbets Field while the Giants swept three encounters with the Braves. Just like that, the contenders were separated by only 2½ games. A day later, when Hearn hurled the Giants to a 5-1 victory in Philadelphia and the Dodgers dropped a doubleheader to Warren Spahn and Jim Wilson in Boston, the Brooklyn lead shriveled to one game.

Only five days of the season remained. Both teams won on September 26, but the Giants were idle the next two days while the Dodgers were engaged in Boston and Philadelphia. On September 27, the Braves beat Brooklyn's Preacher Roe, 4-3, and the next night the Phillies, after trailing 3-0 in the sixth inning, bounced back to post a 4-3 victory on Andy Seminick's ninth-inning homer.

The last vestige of the Dodgers' once formidable lead had evaporated: The teams were deadlocked for first place with 94-58 records. A misstep by either team in the last two games could spell failure, but neither club faltered. As the Giants took two from Boston, the Dodgers captured a pair in Philadelphia, the finale on second baseman Jackie Robinson's home run in the 14th inning.

The Giants had done it. They had posted a 37-7 record over their last 44 games, including victories in 12 of their last 13 contests, to overcome a 13-game deficit in the standings. The Dodgers, meanwhile, had gone 26-22 during that same span. The result was identical 96-58 records for both clubs at the end of the regular season.

The Giants, however, had not yet won the right to go to the World Series. Their remarkable comeback would all be for naught if they failed to win two out of three games in a playoff for the N.L.

pennant. Only once before—when the Dodgers and the Cardinals were tied at the end of the 1946 season —had a playoff been necessary in the senior circuit. So, all eyes focused on Ebbets Field on October 1 as Dressen's Dodgers hosted Leo Durocher's Giants to determine which team would meet the Yankees in the World Series.

The home-field advantage didn't help the Dodgers as the first game produced a 3-1 New York victory, with third baseman Bobby Thomson and left fielder Monte Irvin clouting homers in support of Hearn's five-hit pitching. When the series shifted to the Polo Grounds on October 2, the Giants were similarly stymied at home. They collected only six hits off rookie Clem Labine, who posted a 10-0 victory behind a 13-hit attack that included home runs by Robinson, Gil Hodges, Andy Pafko and Rube Walker.

With the series tied at one game apiece, the N.L. pennant race came down to one final game at the Polo Grounds. The October 3 contest matched Maglie and Newcombe. For seven innings the right-handers dueled on even terms, each permitting one run. The Dodgers scored first, pushing across a run in the first inning after a pair of walks by Maglie set up a run-scoring single by Robinson. Newcombe held that 1-0 lead until the seventh, when the Giants evened the score on a

double by Irvin, a sacrifice by first baseman Whitey Lockman and a run-scoring fly ball by Thomson. But in the top of the eighth, the Dodgers tagged Maglie for three runs. Singles by shortstop Pee Wee Reese and center fielder Duke Snider put runners at first and third with one out, and Reese scored and Snider advanced to third when Maglie threw a wild pitch. The other two Dodger runs came when Maglie surrendered a walk and singles by left fielder Pafko and third baseman Billy Cox. That was it for Maglie, who was replaced in the ninth by right-hander Larry Jansen.

With Brooklyn holding a 4-1 lead after eight innings and Big Newk coasting on a four-hitter, the spirits of the Dodger partisans in the crowd of 34,320 took flight. It appeared to all that the Giants' good fortune finally had run out. In the press box, writers already were being informed where they could procure credentials for the Brooklyn portion of the World Series.

But then, like all bona fide miracles, it happened. Shortstop Alvin Dark, leading off the last half of the ninth inning, beat out an infield single. Right fielder Mueller followed with a ground single to right that sent Dark to third. A murmur of

Bobby Thomson makes an encore appearance for excited Giants fans at New York's Polo Grounds.

expectancy arose from the crowd, which was evenly split between Dodgers and Giants fans.

Newcombe then induced Irvin to foul out to first baseman Hodges. As Lockman, the next batter, walked toward the plate, he mused to himself, "If I hit one out of here, the score is tied." The first pitch from Newcombe, however, caught the outside corner of the plate for a called strike, and the lefthanded batter abandoned all hope for an inside pitch that he could pull into the beckoning right-field seats.

When Newk's second pitch headed for the outside corner of the plate, Lockman slapped a double to left field. Dark scored easily and Mueller, running full throttle to beat left fielder Pafko's throw, slid heavily into third base, injuring an ankle. He was replaced by Clint Hartung.

Dressen had seen enough. The Brooklyn manager wanted a replacement for Newcombe, so he phoned the bullpen. "Branca is popping the ball," coach Clyde Sukeforth reported. "(Carl) Erskine's not at his best."

"Gimme Branca," Dressen ordered.

Branca's assignment was to protect the Dodgers' precarious 4-2 lead by disposing of Bobby Thomson, a Glasgow-born Scot who had batted .357 after being moved from center field to third base on July

OCTOBER 3, 1951									
Brooklyn	ab	r	h	rbi	New York	ab	r	h	rbi
Furillo, rf	5	0	0	0	Stanky, 2b	4	0	0	0
Reese, ss	4	2	1	0	Dark, ss	4	1	1	0
Snider, cf	3	1	2	0	Mueller, rf	4	0	1	0
Robinson, 2b	2	1	1	1	Hartung, ph	0	1	0	0
Pafko, lf	4	0	1	1	Irvin, lf	4	1	1	0
Hodges, 1b	4	0	0	0	Lockman, 1b	3	1	2	1
Cox, 3b	4	0	2	1	Thomson, 3b	4	1	3	4
Walker, c	4	0	1	0	Mays, cf	3	0	0	0
Newcombe, p	4	0	0	0	Westrum, c	0	0	0	0
Branca, p	0	0	0	0	Rigney, ph	1	0	0	0
					Noble, c	0	0	0	0
					Maglie, p	2	0	0	0
					Thompson, ph	1	0	0	0
					Jansen, p	0	0	0	0
Totals	34	4	8	3	Totals	30	5	8	5

Brooklyn ....1 0 0   0 0 0   0 3 0—4
New York ....0 0 0   0 0 0   1 0 4—5
One out when winning run scored.

Brooklyn	IP	H	R	ER	BB	SO
Newcombe	8⅓	7	4	4	2	2
Branca (L)	0*	1	1	1	0	0
New York	IP	H	R	ER	BB	SO
Maglie	8	8	4	4	4	6
Jansen (W)	1	0	0	0	0	0

*Pitched to one batter in ninth.

DP—Brooklyn 2. LOB—Brooklyn 7, New York 3. 2B—Thomson, Irvin, Lockman. SH—Lockman. WP—Maglie. T—2:28. A—34,320.

Giants Owner Horace Stoneham (left) and Manager Leo Durocher (right) celebrate the thrill of victory made possible by Bobby Thomson's dramatic home run.

...WHEN THOMSON HIT HIS FAMOUS HOMER, WE FELT IT CLEAR OUT HERE ON THE WEST COAST! —BIGGEST THRILL? **THAT WAS IT!!**

KARL HUBENTHAL
LOS ANGELES
CALIFORNIA

23   H.R.

But the impact of Thomson's homer also was felt outside New York, as evidenced by this cartoon.

New York's Staten Island was one of several places that honored Thomson as a conquering hero.

20. Durocher moved Thomson to make room for a 20-year-old rookie named Willie Mays. Mays was on deck, but Branca's immediate concern was Thomson.

The righthander's first pitch was a called strike. Strategy dictated an inside pitch next in order to set the batter up for a curve. Branca threw a fastball, high and tight, just where he wanted it. Ordinarily, such a delivery would handcuff Thomson, or better yet, he'd take it for a ball. But on this late Wednesday afternoon, he drew back from the plate and swung. Bat met ball, and in the radio booth Russ Hodges watched the ball arch toward left field.

"There's a long fly," the veteran announcer reported almost impassively. "It's gonna be . . . I believe . . . the Giants win the pennant, the Giants win the pennant, the Giants win the pennant! Bobby hit

Bobby Thomson and pitching victim Ralph Branca went on to become close friends.

that ball into the lower deck of the left-field stands!"

On the pitching mound, Branca stood dazed, paralyzed, unable to absorb the impact of the Giants' incredible 5-4 victory. From the New York dugout, second baseman Eddie Stanky bounded onto the field and raced to the third-base coaching box, where he wrestled joyfully with Durocher. Thomson, whose first impression was that he had smacked an extra-base hit off the wall, watched Pafko gaze up helplessly. Seeing that, he began a leaping trot around the bases, followed closely by Robinson, who wanted to make certain that Bobby touched every base in order.

In the swirling bedlam, Thomson eventually arrived at home plate, where he was gathered up by hysterical teammates and carried, Caesar-like, to the center-field clubhouse. There, from the top of the wooden steps, he acknowledged cheers from adoring subjects far into the thickening twilight.

On the fringe of the throng, Carl Hubbell turned to a companion. "We won't live long enough," the pitching artist of an earlier Giants age said, "to see anything like it again."

As newspapermen frantically tore up copy made obsolete by one swing of Thomson's bat, the Dodgers went into their death march, trooping de-

jectedly off the field. "One of the saddest sights I've ever seen greeted me," a veteran Boston columnist recorded upon entering the Brooklyn clubhouse. "There was an upper level and a lower level, joined by a broad set of steps. Ralph Branca lay on these steps face down, his feet on the floor, his head buried in his hands on the top step."

In the aftermath of "The Miracle of Coogan's Bluff," Thomson and Branca, who had little more than a nodding acquaintance previously, met frequently at public functions. A warm friendship blossomed as they golfed together and, in response to ceaseless grilling, occasionally re-enacted the moment that projected them into the national spotlight. Faced with these constant reminders, Branca, later a successful insurance executive, and Thomson, a representative of a wood pulp company, formulated philosophical attitudes toward the event.

"Why did such a thing happen?" Thomson often wondered aloud of his three-run homer. "I don't know; it was just meant to be, I suppose."

Branca, a superb pitcher who had won 21 games at the age of 21 in 1947, came to regard his role as a blessing in disguise. "If it hadn't been for that homer," he reasoned, "who would remember Ralph Branca?"

Don Larsen's Perfect Afternoon

The scoreboard tells all as Don Larsen throws the final pitch of his 1956 World Series perfecto.

On the night of October 7, 1956, a cab bearing three passengers rumbled through the streets of New York City. As the taxi neared its destination, the tallest of the occupants turned to one of the others.

"I'm gonna beat those guys tomorrow," he said, "and I'm just liable to pitch a no-hitter."

"A four-hitter should be good enough," replied the other man, a newspaper reporter.

"No," said the first, "I feel that I have a no-hitter in me."

As the cab stopped in front of the midtown hotel, the journalist looked at his watch. It was 12:10 a.m., 10 minutes after curfew for his 6-foot-4 companion, a pitcher with the New York Yankees.

The perfect celebration began with catcher Yogi Berra jumping into Don Larsen's arms . . .

"Hope no one sees you coming in at this hour," Arthur Richman of the New York Mirror said.

"So what," Don Larsen responded. "I'm gonna whip them anyway."

The promise to "whip them" smacked of beery bravado inasmuch as the righthander had failed to survive the second inning when he started the second game of the World Series against the Brooklyn Dodgers. His quick removal by Manager Casey Stengel had rankled Larsen. Granted, he carried a major league career record of 30 wins and 40 losses into Game 5 of the Series. And it was true that he had won only 11 games during the regular season. But Larsen reminded detractors that he had been the Yankees' most effective pitcher the last month of the season, concluding the 1956 campaign with four consecutive victories. He no longer was the hurler, he contended, who had lost 21 games, the most in the major leagues, while pitching for Baltimore two years earlier.

Larsen, an Indiana native who finished high school in California, was regarded widely as a vastly talented individual who enjoyed nothing more than an evening on the town spent quaffing beers with congenial friends. He would be a guaranteed success, it was agreed, if he would only concentrate on the art of pitching and abandon his role as a real-life Li'l Abner.

Larsen's mound opponent on October 8, a chilly Monday afternoon at Yankee Stadium, was a hard-bitten righthander who had compiled a 13-5 record for the Dodgers in 1956. Sal Maglie, nicknamed "The Barber" because he loved to give batters a close shave with pitches that were high and tight, was at his best in crucial games, and this was a critical contest. The winning team would take a lead of three games to two in the Series.

With 64,519 fans looking on, Larsen breezed through the first inning, retiring second baseman Jim Gilliam and shortstop Pee Wee Reese on called third strikes and center fielder Duke Snider

. . . and picked up steam with the arrival of other Yankee coaches and teammates from the dugout and other positions on the field.

on a liner to Hank Bauer in right field.

In that Reese took Larsen to a full count before fanning, his at-bat was significant. As the Yankee Stadium crowd was about to witness, Larsen had pinpoint control that afternoon, and no other Dodger batter would reach three balls against him the rest of the way.

Jackie Robinson, leading off the second inning for Brooklyn, smashed a line drive off third baseman Andy Carey's glove. But the ball caromed directly to shortstop Gil McDougald, who threw out the Dodger third baseman by half a step. After first baseman Gil Hodges struck out on a low outside curve, Larsen retired left fielder Sandy Amoros on a pop fly to second baseman Billy Martin, who fell down while backpedaling but held onto the ball.

The third inning started with a fly ball off the bat of Dodgers right fielder Carl Furillo, but his shot was hauled in by Bauer. Catcher Roy Campanella went down swinging and Maglie hit the first pitch to center fielder Mickey Mantle for the third out.

Gilliam was easy leading off the fourth inning, grounding out to second base on the first pitch. Reese, trying to hold back on his swing, went out the same way. Snider proved more difficult and forced Larsen to make six pitches before taking a called third strike.

The crowd started to stir. This was not the same Larsen who had been shelled by the Dodgers three days earlier. His breaking pitches were snapping into catcher Yogi Berra's mitt. He was working the corners. His control was nigh infallible. He had retired 12 consecutive batters. How long could he continue?

At that point, the same question could have been asked of Maglie. Entering the bottom of the fourth, the Barber had retired all nine Yankees he had faced, and after setting down Bauer and first baseman Joe Collins, he was within one out of matching Larsen batter for batter. But with two out, Mantle clouted a home run just inside the right-field foul pole, and Larsen returned to the mound with the narrowest of leads.

He retired Robinson on a fly to right field before Hodges, who had smacked 32 home runs during the season, hit a drive to deep left-center field. A gasp arose from the spectators, then a cheer as Mantle snared the ball with a backhanded catch. Amoros then rolled out to Martin at second. Five perfect innings! In the radio and television booths, announcers reported the embryonic no-hitter, no

longer fearful of the age-old jinx about mentioning a no-hitter in progress.

They also discussed his unconventional delivery: He didn't use a windup. It was something Larsen had decided to try near the end of the season.

"The pitcher can hide the ball better," he later explained. "It keeps the coaches from calling the pitches. And it keeps the batter on his toes. The batter has got to be ready."

Though his new approach had failed miserably in Game 2 of the Series, it appeared to be working wonders in Game 5. In the sixth inning, Martin retreated into shallow right and then shallow center to haul in pop flies by Furillo and Campanella, respectively, and Maglie fanned. Larsen had gone through the Brooklyn lineup twice without anyone reaching base.

Larsen got a little more breathing room in the home half of the sixth. Carey led off with a single and advanced to second on Larsen's sacrifice bunt. Bauer then singled to left, scoring Carey and extending the Yankees' lead to 2-0. Collins also singled as Bauer scooted around to third. But Maglie averted further disaster by getting Mantle to ground out to Hodges,

Don Larsen's "poifeck game" againt the Dodgers was too much for cartoonist Willard Mullin to resist.

who stepped on first base and then whipped the ball to Campanella to trap Bauer in a rundown.

Nevertheless, Larsen's lead had doubled. But so had the pressure under which he was laboring. A roar accompanied every pitch. Wild applause greeted every putout.

The pesky Gilliam opened the seventh inning with a hard smash to shortstop, where McDougald fielded the ball on a short hop and threw out the batter. Reese and Snider presented no problems, each lifting an outfield fly on the second pitch— Reese to center and Snider to Enos Slaughter in left. For Larsen and the Yankees, only six more outs to go!

The cacophony swelled. Conversations were conducted in shouts, if it all. Only Don James Larsen seemed impervious to the drama raging around him. Between innings, Larsen felt the need to take a quick smoke. He ducked into the runway behind the dugout, where he encountered Mantle. "Think I'll get the no-hitter?" the

Dodger loser Sal Maglie congratulates Don Larsen.

flippant 27-year-old hurler asked. Shocked at Larsen's blatant disregard for no-hit tradition, Mantle shot his teammate a horrified glance and resumed his seat on the bench.

Robinson, ever dangerous and unpredictable at the plate, led off the Brooklyn eighth. Jackie took a called strike and fouled off a pitch, then grounded back to Larsen, who flipped to Collins. Hodges was next. The big first baseman ran the count to 2-and-2 before rapping a sharp drive to the left side of the infield. But Carey stepped nimbly to his left and caught the low liner. Amoros then took a called strike before flying to Mantle in center field.

Larsen, Bauer and Collins were set down on strikes in the eighth, giving Maglie five strikeouts for the game. Maglie also had surrendered only five hits, including a single by Martin in the seventh. But on a day when World Series history was to be made, anything short of perfection simply wouldn't do.

When the Yankees took the field for the ninth inning, Berra gave his batterymate an encouraging slap on the rump and said, "Let's get the first one." Larsen obliged and retired Furillo, who fouled off four pitches, on a fly ball to right field.

Next up was Campanella. The slugging catcher fouled off a pitch before grounding out to second base. Only one out to go and Larsen, the blithe spirit with the sub-.500 pitching record, would reign supreme among pitching immortals.

The 27th batter scheduled to face Larsen was Maglie, but Dodgers Manager Walter Alston, still hoping for a rally to overcome the 2-0 deficit, instead sent pinch-hitter Dale Mitchell to the plate. Mitchell, a lefthanded swinger, was familiar with Larsen from his days as an American Leaguer with Cleveland.

"He really scared me," Larsen later related. "I knew how much pressure he was under. He must have been paralyzed. That made two of us."

OCTOBER 8, 1956									
Brooklyn	ab	r	h	rbi	New York	ab	r	h	rbi
Gilliam, 2b	3	0	0	0	Bauer, rf	4	0	1	1
Reese, ss	3	0	0	0	Collins, 1b	4	0	1	0
Snider, cf	3	0	0	0	Mantle, cf	3	1	1	1
Robinson, 3b	3	0	0	0	Berra, c	3	0	0	0
Hodges, 1b	3	0	0	0	Slaughter, lf	2	0	0	0
Amoros, lf	3	0	0	0	Martin, 2b	3	0	1	0
Furillo, rf	3	0	0	0	McDougald, ss	2	0	0	0
Campanella, c	3	0	0	0	Carey, 3b	3	1	1	0
Maglie, p	2	0	0	0	Larsen, p	2	0	0	0
Mitchell, ph	1	0	0	0					
Totals	27	0	0	0	Totals	26	2	5	2

Brooklyn	0	0	0	0	0	0	0	0	0—0
New York	0	0	0	1	0	1	0	0	x—2

Brooklyn	IP	H	R	ER	BB	SO
Maglie (L)	8	5	2	2	2	5
New York	IP	H	R	ER	BB	SO
Larsen (W)	9	0	0	0	0	7

DP—Brooklyn 2. LOB—Brooklyn 0, New York 3. HR—Mantle. SH—Larsen. T—2:06. A—64,519.

Larsen's first pitch was wide of the plate. The second, a slider, caught the strike zone. The third, a fastball, was swung at and missed. On the fourth pitch, Mitchell sliced the ball foul into the stands.

Larsen fidgeted on the mound, preparing to deliver his 97th pitch of the game. "I blacked out," he recounted later. "I don't remember making the last pitch."

Larsen fired. The ball appeared to head for the outside of the plate. Mitchell cocked his bat as though to swing, then held up.

Babe Pinelli, umpiring behind the plate for the final time in his distinguished career, watched the ball intently. His right arm shot outward. If he called "Yer out!" his voice was drowned out by the roar of the multitudes who interpreted the gesture perfectly and turned Yankee Stadium into bedlam.

As Mitchell turned to protest the call—and discovered Pinelli running off the field—Larsen snapped from his temporary fog and into the world of reality. Teammates descended on him from all directions, but the first to arrive was Berra, who leaped at the pitcher and wrapped his legs around Larsen's midsection. Security guards then formed a passageway for the hysterical Yankees to race to their clubhouse, where Larsen stood for hours, patiently answering all manner of queries.

After answering the last of the questions and taking a shower, Larsen returned to his hotel apartment, only to discover the premises overrun with uninvited guests. All were eager to share in his glory, some to suggest ways to convert his new-found fame to instant wealth. Finally, Larsen took to the streets to celebrate at his favorite oasis on 57th Street. But once more the sycophants made the place untenable. In the company of a friend and two female companions, he went to the Copacabana, where comedian Joe E. Lewis summoned Larsen to the spotlight.

There was no escape from the spotlight that night, but the heretofore undistinguished pitcher didn't really mind all the attention.

"If you think I'm not enjoying all this," Larsen whispered to a friend, "you're crazy. Just imagine. Last night I was a bum. Tonight, everyone wants to meet me."

After answering endless questions, acknowledging interminable applause and signing innumerable autographs, Larsen and his party ambled out of the nightclub and into the gray light of dawn.

As quickly as Larsen's star brightened the firmament, so swiftly it faded from view. After sparking the Yankees to their seven-game triumph over the Dodgers, Larsen never again approached his perfect-game form. He won 10 games for New York in 1957, but that was the last time he reached double figures. The Yankees traded him in 1959, and he pitched for six more major league clubs, drifted into the minors and finally retired in 1968. He never did become a career .500 pitcher, and when he walked off the mound after throwing his last major league pitch for the Chicago Cubs in 1967, he took with him a lifetime 81-91 record.

"I still find it hard to believe I really pitched the perfect game," he said after retiring. "It's almost like a dream, like something that happened to somebody else."

But it didn't. It happened to Don Larsen, and on October 8, 1956, no one could dispute that he was on top of the world.

Don Larsen enjoys a post-perfect game moment with Yankee co-Owners Dan Topping and Del Webb.

Haddix Discovers Perfect Way to Lose

The long-distance telephone lines between Winston-Salem and St. Louis quivered with excitement in the summer of 1947.

In the North Carolina city, the business manager of the local Carolina League club rhapsodized over the talents of a little lefthander who was bewildering batters by the bushel.

"He can beat Brooklyn any day of the week," George Sisler Jr. bubbled.

In the Missouri port city, Joe Mathes listened attentively but with little taste for Sisler's zeal.

"Maybe he could win for one of our Triple-A clubs," the Cardinals' farm director replied, "but I don't think he would win with St. Louis. After all, George, did you ever hear of a pitcher jumping from a Class-C league to the majors and winning? Let's forget about the boy for the time being."

But Sisler was not allowed to forget. A few days later the 21-year-old phenom pitched the first game of a doubleheader against Danville. In the first inning he threw 11 consecutive strikes, two of them

Harvey Haddix still found reason to smile after his heartbreaking loss.

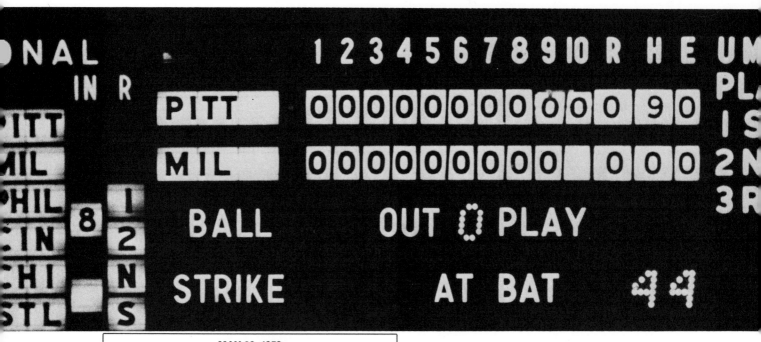

MAY 26, 1959								
Pittsburgh	ab	r	h	rbi	Milwaukee	ab	r	h	rbi
Schofield, ss	6	0	3	0	O'Brien, 2b	3	0	0	0
Virdon, cf	6	0	1	0	Rice, ph	1	0	0	0
Burgess, c	5	0	0	0	Mantilla, 2b	1	1	0	0
Nelson, 1b	5	0	2	0	Mathews, 3b	4	0	0	0
Skinner, lf	5	0	1	0	Aaron, rf	4	0	0	0
Mazeroski, 2b	5	0	1	0	Adcock, 1b	5	0	1	1
Hoak, 3b	5	0	2	0	Covington, lf	4	0	0	0
Mejias, rf	3	0	1	0	Crandall, c	4	0	0	0
Stuart, ph	1	0	0	0	Pafko, cf	4	0	0	0
Christopher, rf	1	0	0	0	Logan, ss	4	0	0	0
Haddix, p	5	0	1	0	Burdette, p	4	0	0	0
Totals	47	0	12	0	Totals	38	1	1	1

Pittsburgh .... 0 0 0   0 0 0   0 0 0   0 0 0   0—0
Milwaukee .... 0 0 0   0 0 0   0 0 0   0 0 0   1—1
Two out when winning run scored.

Pittsburgh	IP	H	R	ER	BB	SO
Haddix (L)	12⅔	1	1	0	1	8

Milwaukee	IP	H	R	ER	BB	SO
Burdette (W)	13	12	0	0	0	2

E—Hoak. DP—Milwaukee 3. LOB—Pittsburgh 8, Milwaukee 1. 2B—Adcock. SH—Mathews. T—2:54. A—19,194.

Milwaukee's scoreboard shows Harvey Haddix's progress through 9 ½ innings.

the time that Mathes was ready to abandon his mission, the pitcher arrived at the ball park. He somehow had received word that Mathes was in town to evaluate him. Sick or not, he did not intend to let the boss go home empty-handed.

Winston-Salem was trying to protect a half-game league lead, so Manager Zip Payne agreed to start the 5-foot-10, 170-pound youngster against the heavy-hitting Durham Bulls. In a box seat, Mathes sat motionless, his gaze trained on the subject of Sisler's fervor.

The hurler fanned the side in the first inning. Roughly five innings later, Mathes proclaimed Harvey Haddix "the greatest young pitcher I've ever seen." Despite being sick, Haddix went the distance and allowed only one hit, a seventh-inning double by the Durham manager, while striking out 19. He walked only three en route to the 5-0 victory.

At the close of the season, Haddix's record showed 19 victories and five defeats, 204 innings pitched, 268 strikeouts, 70 walks and a 1.90 earned-run average. He was named the Most Valuable Player in the Carolina League and earned a promotion to Columbus (American Association) the next year.

Haddix had signed a Columbus contract in 1943 after impressing a Cardinals scout at a tryout camp. Not yet 18, Harvey had yearned for an opportunity to begin his baseball career, but World War II was in progress and he received a deferment to work on his father's farm in Ohio.

After his spectacular season at Winston-Salem,

fouls, to strike out the side. He fanned the first two batters in the second inning and went on to a seven-inning no-hitter. In the abbreviated contest the youngster made 69 pitches, struck out 14 and let only one batter reach first base—on his own fielding error. It was his 15th victory of the season.

Again Sisler went to the telephone. He reported the no-hitter to Mathes and added, "I'm telling you again, this kid can win for you."

This time Mathes displayed more interest. After listening to Sisler's 10-minute eulogy, Mathes promised to visit Winston-Salem for a personal inspection of the organization's newest prodigy. On his arrival, however, Mathes learned that the pitcher was confined to bed with a temperature of 104 degrees.

According to doctors, the lefthander would be incapacitated for six or seven days. But just about

Haddix pitched for Columbus until 1950. His 18 victories, 2.70 ERA and 160 strikeouts in 1950 topped the American Association, where he picked up the nickname "Kitten" for his resemblance while pitching to Harry (The Cat) Brecheen. But while he was ripe for the majors, another deterrent barred his way. He entered military service in September 1950 and was not discharged until late in the 1952 season, just in time to post a 2-2 record for the St. Louis Cardinals.

Haddix disappointed no one in 1953, his first full major league season. He went 20-9, led the National League with six shutouts and came within a shade of hurling a no-hitter against Philadelphia. Haddix held the Phillies hitless for eight innings, but in the ninth, Richie Ashburn rapped a curve to right field for a single. Del Ennis later bounced another single through the middle before Haddix retired the side to protect a 2-0 victory.

Haddix never won 20 games again. Eighteen wins in 1954 were to be his highest total thereafter.

In May 1956, Haddix was traded to Philadelphia. In 1958 he wore a Cincinnati uniform, and the following year he was a member of the Pittsburgh Pirates, for whom he inscribed his most memorable achievement.

By May 26, 1959, Haddix had won three games and lost two. On that day, Harvey awakened at 7 a.m. in Pittsburgh in order to catch the Pirates' 10 a.m. flight to Milwaukee.

"When we got to Milwaukee, I headed straight for my hotel room and slept until 4," the pitcher recalled. "I got up, ate a steak and boarded the team bus for the ball park."

In the pregame clubhouse meeting, Haddix informed his teammates how he intended to pitch to the Braves. When the meeting ended, third baseman Don Hoak told Harvey: "That was a pretty good rundown. If you pitch that way, you'll have a no-hitter."

Haddix laughed. He wasn't thinking no-hitter. All he wanted to do was win. The circumstances, however, were not favorable. It was cloudy and gloomy, with a threat of rain in the air, and Haddix was not feeling in the peak of condition. "I felt a cold coming on," he said, "and had a touch of a sore throat."

Despite his infirmity, Haddix pitched as he had 12 years earlier when he arose from a sick bed in Winston-Salem. He was superb. In the first inning, he retired second baseman Johnny O'Brien on a grounder to shortstop Dick Schofield, third baseman Eddie Mathews on a liner to first base and right fielder Hank Aaron on a fly ball to center field.

The second inning proved equally routine. First baseman Joe Adcock struck out, left fielder Wes Covington grounded to second baseman Bill Mazeros-

Harvey Haddix and the Pittsburgh Pirates were the subjects of this 1959 Willard Mullin cartoon.

ki and catcher Del Crandall grounded to Hoak at third. Haddix breezed through the third frame, retiring center fielder Andy Pafko on a fly to right field, shortstop Johnny Logan on a liner to Schofield and Lew Burdette, his pitching opponent, on a called third strike.

The fourth inning came and went without mishap. O'Brien was called out on strikes and Mathews and Aaron flied to Bill Virdon in center field. Harvey, using an explosive fastball and a slider almost exclusively throughout the game, retired Adcock on a grounder to third and Covington and Crandall on drives to left fielder Bob Skinner in the fifth.

Fifteen batters had come and gone by this time, and Haddix was well aware that a no-hitter was building. "I knew I had a no-hitter because the scoreboard is in full view," he said, "but I wasn't so certain about it being a perfect game. . . . Somewhere along the way I thought somebody may have gotten on base."

In the sixth inning, Pafko popped to first baseman Rocky Nelson before Logan grounded deep in the hole to short, where Schofield fielded the ball and nipped the runner with a long throw. Burdette then fanned. A Mathews strikeout was sandwiched between groundouts to third by O'Brien and Aaron in the seventh.

In the Pittsburgh dugout, teammates gave Haddix a wide berth, fearful that the mere mention of a hitless game would jinx the hurler. Dick Groat, who did not play in the game because of a batting slump, more than once lighted a cigarette for Harvey between innings, then beat a hasty retreat lest the hoodoo remark escape his lips.

"I should have known something special was up," Haddix confessed, "but I was busy concentrating on the work at hand."

Entering the last half of the eighth frame, the 33-year-old Haddix was within six putouts of a perfect nine-inning no-hitter. The Pirates, however, also were being handcuffed by Burdette. The 32-year-old righthander effectively scattered the Pittsburgh hits —12, all singles, by the end of the game—and prevented any Pirates from crossing the plate. The only Pittsburgh rally had come in the third inning, when Hoak led off with an infield single and was forced at second by right fielder Roman Mejias. Haddix then rocketed a shot off Burdette's hand for another infield single, but Logan raced to pick up the ball behind the mound and whipped it to Mathews, who tagged out Mejias at third. Schofield followed with a single that would have scored Mejias had he not tried to take an extra base, and Virdon flied out to end the uprising. The Pirates' bats remained fairly quiet after that.

The scoreless deadlock prevailed through the eighth as Haddix struck out Adcock, Covington flied to left field and Crandall grounded to third. Haddix showed no symptoms of weakening in the ninth as Pafko struck out, Logan flied to left and Burdette fanned for the third time. As catcher Smoky Burgess flipped the ball to home-plate umpire Vinnie Smith and headed to the dugout for the start of the 10th inning, the 19,194 spectators at County Stadium gave Haddix a standing ovation in tribute to his flawless performance.

The Pirates failed to score in the top of the 10th. Del Rice batted for O'Brien to open the home half of the 10th inning and became the 28th consecutive batter to be retired when his long fly ball to center was caught by Virdon. Mathews also flied deep to Virdon, and Aaron rapped a grounder to shortstop that Schofield handled. The 11th inning was similarly non-productive as Adcock grounded to shortstop and Covington and Crandall flied to center. In the 12th inning, Pafko grounded out to Haddix, Logan flied to center field and Burdette smacked a grounder to Hoak, who made a great stop and threw out the pitcher.

By this time, Haddix had "lost track of the innings since the scoreboard only carries 10 innings," he said. His body, still feeling the effects of a cold, also was beginning to tire. Burdette, meanwhile, continued to match Haddix zero for zero. The Pirates were unable to mount any scoring threats, although pinch-hitter Dick Stuart's long drive to center field with one on in the 10th lifted the visitors' hopes until Pafko hauled in the ball at the fence.

After the Pirates were retired in the top of the 13th inning, Haddix faced his 37th batter, Felix Mantilla, who had replaced O'Brien at second base. A ground ball to third base seemed unlikely to break Harvey's perfect string, but Hoak, in his eagerness to preserve the pitcher's streak, threw low toward first base. Nelson was unable to dig it out and Mantilla was safe on the throwing error, thus becoming the Braves' first baserunner of the night. After picking up the ball, Nelson tagged Mantilla, insisting that the runner had made his turn toward second base, but umpire Frank Dascoli disallowed the claim.

Mathews sacrificed Mantilla to second, leaving first base open. In order to set up a double play, Haddix was told to walk Aaron, which he did. That brought up Adcock, who was yet to hit the ball beyond the infield. The first pitch to Adcock missed the strike zone. The second, a high slider, was rapped to deep right-center field, where Virdon made a desperate leap for the ball. It barely eluded his glove and fell just beyond the wire fence.

Mantilla scored easily. Aaron, thinking that the ball had dropped inside the fence and that the game was over when Mantilla crossed home plate, touched second base and then headed for the dugout. Adcock, running with his head down, passed second base. At the frantic urging of Milwaukee coaches, Aaron returned to the field and completed the tour of the bases, followed closely by Adcock.

Without question, the game was over, with Burdette the winner and Haddix, despite pitching 12 perfect innings and allowing just one hit in the 13th, the hard-luck loser. But what was the score? Was it 3-0, in recognition of Adcock's homer? Or 2-0, as the umpires ruled that night, because Adcock had passed Aaron on the bases, thus nullifying his run? Or 1-0, with only Mantilla's run counting? The issue was referred to Warren Giles. The next day, the N.L. president decided that the game would be recorded as a 1-0 Milwaukee victory. Giles ruled that even though Adcock had hit the ball over the fence, he was entitled only to a double for having passed Aaron on the bases and that the game therefore ended the moment Mantilla stepped on the plate.

In tribute to Haddix having pitched the majors'

Harvey Haddix pitched and sweated his way through 12 perfect innings, only to lose in the 13th.

first "perfect extra-inning game," Giles later presented the pitcher a silver tray and 12 silver goblets, one for each flawless inning. The names of the batters he retired in each inning were inscribed on each respective cup.

Immediately after the game, Haddix was far more disturbed about losing the game than the no-hit perfecto.

"My main aim was to win," he said. "It was just another loss, but it hurt a little more."

When the lefty asked a group of reporters assembled around him the inning in which the game finally ended and was told the 13th, he simply shook his head in wonderment.

Haddix's victory totals dropped steadily over the next four years, and he was traded to Baltimore after the 1963 season. He won five games for the Orioles in 1964 and wound up his active career with a 3-2 record in 1965. He spent two years as a pitching coach in the Pirates' minor league system and many more at the major league level with the Mets, Reds, Red Sox, Indians and Pirates before retiring to his farm after the 1984 season.

"It makes me very proud," he once said, "that a small-town farm boy from South Vienna, Ohio, made a little bit of baseball history."

	1	2	3	4	5	6	7	8	9	R	H
Vaughn	0	0	0	0	0	0	0	0	0	0	0
Toney	0	0	0	0	0	0	0	0	0	0	0

He was discovered by an official of a minor league baseball club while on a squirrel-hunting excursion near a place called Goat Hill in the mountains of Tennessee.

The teen-ager, barefooted and attired only in well-worn overalls, was walking down a mountain when the baseball man spotted him. In one hand the boy carried three dead squirrels, victims of his unerring marksmanship. To the enormous surprise of the baseball man, however, there was no evidence of a rifle. How, he wondered, were the rodents brought to earth?

In response, the youth simply tapped an overall pocket that was packed with stones. Then, holding one of the squirrels in the air, he shyly admitted that it had taken two stones to knock this creature from a nearby hickory tree. The other two squirrels had been felled with just one shot each.

Clearly, the boy had an arm worthy of any baseball pitcher. But the veteran baseball executive was curious about one more thing. From his knapsack, the stranger withdrew a flask and invited the native to partake. The young mountaineer accepted gladly and, it was said, his Adam's apple rippled only twice as he drained the contents.

In a day when players often were judged on their ability to handle liquid corn, the baseball man concluded that the boy had the essentials for instant success on the professional diamond. He could throw with amazing accuracy and was accomplished as well in extracurricular endeavors.

By 1909, the 20-year-old phenom was blazing his fastball past befuddled batters in the Class-D Blue Grass League. On May 10 of that season he hurled a 17-inning no-hitter for Winchester, Ky., beating archrival Lexington, 1-0. The righthander struck out 19 batters.

After two seasons at Winchester, during which he won 45 games and lost 25, the 6-foot-1, 195-pound youth was purchased by the Chicago Cubs. But life with the National League club was unpleasant for the unbridled spirit from Tennessee. In 1913 he clashed with Manager Johnny Evers and was shipped to Louisville after splitting four decisions.

He found conditions in the American Association more congenial. He won 18 games the remainder of the 1913 campaign and 21 the next season. The Brooklyn Dodgers drafted him after the 1914 season but, unable to come to terms with club management, he requested a trade. The Dodgers accommodated him with his sale to Cincinnati, and it was as a Redleg on May 2, 1917, that Fred Arthur Toney scored his most notable pitching triumph.

On a bitterly cold and windswept afternoon, the Reds opposed the Cubs at Weeghman Park, which later was renamed Wrigley Field. Toney, known as "the man who walks like a bear," drew as his rival James Leslie Vaughn, a 6-4 lefthander from Texas who was nicknamed "Hippo" because of his lumbering gait on the basepaths.

Vaughn, 29, was an established major leaguer. He had won 21, 20 and 17 games for the Cubs in the three previous seasons, respectively, and was so highly regarded by Christy Mathewson that the Cincinnati manager sent nine righthanded batters (including two switch-hitters) into the game against him. Even lefthanded outfielder Edd Roush, who went on to lead the National League in hitting that season with a .341 average, rode the bench that Wednesday afternoon.

It was not the first encounter of the two hurlers. "We had met several times, dating back to our days in the American Association," Toney recalled in later years. "I usually won because I'd let Vaughn get a hit off me, and he'd get so tired from running the bases our batters would get to him and we'd win."

On this day, however, the old strategy was scrapped. The Tennessean and the Texan were superb. To the delight of the 3,500 fans in attendance, Vaughn disposed of the first nine Cincinnati batters before issuing a leadoff walk to Heinie Groh in the fourth inning. Groh was retired when shortstop Larry Kopf hit into a double play. An error by Cubs shortstop Rollie Zeider permitted center fielder Greasy Neale to reach base, but the future coach of the two-time National Football League champion Philadelphia Eagles was cut down trying to steal, thus ending the inning.

Firing his fastball on almost every pitch, Vaughn struck out first baseman Hal Chase, right fielder Jim Thorpe and second baseman Dave Shean in the fifth, plus left fielder Manuel Cueto to start the sixth. The only other Cincinnati batter to reach base in the regulation nine innings was Gus Getz, who had replaced Groh after the third baseman was banished for his vigorous protests of umpire Al Orth's ball-and-strike decisions. Getz drew a leadoff walk in the seventh, but like Groh earlier, he was erased when Kopf hit into another double play. The next seven batters went down in order, so after nine innings, Vaughn had faced the minimum 27 batters, struck out 10 and allowed no hits.

Toney, in the meantime, was equally unhittable. In the second inning he walked Cy Williams, the Chicago center fielder who normally found favor with Toney's pitching. Williams advanced to second on a fielder's choice but was stranded.

Williams walked again in the fifth but was forced when Shean, hoping to set up a double play, intentionally dropped catcher Art Wilson's pop fly. The maneuver was half successful. Williams was nipped, but Wilson beat the relay to first base. Neale's fine running catch of third baseman Charlie Deal's long drive, however, ended the inning.

Over the next four innings, Toney was in complete control. Twelve Cubs came to the plate during that span, and all 12 went away empty-handed. When Toney returned to the dugout after retiring Vaughn, Zeider and right fielder Harry Wolter in the bottom of the ninth, he knew that both he and Vaughn had gone through nine innings without allowing a hit. There had been several no-hit games pitched in the major leagues before that day, but never one in which both teams' pitchers threw them simultaneously for nine innings.

Both hurlers, in fact, were aware that a double no-hitter was in progress. In a late inning while sitting on the bench, Vaughn overheard a conversation among teammates. One cried out, "Come on, let's get a run off this fellow."

A second replied, "Run, hell, we haven't even got a hit off him."

To which a third responded, "Well, they haven't got a hit off Vaughn, either."

Toney, throwing an assortment of changeups to complement his fastball, was apprised of the bud-

Cubs lefthander Jim Vaughn was unhittable through nine innings of a 1917 game against Cincinnati, but buckled in the 10th and lost a 1-0 heartbreaker.

ding no-hitter in similar fashion in the seventh inning. "Don't think I didn't bear down after listening to my teammates talking," he said.

The visiting Reds broke Vaughn's spell in the top of the 10th inning. With one out, Kopf lined a clean single to right field, the first hit of the game. After Neale was retired on a fly ball to Williams, Chase smacked another drive to center field. Williams drifted under the ball, raised his hands—and dropped it. Kopf raced to third and Chase later stole second while Thorpe was at bat.

Thorpe, a football great who had won a gold medal in the decathlon in the 1912 Olympics, took a mighty swipe at a Vaughn pitch and dribbled it weakly along the third-base line. Hippo lumbered across the all-dirt infield and grabbed the ball.

"As soon as the ball was hit," Vaughn recalled, "I knew I had no chance to get Thorpe, so I fielded the ball and scooped it toward Art Wilson, our catcher. Kopf was running and stopped when he saw me field the ball. I didn't see him or I could have turned and tagged him out."

To many, it appeared that Wilson did not expect the throw because the ball bounced off his chest protector and fell at his feet. But that wasn't the way Hippo saw it.

"He just was paralyzed," Vaughn said. "The moment Kopf saw the ball drop he started for the plate, but Wilson just stood there. I looked over my shoulder and saw Chase round third and head home, too, so I shouted at Art, 'Are you going to let him score, too?' "

Finally awakened, Wilson snatched up the ball and made an easy tag on Chase. But a run was in.

Toney still had to retire the Cubs in the bottom of the 10th to preserve his no-hitter and earn the 1-0 victory. Second baseman Larry Doyle, the league's batting champion two years earlier, led off for the Cubs and went down on strikes. It was only the second strikeout of the day for Toney.

Next up was first baseman Fred Merkle, who brought a momentary roar from the crowd with a drive to deep left field. It was the hardest-hit ball of the day off Toney, but Cueto backed against the fence and made the catch.

Williams, Toney's nemesis in the past, represented the Cubs' last hope. Toney, exceedingly cautious at this point, fired two pitches just off the plate. Williams then took two on the corner for strikes. He fouled off the next two pitches, the second of which bounced off the grandstand.

The ball was returned to Orth for inspection. It contained a large scuff mark from its contact with the grandstand, but for reasons known only to the arbiter, he tossed it back to Toney.

Fred also examined the ball and, almost perceptibly, emitted a gasp of joy. With the blemish, Toney could make the ball do tricks, just as if it had been

nicked with a knife. "I knew I had him this time," he said. After throwing a ball that brought the count full, Toney threw the soiled sphere once more and let physics take over. The ball danced toward the plate and Williams missed it by an estimated eight inches. It was all over.

Although Toney and Vaughn performed a feat unmatched in the majors' first 11 decades, daily newspapers made little of it. The New York Times carried a four-paragraph account of the game. The headline mentioned neither pitcher's name, reporting only: "No Hits, No Runs for Nine Innings / Reds Nose Out Cubs in Tenth by 1 to 0 When Kopf and Jim Thorpe Get Singles."

In Toney's hometown, the local newspaper was even less excited. The Nashville Banner headline read, "Toney In Form."

Several weeks after the Toney-Vaughn masterpiece, Hod Eller hurled a doubleheader for the Reds (although the second game was stopped by darkness after six innings). The iron-man stunt aroused Toney's admiration and he requested permission for a similar chance. His opportunity arrived July 1 when Mathewson let him pitch both games against Pittsburgh. Toney responded in grand style. He hurled a couple of three-hitters and won, 4-1 and 5-1. The sweep accounted for two of Toney's 24 season victories, one more than Vaughn, in 1917.

Prior to the 1918 season, Toney ran afoul of the draft laws, and it was not until after considerable legal wrangling—and the start of the season—that he was able to rejoin the Reds. By that time he was unable to find a groove, so the Reds sold him to the New York Giants in midseason. He remained with the Giants through the 1922 season and appeared in two World Series games against the Yankees in 1921, pitching 2⅔ innings. He was with the Cardinals in 1923, then sat out a year before completing his professional career with his hometown Nashville team of the Southern Association in 1925.

For a number of years, Toney served as an officer in the Davidson County Criminal Court in Nashville. He was 64 at the time of his death, which was attributed to a heart ailment, on March 11, 1953.

Vaughn remained with the Cubs for four years after his historic encounter with Toney. He posted victory totals of 22, 21 and 19 before dropping to three in 1921. In the 1918 World Series, Hippo made three appearances against the Red Sox and, although he allowed only three runs in 27 innings, he lost two of three decisions. He bowed to Babe Ruth, 1-0, in the opening game, then returned in the third game and lost to Carl Mays, 2-1. His teammates finally provided some run support in the fifth contest and Hippo registered a 3-0 triumph.

In his final major league appearance on July 9, 1921, Vaughn opposed the Giants at the Polo Grounds. For three innings he held the Giants to one run. But a grand-slam homer by Frank (Pancho) Snyder in the fourth inning delivered a staggering blow to the 33-year-old veteran. He made his way back to the mound and pitched to Phil Douglas, an excellent pitcher with few batting credentials. Douglas took a savage cut at Hippo's offering and drove it even farther over the fence than Snyder had done. That was enough for Vaughn. Cubs Manager Evers came out to remove him from the game, but by that time Vaughn already was stomping off the hill. His shoulders hunched, the old warrior marched into retirement.

The giant lefthander pitched semipro ball for years around Chicago. He died at his Chicago home on May 29, 1966, at the age of 78.

Fred Toney later pitched for the Giants.

MAY 2, 1917

Cincinnati	ab	r	h	rbi	Chicago	ab	r	h	rbi
Groh, 3b	1	0	0	0	Zeider, ss	4	0	0	0
Getz, ph-3b	1	0	0	0	Wolter, rf	4	0	0	0
Kopf, ss	4	1	1	0	Doyle, 2b	4	0	0	0
Neale, cf	4	0	0	0	Merkle, 1b	4	0	0	0
Chase, 1b	4	0	0	0	Williams, cf	2	0	0	0
Thorpe, rf	4	0	1	1	Mann, lf	3	0	0	0
Shean, 2b	3	0	0	0	Wilson, c	3	0	0	0
Cueto, lf	3	0	0	0	Deal, 3b	3	0	0	0
Huhn, c	3	0	0	0	Vaughn, p	3	0	0	0
Toney, p	3	0	0	0					
Totals	30	1	2	0	Totals	30	0	0	0

Cincinnati	0	0	0	0 0 0	0 0 0		1—1		
Chicago	0	0	0	0 0 0	0 0 0		0—0		

Cincinnati	IP	H	R	ER	BB	SO
Toney (W)	10	0	0	0	2	3

Chicago	IP	H	R	ER	BB	SO
Vaughn (L)	10	2	1	0	2	10

E—Zeider, Williams. DP—Chicago 2. LOB—Cincinnati 1, Chicago 2. SB—Chase. T—1:50.

Mazeroski Stuns Powerful Yankees

From the moment he fielded his first ground ball as a second baseman for the Pittsburgh Pirates, William Stanley Mazeroski was heralded as a defensive superstar, a youngster with unlimited capabilities.

Benny Bengough, grizzled coach of the Phillies, likened the youth to Eddie Collins, a hero with the early-day Philadelphia Athletics and later the Chicago White Sox, and to Charlie Gehringer, the "Mechanical Man" of the Detroit Tigers of the 1920s and '30s.

Bobby Bragan, who managed Maz in the minors and the majors, was a bit more colorful in his evaluation of Bill's lightning-quick hands. "If he were a pickpocket," Bragan declared, "he'd be the best in the business."

When Mazeroski once made an especially acrobatic stop of a sharply hit ball by Chico Fernandez and then threw him out, the Phillies' shortstop returned to the bench fuming in his loud Cuban accent, "He eez not *human.*"

The accolade evoked a passel of chuckles, but George Sisler was more realistic.

"He's one of the greatest second basemen I've

The sequence of photographs below and on the following pages shows Bill Mazeroski's triumphant trot around the bases and the home-plate celebration that followed his 1960 World Series-winning home run.

ever seen," said the Hall of Famer, a hitting instructor for the Pirates when Maz broke in. "He has all the tools and he has the desire. Initially, there was some doubt about his ability to hit, but I always had confidence in him. He has that good eye, and he can flick his wrists with the best of them."

Mazeroski, a native of Wheeling, W.Va., who attended school in Tiltonsville, O., was a shortstop and pitcher in high school, where he pitched three one-hitters. He was wooed by several major league clubs, but the Pirates captured the prize with a $4,000 signing bonus and a contract with Williamsport of the Class-A Eastern League. The other organizations wanted him to start with a Class-D farm team.

Bill originally was a shortstop, but one glance from Branch Rickey, the Pirates' vice president and general manager, changed his course. "He's a natural second baseman," snorted the Mahatma, and with only a few exceptions in the twilight of his career, Maz was a keystoner thereafter.

Mazeroski still was two months short of his 20th birthday when, in July 1956, the Pirates recalled him from Hollywood of the Pacific Coast League. It was the last time he ever played in the minors. When he retired 16 years later, he owned major league records for a second baseman for most dou-

ble plays in a season, most years leading a league in assists, most years leading a league in double plays and most double plays in a lifetime, among others. His National League records for a second baseman included most years leading the league in chances accepted and lifetime marks for most chances accepted, putouts and assists.

Obviously, Mazeroski was one of the greatest second basemen of all time. At the plate, however, he was solid but not spectacular. He never hit as high as .285 as a major leaguer, and his season high for home runs was 19. It is a great irony, then, that the feat for which Mazeroski's name is etched in the minds of baseball fans was achieved not with his glove, but his bat.

Mazeroski enjoyed his finest moment in the spotlight in 1960, a year in which he batted .273 and drove in 64 runs to help the Pirates finish seven games ahead of the second-place Milwaukee Braves in the National League. The pennant was the Pirates' first since 1927, and as in the earlier year, their World Series opponents were the Yankees, who had crushed them in four straight games in their first meeting.

Righthander Vern Law, a 20-game winner for the first time in 1960, pitched the Pirates to a 6-4 victory in the opening game October 5 at Pittsburgh's

Forbes Field. Law was aided by relief from Roy Face and two hits, including a two-run home run, by Mazeroski. In the second game, a 16-3 New York runaway, Bill belted a double. The Yankee offensive domination continued when the Series moved to New York on October 8 for Game 3, a 10-0 shutout by lefthander Whitey Ford in which Mazeroski had one of only four Pittsburgh hits. He also contributed a single in the fourth contest, a 3-2 Pirates victory in which Law won his second Series game.

Maz bounced a two-run double down the left-field line and Face provided his third stellar relief performance the next day to help the Pirates and Harvey Haddix post a 5-2 victory in Game 5. The Pirates could have wrapped up the world championship when the Series returned to Pittsburgh on Columbus Day, but the Yankees had other ideas. The Bucs were humiliated in a 12-0 whitewashing by Ford, who registered his second consecutive shutout. Second baseman Bobby Richardson, who

had hit a grand-slam homer and a two-run single in support of Ford in Game 3, hit two triples to boost his runs batted in total to 12, a Series record, as the Yankees evened the classic at three games apiece.

When the teams took the field for the deciding game, played October 13 at Forbes Field, Law again was on the mound for the Pirates. The righthander began most impressively, holding the Bombers hitless in the first two innings as the Pirates built up a 4-0 lead against Yankees starter Bob Turley and reliever Bill Stafford.

Turley's problems began when he issued a two-out walk to left fielder Bob Skinner in the first inning. The next batter, first baseman Rocky Nelson, homered into the lower right-field stands. The righthander induced right fielder Roberto Clemente to pop up to Richardson, but the first man he faced in the second inning, catcher Smoky Burgess, singled. Yankees Manager Casey Stengel had seen enough. He brought in Stafford, who promptly walked third baseman Don Hoak. Mazeroski then bunted toward third and beat Stafford's throw to first, filling the bases. Law hit into a double play via the plate, but center fielder Bill Virdon singled to drive in Hoak and Mazeroski.

Law blanked the Yanks on two singles over the next two innings, but an opposite-field home run by first baseman Bill Skowron leading off the fifth frame launched a New York comeback. After Richardson and shortstop Tony Kubek opened the sixth inning with a single and a walk, respectively, Pirates Manager Danny Murtaugh summoned Face from the bullpen to take over for Law. Face retired right fielder Roger Maris on a foul pop, but center fielder Mickey Mantle followed with a run-scoring single. Left fielder Yogi Berra then smacked a three-run homer into the upper right-field stands to give the Yankees a 5-4 lead.

The Pirates, who had been blanked on only one hit in five innings by lefthander Bobby Shantz, fell farther behind in the eighth inning. The Yankees combined a walk, singles by Skowron and catcher John Blanchard and a double by third baseman Clete Boyer—all with two out—to score twice, extending their lead to 7-4.

Only six outs remained for the Pirates. With Shantz pitching masterfully, the 36,683 fans in attendance had little hope that the Pirates would prevent the Yanks from winning their 19th world championship—and their eighth in 12 years under Stengel.

Gino Cimoli batted for Face to lead off the last of the eighth, and his single appeared to pose no threat to the Yankees, particularly when Virdon slapped a bouncer toward shortstop that seemed tailor-made for a double play. As Kubek braced for the stop, however, the ball took an erratic hop and struck him on the throat. Kubek was knocked down and had to be replaced by Joe DeMaestri. Cimoli raced safely to second on the play and Virdon received credit for a single in one of the most bizarre and crucial of all World Series plays.

After shortstop Dick Groat singled in a run, Shantz was replaced by righthander Jim Coates. "I wasn't tired and still had good stuff," explained Shantz, who added that Cimoli's hit "was on the fist. He just plopped it into right field."

Stengel's selection of Coates to relieve the little lefthander was uncomplicated. "It was because he had his slider and sinker ready," the Old Perfessor rasped. The choice appeared justified when Coates recorded two outs, the first on Skinner's sacrifice (which advanced both runners) and the second on Nelson's fly ball to right field.

The Pirates were within one out of ending their own rally. But Clemente beat out a chopper to the right side on which Coates was tardy in covering first base, and Virdon crossed the plate to make the score 7-6. Stengel ambled to the mound and urged Coates to exert extreme caution with the next batter, Hal Smith, who had replaced Burgess behind

the plate in the top of the inning. Ol' Case was scarcely back in the dugout, however, when the second-string catcher clouted a pitch over the left-field wall. The Forbes Field crowd went berserk as three Pittsburgh runs crossed the plate, giving the Pirates a 9-7 lead. Ralph Terry came on to retire Hoak for the last out of the inning, but the fans continued to cheer wildly as Bob Friend went out to the mound for the Pirates. Three more outs and Pittsburgh would have its second World Series title.

But then it was the Yankees' turn to rally. Friend, an 18-game winner during the season but a loser in his two previous appearances in the Series, failed to retire a batter. The righthander yielded singles to Richardson and pinch-hitter Dale Long before Murtaugh waved in Haddix, a lefty, to face Maris, a lefthanded swinger. Haddix retired Maris on a foul pop, but Mantle's single scored Richardson and sent Long to third. Long was replaced by Gil McDougald, who then scored the tying run on Berra's infield out. Haddix finally got the third out when Skowron hit into a force play, but it was 9-9. The

home crowd was suddenly subdued as the Pirates were forced to bat in the bottom of the ninth.

As the Bombers took the field, several facts stamped the Series as one of the most unusual of the 57 fall classics. The Yankees had batted .338 as a team, a new Series record. At this point, too, New York had scored 55 runs, compared with 26 for Pittsburgh, and had rapped 91 hits, in contrast with 59 for the Bucs. And yet there were the Yanks in the bottom of the ninth, praying that Terry could record three more outs so they could get another chance at the plate.

Leading off the ninth for the Pirates was their eighth-place hitter—Bill Mazeroski. Terry was relieved not to be facing the meat of the Pittsburgh lineup, but he still pitched carefully to the 24-year-old second baseman. Mazeroski took the righthander's first delivery for a ball. Then he waited.

"On my previous at-bat, I overswung and grounded out," Maz said. "I wanted to make certain I didn't do the same thing again."

Terry pitched once more and Mazeroski swung. From the moment of impact it was obvious that he had not overswung. The ball arched toward left field and crossed the fence at approximately the

Pittsburgh players struggle through a jubilant crowd of Pirates fans after Bill Mazeroski's dramatic World Series home run.

OCTOBER 13, 1960

New York	ab	r	h	rbi	Pittsburgh	ab	r	h	rbi
Richardson, 2b	5	2	2	0	Virdon, cf	4	1	2	2
Kubek, ss	3	1	0	0	Groat, ss	4	1	1	1
DeMaestri, ss	0	0	0	0	Skinner, lf	2	1	0	0
Long, ph	1	0	1	0	Nelson, 1b	3	1	1	2
McD'g'ld, pr-3b	0	1	0	0	Clemente, rf	4	1	1	1
Maris, rf	5	0	0	0	Burgess, c	3	0	2	0
Mantle, cf	5	1	3	2	Christopher, pr	0	0	0	0
Berra, lf	4	2	1	4	Smith, c	1	1	1	3
Skowron, 1b	5	2	2	1	Hoak, 3b	3	1	0	0
Blanchard, c	4	0	1	1	Mazeroski, 2b	4	2	2	1
Boyer, 3b-ss	4	0	1	1	Law, p	2	0	0	0
Turley, p	0	0	0	0	Face, p	0	0	0	0
Stafford, p	0	0	0	0	Cimoli, ph	1	1	1	0
Lopez, ph	1	0	1	0	Friend, p	0	0	0	0
Shantz, p	3	0	1	0	Haddix, p	0	0	0	0
Coates, p	0	0	0	0					
Terry, p	0	0	0	0					
Totals	40	9	13	9	Totals	31	10	11	10

New York.............................0　0　0　　0　1　4　　0　2　2— 9
Pittsburgh..........................2　2　0　　0　0　0　　0　5　1—10
　　None out when winning run scored.

New York	IP	H	R	ER	BB	SO
Turley	1*	2	3	3	1	0
Stafford	1	2	1	1	1	0
Shantz	5‡	4	3	3	1	0
Coates	⅔	2	2	2	0	0
Terry (L)	⅓	1	1	1	0	0
Pittsburgh	IP	H	R	ER	BB	SO
Law	5†	4	3	3	1	0
Face	3	6	4	4	1	0
Friend	0§	2	2	2	0	0
Haddix (W)	1	1	0	0	0	0

　*Pitched to one batter in second.
　†Pitched to two batters in sixth.
　‡Pitched to three batters in eighth.
　§Pitched to two batters in ninth.

　E—Maris. DP—New York 3. LOB—New York 6, Pittsburgh 1. 2B
—Boyer. HR—Nelson, Skowron, Berra, Smith, Mazeroski. SH—
Skinner. T—2:36. A—36,683.

same spot that Smith's home run had left the park an inning earlier.

Uncertain of the ball's destination, Mazeroski raced past first base. Then, seeing the ball disappear, he broke into a jubilant lope. Rounding second base, he took off his hat and waved it wildly, and as he approached third base he was greeted by droves of ecstatic fans who formed an escort for the final 90 feet of his triumphant tour. Wildly cheering teammates awaited Maz at home plate, and it was all that umpire Bill Jackowski could do to make certain that the new hero stepped on the plate in keeping with the rules. That made it official: The Pirates, 10-9 victors in the seventh game, were world champions.

Mazeroski shoved his way to the Pirates' dressing room, where he was swamped by reporters. "I think I hit a fastball," he shouted above the rowdy din, "but I don't know for sure and I don't care. I didn't know whether it would get out or not; that's why I was running so hard."

While the Pirates celebrated noisily, the losers lamented the misfortune that had left them superior in every phase of the Series except the final score.

World Series hero Bill Mazeroski gets a playful pinch on the cheek from Manager Danny Murtaugh after the final game of the 1960 World Series.

"It's impossible for the Pirates to get any more breaks than they got in this Series," groused one Yankee, and there was little dissent.

In another corner of the somber clubhouse, Terry was trying to answer questions from a flock of reporters. In the midst of the interview, the pitcher excused himself to take a telephone call. On his return, a journalist asked:

"Who was the call from?"

"My wife," Terry replied.

"What was she doing?" the persistent media person asked.

"Nursing out new baby," answered Terry, straining for composure.

"Breast or bottle?" rejoined the newsman, and for a moment at least, a round of laughs shattered the otherwise gloomy quarters.

Mazeroski, who would be remembered forever for his dramatic home run rather than his fielding wizardry, discovered that his title-clinching blow was not without cost. When he donned his batting helmet for his final trip to the plate, Bill laid his cap, together with his trusty glove, on the lip of the dugout. He never saw either again. In the wild melee that capped the remarkable afternoon, a spectator made off with the prized souvenirs.

As he left the park, Maz encountered a fan offering to sell him the ball that had crowned the Pirates as world champions. A few steps farther a second fan, with another baseball, made an identical offer. Before he reached his car he had received five offers, each purporting to have the home run ball for sale. Maz did not reach for his wallet.

Bill appeared in a second World Series, but in a subordinate role. In 1971, when the Bucs defeated the Orioles, Maz made one unsuccessful pinch-hitting appearance. After retiring at the close of the 1972 season, Maz coached briefly for the Pirates and later the Seattle Mariners. His last job in the game he graced for 17 seasons was as a minor league instructor for the Montreal Expos in 1984. He was helping players with their fielding, but the youngsters he was tutoring probably wondered why. After all, this was the home run hero of the 1960 World Series!

"I guess it's nice that they remember me for something," the seven-time Gold Glover once said. "I would rather be remembered for my fielding, but it can't be. That homer was the greatest thrill of my baseball life."

Boston Marathon: Oeschger vs. Cadore

The 2,000 or so intrepid souls who huddled in a drizzle and a sharp wind at Braves Field in Boston on May 1, 1920, had little reason to expect a slugging match in that afternoon's game against the Brooklyn Dodgers.

The starting pitchers, Joe Oeschger for the home team and Leon Cadore for the visitors, had hooked up only 11 days earlier, on April 20 in Brooklyn, with Cadore winning, 1-0, in 11 innings. Another duel of the same quality was doubtful, but a well-pitched game was an excellent possibility.

Oeschger and Cadore were similar in many respects. Both stood 6 feet tall, weighed about 190 pounds and threw righthanded. Oeschger was approaching his 28th birthday later that month, while Cadore would not light his 28th candle until November. In addition, both were natives of Chicago.

Oeschger's parents migrated to California when Joe was a youngster. He graduated from St. Mary's College with a degree in engineering before accepting a $5,000 bonus to sign with the Phillies in 1914.

Ordinarily, Oeschger pitched on Sunday. His manager, George Stallings, was a highly superstitious Georgian, and inasmuch as Oeschger was a regular churchgoer, Stallings thought that the Braves enjoyed an advantage if Oeschger, rather than a less devout hurler, pitched on the Sabbath. But because Sunday baseball was illegal in Boston at that time and the Braves' next game, also against

Brooklyn, would not be until the following Monday, Joe drew the starting assignment on this Saturday afternoon.

Cadore spent his first 13 years in Chicago. Orphaned at that age, he was sent to live with an uncle in Idaho, where he developed a love for baseball. He studied at Gonzaga University before entering professional baseball with Vancouver of the Northwest League in 1911.

Prior to the 1920 campaign, Cadore had won 28 games for the Dodgers but had missed most of the 1918 season to serve in World War I, during which he rose from the rank of private to captain. Oeschger had 31 major league victories to his credit entering the 1920 season, including 15 for the Phillies in 1917.

The Boston hurler had pitched remarkably well prior to his May Day encounter with Cadore. In his three previous outings that season, Oeschger had allowed only two earned runs, an achievement that he was about to surpass in one afternoon of work.

Precisely at 3 p.m., home-plate umpire Barry McCormick cried, "Play ball!" and Bob Hart, his partner, took his position at first base. For four innings, both pitchers held their opponents scoreless. The Dodgers finally broke the deadlock in the top of the fifth when they reached Oeschger for one run on a walk to catcher Ernie Krueger, an infield out and second baseman Ivy Olson's broken-bat single over shortstop Rabbit Maranville's head.

"I was to blame for letting the run score," Oeschger recalled years later. "I started the inning off badly by pitching too carefully to Krueger, a good pull-hitter. I walked him. Cadore then followed with a sharp bounder to the mound. In my anxiety to get the double play, I juggled the ball long enough to let Krueger reach second and had to content myself with throwing out Cadore at first base."

The Braves tied the score, 1-1, in the home half of the sixth. Right fielder Walton Cruise smashed a one-out triple off the scoreboard in left field, then held third when Zack Wheat made a shoestring catch of first baseman Walter Holke's sinking liner in left field. Third baseman Tony Boeckel followed with a single that drove in Cruise, Boeckel taking second on the throw to the plate. The rally ap-

MAY 1, 1920									
Brooklyn	ab	r	h	rbi	Boston	ab	r	h	rbi
Olson, 2b	10	0	1	1	Powell, cf	7	0	1	0
Neis, rf	10	0	1	0	Pick, 2b	11	0	0	0
Johnston, 3b	10	0	2	0	Mann, lf	10	0	2	0
Wheat, lf	9	0	2	0	Cruise, rf	9	1	1	0
Myers, cf	2	0	1	0	Holke, 1b	10	0	2	0
Hood, cf	6	0	1	0	Boeckel, 3b	11	0	3	1
Konetchy, 1b	9	0	1	0	Maranville, ss	10	0	3	0
Ward, ss	10	0	0	0	O'Neil, c	2	0	0	0
Krueger, c	2	1	0	0	Christenbury, ph	1	0	1	0
Elliott, c	7	0	0	0	Gowdy, c	6	0	1	0
Cadore, p	10	0	0	0	Oeschger, p	9	0	1	0
Totals	85	1	9	1	Totals	86	1	15	1

Brooklyn.................... 000 010 000 000 000 000 000 000 00—1
Boston......................... 000 001 000 000 000 000 000 000 00—1

Brooklyn	IP	H	R	ER	BB	SO
Cadore..........................	26	15	1	1	5	7
Boston	IP	H	R	ER	BB	SO
Oeschger.....................	26	9	1	1	4	7

E—Olson, Ward, Pick 2. DP—Brooklyn 1, Boston 1. LOB—Brooklyn 11, Boston 16. 2B—Oeschger, Maranville. 3B—Cruise. SB—Myers, Hood. SH—Powell, O'Neil, Cruise, Hood, Holke, Oeschger. WP—Oeschger. T—3:50.

PITCHERS HURLING 20 OR MORE INNINGS IN ONE GAME

Leon Cadore, Bkn. NL vs. Bos., May 1, 1920
Joe Oeschger, Bos. NL vs. Bkn., May 1, 1920   26

Jack Coombs, Phil. AL vs. Bos., Sept. 1, 1906
Joe Harris, Bos. AL vs. Phil., Sept. 1, 1906   24

Bob Smith, Bos. NL vs. Chi., May 17, 1927   22

Babe Adams, Pit. NL vs. N.Y., July 17, 1914
Rube Marquard, N.Y. NL vs. Pit., July 17, 1914
Lefty Tyler, Chi. NL vs. Phil., July 17, 1918   21
Art Nehf, Bos. NL vs. Pit., Aug. 1, 1918
Ted Lyons, Chi. AL vs. Det., May 24, 1929

Addison Gumbert, Chi. NL vs. Cin., June 30, 1892
Tony Mullane, Cin. NL vs. Chi., June 30, 1892
Rube Waddell, Phil. AL vs. Bos., July 4, 1905
Cy Young, Bos. AL vs. Phil., July 4, 1905   20
Ed Reulbach, Chi. NL vs. Phil., Aug. 24, 1905
Tully Sparks, Phil. NL vs. Chi., Aug. 24, 1905
Milt Watson, Phil. NL vs. Chi., July 17, 1918
Burleigh Grimes, Bkn. NL vs. Phil., Apr. 30, 1919
Joe Oeschger, Phil. NL vs. Bkn., Apr. 30, 1919
George Uhle, Det. AL vs. Chi., May 24, 1929

Brooklyn righthander
Leon Cadore.

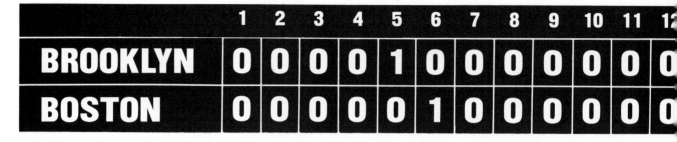

	1	2	3	4	5	6	7	8	9	10	11	12
BROOKLYN	0	0	0	0	1	0	0	0	0	0	0	0
BOSTON	0	0	0	0	0	1	0	0	0	0	0	0

peared to be continuing when Maranville smacked a double to center field, but Wally Hood's strong throw nailed Boeckel at the plate to end the inning.

After two scoreless innings, the Braves threatened to win the game in the ninth. Maranville started the uprising with a single and went to second on pinch-hitter Lloyd Christenbury's infield hit. Oeschger's sacrifice advanced the runners before center fielder Ray Powell was issued an intentional pass to load the bases. The threat died, however, when second baseman Charlie Pick's grounder was fielded by Olson, who tagged Powell and threw to first baseman Ed Konetchy for the final out of the inning.

It was overtime again for Oeschger and Cadore, just as it had been in their last previous engagement. The next four frames passed without a major disturbance. In the 14th, Wheat singled for the Dodgers, but two were out and Hood's outfield fly retired the side. The Braves drew a rise from the crowd when they put two men on base in the 15th, but Cadore retired Boeckel, Maranville and catcher Hank Gowdy to escape damage.

The Dodgers wasted a two-out single by right fielder Bernie Neis in the 16th, after which Oeschger attempted to win his own game with a clout to deep left field. The drive was just deep enough for Wheat to race to the wall and make a fantastic leaping catch. "It would have been a sure triple if it had been a few inches higher," said Joe, who had hit a double previously.

Back came the Dodgers. Wheat opened the 17th with a single and took second on Hood's sacrifice. He advanced to third on Konetchy's single and remained there when shortstop Chuck Ward grounded to Maranville, who held the ball for fear that Wheat would attempt to score if he tried for the putout at first base. That left the bases full with one out, but nevertheless, Rabbit's decision turned out to be a shrewd one.

The next batter, catcher Rowdy Elliott, grounded to the mound, where Oeschger grabbed the ball and started a unique double play. His throw to Gowdy forced Wheat at home, but Gowdy's throw to first was low and eluded Holke for a moment, inspiring Konetchy to break for home. Retrieving the ball, the first baseman fired blindly toward the plate. The throw was off target, but Gowdy grabbed it, dived across the plate and tagged Konetchy's spikes

for the second out at home on the same play. The Dodgers, long famous for wacky baserunning, were in true form.

According to Oeschger, the odd double play "brought the small crowd to its feet with a cheer that could be heard to the Charles River."

As the pitchers returned to the mound for another round of work, they received encouragement from the bench. "Hold 'em, we'll get 'em next inning," Stallings reassured Oeschger.

Brooklyn Manager Wilbert Robinson said nothing to Cadore. "If he had tried to take me out of the game," Leon said, "I think I would have strangled him."

The 18th inning passed without incident, at which point the pitchers had worked the equivalent of two complete games. The 19th . . . the 20th . . . the 21st went by. Hood raised Brooklyn hopes in the 22nd with a two-out walk and a steal of second, but he got no farther as Konetchy grounded out.

Darkness was creeping in as both teams went down in order in the 23rd, 24th and 25th innings and the Dodgers as well in the 26th. Holke's safe bunt with two out in the last of the 26th was the Braves' last gasp. Boeckel was retired for the third out.

The crowd, which had swelled to about 3,000 when word circulated through town that an unusual game was in progress at Braves Field, was speculating on still more action when umpire McCormick turned to the stands and shouted, "This game is called because of darkness."

"One more inning, one more inning," Olson pleaded in a voice that carried to the press box.

"What for?" the arbiter asked.

"So we can say we played three games in one day," Olson replied.

"Not without miners' lamps on your caps," McCormick said, and on that note the longest game in major league history came to a close.

The scoreboard showed 6:50. Three hours and 50 minutes had elapsed since Oeschger delivered his first pitch. Except for the fact that daylight-saving time had arrived a few days before, the marathon would have been called an hour earlier.

Neither Cadore nor Oeschger quarreled with McCormick's action. Each believed he could have continued a bit longer, although Joe estimated that

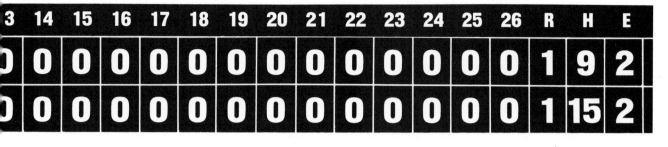

3	14	15	16	17	18	19	20	21	22	23	24	25	26	R	H	E
0	0	0	0	0	0	0	0	0	0	0	0	0	0	1	9	2
0	0	0	0	0	0	0	0	0	0	0	0	0	0	1	15	2

he had made 250 pitches, mostly fastballs, and Leon, featuring curves and slow stuff, guessed that he had thrown "at least 300 curves."

After the fifth inning, Oeschger chalked up 21 consecutive scoreless innings, one more than Cadore. Oeschger, who appeared to grow stronger as the game progressed, allowed nine hits while striking out seven and walking four; Cadore surrendered 15 hits, fanning seven and walking five.

Each team used only 11 players. The Dodgers called on two catchers and a pair of center fielders, the Braves two catchers and a pinch-hitter.

On the day after setting the longevity record, Joe and Leon received congratulatory messages from John Heydler. The N.L. president expressed particular delight that the record had been set in the first season after the major leagues had begun eliminating the spitball and other freak pitches.

Because of Boston's blue law, the teams' three-game series would not resume until Monday. In the meantime, the Dodgers boarded a train and headed for New York to fill a May 2 date with the Phillies at Ebbets Field. By that time the overtime virus had infected the club. The Brooks bowed, 4-3, in 13 innings. That evening they hopped another train. They returned to Boston for their Monday game and, true to form, played 19 innings before losing, 2-1. The three-day adventure gave the Dodgers the unenviable distinction of having played 58 innings with one tie and two losses to show for their labors.

After their 26-inning exercise, neither Oeschger nor Cadore pitched for more than a week. "It wasn't my arm," Oeschger explained. "It was my leg. I pulled a leg muscle while running the day after the game."

Cadore confessed that his arm "was a bit tired" after his strenuous workout, and for three days he was unable to raise his arm to comb his hair. After eight days, however, he returned to the regular rotation and posted 15 victories for the year, the same number achieved by Oeschger.

The Braves finished seventh that year while the Dodgers won the pennant, enabling Cadore to make two appearances in the World Series against Cleveland. He pitched a hitless inning of relief in the first game, which the Indians won, 3-1, but he failed abysmally as a starter in the fourth contest. Two runs in the first inning and a pair of singles leading

off the second preceded his early exodus from the game and the Series.

Fears that Oeschger and Cadore may have suffered irreparable arm damage from their exertions of May 1, 1920, were dispelled the next season when Joe registered 20 victories and Leon 13. Many people believed, however, that the strain of that day ultimately shortened their careers.

Oeschger left the majors after the 1925 season, explaining, "I want to return to California and carve out a new career." He still had the urge to pitch, however, and it was not until 1927, after terms in the Pacific Coast League and the Southern Association, that he hung up his glove.

Oeschger then enrolled at Stanford University and earned a degree in physical education. He taught that subject at Portola Junior High School in the San Francisco area for more than 25 years, stepping down only because of a mandatory retirement law when he was 65. He took up residence in Ferndale, 250 miles north of San Francisco, on property acquired by his Swiss immigrant parents in 1900.

His first opportunity to discuss the historic marathon with Cadore occurred in 1957, when both were guests of the San Francisco Seals at an Old-Timers Day that highlighted a Pacific Coast League game.

"We agreed," Oeschger said, "that on that day we had the edge on the hitters and were sorry to see the game ended."

Cadore's last major league affiliation was with the New York Giants in 1924. He pitched in two games before being sent home, allegedly for breaking training rules.

For a number of years, Leon made his home in New York with his wife, the former Maie Ebbets, daughter of Dodgers President Charles H. Ebbets. He enjoyed an excellent life style while working with a brokerage firm, but the stock market crash of 1929 put an end to that. Cadore and his wife moved to Hope, Idaho, to mine some family copper, but by 1955 it was reported that he was "badly in need of a job."

Cadore spent his last years in Hope as a widower, living with a friend. Death came on March 16, 1958, six weeks after he had entered a veterans hospital in Spokane, Wash., to undergo surgery for cancer. He was 65.

Boston Braves righthander Joe Oeschger.

No. 7

Fred Merkle's Brush With Destiny

The 20th Century was still in its infancy when John T. Brush, the gaunt owner of the New York Giants, was said to have visited Mount Clemens, Mich., in search of a health cure that always seemed just beyond the reach of medical science. While there, John T. visited a barbershop. He asked for Charlie, the taciturn member of the tonsorial crew, because Charlie talked only when he had something to say.

On this particular day, when prompted by Brush, Charlie was inclined to talk. His subject was a teen-ager playing first base for a local team in the nether reaches of the minor leagues.

"I've seen enough baseball games in my life to know a good prospect when I see one," the barber declared, "and this kid's good."

"All right," said Brush, who always was on the lookout for young talent, "send the boy over to my hotel tonight and I'll sign him."

When the prospect arrived, Brush was impressed with his rangy physique, ideal for an athlete. He also admired the youngster's politeness and his steady gaze, which never seemed to waver. The young player signed the contract proffered by Brush, who told him: "Stay around here and when I get back to New York I'll tell John McGraw about you. He'll wire whatever instructions are necessary."

What the Giants' manager thought of his boss signing a prospect virtually sight unseen is not recorded, but he undoubtedly was familiar with the owner's irregular habits. It was Brush's money to spend as he pleased.

The Mount Clemens barber passed quickly into oblivion. But the player he recommended so highly, and on whom a New York club owner took a blind chance, went on to lasting notoriety in baseball history.

Fred Merkle, a native of Wisconsin but a graduate of a high school in Toledo, justified the high praise of his sponsor. After being acquired in 1907, he appeared in 15 games for the Giants near the end of the season, batting a respectable .255. The following year, at the tender age of 19, he was the backup

Fred Merkle, a backup first baseman in 1908, carved his own little niche in baseball history.

Chicago second baseman Johnny Evers called for the ball and forced Merkle at second.

New York's Al Bridwell set off the bizarre chain of events by singling to center.

to veteran first baseman Fred Tenney. He batted .268 in only 41 at-bats.

One of Merkle's 11 hits in 1908 was registered on September 23, the only day in which Tenney's name did not appear in a Giants box score that season. It also was the day that Merkle ran into endless controversy.

On the morning of the game, the Giants were in first place with an 87-50 record, six percentage points ahead of the Cubs (90-53), their opponents that afternoon. All portents pointed to an excellent game. McGraw named righthander Christy Mathewson, who was on his way to a 37-victory season, to start for the Giants, while lefthander Jack (The Giant Killer) Pfiester was the nomination of Cubs Manager Frank Chance, who also played first base.

Both pitchers were superb, and after 8½ innings the teams were deadlocked, 1-1. Mathewson had struck out nine Chicago batters and allowed only five hits, although one was a solo home run by shortstop Joe Tinker in the fifth inning. Pfiester, meanwhile, had struck out no one but had surrendered just four hits through the first eight frames. The only New York run was scored in the sixth inning when second baseman Buck Herzog reached base on third baseman Harry Steinfeldt's throwing error, advanced to second on catcher Roger Bresnahan's sacrifice and scored on right fielder Mike Donlin's single.

The Giants finally began to sense a rally developing in the last half of the ninth inning when third

Umpire Hank O'Day wrestled with his controversial decision and finally called Merkle out.

baseman Art Devlin singled to center with one out. Devlin was forced at second on left fielder Moose McCormick's grounder, but Merkle followed with a long single to right field that sent McCormick scooting around to third base. When shortstop Al Bridwell ripped a single to center field, McCormick crossed the plate with what appeared to be the winning run.

From that point, however, utter confusion engulfed the Polo Grounds. Versions of what happened next were as numerous as the 20,000 or so spectators who tried to make sense out of the chaos.

Most accounts reported that Merkle, seeing McCormick step on home plate, did what other players had done for years. Before reaching second, he veered from the base line and headed toward the clubhouse in center field.

Johnny Evers, the Cubs' brainy second baseman, had been waiting for just such a moment for nearly three weeks, ever since a similar play had occurred September 4 in a Cubs-Pirates game at Pittsburgh. On that occasion, Evers retrieved the baseball, stepped on second base and insisted that umpire Hank O'Day call the runner out on a force play and nullify the run that scored on the play.

O'Day denied the claim on the basis of precedence. Later, mulling over the play, he decided Evers was correct. He assured the second baseman that on the next such occasion he would rule a force play. O'Day made some public acknowledgement of his new interpretation of the rule, but Merkle was

Manager John McGraw refused to censure anybody for what came to be known as "Merkle's Boner."

Fred Merkle's Blunder

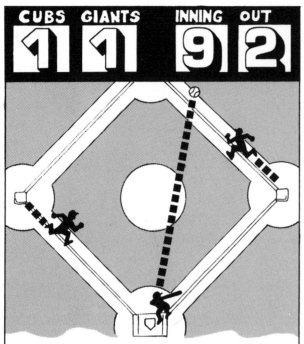

With runners on 1st and 3rd, Bridwell hits Pfiester's pitch to center field for what appears to be a clean hit and McCormick trots home with the run that should give the Giants a 2-1 victory.

However, Merkle, assuming game was over when McCormick touched home, did not run all the way to second base, but ran to Giants clubhouse.

Evers realizes that if Cubs retrieve ball and tag second base, Merkle will be forced for third out of inning and McCormick's run will not count.

Thinking game is over, fans swarm onto field. Meanwhile, members of both teams wrestle over possession of ball. Cubs finally recover a baseball and touch second, claiming Merkle is out. Umpire O'Day agrees and game is declared a 1-1 tie.

not aware of it. He had been in and out of action for quite some time, recovering from a foot injury that at one point earlier in the summer had threatened amputation.

O'Day was behind the plate and Bob Emslie was working the bases on this Wednesday afternoon when Evers spotted Merkle's dereliction. Evers hollered frantically to center fielder Artie Hofman to throw the ball for the forceout Evers knew would be awarded.

Hofman's throw was wide of the mark and, for a while, the ball was lost in the mass of exuberant Giants fans surging onto the field. Seeing what was happening, New York pitcher Joe McGinnity, who had spent the day in the third-base coaches box, located the ball and threw it into the stands, according to most accounts. From some undisclosed source, Evers apparently obtained a second ball. He tagged the bag and appealed to Emslie.

"I didn't see the play," replied the umpire, who had dived to the dirt when Bridwell's vicious liner came his way and was dusting himself off when the uproar commenced.

Many minutes elapsed before the umpires could discuss the situation and render a verdict.

"Did you see what happened?" Emslie asked his partner.

"I did," O'Day answered. "The runner is forced at second base and the game is a tie."

Mathewson's version of events differed drastically. "I had started from the field," Matty revealed, "when I heard Evers yell to Hofman, 'Throw the ball to second.' I remembered the trick they had tried to play in Pittsburgh, and I got Merkle by the arm and told him to go to second. . . . Merkle touched the bag, and I was near him when he did it."

No other account coincided with Mathewson's— not even Merkle's.

After eating dinner, O'Day wrote a report in which he apprised National League President Harry C. Pulliam of all the details concerning that muddled ninth-inning play. He ruled the game a tie, O'Day said, because the field was swamped with people, making further play impossible, and besides, it was getting dark.

When McGraw learned of O'Day's report later that night, he phoned Merkle at his hotel. Anticipating possible developments, McGraw told Merkle, "Go to the Polo Grounds immediately and tag second base so that, if necessary, you can say under oath that you did indeed tag the bag on September 23." Merkle obeyed his orders to the letter, but he never was asked to testify.

In the meantime, both clubs screamed for justice. The Cubs demanded a forfeit because of the Giants' refusal to play off the tie on the following day, as provided by league rules. The Giants maintained that they were entitled to a 2-1 victory because they were being penalized for a baserunning habit that had gone uncalled by umpires in the past.

The disputants took their case to Pulliam, who supported O'Day's tie-game ruling. The Giants then presented their appeal to the league board of directors. Again they were rebuffed. They received instead an edict that, if the teams finished the race in a dead heat, the tie game would have to be replayed October 8 at the Polo Grounds.

The final day of the race found the teams with identical records of 98 wins and 55 losses. After nearly six months of heated competition, the N.L. championship would hinge on a single game—a game that the Giants thought they already had won.

Ideal baseball weather prevailed when the Cubs arrived at Grand Central Station. Their reception, however, was anything but cordial. Approximately 5,000 rowdies showered the players with all manner of epithets. It appeared that a fight might break out before a cordon of policemen whisked the players away to the Polo Grounds, where fans had been gathering since before sunrise. When the gates to the park finally were unlocked, about 27,000 rabid fans pushed their way inside before the gates were relocked to keep the crowd manageable. Another 20,000 people were seated on the bluffs surrounding the park.

As on September 23, the starting pitchers were Pfiester and Mathewson. But this time Pfiester was wild. He hit the first New York batter with a pitch and walked the second one, and when Donlin's double pushed across one run and the next batter walked, Chance summoned Mordecai (Three Finger) Brown from the bullpen.

Mathewson held the Cubs in check for two innings, but in the third his old nemesis, Tinker, belted a triple to launch a four-run rally that also featured doubles by Chance and right fielder Frank

SEPTEMBER 23, 1908								
Chicago	ab	r	h	rbi	New York	ab	r	h	rbi
Hayden, rf	4	0	0	0	Herzog, 2b	3	1	1	0
Evers, 2b	4	0	1	0	Bresnahan, c	3	0	0	0
Schulte, lf	4	0	0	0	Donlin, rf	4	0	1	1
Chance, 1b	4	0	1	0	Seymour, cf	4	0	1	0
Steinfeldt, 3b	2	0	0	0	Devlin, 3b	4	0	2	0
Hofman, cf	3	0	1	0	McCormick, lf	3	1	0	0
Tinker, ss	3	1	1	1	Merkle, 1b	3	0	1	0
Kling, c	3	0	1	0	Bridwell, ss	4	0	0	0
Pfiester, p	3	0	0	0	Mathewson, p	3	0	0	0
Totals	30	1	5	1	Totals	31	2	6	1

Chicago .... 0 0 0   0 1 0   0 0 0—1
New York .... 0 0 0   0 0 1   0 0 0—1

Chicago	IP	H	R	ER	BB	SO
Pfiester	9	6	1	0	2	0

New York	IP	H	R	ER	BB	SO
Mathewson	9	5	1	1	0	9

E—Steinfeldt, Tinker 2. DP—Chicago 3, New York 1. LOB—Chicago 3, New York 7. HR—Tinker. SH—Steinfeldt, Bresnahan. HBP—By Pfiester (McCormick). T—1:30.

Long after retirement, Fred Merkle returned to New York and posed with John McGraw's widow.

(Wildfire) Schulte. The Giants touched Brown for their second run in the seventh before losing, 4-2.

The Cubs went on to defeat the Tigers in the World Series. McGraw, meanwhile, screamed that he had been robbed of the pennant, a charge he repeated frequently the rest of his life.

As for Merkle, the 19-year-old first baseman was saddled by cruel fans and writers with the name "Bonehead," an unfair designation considering his actual offense. To be sure, his failure to touch second base was a major gaffe considering the importance of the game. But in his defense, he had done nothing more than what had been accepted as proper for years.

McGraw never censured his first baseman. He regarded Merkle as one of his more intelligent players and retained him on the Giants until August 1916, when Fred was traded to the Dodgers. He also played with the Cubs, the Yankees and a couple of minor league clubs before retiring in 1927.

Merkle moved to Florida, where he avoided any contact with major league baseball and refused interviews while working in real estate and various private enterprises. After years of being called a bonehead, he merely wanted to live in peace and disassociate himself from the game that had caused him such grief.

For nearly a quarter of a century, Merkle remained away from the major league scene. Then in 1950 he received a letter from Horace Stoneham. The owner of the Giants informed the ex-player

that the club had scheduled an Old-Timers Day in July and invited Merkle to attend. The old Giant considered the invitation at some length and eventually notified Stoneham that he would be there under one provision. At 61, he flatly rejected any thought of donning a uniform again. Stoneham agreed.

In the company of his daughter, Merkle returned to New York. The reception accorded him exceeded all expectations. Everywhere he went he was lionized. He held a reunion with McGraw's widow. He rehashed old times with Larry Doyle, his teammate at second base. He was interviewed on radio. When he was introduced at the Polo Grounds, the crowd gave him a standing ovation. He enjoyed the ball game and the festive hours that followed. When he boarded the train for Florida, Fred Merkle conceded that "I never had such a good time."

Back at Daytona Beach, Merkle lived out his remaining years far less bitter than he had been before returning to his old haunts in New York. He died March 2, 1956, at the age of 67.

The months following the Merkle incident in 1908 were even more tragic for Pulliam than for the unfortunate player. Beset by melancholy that at least partly was a result of his ruling that cost the Giants a flag, the bachelor president retired to his room at the New York Athletic Club on the evening of July 28, 1909. About 9:30 p.m. he picked up a revolver, pulled the trigger and fired a bullet into his brain.

Vander Meer Gets Double Dose

Cincinnati lefthander Johnny Vander Meer made his 1938 season one to remember.

In the summer of 1932, John Heydler devised a scheme to enhance the attractiveness of professional baseball as a livelihood for young athletes. But the National League president needed assistance in executing the project.

Heydler contacted Dave Driscoll, the business manager of the Brooklyn Dodgers. "Find me a boy," he told Driscoll, "who has a modest background, whose people are of the middle class and whose father has an industrial background." The idea was to feature the youngster in a propaganda film designed to lure young men away from golf and tennis and into Organized Baseball.

Driscoll's talent search took him no farther than Midland Park, N.J., to the home of first-generation Dutch immigrants. Driscoll explained his mission to the deeply religious parents, who shrank from the notion that their 17-year-old son, who already had three no-hit games in semipro ball to his credit, would be associated with moving pictures and their carnal implications.

Their resistance melted when Driscoll guaranteed them that their handsome, curly-haired son could return to his church baseball league as soon as the picture was completed. The son endorsed the project enthusiastically as soon as he learned that he would receive a spring training trip with the Dodgers in 1933. In Miami, the cameras would show him realizing his lifelong dream of pitching in a major league camp.

The project could have ended at that point and no one ever would have heard of the subject of Heydler's promotional film. But the young left-hander in the starring role was Johnny Vander Meer, and even though he wasn't considered a prospect at that time, it wouldn't be too many more years before he would leave his imprint on baseball —and particularly the Dodgers.

While Vander Meer was in Miami, he was befriended by Joe Shaute, an aging lefty whose best years had been spent with the Cleveland Indians. Shaute liked the unpolished kid, and he urged Dodgers Manager Max Carey to use him in an in-

Johnny Vander Meer pitches to the Dodgers en route to his second straight no-hitter.

trasquad game. But Carey, who was more interested in the bona fide rookies in his camp, considered Vander Meer's presence merely a nuisance. Max did agree, however, to send Johnny to Dayton of the Class-C Middle Atlantic League.

Vander Meer won 11 games and lost 10 in his first season as a professional. He also struck out 132 batters and walked 74 in 183 innings and earned a promotion to Scranton of the Class-A New York-Pennsylvania League. In 1936, after compiling a two-year record of 18-18 at Scranton, Johnny jumped to Nashville. But he had problems with his control, and after losing his only decision in the Southern Association, he was transferred to Durham of the Piedmont League. Vandy finally found a groove with the Class-B club. He won 19 of 25 decisions, led the league with 295 strikeouts and a

2.65 earned-run average and walked 116 batters in 214 innings. The young lefty was an overwhelming choice as The Sporting News' first Minor League Player of the Year.

The youngster's next step upward was to Cincinnati. But wildness plagued him again, and after going 3-5 for the Reds he was demoted to Syracuse (International), where he slumped to 5-11.

Back with the Reds for spring training in 1938, Vander Meer encountered his old bugaboo. Despite his own strenuous efforts and those of Manager Bill McKechnie and coach Hank Gowdy, Johnny was unable to master his control.

The problem was at its frustrating peak when the Reds met the Boston Red Sox in an exhibition contest. In the pregame drills, Gowdy summoned Vander Meer. "I've been talking to you and Mc-

Johnny Vander Meer was the center of attention in Cincinnati after his incredible pitching feat.

Kechnie has been talking to you," the coach grumbled. "Today I'm not going to talk to you. I'm going to let you look."

At that, Gowdy pointed across the field to Lefty Grove, the grizzled and sometimes grumpy veteran of the Red Sox. "Watch him closely," Gowdy advised. "See how he keeps the ball in front of him when he pitches."

Vandy did as instructed. Then he introduced himself to the legendary pitcher, who lent a sympathetic ear to the confused youngster. By words and demonstrations, Lefty explained the methods he had employed in curbing wildness.

The impromptu clinic produced immediate results. On May 20, the 6-foot, 190-pound lefty blanked the Giants, 4-0, on a five-hitter, and Johnny beat the same team, 4-1, on a three-hitter June 5. By that time he had a 5-2 record in 11 appearances.

Vander Meer's next outing was June 11 against the Boston Bees at Cincinnati's Crosley Field. The crowd of less than 10,000 fans had no idea what was in store that Saturday afternoon when Vandy started by retiring Gene Moore, Johnny Cooney and

Vince DiMaggio in order in the first inning. When he forced pinch-hitter Ray Mueller to ground out almost two hours later, Johnny had posted a no-hitter, the first by a Redleg in 19 years. He lacked pinpoint control, issuing three walks, but he faced only 28 batters in the course of his 3-0 masterpiece.

It was Vander Meer's turn to pitch again four days later when the Reds traveled to Brooklyn to face the Dodgers at Ebbets Field. On this occasion, 38,748 wild-eyed Flatbush fanatics poured through the gates. They were there not so much because a no-hit hurler was scheduled to pitch, although that did make the occasion even more special, but because it was the first night game in Brooklyn history.

The bleacher gates were opened at 5 p.m., and within minutes they were closed, that section having filled to capacity. Larry MacPhail, the Dodgers' majordomo who had arrived from a similar position in Cincinnati a short while before, overlooked no opportunities to make this night one that would be remembered for decades to come.

Jesse Owens, the gold-medal Olympic sprinter of

1936, was a feature of the pregame entertainment. In one event, Owens spotted Ernie Koy, the Dodgers' fleet center fielder, a 10-yard handicap in a 100-yard dash. Koy won, barely. In a second event, Owens ran the 120-yard hurdles in competition with outfielder Gil Brack, who ran the course in the flat. Again Owens lost. He also gave a broad-jumping exhibition.

The main gates to the park were locked at 8:36 on that Wednesday evening. A moment later, 615 floodlights, representing the illumination of 92 million candles, bathed the field in light amid the thunderous applause of the multitudes. A bomb exploding behind second base was the signal for the massed bands to strike up the national anthem, and at 9:23, Max Butcher fired the first pitch of the historic night.

Butcher was not long for the game. The right-hander departed under fire in the third inning when the Reds erupted for four runs, three riding home on first baseman Frank McCormick's home run. A walk to catcher Ernie Lombardi and singles by center fielder Harry Craft and third baseman Lew Riggs made the score 4-0.

Tot Pressnell, who replaced Butcher, held the Reds in check until the seventh inning. With one out, right fielder Ival Goodman smacked a line drive off Pressnell's kneecap, and the righthander was taken off the field on a stretcher. Luke Hamlin came out to pitch for Brooklyn, but the Reds made it 5-0 when Goodman stole second and scored on Craft's single. Vander Meer scored Cincinnati's final run in the eighth when left fielder Wally Berger tripled him home.

While the Reds were accumulating 11 hits off

four pitchers, Vander Meer was dispatching Brooklyn batters with regularity. In the first inning he retired right fielder Kiki Cuyler on a fly ball, fanned second baseman Pete Coscarart and set down left fielder Buddy Hassett on a ground ball. Grounders off the bats of catcher Babe Phelps and third baseman Cookie Lavagetto, a walk to first baseman Dolph Camilli and Koy's pop-up took care of the Dodgers in the second. Shortstop Leo Durocher grounded out and Pressnell struck out to start the third, but Cuyler then became the second Dodger to reach base when Vandy surrendered another base on balls. Coscarart flied out, however, to end the inning.

Succeeding innings came and went thusly:

FOURTH—Hassett grounded out. Phelps fanned. Lavagetto flied out.

FIFTH—Camilli and Koy grounded back to the mound. Durocher fouled out.

SIXTH—Pressnell grounded out. Cuyler walked. Brack, batting for Coscarart, struck out. Hassett grounded out.

SEVENTH—Phelps grounded out. Lavagetto and Camilli walked. Koy fanned. Durocher forced Camilli.

EIGHTH—Woody English, batting for Hamlin, struck out. Cuyler flied out. Johnny Hudson, who had taken Coscarart's place at second, went down on strikes.

By the time Vander Meer walked out to the mound for the bottom of the ninth inning, jam-packed Ebbets Field was a madhouse. The Flatbush crowd had been roaring with every pitch, giving the 23-year-old lefty plenty of vocal support as he faced the home team. Seemingly everyone in attendance that night knew that Vandy was three outs away from an unprecedented feat: Two no-hitters in a row.

The inning started well enough for Vander Meer. Hassett hit a grounder back to the pitcher, who tossed over to McCormick for the first out. Within minutes, however, the bases were loaded as Johnny walked Phelps, Lavagetto and Camilli in succession. Sitting in his dugout, Dodgers Manager Burleigh Grimes was thinking that Vander Meer might just be ready to buckle under the pressure.

McKechnie decided to make sure he didn't. The Cincinnati skipper ambled out to the mound, where he huddled with Vandy, Lombardi and the entire Reds infield. "Take your time, Johnny," McKechnie said. "Quit pitching so fast and pitch the way you know how to pitch."

That pep talk did Johnny a world of good. He induced the next batter, Koy, to hit a grounder to third, where Riggs fielded the ball and fired home for the forceout on pinch-runner Goody Rosen.

"You know," Vandy recalled years later, "Lombardi was going to throw down to first for the dou-

JUNE 15, 1938									
Cincinnati	ab	r	h	rbi	Brooklyn	ab	r	h	rbi
Frey, 2b	5	0	1	0	Cuyler, rf	2	0	0	0
Berger, lf	5	1	3	1	Coscarart, 2b	2	0	0	0
Goodman, rf	3	2	1	0	Brack, ph	1	0	0	0
McCormick, 1b	5	1	1	3	Hudson, 2b	1	0	0	0
Lombardi, c	3	1	0	0	Hassett, lf	4	0	0	0
Craft, cf	5	0	3	1	Phelps, c	3	0	0	0
Riggs, 3b	4	0	1	1	Rosen, pr	0	0	0	0
Myers, ss	4	0	0	0	Lavagetto, 3b	2	0	0	0
Vander Meer, p	4	1	1	0	Camilli, 1b	1	0	0	0
					Koy, cf	4	0	0	0
					Durocher, ss	4	0	0	0
					Butcher, p	0	0	0	0
					Pressnell, p	2	0	0	0
					Hamlin, p	0	0	0	0
					English, ph	1	0	0	0
					Tamulis, p	0	0	0	0
Totals	38	6	11	6	Totals	27	0	0	0

Cincinnati	0	0	4	0	0	0	1	1	0—6
Brooklyn	0	0	0	0	0	0	0	0	0—0

Cincinnati	IP	H	R	ER	BB	SO
Vander Meer (W)	9	0	0	0	8	7
Brooklyn	IP	H	R	ER	BB	SO
Butcher (L)	2⅔	5	4	4	3	1
Pressnell	3⅔	4	1	1	1	3
Hamlin	1⅔	2	1	0	1	3
Tamulis	1	0	0	0	0	0

E—Lavagetto 2. LOB—Cincinnati 9, Brooklyn 8. 2B—Berger. 3B—Berger. HR—McCormick. SB—Goodman. T—2:22. A—38,748.

ble play but didn't want to chance it. During one of his frequent walks out to me on the mound, he built my confidence by saying, 'I know you can get the next guy.' "

Only one guy was left, and Johnny got him. Durocher flied out to center field, giving Vandy his second consecutive no-hit shutout, this time 6-0.

As the ball settled into Craft's glove, Johnny's teammates rushed to the mound to congratulate him—and to protect him from the oncoming throng of well-wishers. Quickly they whisked Vandy to the safety of the clubhouse. Reporters who wanted to interview the game's first double no-hit hurler were left to chat with Vandy's parents, who were among the 700 townfolk from nearby Midland Park who attended the game.

Johnny spent the night at his parents' home, then went fishing with Midland Park's police chief the next day. Meanwhile, the Ohio state Senate passed a resolution in "tribute to the newly crowned king of the baseball world."

Vander Meer, who had walked eight of the 35 batters he faced in his second no-hit gem, extended his hitless string to 21⅔ innings before Bees third baseman Debs Garms broke the spell with a fourth-inning single in a game at Boston. "The hit came on a 3-and-2 pitch and went right up the middle," Vandy recalled. "I was so relieved that the tension was broken, I could have kissed him." Johnny won the game, 14-1.

Vandy pitched three scoreless innings of one-hit ball for the victorious National Leaguers in the 1938 All-Star Game at Cincinnati and finished the season with a 15-10 record. He also struck out 125 batters and walked 103 in 225 innings while compiling a 3.12 ERA. Just two years after he was hailed as the No. 1 minor league player, Vander Meer was selected as The Sporting News' Major League Player of the Year for 1938.

Except for a brief stint with Indianapolis (American Association) in 1940 and two years in the U.S. Navy (1944-45), Vandy remained with the Reds through 1949. His most productive season was 1942, when he posted 18 victories. That also was the second of three consecutive years in which he led the league in strikeouts. He pitched for the Chicago Cubs in 1950 and made one appearance with the Cleveland Indians—his last as a major leaguer—in 1951. He had 119 victories and 121 losses to his credit in his career.

In 1952, the Dutch Master pitched for Tulsa of the Texas League. At 37, he still possessed some of his old cunning and on July 15, exactly 14 years and one month after his epochal performance in Brooklyn, Johnny spun another hitless game. He hurled the 12-0 gem before 335 paying customers at Beaumont, Tex. Ironically, the Beaumont manager was Harry Craft, the former center fielder who had accounted for the final putout at Brooklyn on June 15, 1938.

Vander Meer spent several more years in the minors as a pitcher-manager and as a non-playing manager. He also had a partnership in a hardware business and worked as a salesman for a brewery before retiring to his home in Tampa. In all that time, no one has matched his feat of throwing consecutive no-hitters.

"Someone may tie the record," he once said, "but I don't think anyone will break it. If someone does, it will be unbelievable."

Long after retirement, Johnny Vander Meer enjoyed reliving the moments that made his name one of the most memorable in baseball history.

Cookie Crumbles Bevens' Bid

Cookie Lavagetto strokes the double that sends Bill Bevens down to gut-wrenching defeat.

If the big righthander for the New York Yankees had been a triskaidekaphobiac, living in mortal dread of the number 13, he would have suspected that sinister influences were at work on an autumn afternoon in 1947.

For three consecutive years, the won-and-lost columns in the statistical record of Floyd Clifford (Bill) Bevens had contained the number 13. In 1945, Bevens won 13 games for the Bronx Bombers, while in each of the next two seasons he lost the same number for the same team. Bearing in mind that everything seems to come in threes and he was a triple crown champion in the unluckiest of numbers, he should have known that 1947 was not going to be his lucky year.

In all likelihood, though, Bevens paid scant attention to the figures. He was a taciturn type of whom a teammate once said, "If Bill nods to you, he's practically boisterous."

Bevens' job was to throw baseballs with great velocity and little finesse. Joe McCarthy, who managed the Yankees when Bevens broke into the majors, assured the rookie: "You're big and strong and have a live fastball. Never mind trying to pitch to spots. Just rear back and fire away. If you're around the plate, they're going to be swinging. And they're not going to be able to do much with your stuff."

But, as often is the case with players of vast potential, Bevens experienced a tinge of misfortune, too. In 1946, when Bill compiled his best major league record of 16 victories (against 13 losses), he dropped two 1-0 heartbreakers, one to Tex Hughson of Boston when a walk to Ted Williams with the bases loaded forced in the only run of the game, and another to Cleveland when Bob Feller pitched

The flight of Cookie Lavagetto's ninth-inning double in Game 4 of the
1947 World Series at Ebbets Field is diagrammed.

a no-hitter and catcher Frank Hayes tagged him for
a home run in the ninth inning. In 1947, Bevens
won his first two games and then fell off. For the
campaign, he won seven games (compared with 13
losses) but remained in the starting rotation, a tribute to the confidence reposed in him by his manager, Bucky Harris. Bevens completed 11 of 23 starts
and hurled one shutout, a 6-0 decision over Philadelphia a week before the close of the season.

In the World Series against the Brooklyn
Dodgers, Bevens drew the fourth-game assignment,
by which time the Yankees had gained a two-to-one
edge in games. His mound opponent for the October 3 contest at Ebbets Field was Harry Taylor, a
righthander who had won 10 games for the National League champions and boasted an earned-run average of 3.11, the sixth-lowest figure in the circuit.
The Friday afternoon game marked Taylor's World
Series debut, but it was an effort that he would have
preferred to forget. He failed to retire a solitary batter.

Second baseman Snuffy Stirnweiss and right
fielder Tommy Henrich led off the game with back-
to-back singles. When shortstop Pee Wee Reese
dropped Jackie Robinson's relay on a potential
double-play ball, the bases were loaded. A walk to
center fielder Joe DiMaggio scored Stirnweiss and
convinced Burt Shotton that a change was in order.
The Brooklyn manager summoned Hal Gregg,

who retired the side without further scoring. Gregg
yielded a second run in the fourth inning when
third baseman Billy Johnson tripled and left fielder
John Lindell doubled, but the righthander was
faultless otherwise as he scattered four hits in seven
innings before being lifted for a pinch-hitter.

In the meantime, Bevens held the Dodgers without a hit, but he was doling out walks most gra-
ciously. He issued two free passes in the first inning,
one each in the second and third, two in the fifth,
one in the sixth and another in the seventh before
retiring the Brooks in order in the eighth.

Despite all that generosity, Bevens wriggled out of
danger in all but one of those innings. In the fifth,
he walked the first two batters, third baseman Spi-
der Jorgensen and Gregg, both of whom advanced
another base on second baseman Eddie Stanky's
sacrifice bunt. Reese followed with a grounder to
shortstop Phil Rizzuto, who nailed Gregg going into
third while Jorgensen scored. Bevens struck out
Robinson to end the inning, but the Dodgers had
reduced the Yankees' lead to 2-1.

The Yankees mounted a threat in the ninth inning against Hank Behrman but, with one out and
the bases loaded, righthander Hugh Casey shuffled
out of the bullpen. The implacable reliever—the
fourth Dodger pitcher of the day—made one pitch,
a changeup screwball that Henrich rapped into a
double play.

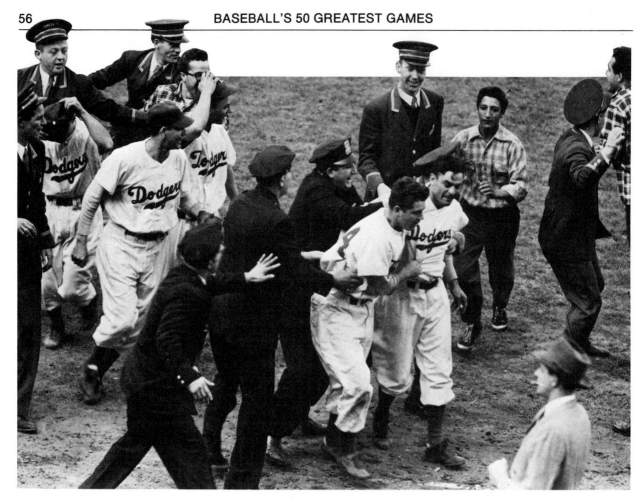

Cookie Lavagetto is escorted from the field by police and happy teammates after ending Bill Bevens' no-hit bid.

As the 29-year-old Bevens trudged to the mound for the ninth time, he was only three outs away from a pitching pinnacle that had resisted the finest efforts of Cy Young, Christy Mathewson, Walter Johnson and other mound masters. At that time, no one ever had pitched a World Series no-hitter. Bevens drew even closer to that unprecedented feat when the first Brooklyn batter, catcher Bruce Edwards, flied deep to left field, but then the old ogre, the base on balls, reared its ugly head once more. Center fielder Carl Furillo walked.

After Jorgensen fouled out to first baseman George McQuinn, bringing the Yankees within one out of a 3-1 Series lead and Bevens just as close to everlasting fame, Shotton scanned the bench for somebody to bat for Casey. His glance fell on Pete Reiser, a .309 hitter in 1947 who had sprained his ankle while sliding the previous day. Pistol Pete had spent the early hours of this game in the whirlpool bath and when, at last, he appeared in the dugout, Shotton had given him a puzzled look and inquired: "What are you doing here? You can't even stand on your feet."

"Maybe I can't," Reiser responded, "but if you need me I'll give it one hell of a try."

Shotton had no doubt about that; he sent the gimpy outfielder up to bat for Casey. He also sent Al Gionfriddo in to run for Furillo. After the count went to two balls and one strike, Shotton decided on a daring piece of strategy. He flashed the steal sign to Gionfriddo, who belly-flopped safely into second base ahead of catcher Yogi Berra's high throw.

"I slipped when I started my break and thought I was a dead duck with that lost step," Gionfriddo said afterward. "I would have been out had Berra's throw not been high."

Then it was Harris' turn to gamble. He ordered Bevens to walk Reiser intentionally.

"I knew it was against baseball tradition to put the winning run on base," the manager later explained, "but this was an exceptional case. Who would you rather pitch to—Reiser or the next batter, Eddie Stanky? And Brooklyn was without left-handed pinch-hitters. They had already used Arky Vaughan. Reiser could have hit the ball over the fence. He had done it before in a World Series."

As Reiser limped to first base, Shotton surveyed his bench again. His gaze fell on 32-year-old Cookie Lavagetto.

"Want me to run for Pete?" asked Cookie, a .261 hitter that season in a part-time role.

"I want you to bat for Stanky," answered Shotton, replacing a righthanded regular with a righthanded irregular and sending Eddie Miksis in to run for Reiser.

Bevens thought he knew how to handle Lavagetto. "We had received printed instructions on how to pitch to the Dodgers," Bevens recalled. "The word on Lavagetto was fastballs outside."

But Cookie knew better.

"If they were pitching outside to me, they were almost entirely wrong," he said. "Fast and tight was the way to handle me."

Lavagetto swung at Bevens' first pitch and missed. Once more Bevens was within two strikes of no-hit immortality. Again Bill threw. The ball was on the outside part of the plate—"just where I wanted it," according to the pitcher.

"This is it," Lavagetto muttered to himself as he went with the pitch and drove it toward right field, where Henrich considered his options. Old Reliable could either try for a leaping catch or play the carom off the wall and try to hold the go-ahead run at third base.

Henrich chose the latter course. But after crashing off the fence, the ball bounced off his shoulder and trickled to the ground. By the time Henrich retrieved the ball and fired it to the cutoff man, Gionfriddo had scored and Miksis had slid safely across the plate with the winning run.

Cookie Lavagetto was the toast of the Dodger locker room after his big hit.

"As soon as the ball was hit," Bevens recalled, "I ran to back up the plate. After Miksis slid across the plate, almost on Gionfriddo's heels, I saw umpire Larry Goetz move up to dust off the plate. He was so wrapped up in the game, he didn't know it was over. But I did."

The Ebbets Field clock showed that the double by Lavagetto that produced the 3-2 victory was struck at 3:50 p.m. But, for Bevens, it was midnight, when fairy-tale carriages and pitchers' no-hit dreams turn into pumpkins. There was little consolation for Bevens when newsmen informed him that Lavaget-

OCTOBER 3, 1947

New York	ab	r	h	rbi	Brooklyn	ab	r	h	rbi
Stirnweiss, 2b	4	1	2	0	Stanky, 2b	1	0	0	0
Henrich, rf	5	0	1	0	Lavagetto, ph	1	0	1	2
Berra, c	4	0	0	0	Reese, ss	4	0	0	1
DiMaggio, cf	2	0	0	1	Robinson, 1b	4	0	0	0
McQuinn, 1b	4	0	1	0	Walker, rf	2	0	0	0
Johnson, 3b	4	1	1	0	Hermanski, lf	4	0	0	0
Lindell, lf	3	0	2	1	Edwards, c	4	0	0	0
Rizzuto, ss	4	0	1	0	Furillo, cf	3	0	0	0
Bevens, p	3	0	0	0	Gionfriddo, pr	0	1	0	0
					Jorgensen, 3b	2	1	0	0
					Taylor, p	0	0	0	0
					Gregg, p	1	0	0	0
					Vaughan, ph	0	0	0	0
					Behrman, p	0	0	0	0
					Casey, p	0	0	0	0
					Reiser, ph	0	0	0	0
					Miksis, pr	0	1	0	0
Totals	33	2	8	2	Totals	26	3	1	3

New York	1 0 0	1 0 0	0 0 0—2
Brooklyn	0 0 0	0 1 0	0 0 2—3

Two out when winning run scored.

New York	IP	H	R	ER	BB	SO
Bevens (L)	8⅔	1	3	3	10	5
Brooklyn	IP	H	R	ER	BB	SO
Taylor	0*	2	1	0	1	0
Gregg	7	4	1	1	3	5
Behrman	1⅓	2	0	0	0	0
Casey (W)	⅔	0	0	0	0	0

*Pitched to four batters in first.

E—Berra, Reese, Edwards, Jorgensen. DP—Brooklyn 3. LOB—New York 9, Brooklyn 8. 2B—Lindell, Lavagetto. 3B—Johnson. SB—Rizzuto, Reese, Gionfriddo. SH—Stanky, Bevens. WP—Bevens. T—2:20. A—33,443.

to's hit was, as far as they could tell, his first of the year to right field.

Of the 600 writers covering the Series, only one—from Bevens' hometown of Salem, Ore.—and his wife knew that there was a second development at Ebbets Field that October day, equally as significant to the career of Bill Bevens as his near no-hitter. During the game the pitcher injured his arm. On the night before the seventh Series game, Bevens' wife massaged the shoulder through many sleepless hours. He pitched 2⅔ scoreless innings during the Yankees' Series-clinching victory and then returned to Salem, where he was greeted as a conquering hero. Bill was feted at civic celebrations and groups vied for a chance to heap praise on the native son who had come so close to every pitcher's dream. A beer company gave Bill a job that paid $600 a month. All he had to do was shake hands with endless columns of adulators and sell beer to those who clamored for an opportunity to mingle with the celebrity.

Cookie Lavagetto (left) offers Bill Bevens a sympathetic hand after breaking up his no-hit bid.

When Bevens reported to training camp in 1948, his worst fears were realized. The five-month rest had not cured his ailing arm. That year he pitched only eight innings for Newark of the International League.

When he returned home at the close of the 1948 season, his right arm now dead, Bill was rehired by the beer company. Only this time he was paid $300 a month, half his salary of a year earlier, and he was assigned the job of loading heavy beer cases onto trucks. In 1949, after an unsuccessful stint with the Pacific Coast League's Seattle club, the World Series hero of two years before was reduced to playing first base and the outfield for a Salem softball team.

After months of treatment, much of which was excruciatingly painful, Bevens felt encouraged to try again the next year. In 77 innings for Sacramento and San Diego of the Pacific Coast League he compiled a 7.48 ERA. In 1951 he was down in the Class-B Western International League, where he won 20 games for the Salem club. The arm that once had propelled a baseball with blinding speed had lost much of its resiliency, but based on his performance in Salem, the Cincinnati Reds drafted him the following November. Still it was no go. Bevens never pitched in the major leagues after his relief appearance in Game 7 of the 1947 World Series.

For Hugh Casey, who had defeated Bevens with only one pitch in Game 4 (and also had won Game 3 in relief), the years were even more cruel. On July 3, 1951, while Bevens' Salem club was in Tacoma, Wash., for a series of games, Casey telephoned his estranged wife from an Atlanta hotel room. As they chatted, the onetime imperturbable relief pitcher calmly discharged a 16-gauge shotgun into his head.

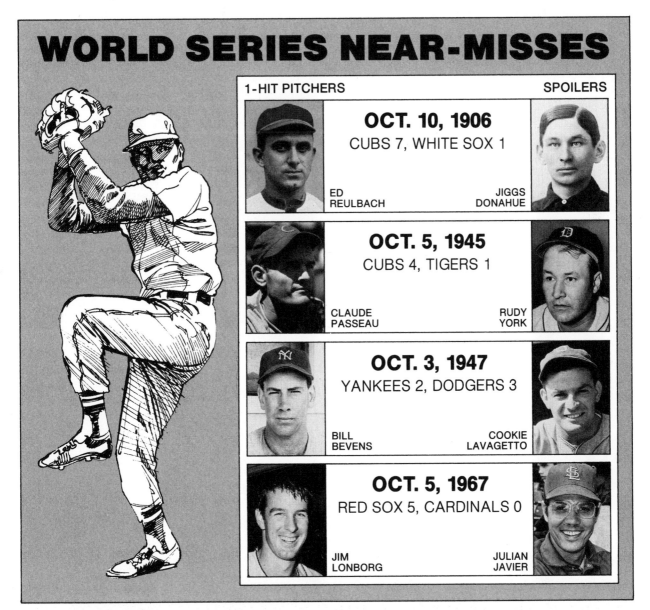

WORLD SERIES NEAR-MISSES

1-HIT PITCHERS   **SPOILERS**

OCT. 10, 1906
CUBS 7, WHITE SOX 1
ED REULBACH   JIGGS DONAHUE

OCT. 5, 1945
CUBS 4, TIGERS 1
CLAUDE PASSEAU   RUDY YORK

OCT. 3, 1947
YANKEES 2, DODGERS 3
BILL BEVENS   COOKIE LAVAGETTO

OCT. 5, 1967
RED SOX 5, CARDINALS 0
JIM LONBORG   JULIAN JAVIER

The Game That Got Away

As a teen-ager in Los Angeles in the early 1930s, Arnold Malcolm Owen made an inspired decision. If, as he fully intended, he someday would play for the St. Louis Cardinals, a gritty crew that featured such names as Pepper, Ripper, Dizzy and Lippy, his baptismal name simply would not do. He needed a name that denoted the aggressive style of the Gas House Gang.

After giving the matter some thought, the youngster settled on a name that clearly reflected the scrappy, sometimes brawly nature of the Cardinals: Mickey. That sobriquet had been worn with distinction by some of the game's finest players, including another catcher named Cochrane. Mickey it was!

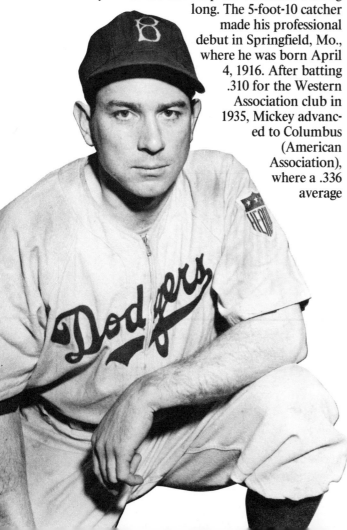

Mickey Owen did not keep the Cardinals waiting long. The 5-foot-10 catcher made his professional debut in Springfield, Mo., where he was born April 4, 1916. After batting .310 for the Western Association club in 1935, Mickey advanced to Columbus (American Association), where a .336 average

earned him a quick promotion to the Cardinals for 1937. His fondest boyhood dream had been realized in two years.

Owen wore the St. Louis uniform for four seasons, but he became expendable with the emergence of Walker Cooper, another native Missourian who swung a more productive bat. In December 1940, Mickey became a Brooklyn Dodger. Owen's temperament was well suited to the Dodgers, who mirrored the personality of their aggressive chief executive officer, Larry MacPhail.

In Flatbush, Owen handled the pitches of Whitlow Wyatt, Kirby Higbe, Curt Davis and Fred Fitzsimmons and battled side by side with first baseman Dolph Camilli, second baseman Billy Herman, center fielder Pete Reiser, left fielder Joe Medwick, right fielder Dixie Walker, shortstop Pee Wee Reese and third baseman Cookie Lavagetto. None exemplified the fighting spirit of the organization better, however, than the expatriate from St. Louis.

Mickey was behind the plate in 128 games for the 1941 Dodgers, who won the National League pennant by 2½ games over the Cardinals. He tied for the league lead among catchers in putouts and fielding percentage while setting a record for most consecutive chances without an error (476) and, on August 4, entered the record book by making three putouts in one inning on fouls. The Dodgers prized Owen, who hit .231 with only 44 runs batted in that year, for his steady, agile glove more than anything else.

In the first World Series game, played October 1 at Yankee Stadium, Owen contributed a run-scoring triple. But the Dodgers were able to tally just once more against Yankees righthander Red Ruffing, who beat Brooklyn and Davis, 3-2. The Yankees' 10-game Series winning streak finally came to an end the next day, however, as Wyatt handed the Bombers a 3-2 setback. Owen singled in the tying run to help the Dodgers even the Series at one game apiece. But the Yankees resumed the lead in Game 3 at Brooklyn, where Marius Russo blanked Owen and many of his teammates on a four-hitter, 2-1. The game was scoreless in the seventh inning when

Brooklyn catcher Mickey Owen was known for his steady glove work.

Yankee Tommy Henrich heads toward first base as the ball eludes Dodger catcher Mickey Owen.

Russo knocked Fitzsimmons out of the game with a savage line drive that caromed off the Brooklyn starter's leg. The Yanks then reached reliever Hugh Casey for both of their runs in the eighth.

By most calculations, the fourth game was pivotal. If the Dodgers could win the Sunday game at Ebbets Field and square the Series at two victories apiece, they stood a good chance of winning their first World Series in three tries.

An unseasonal heat wave gripped New York on October 5, with the temperature in the 90s, as 33,813 fans jammed the Flatbush park for what was expected to be a pitching duel between Higbe and Atley Donald, a pair of righthanders. But Higbe, who had gone 22-9 during the regular season, got off to a shaky start. Singles by third baseman Red Rolfe and left fielder Charlie Keller produced one Yankee run in the first inning. Higbe surrendered just one hit over the next two frames, but he was KOd in the fourth. Keller led off with a double, after which catcher Bill Dickey walked and second baseman Joe Gordon singled to load the bases. Higbe appeared to be wiggling out of danger when shortstop Phil Rizzuto forced Keller at the plate and Donald fanned on three pitches, but first baseman Johnny Sturm followed with a single that drove in Dickey and Gordon. Larry French came on to record the last out of the inning, holding the Yankees' lead to 3-0.

The Dodgers stormed back with a pair of runs in each of their next two tries. Donald retired the first two batters in the bottom of the fourth before issuing consecutive walks to Owen and second baseman Pete Coscarart. Both runners then scored on pinch-hitter Jimmy Wasdell's double. In the fifth, Walker led off with a double and scored when Reiser hit Donald's first pitch over the scoreboard in right field for a home run. That blast sent Donald to the showers and lifted the Dodgers into the lead, 4-3.

That was the score after eight innings. On the mound for the Dodgers was Casey, who had come to the rescue of Johnny Allen with two out and the bases loaded in the fifth inning. The redoubtable reliever had induced Gordon to fly out to end the threat, and over the next three innings he had checked the Yankees on two harmless singles. Who could doubt that sweet victory was just moments away?

The noise level rose appreciably when the Dodgers took the field for the start of the ninth inning. It soared higher when Casey retired Sturm, the leadoff batter, on a grounder to second base.

The chorus of cheers grew even louder as the right-hander forced Rolfe to tap back to the mound. Only one more out and Ebbets Field would erupt, perhaps as never before.

As right fielder Tommy Henrich stepped into the batter's box, Rizzuto waited nervously in the runway leading from the visitors' dugout to the clubhouse. He was holding the gloves of several of his teammates to avoid the risk of having them stolen by overzealous Brooklyn fans after the game.

Henrich, who had hit two outfield flies, popped out and been hit by a pitch on his previous plate appearances that day, worked the count to 3-and-2. Casey rocked and fired once more. The lefthanded batter swung . . . and missed. The right arm of umpire Larry Goetz shot out convulsively . . . strike three . . . the game was over . . . the Dodgers had won, 4-3 . . . the Series was tied . . . the expected roar rocked the old park.

Then, as if it had suffered a collective punch in the stomach, the crowd gasped. The game wasn't over. The strike-three pitch had bounced off Owen's mitt, and Henrich was racing toward first base. Rizzuto, alerted by the yells of the spectators, stopped in his retreat and returned to the dugout to see what was happening.

"There was Tommy running to first base and Owen chasing the ball over by his own dugout," the little shortstop recalled. "By the time he got it, Tommy was on first and there wasn't any play."

At third base, umpire Bill Grieve surveyed the situation. "It doesn't matter," he thought. "Casey will get the next batter, and it will all be over." It was his only incorrect decision of the day.

As center fielder Joe DiMaggio strode to the plate, Casey stood on the pitching mound, a solitary figure devoid of counsel or comfort from his catcher, a coach or Manager Leo Durocher. Perhaps the Dodgers were in shock, but after Henrich reached base on Owen's error, no one went out to the mound to console the pitcher.

That oversight immediately became apparent as DiMaggio whistled a single to left field. Still, Owen remained behind the plate and Durocher sat motionless in the dugout.

Keller was next. Casey got two quick strikes on the left fielder, who drilled the next pitch against the right-field wall for a double. Henrich and Di-Maggio scored, giving the Yankees a 5-4 lead. Dickey then coaxed a walk from the obviously unnerved Casey, and Gordon blasted a double to deep left field to drive in the third and fourth unearned runs of the inning. After Casey walked Rizzuto, the inning finally came to a merciful end when pitcher Johnny Murphy grounded out.

Dodger reliever Hugh Casey couldn't close the Yankee flood gates.

OCTOBER 5, 1941

New York	ab	r	h	rbi	Brooklyn	ab	r	h	rbi
Sturm, 1b	5	0	2	2	Reese, ss	5	0	0	0
Rolfe, 3b	5	1	2	0	Walker, rf	5	1	2	0
Henrich, rf	4	1	0	0	Reiser, cf	5	1	2	2
DiMaggio, cf	4	1	2	0	Camilli, 1b	4	0	2	0
Keller, lf	5	1	4	3	Riggs, 3b	3	0	0	0
Dickey, c	2	2	0	0	Medwick, lf	2	0	0	0
Gordon, 2b	5	1	2	2	Allen, p	0	0	0	0
Rizzuto, ss	4	0	0	0	Casey, p	2	0	1	0
Donald, p	2	0	0	0	Owen, c	2	1	0	0
Breuer, p	1	0	0	0	Coscarart, 2b	3	1	0	0
Selkirk, ph	1	0	0	0	Higbe, p	1	0	1	0
Murphy, p	1	0	0	0	French, p	0	0	0	0
					Wasdell, ph-lf	3	0	1	2
Totals	39	7	12	7	Totals	35	4	9	4

New York	1	0	0	2	0	0	0	0	4—7
Brooklyn	0	0	0	2	2	0	0	0	0—4

New York	IP	H	R	ER	BB	SO
Donald	4*	6	4	4	3	2
Breuer	3	3	0	0	1	2
Murphy (W)	2	0	0	0	0	1

Brooklyn	IP	H	R	ER	BB	SO
Higbe	3⅔	6	3	3	2	1
French	⅓	0	0	0	0	0
Allen	⅔	1	0	0	1	0
Casey (L)	4⅓	5	4	0	2	1

*Pitched to two batters in fifth.

E—Owen. DP—New York 1. LOB—New York 11, Brooklyn 8. 2B—Keller 2, Walker, Camilli, Wasdell, Gordon. HR—Reiser. HBP—By Allen (Henrich). T—2:54. A—33,813.

Yankee Tommy Henrich (left) struck out, but (left to right) Joe DiMaggio, Charlie Keller and Joe Gordon made the Dodgers pay for their mistake.

Murphy, who had taken over for reliever Marv Breuer in the eighth, earned the improbable victory by retiring the shellshocked Dodgers in order in the bottom of the ninth. The Yankees then wrapped up the world championship the next day with a 3-1 victory behind the four-hit pitching of Ernie Bonham.

What had happened on the missed third strike? Had Casey "loaded one up," as he occasionally was accused of doing? Who was to blame for the misplay that had created Brooklyn's day of infamy?

Casey's pitch was not a spitter, insisted Owen, who refused to hide or point a finger. With dozens of reporters ready to crown him with a deluxe set of goat horns, Owen explained patiently for the first of what was to become hundreds of times precisely what had occurred.

"Casey has two kinds of curves," he related. "He has the big, sweeping curve that he tried early in the game, but it hung. He also has the quick curve that was working real good. When I called for the curve (to Henrich), I was looking for the quick one, but Casey rolled off that big one, and it really broke."

Years after the incident, Henrich recalled: "With the count against me, I was guarding the plate. It came in chest high, and that ball broke like no other curve I'd ever seen Casey throw. As I start to swing, I think, 'No good, hold up.' That thing broke so sharp, though, that as I tried to hold up, my mind said, 'He (Owen) might have trouble with it.' If you look at the picture of it, you'll see that I'm already looking back over my shoulder. I'm expecting him to lose that ball."

Mickey assumed full responsibility. The pitch "took me by surprise, too," he said. "I just didn't get

my glove turned enough, and the ball bounced off the heel."

Owen said his first reaction was surprise, followed by disgust. "After that," he recalled, "I was kind of numb, like I'd been hit by a real good right-hand punch. I kept asking myself: 'How did I do it? How did I do it?' Then I made up my mind I'd have to live with it. I'd always been able to take adversity pretty good, and I reasoned that I had been trying my best. At other times I'd dwell for weeks on a pop fly I hadn't gone back on or if I hadn't backed up first base, but this time I had tried."

To all interrogators, Owen denied that the fateful pitch had been a spitball. He was equally vehement in denying Durocher's assertion that he would have had a chance to nail Henrich at first base if the park police, in their zeal to protect the field from mischievous spectators, had not spilled out of the stands the moment Henrich swung. Even Yankees Manager Joe McCarthy tried to spare Owen the burden of guilt, saying Casey's pitch might have been to blame.

In addition, the 25-year-old catcher said he was so stunned by his own miscue that he forgot all about talking to Casey before the pitcher faced DiMaggio. "I should have gone out to the mound and stalled around a little," he said. "It was more my fault than Leo's."

Owen's willingness to accept full blame for the bizarre incident won the media's immediate approbation. One New York newspaper carried an account that said, "They came to interview the goat of the Series, and many of them left with the feeling that the battered catcher was a hero—heroic in the courage he showed by taking all the blame for the latest misfortune of his teammates."

By his singular misadventure, Owen stirred the hearts of thousands. He received about 4,000 wires and letters from sympathetic fans nationwide. Among the communications were marriage proposals from women who were unaware that Mickey had married Gloria Taylor, a Southern California beauty queen, four years earlier.

"Some girls sent their pictures in bathing suits," Owen said. "My wife tore 'em up."

Owen remained with the Dodgers until early in the 1945 season and frequently played infield positions during the talent crunch of World War II. He served in the U.S. Navy in 1945, and prior to his discharge in the spring of 1946 he contacted Dodgers President Branch Rickey.

Attempts by the two to negotiate a salary reached an impasse, whereupon Mickey's wife wrote Jorge Pasquel, asking if the millionaire president of the outlaw Mexican League would be interested in her husband's services. The inquiry drew an affirmative response, and Owen agreed to a five-year contract to manage a Mexican club. The money was good but, as Owen discovered, the quality of the competition was not. The Mexican game was beset by apa-

thy as well as such incidents as one of Pasquel's bodyguards drawing a knife on an umpire and Owen himself being forced to wrestle a pistol away from a pitcher in a clubhouse brawl. Before the '46 season was over, Mickey wanted out.

By early August, Mickey had mapped out his escape plans. With the help of an American friend in Mexico, the Owens, using assumed names, slipped back into the United States. But upon his return, Mickey learned that he, along with the other league jumpers, had been banned from Organized Baseball for five years by Commissioner A.B. (Happy) Chandler.

Deprived of his livelihood, Owen took to barnstorming, squeezing out a few dollars here and there along the back roads of the Midwest. The gypsy life ended in June 1949, when Chandler granted amnesty to all the jumpers. Ten days later, the Dodgers released Owen to the Cubs on waivers. He spent the next three years in Chicago before being released. He did not return to the majors until 1954, when he was with the Red Sox. He played in 32 games, batted .235 and clouted one home run, a very special home run in Mickey's book of memories.

After serving in the U.S. Navy in the mid-1940s, Mickey Owen went to play for Veracruz of the outlaw Mexican League.

In a July 19 game at Fenway Park, the Red Sox trailed the Orioles, 7-5, in the ninth inning. With two Boston runners on base and Ted Williams strolling to the plate, Jimmie Dykes spotted Owen kneeling in the on-deck circle. The Baltimore manager ordered an intentional walk to Williams in order to pitch to light-hitting Mickey, who had hit only 13 homers in his career. The strategy backfired when Owen lifted a curve from Mike Blyzka over the fence for a grand-slam homer and a 9-7 Boston victory.

Released at the end of that season, Mickey became a Red Sox coach for the next two years and then went into scouting for several major league clubs. He ended his association with professional baseball after scouting for the Yankees in 1960.

That did not terminate his relationship with baseball, however. He operated a popular baseball school for boys in Miller, Mo., where hundreds of youngsters learned the rudiments of the game on a seven-diamond layout. Owen also served as sheriff of Greene County in Missouri. For years he maintained not only law and order, but also the contention that the only person to blame for his famous blunder on October 5, 1941, was Mickey Owen. He was simply looking for the wrong curve from Casey.

"Henrich missed it by more than I did," Owen said, laughing, in a 1985 interview. "He's the one that ought to be famous. I at least touched the ball."

Because he played in the Mexican League, Owen was banned from Organized Baseball and had to apply for reinstatement in 1949.

Alexander To the Rescue

Of all the babies born between 1884 and 1888 and named for the 22nd President of the United States, none gained greater renown than the male infant who arrived at St. Paul, Neb., on February 26, 1887.

No political prominence awaited him, no mercantile or industrial eminence. Just the national recognition that accompanies the ability to throw a baseball with uncommon speed and precision.

An aging Grover Cleveland Alexander posed with former great Honus Wagner before the 1926 World Series.

Grover Cleveland Alexander was a star from the moment he stepped onto a major league diamond. As a 24-year-old rookie in 1911, Grover won 28 games for the Phillies. He was a workhorse, leading the National League in innings pitched in six of his seven years in Philadelphia. He won 30 or more games in three successive seasons, after which he was traded to the Cubs in November 1917. The 6-foot-1, 185-pound righthander spent most of the 1918 campaign as an artillery sergeant in World War I, then put in more than seven years with the Cubs.

During his major league career, which also included terms in St. Louis and back in Philadelphia, Alexander won 373 games. Six times he led the National League in shutouts, and once he tied for the lead. One season he hurled 16 shutouts, and in another he authored four one-hit games. What he started he usually finished, a practice that enabled him to set a modern N.L. record with 436 complete games.

But all these accomplishments notwithstanding, Alexander is best remembered for an exceedingly brief stint on an autumn afternoon in 1926.

Alexander was 39 when, in June 1926, he was waived to the Cardinals. Cubs Manager Joe McCarthy had decided that Alex's devotion to a bottle was stronger than to his profession.

Alexander, fondly known as "Old Pete," readily conceded his weakness. "I never said I was an angel," he told St. Louis club officials, "but I know how to pitch."

He proved that point convincingly in the next four months. Fittingly, Old Pete beat the Cubs, 3-2, in his first outing as a Cardinal, and he went on to win eight more games for St. Louis that season. Each victory was important because the Cardinals, under the inspired leadership of player-Manager Rogers Hornsby, won their first pennant in club history by only two games over Cincinnati. Their opponents in the World Series were the New York Yankees, who had edged out Cleveland to return to the classic after a two-year absence.

Lefthander Herb Pennock checked the Cardinals on three hits in the October 2

Series opener as the Yankees posted a 2-1 victory at Yankee Stadium. Alexander, making his first Series appearance in 11 years, then brought the Cards even the next day with a 6-2 decision. The Nebraskan retired the last 21 Yankees in order and allowed only four New York hits while St. Louis pounded out 12, including home runs by right fielder Billy Southworth and shortstop Tommy Thevenow.

When the Series moved to St. Louis on October 5, Cardinals righthander Jesse Haines threw a 4-0 shutout and aided his own cause with a two-run homer and a single. But the visitors battled back to win the next two games at Sportsman's Park. In Game 4, left fielder Babe Ruth clubbed a Series-record three homers to spark righthander Waite Hoyt and the Yankees to a 10-5 victory, while Pennock posted his second Series victory over Willie Sherdel with a 3-2, 10-inning decision in Game 5 to lift New York within one game of the world championship.

The Yanks' hopes of wrapping up the Series with a sixth-game victory at Yankee Stadium were dashed when Alexander coasted to a 10-2 triumph, scattering eight hits and again going the distance. With any control over the events of Game 7 seemingly out of his hands, Alexander was in a position to sit back and ponder what McCarthy, who had given him his walking papers earlier that summer, thought about his 2-0 Series record.

The world championship of baseball now hinged on a single game, which should have attracted a capacity crowd of 65,000. Instead it drew only 38,093, the result of near-freezing temperatures and a widely circulated report that Commissioner Kenesaw M. Landis had postponed the game because of intermittent rain.

The pitching assignments for the October 10 game went to Haines, who had won the third game for St. Louis, and Hoyt, the Yankees' winning pitcher in Game 4. After three innings, Hoyt held a 1-0 advantage, thanks to Ruth's fourth Series homer in the third inning. In the top of the fourth, however, a porous defense betrayed Hoyt. With one out, Cardinals first baseman Jim Bottomley singled. Third baseman Lester Bell hit a ball to shortstop that looked like a probable inning-ending double play, but Mark Koenig fumbled the ball and both runners were safe. Left fielder Chick Hafey then hit a looper that Koenig and left fielder Bob Meusel somehow let fall between them. The bases were loaded.

But more evil still lurked in the New York outfield. Catcher Bob O'Farrell hit a soft fly to medium left-center field that was a routine play for either Meusel or center fielder Earle Combs. Because of Meusel's superior throwing arm, Combs backed away to let Meusel make a throw to the plate if necessary. But the usually reliable Meusel muffed

"Old Pete" made short work of young Yankee Tony Lazzeri.

the ball, permitting Bottomley to score the tying run. Thevenow, who batted .417 in the Series, then drove in Bell and Hafey with a solid single. The frustrated Hoyt retired the next two batters, but the Cardinals, without scoring an earned run, had taken a 3-1 lead.

Hoyt and his reliever, Pennock, kept the Cardinals at bay the rest of the game. The Yankees, however, tagged Haines for a run in the sixth. Third baseman Joe Dugan singled with two out and scored on catcher Hank Severeid's double, cutting the Cards' lead to 3-2. The Yanks then knocked Haines out in the seventh.

Combs led off with a single and was sacrificed to second by Koenig. Hornsby ordered an intentional walk to Ruth, who was forced by Meusel for the second out as Combs took third. First baseman Lou Gehrig then was walked on a 3-2 pitch.

With the bases jammed, Hornsby conferred with Haines on the mound. It was a brief consultation. A blister on Haines' right index finger had burst, making it impossible for him to continue pitching.

Hornsby turned toward the St. Louis bullpen and signaled for a reliever. Herman Bell and Art Reinhart had been warming up for several innings, but to the audible dismay of the spectators, who had the utmost respect for Alexander, it was Old Pete who ambled toward the infield, his cap perched atop his head, a red warmup sweater draped over his arm. He hadn't even thrown a pitch in the bullpen before being summoned.

By most accounts, the hero of the Saturday victory had celebrated far into the night, convinced that his participation in the Series was over. Old Pete, it was said, had arrived at Yankee Stadium only in time to fall asleep in the bullpen.

Many years later, Alexander disavowed the story. After the Game 6 victory, Alex insisted, Hornsby had approached him at his locker, slapped him on the back and said: "You were great today, and I suppose you want to celebrate. Don't do it. I may need you tomorrow."

Alexander maintained that he returned to his hotel room, where he spent the night, "and I didn't celebrate, either," he said. "I don't want to spoil anyone's story, but I was cold sober that night. There were plenty of other nights, before and since, that I wasn't, but that night I was as sober as a judge should be."

Clear-eyed or bleary-eyed, Old Pete gave his sweater to a batboy and was met at the edge of the infield by Hornsby, who reminded him that second baseman Tony Lazzeri was the next batter and that "there is no place to put him."

Supposedly, Old Pete replied, "Guess I'll have to get him out."

As Alexander took his warmup pitches—"I didn't need the last two," he reported later—Lazzeri consulted his manager, Miller Huggins. "What do you want me to do?" inquired Tony, who had clouted 18 home runs and driven in 114 runs as a rookie that season. "Shall I hit the first one?"

"Wait him out," instructed Little Hug, hoping for a walk from Alexander to force home the tying run.

Alex assessed the situation with the aplomb of a seasoned campaigner. "I figured that young fellow was more nervous than I was," he reasoned. "But with all that responsibility, it seemed impossible for anyone not to feel nervous."

"Did you worry?" he was asked.

"If I were the worrying kind," he said, "I wouldn't have pitched these many years in the major leagues."

Taking his time, perhaps to magnify Lazzeri's apprehension, Old Pete threw. It was a curve, just low, and umpire George Hildebrand called ball one after Lazzeri resisted the temptation to swing. Alexander's next pitch was a high fastball that Lazzeri took for a strike. A third time Alexander threw, but not quite where he would have preferred. Lazzeri swung, a trifle early as it turned out, and sent a vicious liner down the left-field line. A cry went up as it appeared that the drive would clear the bases, but the ball finally hooked foul.

The 39-year-old veteran faced the 21-year-old batter again. His fourth pitch was another curve, low and outside. Lazzeri swung . . . and missed.

"He struck him out!" the radio announcer screamed as Lazzeri started to walk dejectedly toward his position at second base. "Alexander the Great comes in and strikes out Tony Lazzeri, retiring the side. The entire Cardinal team has rushed over to Alexander, petting him and patting him on the back, and are simply wild over him."

Old Pete set the Yankees down in order in the eighth and retired Combs and Koenig in the ninth. One out—and Babe Ruth—is all that stood between the Cards and the world championship. Alexander did not back away from the challenge, however, as he chose to pitch to Ruth. The Bambino took a strike and fouled off a pitch before working the count full and then walking on a border-line pitch. It was his 11th walk of the Series.

"Where was that last pitch?" Alexander asked Hildebrand quietly.

The arbiter held the palms of his hands close together.

"If it was that close," Alex replied, "I think you might have given the call to an old guy."

OCTOBER 10, 1926									
St. Louis	ab	r	h	rbi	New York	ab	r	h	rbi
Holm, cf	5	0	0	0	Combs, cf	5	0	2	0
Southworth, rf	4	0	0	0	Koenig, ss	4	0	0	0
Hornsby, 2b	4	0	2	0	Ruth, rf	1	1	1	1
Bottomley, 1b	3	1	1	0	Meusel, lf	4	0	1	0
L. Bell, 3b	4	1	0	0	Gehrig, 1b	2	0	0	0
Hafey, lf	4	1	2	0	Lazzeri, 2b	4	0	0	0
O'Farrell, c	3	0	0	1	Dugan, 3b	4	1	2	0
Thevenow, ss	4	0	2	2	Severeid, c	3	0	2	1
Haines, p	2	0	1	0	Adams, pr	0	0	0	0
Alexander, p	1	0	0	0	Collins, c	1	0	0	0
					Hoyt, p	2	0	0	0
					Paschal, ph	1	0	0	0
					Pennock, p	1	0	0	0
Totals	34	3	8	3	Totals	32	2	8	2

St. Louis ....0 0 0   3 0 0   0 0 0—3
New York ....0 0 1   0 0 1   0 0 0—2

St. Louis	IP	H	R	ER	BB	SO
Haines (W)	6⅔	8	2	2	5	2
Alexander	2⅓	0	0	0	1	1
New York	IP	H	R	ER	BB	SO
Hoyt (L)	6	5	3	0	0	2
Pennock	3	3	0	0	0	0

E—Koenig, Meusel, Dugan. LOB—St. Louis 7, New York 10. 2B—Severeid. HR—Ruth. SH—Haines, Koenig, Bottomley. SF—O'Farrell. T—2:15. A—38,093.

Years after their 1926 encounter, Grover Cleveland Alexander (left) and
Tony Lazzeri traveled down memory lane.

The Babe did not linger long at first base. Hoping to catch the Cardinals napping, he attempted to steal second base and was cut down on O'Farrell's throw to Hornsby. "With Meusel at bat and Gehrig coming up next," a Yankee official said, "anything could have happened. It was the only dumb play I ever saw Ruth make."

The Cardinals were world champions for the first time and Grover Cleveland Alexander was forever enshrined in the hearts of his countrymen. He then won 21 games as a 40-year-old in 1927, followed by 16 in 1928 and nine in 1929. On December 11, 1929, he was traded to Philadelphia, where he had launched his extraordinary career 19 years earlier. He lost his only three decisions for the Phillies in 1930 and caught on with Dallas of the Texas League after his release. One victory and two defeats terminated Old Pete's professional career.

For a number of years, Alex toured with the bearded House of David team, but alcoholism, plus epilepsy and cancer, proved insurmountable obstacles. The National League sent him $100 a month, and a World War I pension added another $60 to his monthly income. He returned to his native St. Paul, barely recognized in the Nebraska village where he had been lionized. In a rented room, Al-

exander the Great died there on November 4, 1950, fondly remembered for his pitching strength and sadly pitied for his bodily weaknesses.

Tony Lazzeri's years after their 1926 encounter were even shorter than Alexander's. But while he was in the majors, Poosh 'Em Up Tony enjoyed some glorious days. He batted .300 or better five times in a 12-year Yankee career. He also smashed seven homers in four straight games and six in three as a member of the Yankee wrecking crew. The San Francisco native played on five more World Series teams, all of them world champions, as a New Yorker. He belted two home runs in one game in the 1932 Series against Chicago, and he pounded a grand slam against the Giants in the 1936 Series.

Lazzeri was with the Cubs in 1938, the year the Yankees swept Chicago in the Series, and with the Dodgers and the Giants in 1939. Tony managed Toronto of the International League as well as Portsmouth (Piedmont) and Wilkes-Barre (Eastern) before retiring from the game in 1944.

Lazzeri was living in San Francisco when his wife, returning from a short vacation, found him slumped at the foot of some stairs at their home on August 7, 1946. Death was attributed to a heart attack or the effects of the fall. He was 41.

Slaughter's Mad, Mad Dash

Enos (Country) Slaughter, the Cardinals' "Old Warhorse," slides across the plate with the winning run of the 1946 World Series.

The catalog of extraordinary baseball games abounds with chapters on dramatic hitting and heroic pitching, but there are precious few devoted to baserunning exploits. This paucity is due, in part, to the fact that there was only one Enos Bradsher Slaughter. While others achieved undying fame with key home runs or no-hit games, the stocky North Carolinian ran his way into baseball immortality by disobeying a stop sign in a World Series.

Known variously as "Country" or the "Old War-

horse," Slaughter was a compulsive runner by the time he reached the major leagues. Earlier, however, when he was a $75-a-month rookie with a Class-D club, he ran only when the mood struck him. When base hits were infrequent or a ground ball escaped his frantic grasp, he could assume a world-class poke.

That attitude changed abruptly in 1936, when the native of Roxboro, N.C., was with Columbus, Ga., of the South Atlantic League. Returning to the dug-

This group of triumphant Cardinals included (left to right) Manager Eddie Dyer, Enos Slaughter, George Munger, Whitey Kurowski and Joe Garagiola.

out from the outfield, Enos slowed from a trot to a walk halfway to his destination. "Hey, kid," Manager Eddie Dyer barked, "if you're tired, I'll get you some help."

Stung deeply by the rebuke, Slaughter started running everywhere, from the moment he left the dugout until the moment he returned. It was his trademark for the remainder of his distinguished career.

From Columbus, Ga., where he batted .325 and hustled his way to a league-leading total of 20 triples, Enos leaped to Columbus, O., the Cardinals' American Association affiliate, in 1937. Here, under the kindly leadership of Manager Burt Shotton, Slaughter blossomed into the prize prospect of the Cards' far-flung farm system. He led the league with a .382 batting average, 245 hits and 147 runs scored.

As a St. Louis rookie in 1938, Enos displayed the spirit of the old Gas House Gang, a go-for-broke approach to the game that had flourished a few years earlier but had fallen into decline. But he also batted only .276, a figure that raised some doubts about the validity of his batting mark a year earlier. The questions faded the next season, however, when he hit .320, the first of 10 .300-or-better seasons he would post in his career.

He also ran the bases and pursued fly balls with reckless abandon, often to his own physical detriment. In August 1941 he suffered a broken collarbone when he dived over teammate Terry Moore to avoid an outfield collision and crashed into the concrete wall at Sportsman's Park in St. Louis. He was sidelined for five weeks, and when he returned —a bit prematurely, as it turned out—he swung so hard striking out that he tore the skin over the collarbone and started bleeding. The injury may have been the difference between the Cards winning the National League pennant and losing it, which they did to the Brooklyn Dodgers by 2½ games.

The 5-foot-9, 190-pound right fielder rebounded impressively in 1942. He led the league in triples with 17 and hits with 188 and was a key performer in the Cards' dash to the pennant and their upset of the New York Yankees in a five-game World Series.

Spring training of 1943 was only weeks away when Enos received a call to help win World War II. He entered the Army Air Force. He spent the next three years, which should have been the most productive period of his career, attending to his GI duties and playing ball on hastily constructed diamonds in such far-off places as Guam and Saipan.

Although his uniform bore no resemblance to his major league attire and the playing sites would never be mistaken for well-groomed, big-league parks, Slaughter's style of play underwent no change. Disregarding the jagged coral that frequently peeked through the playing surface, the Old Warhorse risked gashes to his arms and legs with crunching slides into bases and diving catches in the outfield. When asked why he, unlike many major leaguers, played with such fiery intensity, Slaughter replied, "These servicemen deserve to see how major leaguers play the game."

Enos was 29 when he returned to the Cardinals in 1946 and, if anything, was friskier than ever. Youthful contenders for his right-field position had to be shown, he maintained, that he still was the incumbent, his three years at war notwithstanding. He clinched his argument by batting .300 and leading the league with 130 runs batted in and 23 outfield assists.

The N.L. pennant race of 1946 was similar to the 1942 chase, which involved the Cardinals and the Dodgers. This time the same two teams finished the 154-game schedule in a dead heat, necessitating an unprecedented best-of-three playoff series. But only two games were required as the Cards swept to victory. In the first game, played at St. Louis, Slaughter contributed two singles to a 12-hit attack that produced a 4-2 triumph. Two days later, in Brooklyn, Country cracked a two-run triple as the Cards exploded for 13 hits and wrapped up the pennant with an 8-4 victory.

The frenzied flag race in the senior circuit differed sharply from that in the American League. The Boston Red Sox breezed to the pennant by 12 games over the Detroit Tigers. It was the first Red Sox pennant since 1918; for the Cardinals, it was their ninth championship and their fourth in five years.

Because of the N.L. playoffs, the World Series opened on a Sunday, October 6, in St. Louis, and for the eighth time in postseason play, the Cards started on a losing note. Despite wasting Slaughter's fourth-inning triple, the Cards still were within one out of a 2-1 victory when right fielder Tommy

McBride singled home the tying run in the ninth. First baseman Rudy York's solo homer off starter Howard Pollet in the 10th gave Boston a 3-2 win.

The Cards collected only six hits in the second game, but lefthander Harry Brecheen knocked in the first run of the game and allowed only four hits as he blanked the Red Sox, 3-0. When the Series moved to Boston for Game 3 October 9, the heavily favored Red Sox once more moved ahead in games as righthander Dave Ferriss hurled a six-hit, 4-0 shutout. The St. Louis bats finally awakened in the fourth game as Slaughter (a home run, a double and two singles), third baseman Whitey Kurowski (two doubles and two singles) and catcher Joe Garagiola (a double and three singles) led a 20-hit barrage against six Boston pitchers. The result was a 12-3 St. Louis victory and an evening of the Series at two games apiece.

The alternate victory pattern continued in the fifth game as Red Sox righthander Joe Dobson allowed just three unearned runs and won a 6-3 decision over Al Brazle, who had relieved Pollet in the first inning after the latter could not overcome a back injury. Another casualty was Slaughter, who was struck on the right elbow by a Dobson pitch in the fourth inning. Enos promptly stole second base and later batted again, but the elbow eventually swelled up to the point that he no longer could stand the pain. For the first and only time in his career, Slaughter asked Dyer, the Cardinals' rookie manager, to take him out of the game in the seventh inning.

En route to St. Louis that night, Slaughter underwent hot-pack treatments on his throwing arm. X-rays were taken upon his arrival in Missouri, and a blood clot was discovered. Doctors advised against his playing anymore that year at the risk of ruining his arm and perhaps his career, but Slaughter pleaded with Dyer to leave him in the lineup.

"It's my arm," he told the manager, "and I want to play even if the damn thing falls off."

Dyer finally relented. Although scarcely able to lift a bat, Enos rapped a run-scoring single in the Cards' three-run third inning in Game 6. That was all the support Brecheen needed as he tallied his second Series victory with a 4-1 decision. For the third time the Series was knotted.

The seventh contest, played October 15 before 36,143 fans at Sportsman's Park, was Slaughter's transport to World Series immortality.

Starting for the Red Sox was Ferriss, who had beaten the St. Louis starter, righthander Murry Dickson, in Game 3. The Red Sox wasted no time getting to Dickson, scoring a run in the first inning when right fielder Wally Moses led off with a single, advanced to third on shortstop Johnny Pesky's single and scored on center fielder Dom DiMaggio's fly ball.

Boston stars Ted Williams (left) and Mickey Harris dejectedly contemplate
the agony of defeat brought on by Enos Slaughter's mad dash.

St. Louis got that run back in the second. After
smashing a leadoff double to left-center field,
Kurowski moved to third on Garagiola's grounder
and scored when Harry Walker lined out to his Red
Sox counterpart, left fielder Ted Williams. In the
fifth inning, Walker led off with a single to spark a
two-run rally. He was sacrificed to second by shortstop Marty Marion and scored on Dickson's double. Second baseman Red Schoendienst then singled
in Dickson. After center fielder Moore followed
with another single, Red Sox Manager Joe Cronin
summoned Dobson from the bullpen to replace
Ferriss. Dobson managed to prevent any further
Redbird scoring that inning, but the Cards had a 3-1
lead.

Dickson nursed that lead into the top of the
eighth, retiring 18 of 19 batters. He had not surrendered a hit since the second inning when the first
man up in the eighth, pinch-hitter Glen Russell,
punched a single to center. George Metkovich followed with a pinch double to left, Russell stopping
at third.

In the St. Louis dugout, Dyer, Slaughter's skipper
from his Sally League days, decided Dickson had
had enough. He signaled to the bullpen for Brecheen, who had pitched nine innings in Game 6 two
days earlier. The Cat began impressively. He fanned
Moses and retired Pesky on a line drive to Slaughter, whose quick throw held both runners. But Di-
Maggio slammed a double off the right-center-field

wall to tie the score, 3-3. DiMaggio twisted an ankle while rounding first base and was replaced by Leon Culberson, who was stranded when Williams popped out.

To hold the Cardinals in check, Cronin called on Bob Klinger, a former National Leaguer who had pitched effectively in relief during the regular season but had not appeared previously in the Series. The righthander yielded a leadoff single to Slaughter, who remained on first base as Kurowski, attempting to sacrifice, popped to the pitcher and catcher Del Rice flied to Williams.

The next batter was Walker, who already had six hits in 16 at-bats in the Series. "Dyer flashed the run-and-hit sign," Enos recalled, "(which was) distinguished from the hit-and-run in that if Harry didn't get his pitch, he didn't have to swing and I'd be on my own."

But Walker got his pitch. He slapped a shot over shortstop for what Harry expected to be just a long single. But as Enos rounded second base, he plotted his course. In an earlier game, under similar circumstances, coach Mike Gonzalez had held the 30-year-old veteran at third base. Enos groused at length, insisting that he could have scored on the play. "OK," Dyer told him, "if it happens again and you think you can make it, run on your own. I'll back you up."

This was the moment, Enos decided. As he headed for third base, Gonzalez gestured wildly for Enos to apply the brakes. It did no good. Slaughter ignored his signs and shouts, hurtled past the coach and careened toward home plate.

Culberson, in the meantime, had fielded Walker's hit and thrown the ball to Pesky. The shortstop paused, turning slightly clockwise, perhaps to ascertain Walker's intentions. If a teammate alerted Johnny to Slaughter's full-speed pursuit of home plate, his words were drowned out by the roar of the crowd. Belatedly, Pesky fired toward the plate, but his weak throw drew catcher Roy Partee 10 feet up the third-base line. Enos hit the dirt, but he needn't have bothered. He could have scored just as easily standing up. Walker was credited with a double after reaching second base, where he was stranded.

"If Pesky had turned counterclockwise," Walker explained many years later, "he could have made a stronger throw and had a chance to nail Slaughter."

Trailing 4-3, the Red Sox were not finished. Singles by the first two batters in the ninth, York and second baseman Bobby Doerr, posed another threat. But Brecheen wiggled out of danger and earned his third Series victory with a forceout, a pop foul and another infield roller that hopped up Schoendienst's arm before the second baseman grabbed the ball and tossed it to Marion for a Series-ending force play at second base.

The Series was Slaughter's last as a Cardinal. He remained in St. Louis until he was traded to the Yankees in April 1954. The Old Warhorse was two weeks short of his 38th birthday when the deal was made. A Cardinal born and bred, he had never considered the likelihood of wearing any other uniform. Tears flowed freely before he came to the realization that numerous benefits accrued to those who wore the Yankee pinstripes.

Dry-eyed at last, Enos muttered, "I'll help Casey Stengel win some more pennants."

True to his prediction, Country Slaughter wore a Yankees uniform in the World Series of 1956, '57 and '58, twice emerging as a world champion.

Slaughter managed in the minors for two seasons, the first at Houston of the American Association in 1960 and the second at Raleigh of the Carolina League in 1961. He was 45 when he handled the Class-B club, but his eye still was keen. In 41 pinch-hitting appearances, he batted .341.

The Old Warhorse retired from the game after that season, but it was not until 1985 that he was inducted into the Hall of Fame. It took a special vote of the Veterans Committee to get him into Cooperstown.

"Well, this is it," said Slaughter, who always spoke as aggressively as he played. "It came a long time too late, I thought."

As the crowd at Cooperstown, N.Y., chuckled at his remark, the 69-year-old country boy offered a wide smile.

OCTOBER 15, 1946									
Boston	ab	r	h	rbi	St. Louis	ab	r	h	rbi
Moses, rf	4	1	1	0	Schoend'nst, 2b	4	0	2	1
Pesky, ss	4	0	1	0	Moore, cf	4	0	1	0
DiMaggio, cf	3	0	1	3	Musial, 1b	3	0	1	0
Culberson, pr-cf	0	0	0	0	Slaughter, rf	3	1	1	0
Williams, lf	4	0	0	0	Kurowski, 3b	4	1	1	0
York, 1b	4	0	1	0	Garagiola, c	3	0	0	0
Campbell, pr	0	0	0	0	Rice, c	1	0	0	0
Doerr, 2b	4	0	2	0	Walker, lf	3	1	2	2
Higgins, 3b	4	0	0	0	Marion, ss	2	0	0	0
H. Wagner, c	2	0	0	0	Dickson, p	3	1	1	1
Russell, ph	1	1	1	0	Brecheen, p	1	0	0	0
Partee, c	1	0	0	0					
Ferriss, p	2	0	0	0					
Dobson, p	0	0	0	0					
Metkovich, ph	1	1	1	0					
Klinger, p	0	0	0	0					
Johnson, p	0	0	0	0					
McBride, ph	1	0	0	0					
Totals	35	3	8	3	Totals	31	4	9	4

Boston .... 1 0 0   0 0 0   0 2 0—3
St. Louis .... 0 1 0   0 2 0   0 1 x—4

Boston	IP	H	R	ER	BB	SO
Ferriss	4 1/3	7	3	3	1	2
Dobson	2 2/3	0	0	0	2	2
Klinger (L)	2/3	2	1	1	1	0
Johnson	1/3	0	0	0	0	0
St. Louis	IP	H	R	ER	BB	SO
Dickson	7*	5	3	3	1	3
Brecheen (W)	2	3	0	0	0	1

*Pitched to two batters in eighth.

E—Kurowski. LOB—Boston 6, St. Louis 8. 2B—Musial, Kurowski, Dickson, DiMaggio, Metkovich, Walker. SH—Marion. T—2:17. A—36,143.

Hartnett Hits Homer in Gloamin'

As a youngster in Millville, Mass., Charles Leo Hartnett won 55,000 marbles from less skillful playmates and stored them in three 25-pound sugar sacks, an accomplishment that generally was forgotten in light of later achievements.

He joined the Chicago Cubs as a husky 21-year-old in 1922 and almost immediately was named Gabby because of his incessant chatter. In time he developed into one of the National League's foremost catchers. Twelve times he caught 100 or more games in a single season, and six times he led the league in double plays by a catcher, accomplishments that often are overlooked as well.

He was named the league's Most Valuable Player in 1935, and five times his 6-foot-1, 218-pound frame squatted behind the plate in All-Star Games. These also are infrequently remembered distinctions in the Hall of Fame career of the genial character known as "Tomato Face."

But what is remembered, if nothing else, from Gabby's 20-year major league career is one murderous swing of his bat on a late-September afternoon at Wrigley Field in 1938.

Hartnett was 37 and a veteran of three Chicago pennant-winners when, on July 20, 1938, he was appointed manager of the Cubs. He succeeded Charlie Grimm, who agreed with the decision of Owner Philip K. Wrigley to change skippers. Jolly Cholly had been unable to spark the team as he had in the championship seasons of 1932 and 1935, and both he and Wrigley believed that the talkative catcher could motivate the club.

Hartnett's inspired leadership paid quick dividends. From a position 5½ games off the pace when Gabby took over, the Cubs inched upward. By September 1 they had risen to second place, although the front-running Pittsburgh Pirates still were seven games ahead. Few regarded the Bruins as serious threats, especially Bill Benswanger. The Pirates' president was so confident that his club would win the pennant—and other knowledgeable observers assured him it was true—that he ordered the construction of a new and larger press box on the roof of Forbes Field, approved the installation of equipment for telegraphers and broadcasters and authorized the printing of World Series tickets as well as press buttons to be worn by the hundreds of jour-

nalists who would cover the fall classic.

The Pirates' confidence turned into concern, however, when the Cubs refused to slacken their pursuit. Only 1½ games separated the two contenders when the Bucs invaded Chicago for three games in the last week of the season. "We've got to take this series," Manager Pie Traynor announced, but he added that Chicago's hurlers "will be pitching with insufficient rest. My pitchers are ready."

Righthander Jim Tobin, a knuckleball specialist, was named to pitch the first game for the Pirates. Hartnett pondered his choice. His staff, like Traynor said, was badly frayed from overwork. He ultimately settled on Dizzy Dean, the once great righthander of the St. Louis Cardinals. The Cubs had picked up Dean the previous April when it became apparent to the Cardinals that an injury he had

Gabby Hartnett was Cubs player-manager in 1938.

sustained in the 1937 All-Star Game was eroding his vast talent. Thus handicapped, Dean was trying to get by with soft stuff, control and guile. But the fact remained that Dean had not started a game in more than a month because of a sore arm.

Hartnett had two reasons for his selection. One, Ol' Diz had a way of coming through in a crisis, and two, using Dean would give his other hurlers an extra day of rest.

Dean's reaction to the assignment was altogether predictable. "Gabby's getting smarter every day," he proclaimed. "Who else would he pick but Ol' Diz?"

Dean had little on the ball that day, but his cunning made him just as effective as he had been in his prime. He pitched eight shutout innings while the Cubs nicked Tobin for a pair of runs. In the ninth, however, pinch-hitter Woody Jensen reached base on a fielder's choice and third baseman Lee Handley doubled him to third with two out. That was all for Jay Hanna Dean.

Hartnett summoned Bill Lee, another righthander, and for one terrifying moment, it appeared that Gabby had made an unwise selection. The first thing Lee did was uncork a wild pitch. Jensen raced home and Handley moved to third. But Big Bill brought the situation under control by striking out catcher Al Todd. The Cubs won, 2-1, and were only half a game out of first place.

Wrigley Field was packed with 34,465 vocal parti-

sans September 28 for the second game. Starting for the Cubs was righthander Clay Bryant, who would win 19 games that season. On the mound for the Pirates was righthander Bob Klinger, a 28-year-old rookie who was on his way to 12 victories and a 3.00 earned-run average.

The Cubs staked Bryant to an early lead when they scored an unearned run in the second inning. Klinger threw strike three past Bill Jurges for what should have been the third out, but Todd failed to hold onto the ball and allowed the shortstop to reach base. Bryant then hit a grounder to third, where Handley scooped up the ball and threw it into the stands, allowing first baseman Ripper Collins to score. Bryant nursed that 1-0 lead into the sixth inning, when he was driven to cover by a three-run outburst that included a two-out, solo home run by rookie left fielder Johnny Rizzo and a two-run single by Handley. Jack Russell recorded the last out of the inning for Chicago.

Klinger weathered a two-run Chicago rally in the bottom of the sixth as the Cubs tied the score, 3-3. Hartnett doubled and scored on a double by Collins, who then came around with the tying tally on a bunt and an infield out.

Neither team scored in the seventh, although the Pirates contended bitterly that they were entitled to at least one run. Center fielder Lloyd Waner was on third base, brother Paul on first and Rizzo at bat with one out when, the Buccos maintained, Vance Page committed a balk. They insisted that the rookie righthander had hesitated in his windup before delivering his pitch, which Rizzo smacked into a double play. But the umpires ignored the Pirates' pleas for justice and the Bucs, instead of having a 4-3 lead with one down, were out of the inning and still deadlocked.

Pittsburgh broke the stalemate in the eighth inning. A walk to shortstop Arky Vaughan and a single by first baseman Gus Suhr shelled Page, who was replaced by lefthander Larry French. The former Pirate was cuffed for a run-scoring single by pinch-hitter Heinie Manush and bowed out in favor of Lee, who was making his third appearance in as many games. Handley greeted Lee with a single to drive in Suhr. The Bucs had restored their two-run margin, 5-3, still with none out. But that was the extent of the rally. Jurges fielded Todd's grounder and nailed Manush at the plate, after which Klinger hit into a double play.

As it developed, Traynor would have done well to lift Klinger for a pinch-hitter. The righthander served up a leadoff single to Collins in the bottom of the eighth and was succeeded by Bill Swift, another righthander.

Swift did not solve Traynor's problem. He made matters infinitely worse by walking Jurges and yielding a run-scoring double to pinch-hitter Tony

SEPTEMBER 28, 1938								
Pittsburgh	ab	r	h	rbi	Chicago	ab	r	h	rbi
L. Waner, cf	4	0	2	0	Hack, 3b	3	0	0	1
P. Waner, rf	5	0	2	0	Herman, 2b	5	0	3	1
Rizzo, lf	4	1	1	1	Demaree, lf	5	0	0	0
Vaughan, ss	2	2	1	0	Cavarretta, rf	5	0	0	0
Suhr, 1b	3	2	1	0	Reynolds, cf	5	0	1	0
Young, 2b	2	0	0	0	Hartnett, c	4	2	2	1
Manush, ph	1	0	1	1	Collins, 1b	4	3	3	1
Thevenow, 2b	0	0	0	0	Jurges, ss	3	1	1	0
Handley, 3b	4	0	2	3	Bryant, p	2	0	1	0
Todd, c	4	0	0	0	Russell, p	0	0	0	0
Klinger, p	4	0	0	0	O'Dea, ph	1	0	0	0
Swift, p	0	0	0	0	Page, p	0	0	0	0
Brown, p	0	0	0	0	French, p	0	0	0	0
					Lee, p	0	0	0	0
					Lazzeri, ph	1	0	1	1
					Marty, pr	0	0	0	0
					Root, p	0	0	0	0
Totals	33	5	10	5	Totals	38	6	12	5

Pittsburgh ....0 0 0   0 0 3   0 2 0—5
Chicago ....0 1 0   0 0 2   0 2 1—6
Two out when winning run scored.

Pittsburgh	IP	H	R	ER	BB	SO
Klinger	7	9	4	3	2	6
Swift	⅓	2	1	1	2	0
Brown (L)	1 ⅓	1	1	1	0	0

Chicago	IP	H	R	ER	BB	SO
Bryant	5 ⅔	4	3	3	5	1
Russell	⅓	0	0	0	0	0
Page	1	3	2	2	1	1
French	0	1	0	0	0	0
Lee	1	1	0	0	0	0
Root (W)	1	1	0	0	0	0

E—P. Waner, Vaughan, Handley, Todd. DP—Pittsburgh 1, Chicago 3. LOB—Pittsburgh 7, Chicago 10. 2B—L. Waner, Hartnett, Collins, Lazzeri. HR—Rizzo, Hartnett. WP—Lee. T—2:37. A—34,465.

Lazzeri. Jurges stopped at third and Joe Marty took Lazzeri's place at second. Swift then walked third baseman Stan Hack to fill the bases. Second baseman Billy Herman followed with a single that drove in Jurges, making the score 5-5, but right fielder Paul Waner's throw nailed Marty as he tried to score. That was all for Swift. The third Pittsburgh pitcher was Mace Brown, who quickly ended the inning by forcing left fielder Frank Demaree to hit into a double play.

As the teams prepared to start the ninth inning, darkness was fast falling over Wrigley Field. It was clear to all that the game would be called and declared a draw if the teams still were knotted at the end of the frame.

Charlie Root, the sixth Chicago hurler of the day, retired the Pirates on one hit in the top of the ninth. The sky was growing darker by the minute as Brown disposed of the first two Chicago batters, right fielder Phil Cavarretta and center fielder Carl Reynolds, in the home half. Only one out—and Gabby Hartnett—stood between the Pirates and a tie game, which at that point was the most for which they could hope.

Brown fired twice for strikes. Hartnett took a quick glance at the left-field bleachers, indistinct now in the semi-darkness. In similar circumstances, most pitchers would have teased the batter with a delivery off the plate. Brown reasoned differently. The third pitch was a curve that broke over the plate. Hartnett swung, and the crack of the bat left no doubt as to the destination of the baseball.

Before anyone else, Brown recognized the error of his ways. Not wanting to watch the ball disappear into the left-field bleachers, he started toward the dugout. He knew that the Cubs had won, 6-5, and the Pirates were in second place for the first time since July 11.

As Hartnett passed first base on his triumphal tour, he was joined by delirious fans. In their wake came ushers trying to clear a path for Gabby.

The Chicago Tribune of the next morning reported: "By the time he reached second base, he couldn't have been recognized . . . except for the red face that shone out even in the gray shadows.

"After the skipper had finally struggled to the plate, things became worse. The ushers who had fanned out to form the protective barrier around the infield forgot their constantly rehearsed maneuver and rushed to save Hartnett's life. They tugged and they shoved and finally they started swinging their fists before the players could carry their boss to safety.

"There was further hysteria when Gabby reached the catwalk leading to the clubhouse. But by this time, the gendarmes were organized. Gabby got to the bathhouse without being stripped by souvenir maniacs."

Pirates pitcher Mace Brown knew by the crack of Gabby Hartnett's bat that the game was history.

Hartnett's "homer in the gloamin' " dealt a staggering blow to the Pirates who, thoroughly demoralized, were pummeled the next day, 10-1. The Cubs retained first place until the close of the campaign and were, in turn, thrashed by the Yankees in a four-game World Series.

Gabby managed the Cubs through the 1940 season. In 1941 he was a player-coach for the New York Giants. Several minor league managerial jobs followed. His last major league connection was with the Kansas City Athletics, for whom he coached in 1965 and then scouted and did public relations work. He died of a liver ailment on his 72nd birthday, December 20, 1972, in Park Ridge, Ill.

Mace Brown, the unwilling partner in the Hartnett drama, remained in the majors through the 1946 season when, as a member of the Boston Red Sox, he realized his World Series dream. Again his luck was bad. As a mop-up pitcher in the fourth game he gave up four hits and three runs in one inning of work. The Cardinals won, 12-3.

Bill Benswanger's Series dream never was realized. When Hartnett's home run started on its historic flight, the prostrate form of the Pirates' president was spotted in the box-seat area adjoining the visitors' dugout. It was reported that Bill had fainted, but he always insisted that he had merely fallen. After the Pirates failed to win the pennant, he took the worthless World Series press buttons he had manufactured and gave them away as souvenirs.

Benswanger continued to direct the Bucs until the franchise was sold in 1946. An accomplished pianist, he devoted his later years to the Pittsburgh Symphony Society, which he helped to organize. He died in Pittsburgh on January 15, 1972, following a lengthy illness.

A's Explode
In 1929 Series

For 15 years, Connie Mack labored diligently to rebuild the fortunes of the Philadelphia Athletics, a team that had been dismembered by the threat of fiscal insolvency following its stunning setback to the Boston Braves in the four-game World Series of 1914.

Allurements by Federal League teams had caused players' salary expectations to rise. In addition, the A's were faced with additional expenses related to Shibe Park improvements. So, Mack decided to trim the payroll in order to make ends meet. The A's manager released Chief Bender, Eddie Plank and Jack Coombs, the heart of the pitching staff that had helped the A's win four pennants in five years (1910-14). Gone, too, was Eddie Collins, the superb second baseman. He had a Chicago forwarding address after being sold to the White Sox for $50,000. Jack Barry, the shortstop, was with the Red Sox. Third baseman Frank (Home Run) Baker was playing semipro ball in Upland, Pa., sitting out the 1915 season because of dissatisfaction over salary offers.

From pennant prestige in 1914, the stripped-down A's plunged to the American League cellar in 1915, and they remained in eighth place for seven consecutive years as Mack searched for the building blocks with which to create another empire. The drought finally ended in 1922, when the team climbed to seventh place. In 1923 it found its way to sixth, and civic pride virtually exploded in 1924, when the A's finished fifth.

The reconstruction project received a substantial boost before the 1924 season. Mack purchased a young outfielder who had batted .360 in the Texas League and .398 in 98 at-bats with Milwaukee the previous year. Initially, there were grave concerns about the rookie's unorthodox batting style. A righthanded hitter, he stood with his left foot pointed toward third base. He had his foot in the bucket, it was said, but any suggestions that his stance should be corrected or changed drew an immediate veto from the manager. Anyone who could hit with such authority in the American Association could hit in the American League, Mack insisted. Hands off!

Al Simmons was a regular from the day he arrived in training camp. He hit .308 as a rookie in 1924 and starred with the club for eight more seasons.

During the 1924 season, word filtered into club headquarters of a young firebrand who was displaying extraordinary skills as a catcher and hitter with Portland of the Pacific Coast League. The A's needed a good catcher, but could they engage in spirited bidding with more affluent clubs? Mack and his boss, A's President Thomas Shibe, decided the answer was no, so they bought the Portland franchise to assure spring delivery of Mickey Cochrane. His .331 average as a rookie in 1925 brought him immediate acclaim, and he continued to excel with the A's through 1933.

About that same time, the A's invested more than $100,000 in a rawboned lefthander who had scintillated for Baltimore of the International League in 1924. The pitcher proved to be worth every nickel. Robert Moses (Lefty) Grove won 300 games during his career with the A's and the Red Sox.

In 1926, a broad-beamed farm boy from Maryland joined the A's. When he was discovered by Home Run Baker, who recommended him to Mack, the teen-ager was a catcher. But with Cochrane available, the lad was shifted to first base, where he performed for years. By the end of his major league career, Jimmie Foxx had clouted 534 home runs.

At other times during the rebuilding program, Mack added hard-throwing righthander George Earnshaw, a slick middle infield combination of Joe Boley and Max Bishop, wisecracking infielder Jimmie Dykes and a pair of excellent outfielders, Bing Miller and Mule Haas.

With the influx of young talent, the refurbished A's jumped from fifth place in 1924 to second in '25. They fell to third the next season, then came on again and finished second to the Yankees in 1927 and '28.

By 1929, the A's were ready to crest. They did so in a most impressive style, winning 104 games to outdistance the Yanks by 18 lengths.

Their World Series opponents were the Chicago Cubs, who were back in the winner's circle after a 10-year absence. The National Leaguers were managed by Joe McCarthy, an emerging genius despite the fact that he had never played in the majors.

When the Series opened October 8 in Chicago, it

The Game 4 "goats" for Chicago in the 1929 World Series were center fielder Hack Wilson (below), who turned a routine fly ball into an inside-the-park home run, and four pitchers who could not quell the A's 10-run seventh-inning uprising.

Charlie Root.

Art Nehf.

Sheriff Blake.

A NEW PAIR OF SUN-GLASSES WERE RESPONSIBLE FOR HACK WILSON'S FAMOUS MUFF IN THE 1929 WORLD SERIES — HE HAD JUST BROKEN HIS REGULAR PAIR A FEW DAYS BEFORE —

Pat Malone.

was generally assumed that Grove would start for the A's. The 20-game winner was ready, but Mack was not. When the spectators and players glanced at the bullpen, they spotted a righthander warming up. He was Howard Ehmke, a second-line hurler who had pitched only 54⅔ innings all season. He had won seven games but had not pitched in almost a month and had not even traveled with the team on its last trip of the season.

The outspoken Simmons turned to Mack. "Is that fellow going to pitch for us?" he asked.

"Why yes," Connie replied. "Isn't that all right with you?"

"If it's all right with you, it's all right with me," the outfielder answered.

While the A's had been wrapping up the pennant, Ehmke had been scouting the Cubs, noting their strengths and weaknesses in anticipation of his surprise assignment. How well the 35-year-old pitcher analyzed the Cubs was apparent from the beginning. Throwing his soft pitches to the heavy-hitting Bruins, Ehmke piled one strikeout on top of another, and by late afternoon, 50,740 disgruntled fans headed for the Wrigley Field exits after watching Ehmke fan 13 batters, a Series record that stood for 24 years. Foxx broke a scoreless deadlock with a

home run in the seventh, and the A's went on to win the game, 3-1.

Philadelphia also won the second contest, 9-3, and curiously, 13 Cubs again struck out. Earnshaw, a 24-game winner during the regular season, whiffed seven in 4⅔ innings and Grove added six more in protecting Earnshaw's victory. Foxx again starred for the A's, contributing a single, a double and a home run, and Simmons added a homer and a single.

When the Series resumed in Philadelphia two days later, Earnshaw started again. Big Moose struck out 10 and scattered six hits but lost, 3-1, to righthander Guy Bush as a result of a walk, an error and singles by second baseman Rogers Hornsby and right fielder Kiki Cuyler in the sixth inning. The home team was yet to win a game in the '29 Series.

It appeared as if that pattern would continue in Game 4. Played October 12 at Shibe Park, the fourth game sent 29,921 fans through the entire gamut of emotion. The A's fans went into a deep depression as the Cubs built up an 8-0 lead against starter Jack Quinn and relievers Rube Walberg and Eddie Rommel. A single by Cuyler and a home run by first baseman Charlie Grimm produced two

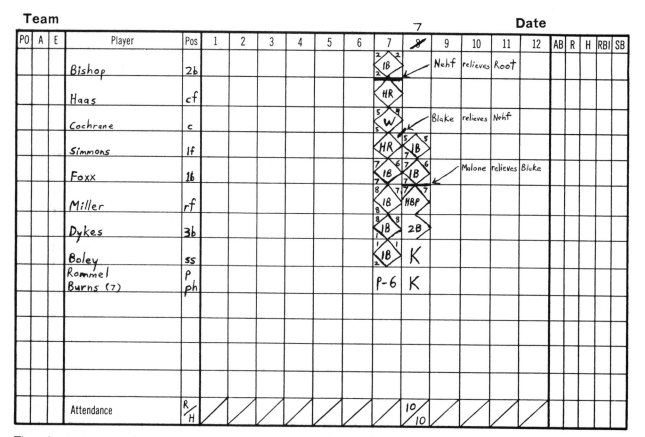

The above scorecard shows the progression of walks and hits that led to Philadelphia's record 10-run seventh inning in Game 4 of the 1929 Series.

runs in the fourth inning, but the Cubs were just warming up. Hornsby, center fielder Hack Wilson, Cuyler, left fielder Riggs Stephenson and Grimm hit consecutive singles—all with none out—and catcher Zack Taylor followed with a run-scoring fly ball to push five more Chicago runners across the plate in the sixth. The Cubs scored another run on a triple by Hornsby and a single by Cuyler to extend their lead to 8-0 after 6½ innings.

It was a somber crowd that greeted the A's as the home team came to bat in the seventh. But the mood at Shibe Park soon would change to mild optimism, then hopeful expectancy and finally wild hysteria as the A's staged one of the most incredible comebacks of all time.

Charlie Root had coasted through the first six frames. Singles by third baseman Dykes and right fielder Miller and a double by Cochrane were the only blemishes on his slate as the righthander toed the rubber to face Simmons, Philadelphia's leadoff batter in the seventh.

The left fielder greeted Root with a home run that hit the roof of the left-field stands. "What a way to waste a perfectly good homer," Simmons mused as he circled the bases.

In quick succession, however, Foxx, Miller and Dykes singled for a second run, and the spectators were no longer sullen.

Boley was next. As the shortstop started for the plate, he was called back. "Root is losing his stuff," Mack said. "Swing at anything near the plate."

Joe did as ordered. He also singled, driving in Miller and sending Dykes to third.

The uprising stalled momentarily when pinch-hitter George Burns popped up, but second baseman Bishop rekindled the flame with another one-base hit. Dykes crossed the plate and the Chicago lead was only four runs.

On the Chicago bench, McCarthy echoed Mack's opinion. Root was losing his stuff. The righthander was relieved by Art Nehf, a 37-year-old lefthander who was in his last major league season. The first batter to face the former Giants mainstay was center fielder Haas, a lefthanded batter who had only three hits in 16 at-bats in the Series thus far.

According to John B. Foster, editor of the Spalding Baseball Guide, Nehf had "orders to make the best batters hit fly balls. Nehf didn't like the sun which shone in his eyes and Wilson lost a drive by Haas because the ball became tangled up with the sun. Wilson ran in, found that he would not get it, tried to block it on the bound, and the ball went by him to the fence, Boley and Bishop scoring ahead of Haas, with the spectators deliriously mad."

The inside-the-park homer cleared the bases for the second time in the inning, and the Cubs' lead was down to 8-7. Nehf was permitted to pitch to Cochrane, who worked the hurler for a walk. That

was it for Nehf, who was replaced by righthander Sheriff Blake. The merry-go-round started afresh as Blake yielded a single to Simmons, whose apparent double-play ball took a bad hop over third baseman Norm McMillan's head. A clean single to center by Foxx scored Cochrane with the tying run.

Blake was excused for the day. His successor was righthander Pat Malone, whose first pitch nicked Miller to load the bases. Dykes, with two hits already to his credit, then belted a liner to left where, Foster reported, "Stephenson played the ball none too well." Old Hoss leaped for the ball, but it eluded his grasp and two more runners pranced home. The A's led, 10-8.

The most spectacular rally in Series history was over. Two runners remained on base with only one out, but Malone fanned Boley and Burns to end the inning.

When the score was 8-0 just minutes before, Mack was considering letting his reserves finish the game. He certainly had no intention of putting his ace pitcher on the mound. But when the bats began to boom, the manager rushed Grove to the bullpen. Lefty set down the last six Cubs in order, striking out four, to close out a most implausible afternoon.

By the rules of scoring, the victory was awarded to Rommel, although the knuckleball artist had allowed two hits, a walk and a run in one inning. The only effective Philadelphia pitcher was Grove, who completed his Series work with a record of 10

OCTOBER 12, 1929

Chicago	ab	r	h	rbi	Philadelphia	ab	r	h	rbi
McMillan, 3b	4	0	0	0	Bishop, 2b	5	1	2	1
English, ss	4	0	0	0	Haas, cf	4	1	1	3
Hornsby, 2b	5	2	2	0	Cochrane, c	4	1	2	0
Wilson, cf	3	1	2	0	Simmons, lf	5	2	2	1
Cuyler, rf	4	2	3	2	Foxx, 1b	4	2	2	1
Stephenson, lf	4	1	1	1	Miller, rf	3	1	2	0
Grimm, 1b	4	2	2	2	Dykes, 3b	4	1	3	3
Taylor, c	3	0	1	1	Boley, ss	3	1	1	1
Root, p	3	0	0	0	Quinn, p	2	0	0	0
Nehf, p	0	0	0	0	Walberg, p	0	0	0	0
Blake, p	0	0	0	0	Rommel, p	0	0	0	0
Malone, p	0	0	0	0	Burns, ph	2	0	0	0
Hartnett, ph	1	0	0	0	Grove, p	0	0	0	0
Carlson, p	0	0	0	0					
Totals	35	8	10	6	Totals	36	10	15	10

Chicago ....0 0 0   2 0 5   1 0 0— 8
Philadelphia ....0 0 0   0 0 0   10 0 x—10

Chicago	IP	H	R	ER	BB	SO
Root	6⅓	9	6	6	0	3
Nehf	0†	1	2	2	1	0
Blake (L)	0†	2	2	2	0	0
Malone	⅔	1	0	0	0	2
Carlson	1	2	0	0	0	1

Philadelphia	IP	H	R	ER	BB	SO
Quinn	5*	7	6	5	2	2
Walberg	1	1	1	0	0	2
Rommel (W)	1	2	1	1	1	0
Grove	2	0	0	0	0	4

*Pitched to four batters in sixth.
†Pitched to two batters in seventh.

E—Wilson, Cuyler, Miller, Walberg. DP—Philadelphia 1. LOB—Chicago 4, Philadelphia 6. 2B—Cochrane, Dykes. 3B—Hornsby. HR—Grimm, Haas, Simmons. SH—Taylor, Haas, Boley. HBP—By Malone (Miller). T—2:12. A—29,921.

Jimmie Dykes collected a single, a double and three RBIs in the A's seventh.

strikeouts, one walk, three hits allowed and an earned-run average of 0.00 over 6⅓ innings. Blake took the loss for Chicago.

One more victory was required before Mack could lay claim to his first world championship since 1913. He realized that goal in Game 5, which President Herbert Hoover and the third consecutive capacity crowd at Shibe Park watched October 14. The Chief Executive witnessed another pulsating performance by the A's, who trailed, 2-0, as they batted against Malone in the ninth inning.

With one out, Bishop lashed a single to left field for his club's third hit of the day. Haas, the spoilsport of the fourth game, repeated his act, this time without the aid of the sun. The Mule lined a home run over the right-field wall to knot the score, 2-2. But the American Leaguers were not finished. After Cochrane went out on a grounder to second, Simmons rifled a double off the scoreboard in center field, missing a home run by inches.

The Cubs saw no advantage in pitching to Foxx, who had collected seven hits, including two homers, and driven in five runs during the Series. He was handed an intentional pass. But Miller shattered the

Mule Haas contributed a three-run, inside-the-park home run to Philadelphia's seventh-inning cause

while teammate Jimmie Foxx singled twice and drove in a run.

Al Simmons led off the big inning with a home run and later added a single.

strategy by bouncing another double off the scoreboard. It was almost a replica of the drive by Simmons, who raced home with the Series-deciding run.

The reaction of the Philadelphia fans to their team's stunning victory was interesting. Rather than rushing onto the field, the joyful spectators stood on their seats and cheered lustily until the President and the First Lady had left safely. Then they swarmed around the A's bench, which already had been vacated by all but one man—Connie Mack. The only manager the A's had ever known was so choked up by the emotional triumph that he just waved his hat, unable to speak.

Not since the A's defeated the Giants in 1913 had the club and the city enjoyed such prestige. Civic pride reached new heights and the city fathers, caught up in the fervor, the next year presented the coveted Bok Award to the 67-year-old manager. Previously awarded to scholars and other learned men in the community, the award was given to the man whom Philadelphians recognized as having rendered the greatest service to their town in 1929.

'The Streak' Comes to an End

Ascertaining the correct spelling of proper names has become an increasingly important part of a journalist's job, as a careful examination of any periodical over the last several decades will show. That practice, however, was not yet fully developed in the summer of 1933.

For example, when the batting streak of a Pacific Coast League outfielder came to an end, the August 3, 1933, issue of The Sporting News carried a front-page headline that announced: "De Maggio Stops at 61, Mob Charges Scorer."

The player was, of course, Joe DiMaggio of the San Francisco Seals. His 61-game streak established a league record but, moreover, brought attention to his misspelled name. Before long, box scores carried his name with the correct letters in the proper order.

The second part of the headline pertained to an incident in Sacramento. A ball hit by DiMaggio to the shortstop's right side had been bobbled momentarily. By the time the ball was firmly grasped, DiMaggio was across the bag, and no throw was made. Steve George, the official scorer, ruled it a hit, infuriating some fans who charged the press box. Only the prompt intervention of gendarmes saved the beleaguered scorer.

DiMaggio, in his first full season of professional ball, was only two years removed from his dual role of newsboy and shortstop on a semipro team in the Bay Area. He played three games at shortstop for the Seals at the tail end of the 1932 campaign—without contract or compensation—as a late-season replacement when the club suffered a shortage of infielders. The youngster remained with the Seals the next spring, but his defensive inconsistency inspired the club to move him to the outfield.

Batting streaks were nothing new to Joe DiMaggio when the 1941 season began.

The 18-year-old's streak, which started May 28, 1933, was snapped in a July 26 game against Oakland. The pitcher who handcuffed Deadpan Joe was Ed Walsh, the son of the famed spitball pitcher by the same name who won 40 games for the White Sox in 1908 and later was elected to the Hall of Fame.

According to the San Francisco correspondent, who concealed his identity behind the pseudonym "Seal," the streak exacted a heavy toll on the teenager's stamina. "His former clean drives were not getting out of the infield," he wrote. "The adulation and publicity that had been heaped on him and the worry over whether he could set a world's record apparently were telling on him, and it became only a question of how soon he would crack."

The attention he received in 1933 was only a foretaste of what DiMaggio would experience eight years later. By 1941, Joe was a veteran of four world championship teams with the New York Yankees. He was the archetypical center fielder and a smooth, powerful batter, already the recipient of one American League Most Valuable Player award (in 1939). He was in his sixth season with the Yankees when he launched a two-month adventure that produced a ponderous pressure known to but few.

The new experience got under way modestly enough May 15 at Yankee Stadium. It took the form of a one-base hit off Edgar Smith, a White Sox lefthander. The next day he belted a triple and a home run off Chicago's Thornton Lee, and on May 17 he tagged John Rigney of the White Sox for a

FACTS ON DiMAGGIO'S STREAK
MAY 15-JULY 16, 1941

22 multiple-hit games

56 singles

55 RBIs

91 hits

Yanks' record before streak: 14-14, 4th place, 5½ games out

Yanks' record after last game of streak: 55-27, 1st place, 6 games in front

16 doubles

56 runs

4 triples

.408 average

Yanks' record during streak: 41-13 (2 ties)

15 home runs

single. After going hitless for two games, DiMag had hit safely in three consecutive games.

On the succeeding days, Joe continued to forge additional links in the lengthening chain, although few paid much attention. There was a slight stir when he rapped three singles and a prodigious homer against Washington on May 27, but it was only a momentary flurry. By the end of May the string stood at 16 games, mildly impressive but hardly awe-inspiring.

By June 7, when the streak stood at 21 games, interest was growing. Game reports generally carried a line or two on Joe's progress. But it wasn't until another two weeks had passed that DiMaggio himself started to take an interest in his accomplishment. On June 20 he hit three singles and a double to tie Rogers Hornsby's feat of hitting in 33 straight games, which had been the modern National League record since 1922. The next day he surpassed the former Cardinal with a single off Dizzy Trout of the Tigers. By this time, with his media entourage growing steadily larger, he couldn't help but get excited about his batting streak.

The Yankee Clipper had hit safely in 37 consecutive games when he narrowly escaped the most serious threat to a break in the string June 26. The Yankees led the St. Louis Browns, 3-1, going into the last half of the eighth inning. DiMag was the fourth scheduled batter. He still was hitless in three at-bats, and unless one of the three preceding batters reached base, he would not get another chance to preserve the streak.

Elden Auker, a righthanded submarine hurler with considerable talent, retired first baseman Johnny Sturm for the first out, but third baseman Red Rolfe coaxed a base on balls as the Yankee Stadium crowd roared its approval. That left it squarely up to right fielder Tommy Henrich. If Old Reliable hit into a double play, DiMaggio's streak would end at 37 games. But Joe McCarthy did not want to risk that, so the manager ordered Henrich to sacrifice. The bunt was executed perfectly and Joe, pleased with that, cracked Auker's first pitch to left field for a double, scoring Rolfe.

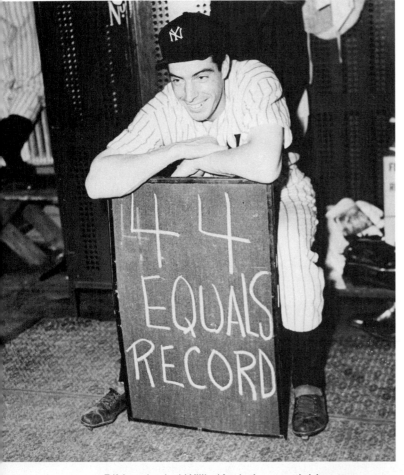

DiMaggio tied Willie Keeler's record 44-game streak with a July 1 single.

A July 2 home run gave DiMaggio the all-time major league record.

DiMaggio was closing in on George Sisler's A.L. and modern major league record of 41 games, set with St. Louis in 1922. His streak had reached 40 and was exciting a nation when the Yankees invaded Washington for a doubleheader June 29. A crowd of 31,000 was kept waiting until Joe's third plate appearance in the opening game before he tied Sisler's record. The hit was a double off Emil (Dutch) Leonard, the Senators' formidable knuckleball artist.

The pressure and the heat under which DiMaggio was laboring that afternoon appeared to be near the boiling point. The temperature at Griffith Stadium was a stifling 98 degrees when DiMag returned to the dugout for the start of the second game, whereupon he discovered that a mischievous fan had pilfered his favorite bat.

Without his pet bludgeon, DiMaggio went hitless in his first three at-bats. In the seventh inning, Henrich offered Joe his bat. Joe accepted and promptly lined a single to left field off the Senators' Red Anderson. The modern record now belonged to DiMaggio. Before day's end he received a congratulatory wire from Sisler, who had declared before the game that if the record was to be broken, the Jolter was the ideal player to do it.

"Sure, I'm tickled," DiMaggio said afterward. "Who wouldn't be? It's a great thing. I've realized an ambition. But I don't deserve the credit all alone. You have to give Mr. McCarthy some of it. I got many a break by being allowed to hit that 3-and-0 pitch. It brought me many a good ball to swing at."

The tension relaxed considerably in the days that followed, but one more goal remained. That was the 44-game streak forged by Willie Keeler of Baltimore in 1897. Joe tied that record July 1 with a single off Boston's Jack Wilson. The next day, against Dick Newsome of the Red Sox, DiMaggio clouted a 2-and-1 fastball into the left-field seats at Yankee Stadium, giving him the all-time major league record for consecutive games hit safely.

How much longer could he continue his phenomenal streak? Not much, many fans thought, figuring that DiMaggio would suffer a letdown after scaling the final summit. But he gained the 50-game mark July 11 with a four-hit salvo against the Browns and then the 55-game plateau July 15 with a double and a single off Edgar Smith, who had surrendered the first hit of the streak exactly two months before.

The Bombers moved into Cleveland for the start of a three-game series July 16, and Joe marked the occasion with a double and two singles in a 10-3 trouncing of Al Milnar and reliever Joe Krakauskas.

On July 17, 67,468 fans rimmed Municipal Stadium to see if this would be the night, after 56 games, when the Clipper would be shoved off course. It was the largest night-game throng in history at that time.

Pitching for New York was DiMaggio's roommate, Lefty Gomez, whom Joe regarded as his good luck charm. Al Smith, a 33-year-old lefthander who had won 15 games for the Indians the previous year following undistinguished terms with the Giants and the Phillies, was on the mound for Cleveland.

The Yanks scored one run in the first inning when Rolfe beat out an infield single and Henrich doubled. With one out, Henrich pranced nervously off second base as Smith prepared to pitch to DiMaggio. His first delivery missed the strike zone. On the second offering, a fastball, the Jolter turned viciously and blasted a grounder down the third-base line. Ken Keltner, playing deep, made a sensational backhanded stab and nailed Joe by a whisker at first base.

In the fourth inning, with Gomez keeping the Yankees in front, 1-0, DiMaggio faced Smith again. Pitching with extreme caution, Smith worked the count to 3-and-2 and then walked the batter with a pitch in the dirt. The shower of boos told Smith of the crowd's displeasure.

Cleveland left fielder Gerald Walker hit an inside-the-park home run in the bottom of the fourth inning to tie the score. The teams still were deadlocked when DiMaggio came to bat for the third time in the seventh inning. Smith's first pitch was a sweeping curve, and DiMag liked it well enough to unleash a powerful swing. It was another screamer toward third base and directly at Keltner. Like the All-Star third baseman he was, Keltner fielded the ball cleanly and again nipped DiMaggio by a step.

Moments later, second baseman Joe Gordon homered into the left-field seats to give the Yanks a 2-1 edge. The Yankees extended their lead to 4-1 in the

JULY 17, 1941									
New York	ab	r	h	rbi		Cleveland	ab	r	h	rbi
Sturm, 1b	4	0	1	0		Weatherly, cf	5	0	1	0
Rolfe, 3b	4	1	2	1		Keltner, 3b	3	0	1	0
Henrich, rf	3	0	1	1		Boudreau, ss	3	0	0	0
DiMaggio, cf	3	0	0	0		Heath, rf	4	0	0	0
Gordon, 2b	4	1	2	1		Walker, lf	3	2	2	1
Rosar, c	4	0	0	0		Grimes, 1b	3	1	1	0
Keller, lf	3	1	1	0		Mack, 2b	3	0	0	0
Rizzuto, ss	4	0	0	0		Rosenthal, ph	1	0	1	2
Gomez, p	4	1	1	1		Hemsley, c	3	0	1	0
Murphy, p	0	0	0	0		Trosky, ph	1	0	0	0
						Smith, p	3	0	0	0
						Bagby, p	0	0	0	0
						Campbell, ph	1	0	0	0
Totals	33	4	8	4		Totals	33	3	7	3

New York ....1 0 0   0 0 0   1 2 0—4
Cleveland ....0 0 0   1 0 0   0 0 2—3

New York	IP	H	R	ER	BB	SO
Gomez (W)	8	6	3	3	3	5
Murphy	1	1	0	0	0	0
Cleveland	IP	H	R	ER	BB	SO
Smith (L)	7⅓	7	4	4	2	4
Bagby	1⅔	1	0	0	1	1

DP—Cleveland 1. LOB—New York 5, Cleveland 7. 2B—Henrich, Rolfe. 3B—Keller, Rosenthal. HR—Walker, Gordon. SH—Boudreau. PB—Hemsley. T—2:03. A—67,468.

Cleveland pitchers Al Smith and Jim Bagby Jr. checked DiMaggio's streak at 56 games.

eighth. Left fielder Charlie Keller led off with a triple and scored on Gomez's one-out single. Sturm then singled and advanced to third on Rolfe's run-scoring double. When Smith walked Henrich to load the bases, bringing up DiMaggio, Indians Manager Roger Peckinpaugh walked out to the mound. Peckinpaugh lifted Smith in favor of righthander Jim Bagby Jr., the 24-year-old son of Cleveland's 31-game winner of 1920.

Bagby started Joe off with a ball. One more ball and a strike later, Bagby threw a fastball on the inside edge of the plate that was to Joe's liking. He smashed it up the middle "as hard as I ever hit any ground ball."

From his shortstop position, Lou Boudreau took several steps to his left and reached for the ball. But the ball bounced erratically and was about to carom off his shoulder when Boudreau reacted with lightning-like reflexes and speared the ball. An inning-ending double play by·way of second baseman Ray Mack was the result.

As he was waved out at first base, DiMaggio displayed no trace of emotion, no hint of frustration or anger. He retrieved his glove and trotted to center field.

When the Indians scored two runs in the ninth inning to make the score 4-3 with none out, it appeared possible that the Indians would tie the score and send the game into extra innings, perhaps giving Joe another chance to preserve his streak. But reliever Johnny Murphy, after surrendering a two-run triple to Larry Rosenthal, shut the Tribe down without further scoring. The game and the streak were over.

"The memory of that game is clear to me, very

clear," DiMaggio said many years later. "Strangely enough, I wanted to keep on going. I felt a little downhearted. I was stopped, but I quickly got over that. It was like going into the seventh game of the World Series and losing it. That's how I felt. But I did want to keep on going. I wanted it to go on forever."

During the 56-game streak, DiMaggio batted .408 in 223 at-bats with 91 hits, including 16 doubles, four triples and 15 homers. He also drove in 55 runs.

When the streak began, the Yankees were in fourth place, 5½ games behind the Indians. When it ended the Bombers were in first place, six games ahead of the Tribe. Sparked by DiMag, the Yanks won 41 games, lost 13 and played two ties during that span.

After the July 17 heartbreaker in Cleveland, DiMaggio launched another streak. It reached 16 games before he was blanked twice in an August 3 doubleheader at Yankee Stadium. Curiously, the culprits were members of the second-division Browns, who won both games behind Johnny Niggeling and Bob Harris. But the Yankees recovered and won the pennant by 17 games over the Red Sox. DiMaggio and the Yanks then climaxed the most wondrous of years with a World Series conquest of the Brooklyn Dodgers in five games.

When the A.L. Most Valuable Player ballots were tabulated, it was discovered that the electorate regarded DiMaggio, with his .357 batting average, 125 runs batted in and 56-game hitting streak, of greatest value to his team. What had the runner-up, Boston's Ted Williams, done to distinguish himself?

Batted .406 and hit 37 home runs, that's all.

Fisk's Home Run Deadlocks '75 Series

For Carlton Fisk, the 1975 baseball season started with all the exhilaration of a passed ball or an errant pickoff throw or a botched pop foul.

It commenced, in fact, in much the same manner that the 1974 campaign had ended. In June 1974, the husky Boston catcher was involved in a violent home-plate collision with Indians outfielder Leron Lee in Cleveland. Fisk, who had missed the start of the season with a groin injury, suffered torn ligaments in his left knee and spent the rest of the year on the disabled list.

Months of exhaustive and painful rehabilitation followed, but by the start of the next spring training, the 6-foot-2, 200-pounder was fully restored. He arrived at Winter Haven, Fla., the club's training base, fully expecting a return to the form that had earned him American League Rookie of the Year honors in 1972 and produced 26 homers and 71 runs batted in a year later.

In the first exhibition game, Fisk played five innings. Even though the Expos stole five bases against him, the performance was encouraging and

Boston's Carlton Fisk swings and Game 6 of the 1975 World Series comes to a dramatic conclusion.

few, if any, would have doubted that the Vermont native would be a serious contender for the All-Star Game honors he had received in 1972 and '73.

In the second exhibition game, however, disaster struck once again. Fisk was hit by a pitch from Detroit's Fred Holdsworth and suffered a fractured right forearm. He dejectedly assumed his now familiar spot on the disabled list.

The season was in its third month when the 27-year-old catcher made his 1975 debut. It happened June 23 at Fenway Park and was accompanied by a standing ovation.

"It was just like getting married," he quipped. "You plan for it, you know it's coming. And when the day arrives, you're still nervous."

As a result of the two extended layoffs, Carlton played in fewer games in the combined seasons of 1974 and '75 than he did in 1973, when he appeared in 135 contests. But to the enormous delight of the Red Sox, the lengthy idleness failed to dim Fisk's

batting eye. In the 79 games remaining to him in 1975 he batted .331, cracked 10 homers and drove in 52 runs. He was a major factor in Manager Darrell Johnson's team winning the A.L. East championship by 4½ games over Baltimore and sweeping the A's in the League Championship Series. He batted .417 (five hits in 12 at-bats) against Oakland as a pennant was raised over Boston for the first time since 1967.

Boston's opponent in the World Series was Cincinnati, which had swept Pittsburgh in the playoffs to win the National League pennant for the third time in six years, all under the leadership of Manager Sparky Anderson. The Reds' lineup bulged with talented players who excelled in all phases of the game—third baseman Pete Rose, second baseman Joe Morgan, catcher Johnny Bench, first baseman Tony Perez, left fielder George Foster, shortstop Dave Concepcion, right fielder Ken Griffey and center fielder Cesar Geronimo. There was no weakness

Fisk implores his drive to stay fair.

Fisk (right) and teammate Fred Lynn celebrate as the

in the offense that had batted .271 and led the league in runs scored and stolen bases.

Luis Tiant, who had won 18 games during the regular season, refused to be intimidated by the imposing array of Cincinnati hitters in Game 1 on October 11 at Fenway Park. The righthander muffled the Reds' big guns, allowing only five hits and posting a 6-0 shutout. All the Boston runs were scored in the seventh inning, which Tiant launched with a single. Four batters later, after starter and loser Don Gullett had been knocked out of the game, Fisk drew a bases-loaded walk off reliever Clay Carroll.

Fisk contributed a run-scoring single in the second game, but the Red Sox's seven-hit attack fell short. Trailing 2-1 in the top of the ninth, the Reds parlayed a double by Bench, an infield single and a stolen base by Concepcion and a double by Griffey into two runs to pull out a 3-2 victory.

When the Series moved to Cincinnati for the third contest October 14, Fisk hammered a solo home run leading off the second inning. But Bench, Concepcion and Geronimo also homered for the Reds as Cincinnati took a 5-1 lead. The Red Sox battled back, however, scoring a run on center fielder Fred Lynn's sacrifice fly in the sixth and another on pinch-hitter Bernie Carbo's solo home run in the seventh. The key blow—and the sixth homer of the game—was provided by Boston right fielder Dwight Evans, whose two-run blast tied the score, 5-5, in the ninth inning.

The teams remained deadlocked until the bottom of the 10th, when controversy propelled Fisk into the spotlight. With Geronimo on first base, pinch-hitter Ed Armbrister bunted. The catcher and the batter became entangled in front of the plate and Fisk, throwing off-balance, fired wildly into center field. Claims of interference by the Red Sox were dismissed by umpire Larry Barnett, and Geronimo and Armbrister advanced to third and second, re-

ball caroms off the left-field foul pole.

Fisk receives a warm reception at home plate.

spectively. Geronimo eventually scored on Morgan's single, giving the Reds a 6-5 victory.

The combatants split the next two games at Riverfront Stadium, the Red Sox and Tiant winning the fourth game, 5-4, and the Reds and Gullett capturing the fifth game, 6-2. By this time, the reaction to Barnett's non-call against the Red Sox in Game 3 had become nasty. The umpire, his wife and his daughter had received death threats through the mail. One extortion letter demanded payment of $10,000. For the remainder of the Series, the Barnetts were given round-the-clock protection by FBI agents.

The sixth game, scheduled for October 18 at Fenway Park, was postponed three times as a storm struck New England in all its unbridled fury. Boston merchants loved the rain, which forced transients to eat, drink and buy to excess while idling the hours away. Club officials and media people, however, were less enamored of the meteorological mischief. As journalists looked at dwindling cash reserves and mounds of soiled laundry, the Red Sox saw their revenue being nibbled away by a myriad of extra expenses. Television executives, meanwhile, wondered whether the days of inactivity would diminish national interest and slash the viewing audience.

They needn't have worried. When the storm swirled out to sea and permitted the sixth game to be played October 21, a sellout crowd of 35,205 crammed into historic Fenway Park while millions more watched on television. The wait was worth it. The game was to be one of the most exciting in baseball history.

The fireworks started early—too early, in fact, for Barnett, who had not been forgotten during the five days since the Red Sox and the Reds had last met. While walking to his post at third base before the start of the game, the arbiter wondered whether he was drifting too close to the stands. Just then, "somebody threw a string of firecrackers on the field and I almost fainted," he recalled. "I was sure they'd gotten me. I was waiting for something to start hurting."

More fireworks—this time the between-the-white-lines variety—commenced anew in the home half of the first inning. With two out, left fielder Carl Yastrzemski and Fisk singled. Lynn, the league's Most Valuable Player as a rookie that year, followed with a three-run homer off starter Gary Nolan.

The Reds knotted the score with three runs in the fifth inning. Griffey knocked in two runs with a triple off Tiant and then scored himself on Bench's single.

The Reds went ahead, 5-3, in the seventh when,

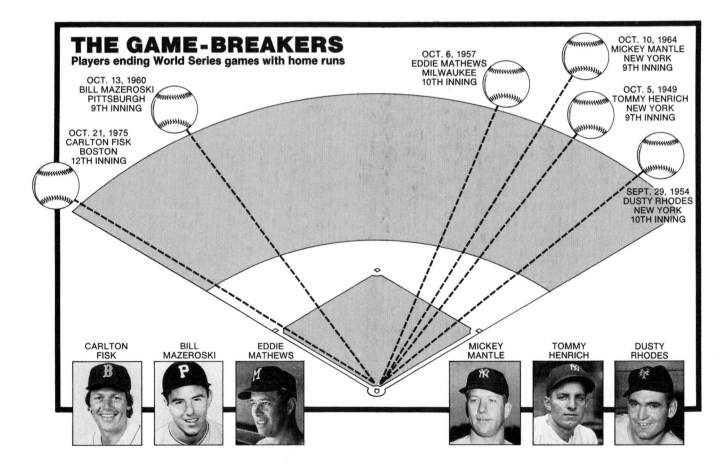

THE GAME-BREAKERS
Players ending World Series games with home runs

OCT. 6, 1957
EDDIE MATHEWS
MILWAUKEE
10TH INNING

OCT. 10, 1964
MICKEY MANTLE
NEW YORK
9TH INNING

OCT. 13, 1960
BILL MAZEROSKI
PITTSBURGH
9TH INNING

OCT. 5, 1949
TOMMY HENRICH
NEW YORK
9TH INNING

OCT. 21, 1975
CARLTON FISK
BOSTON
12TH INNING

SEPT. 29, 1954
DUSTY RHODES
NEW YORK
10TH INNING

CARLTON FISK   BILL MAZEROSKI   EDDIE MATHEWS   MICKEY MANTLE   TOMMY HENRICH   DUSTY RHODES

with two out, Foster doubled in Griffey and Morgan. A leadoff homer by Geronimo in the eighth finished Tiant and gave the Reds a three-run cushion, pushing the Red Sox one step closer to the precipice.

But the Red Sox were not ready to knuckle under. Lynn, who had been shaken up when he crashed against the wall while chasing Griffey's hit in the fifth, opened the bottom of the eighth with a single. Third baseman Rico Petrocelli then was walked, driving righthander Pedro Borbon to the showers. The new pitcher—Cincinnati's sixth of the day—was righthander Rawly Eastwick, who began his tour of duty in a style consistent with his 22 saves and 2.60 earned-run average in the regular season. He struck out Evans and retired shortstop Rick Burleson on an outfield fly. His only remaining obstacle to a scoreless inning was Carbo, the part-time outfielder who had socked 15 homers and driven in 50 runs during the A.L. campaign. Johnson sent him to the plate for Roger Moret, the second of four Boston hurlers, and he delivered just as handsomely as he had in Game 3. Bernie's line-drive homer into the center-field seats tied the score, 6-6, as well as a Series record. His two pinch homers matched a feat performed only once before, by Chuck Essegian of the Dodgers in 1959.

The Red Sox shelled Eastwick in the ninth inning and made serious overtures toward an early climax by loading the bases with none out. Only a piece of bizarre baserunning stymied their efforts.

Lefthanded reliever Will McEnaney induced Lynn to lift a foul fly to Foster in left field, an estimated 180 feet from the plate. From a Boston viewpoint, the easy putout was disappointing, but it became positively distressing when second baseman Denny Doyle ignored coach Don Zimmer's shouts and broke off third base. Foster's throw was several feet off target but still in time for Bench to complete the double play. Petrocelli's groundout snuffed out what only moments before had all the earmarks of a game-winning charge.

The Reds advanced a runner to second base in the 10th inning without bringing him home and mounted an even more serious threat in the 11th when Morgan smashed a Dick Drago pitch to deep right field. The ball appeared headed for the second or third row of the bleachers, but Evans made a leaping one-handed catch. His throw to the infield easily doubled up Griffey, who already had rounded second base.

"It was just about the greatest catch I've ever seen," Anderson said.

The Reds made yet another move toward dissolving the stalemate in the 12th inning when one-out singles by Perez and Foster sent tremors through the crowd. The uprising foundered when Concepcion flied out and Geronimo struck out against

righthander Rick Wise, the fourth (and last) Boston pitcher on that Tuesday night.

As Fisk shucked off his catching gear and walked, bat in hand, toward the plate to open the home half of the third overtime inning, the hands on the clock atop the right-field stands revealed that Tuesday had slipped into Wednesday. Four hours had passed since Tiant had delivered the game's first pitch to Rose.

On the mound for Cincinnati was righthander Pat Darcy, the eighth visiting pitcher to appear that night. Darcy had retired six batters in a row since entering the game in the 10th inning.

Darcy threw once, and the batter took the pitch for a ball. On Darcy's second pitch, Carlton Ernest Fisk swung with all his might. The crash of bat against ball turned 35,000-plus pairs of eyes peering into the New England darkness and searching for the target area. A couple of steps from the plate, Fisk stopped and, like a schoolboy at recess, did a slight jig. He knew the ball had home run distance; the question was whether it would drift foul. He applied some body English, trying to wave the ball

OCTOBER 21, 1975

Cincinnati	ab	r	h	rbi	Boston	ab	r	h	rbi
Rose, 3b	5	1	2	0	Cooper, 1b	5	0	0	0
Griffey, rf	5	2	2	2	Drago, p	0	0	0	0
Morgan, 2b	6	1	1	0	Miller, ph	1	0	0	0
Bench, c	6	0	1	1	Wise, p	0	0	0	0
Perez, 1b	6	0	2	0	Doyle, 2b	5	0	1	0
Foster, lf	6	0	2	2	Y'strz'mski, lf-1b	6	1	3	0
Concepcion, ss	6	0	1	0	Fisk, c	4	2	2	1
Geronimo, cf	6	1	2	1	Lynn, cf	4	2	2	3
Nolan, p	0	0	0	0	Petrocelli, 3b	4	1	0	0
Chaney, ph	1	0	0	0	Evans, rf	5	0	1	0
Norman, p	0	0	0	0	Burleson, ss	3	0	0	0
Billingham, p	0	0	0	0	Tiant, p	2	0	0	0
Armbrister, ph	0	1	0	0	Moret, p	0	0	0	0
Carroll, p	0	0	0	0	Carbo, ph-lf	2	1	1	3
Crowley, ph	1	0	1	0					
Borbon, p	1	0	0	0					
Eastwick, p	0	0	0	0					
McEnaney, p	0	0	0	0					
Driessen, ph	1	0	0	0					
Darcy, p	0	0	0	0					
Totals	50	6	14	6	Totals	41	7	10	7

```
Cincinnati .........0  0  0    0  3  0    2  1  0    0  0  0—6
Boston .............3  0  0    0  0  0    0  3  0    0  0  1—7
```
None out when winning run scored.

Cincinnati	IP	H	R	ER	BB	SO
Nolan	2	3	3	3	0	2
Norman	⅔	1	0	0	2	0
Billingham	1⅓	1	0	0	1	1
Carroll	1	1	0	0	0	0
Borbon	2†	1	2	2	2	1
Eastwick	1‡	2	1	1	1	2
McEnaney	1	0	0	0	1	0
Darcy (L)	2§	1	1	1	0	1

Boston	IP	H	R	ER	BB	SO
Tiant	7*	11	6	6	2	5
Moret	1	0	0	0	0	0
Drago	3	1	0	0	0	1
Wise (W)	1	2	0	0	0	1

*Pitched to one batter in eighth.
†Pitched to two batters in eighth.
‡Pitched to two batters in ninth.
§Pitched to one batter in twelfth.

E—Burleson. DP—Cincinnati 1, Boston 1. LOB—Cincinnati 11, Boston 9. 2B—Doyle, Evans, Foster. 3B—Griffey. HR—Lynn, Geronimo, Carbo, Fisk. SB—Concepcion. SH—Tiant. HBP—By Drago (Rose). T—4:01. A—35,205.

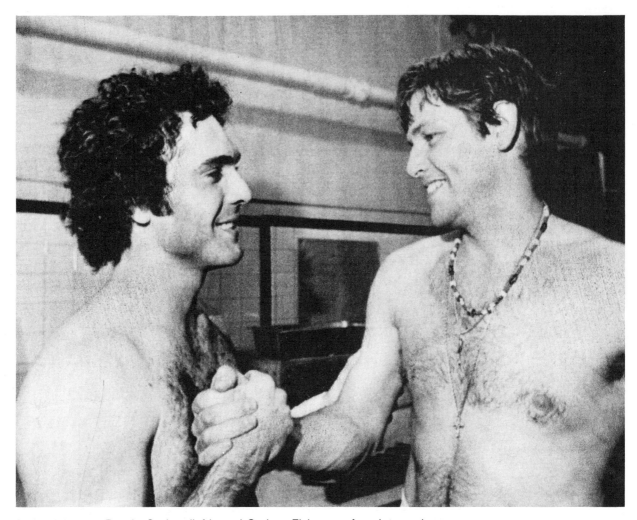

Game 6 heroes Bernie Carbo (left) and Carlton Fisk pose for pictures in the jubilant Red Sox clubhouse.

into fair territory as he watched the high trajectory of the ball in its flight toward the left-field wall. The hand signals must have worked because the ball caromed off the foul pole for a game-winning and Series-tying home run. Fisk leaped convulsively and undertook his tour of the bases.

Simultaneously, kids popped out of the stands, oblivious of park attendants and security personnel and eager to bestow their own special idolatry on the man of the moment.

"I was going to make certain that I stepped on every little white thing out there," Fisk explained, "even if I had to straight-arm or kick somebody to do it."

When Fisk stepped triumphantly on home plate, where he was engulfed by hysterical teammates, the husky catcher rang down the curtain on one of baseball's all-time thrillers. As the organist saluted the victorious Red Sox with "Stout-hearted Men," "The Hallelujah Chorus" and "Beer Barrel Polka," spectators lingered in the pews. They were emotion-

ally drained, but they overflowed with the jubilation that only a superior baseball game can provide. The lateness of the hour was no deterrent. They wanted to savor a hero's finest moment, a moment that suffered not at all when the Reds captured the world championship on Morgan's run-scoring single in the ninth inning the next night.

Fisk remained with the Red Sox through the 1980 season, after which an arbitrator granted him his free agency. He signed a lucrative contract with the White Sox, for whom he continued to excel as a versatile slugger who could play catcher, first base, third base, the outfield and designated hitter. But he still is best remembered for his wild gyrations as he watched his 12th-inning homer force a seventh game of the 1975 World Series. It was a dramatic finish to a game that was so spine-tingling, even the losers were impressed.

"What a game!" Rose bubbled afterward. "If this isn't the national pastime . . . well, it's the best advertisement you could have for baseball."

Amoros Catches Brooklyn's Fancy

The 5-foot-7 outfielder never appeared in more than 119 games in a single major league season. He never batted more than .277 nor collected as many as 100 hits in one campaign. His was not the type of career that inspires awe among baseball historians.

Yet when listing the names of the key figures in baseball's greatest games—Ruth, Mays, Williams, Alexander, Slaughter, Drysdale, DiMaggio and so on—one must include the name Amoros. If pronounced rapidly, it could be made to sound like "amorous," an adjective that captured the sentiments of Dodgers aficionados on October 4, 1955. On that date, long-suffering Brooklyn fans absolutely fell in love with the young outfielder whose superlative defensive play in the final game of the World Series not only provided the thrill of the year for hundreds of callous sportswriters, but also earned him an indelible spot in baseball history.

Christened Edmundo in his native Matanzas, Cuba, Amoros was nicknamed Sandy because somebody detected his resemblance to a fighter named Sandy Saddler. He was tabbed with that moniker shortly after being discovered by Al Cam-

Spectators in the left-field seats at Yankee Stadium get a backseat view of Brooklyn's Sandy Amoros making his game-saving catch in Game 7 of the 1955 World Series.

With his eye on the ball, Brooklyn left fielder Sandy Amoros glides toward the foul line.

panis, then a Spanish-speaking Brooklyn scout, during a winter visit to Cuba to check on another prospect. Sandy's Cuban manager, Mike Gonzalez, insisted that the youngster was an ordinary player, but Campanis was smitten with Sandy's blinding speed and secured the player's services in 1952.

As a 20-year-old rookie, Amoros batted .337 for St. Paul of the American Association. Less than two seasons with Montreal of the International League completed Sandy's apprenticeship, and he joined the Dodgers midway through the 1954 season.

From the start he was a Flatbush favorite. An ear-splitting smile was his unmistakable trademark. His English vocabulary, however, was severely limited, and for a long time it consisted of one word, "hokay." Sandy generally communicated through interpreters such as pitcher Joe Black or catcher Roy Campanella.

How much of the English language Amoros understood was debatable. Buzzie Bavasi, the Dodgers' vice president, never was certain, particularly when he tried to censure Sandy for arriving late to spring training, as was the Cuban's annual habit. The dialogue, as recounted by columnist Frank Graham of the New York Journal-American, went something like this:

"You are four days late," Buzzie said sternly.

"Yes?" Sandy said, grinning.

"Yes," Buzzie said, "What is your excuse?"

"What?"

"Your excuse! Why were you late?"

"Late," Sandy said. "Yes."

"Well, it will cost you $100," Buzzie said. "Understand?"

"Hundred dollars," Sandy said, his grin widening. "Good."

"No," Buzzie said. "It's not good. It means you are fined $100. Do you know what 'fine' means?"

"Fine!" he said. "Hundred dollars! Fine!"

"He thinks," Buzzie said, "I'm going to give him $100. He's going to get an awful shock when he sees his first paycheck."

A lefthanded batter and thrower, Amoros hit .274 in 79 games in his freshman season of 1954. The next year, playing in 119 games, he dropped to .247. He smacked 10 home runs and stole as many bases while being thrown out five times. His fielding was not exceptional. He committed six errors in 217 chances for a percentage of .972, which ranked well down the list for National League outfielders who appeared in 10 or more games.

The 1955 Dodgers were not dependent on Sandy's contributions to win their fifth pennant in nine years. They batted .271 to lead the league. Their .978 fielding percentage was only three points below league-leading Philadelphia's. They finished 13½ games ahead of second-place Milwaukee. They drew 1,033,589 fans through the gates of tiny Ebbets Field, the second-highest home attendance in the league. On the road, the Dodgers were the second-

As he nears the line and stands, Amoros reaches out for a do-or-die snare at the ball.

most popular draw in the majors, trailing the Yankees by less than 70,000.

As a World Series participant, though, Brooklyn had been an unmitigated failure. Starting in 1916, when they were defeated by the Boston Red Sox, the Brooks had lost seven postseason tournaments. The last five classics had been against the Yankees, who once again were poised to beat up the Dodgers after edging the Cleveland Indians by three games in the American League.

Would it be New York winning its 17th world title? Or Brooklyn winning its first? The odds-makers for the 12th "subway series" established the Dodgers in their familiar role as underdogs, and after the first two games at Yankee Stadium it appeared that the smart money had called the turn correctly.

In the September 28 opener, Whitey Ford and the Yankees beat Don Newcombe and the Dodgers, 6-5. Big Newk got plenty of offensive support, including solo home runs by right fielder Carl Furillo and center fielder Duke Snider, but a pair of homers by New York first baseman Joe Collins and another by left fielder Elston Howard did him in. Newcombe did not reappear in the Series. The next afternoon, lefthander Tommy Byrne pitched a complete game and boosted his own cause with a two-run single as the Yanks won again, 4-2.

But the complexion of the Series changed abruptly when the teams shifted to Brooklyn on Septem-

ber 30. In cozy Ebbets Field, with its 32,111-seat official capacity (although more people could be crammed inside), fanatical loyalists, inviting fences and inspirational atmosphere, the Dodgers regained their touch.

Johnny Podres, a lefthander with a season mark of 9-10, celebrated his 23rd birthday by pitching the Dodgers to an 8-3 victory in Game 3. Campanella sparked the Brooklyn attack with a two-run homer, a double and a single.

The N.L. champions deadlocked the Series on October 1, winning 8-5 as righthander Clem Labine beat Don Larsen with 4⅓ innings of effective relief work. Six of the Brooklyn runs came on homers by Campanella, Snider and first baseman Gil Hodges. Rookie righthander Roger Craig received credit for Brooklyn's 5-3 triumph in the fifth contest as the Dodgers took a three-games-to-two lead with its home-field sweep of the Yanks. Two homers and a double by Snider and a homer by Amoros highlighted Brooklyn's offensive show.

Ford was too much for the Dodgers in the sixth game, played at Yankee Stadium. The lefthander posted a 5-1 decision as the Bombers scored all their runs in the first inning, shelling young lefty Karl Spooner with a bombardment that included a three-run homer by first baseman Bill Skowron.

For the decisive encounter October 4 at Yankee Stadium, Managers Walter Alston and Casey Stengel nominated a pair of starting pitchers with one

Amoros saves the day for the Dodgers as he clutches the ball in the webbing of his glove.

Series victory apiece under their belts—Podres for the Dodgers, Byrne for the Yankees. Byrne held the Dodgers hitless in the first three innings, while the Yankees tagged Podres for one hit in the second inning and two in the third without scoring.

Byrne struck out Snider to open the fourth, but Campanella doubled into the left-field corner for the Dodgers' first hit. After Furillo grounded out, Hodges knocked in Campanella with a single to give Brooklyn a slim 1-0 lead.

The Dodgers doubled their lead in the sixth inning, which shortstop Pee Wee Reese opened with a single to center field. Snider laid down a sacrifice bunt that Byrne fielded, but the pitcher's throw to Skowron pulled him off the bag. In trying to tag Snider, the first baseman dropped the ball for an error. A sacrifice by Campanella advanced the runners, and an intentional walk to Furillo loaded the bases.

At this point, Stengel brought in righthander Bob Grim to face Hodges, a righthanded batter. But Hodges negated the strategy with a fly ball to Bob Cerv in deep right-center field that allowed Reese to score. A wild pitch and a walk to third baseman Don Hoak reloaded the bases, but George Shuba, batting for second baseman Don Zimmer, grounded out to end the inning.

In shuffling his lineup to fill the void created by the removal of Zimmer, Alston shifted Jim Gilliam from left field to second base and inserted Amoros

in the vacated outfield spot. Alston could not know it at the time, but the second-year Brooklyn manager's move was a stroke of genius.

Podres opened the home half of the sixth inning on a down note. He walked second baseman Billy Martin on four pitches and instantly sank deeper into trouble when third baseman Gil McDougald surprised the defense with a bunt that he beat out easily for a base hit. Martin stopped at second.

With catcher Yogi Berra approaching the plate, the Brooklyn defense shifted toward right for the lefthanded hitter. Amoros was stationed far toward center field when Berra slapped Podres' outside pitch down the left-field line. Sandy had a long way to run, and it looked as if the ball would fall inches inside the foul line for an extra-base hit. The New York runners thought so, particularly McDougald, who took off at full tilt with the intention of scoring behind Martin with the tying run.

The speedy Amoros, meanwhile, was gliding across left field with his eye on the ball. At the last second, just inside fair territory, Amoros thrust out his glove. The ball stuck. Seeing the incredible catch, McDougald, who already had touched second base, and Martin quickly reversed direction— but not quickly enough. Sandy fired a perfect throw to Reese, whose relay to Hodges doubled up McDougald. So, rather than having a 2-2 game with Berra on base with none out, the score was 2-0 with Martin on second and two out. Right fielder Hank

Having dodged a sixth-inning bullet, Brooklyn went on to record a 2-0 Game 7 victory and the celebration began.

Bauer then grounded out to end the uprising as 62,465 fans stared in disbelief while Amoros trotted to the dugout.

"I don't see how Amoros caught the ball," Berra said later. "If he misses, we have two runs and I'm on third with none out. It was that close."

Howard's two-out single created a minor threat to Podres in the seventh, but Mickey Mantle, who played in only three games because of leg ailments, popped up as a pinch-hitter. In the eighth, singles by shortstop Phil Rizzuto and McDougald placed two runners aboard with one out, but Berra flied out to Furillo in short right field and Bauer, who batted .429 in the Series despite playing with a severely pulled leg muscle, struck out.

Having escaped the Yankee clutches in those two innings, Podres made quick work of the American Leaguers in the ninth. After Skowron grounded back to the mound and Cerv flied to Amoros, Johnny induced Howard to ground to Reese. The shortstop's throw to Hodges was on target, and Brooklyn's Series famine was snapped. After seven failures, the Dodgers were world champions! Podres was king of the hill, enriched by $9,768 like all of his teammates, and Amoros was praised widely for his defensive wizardry.

"That was a great catch and play," Stengel told reporters afterward. "That play was the play that won the game for them."

Amoros, who was hailed in his native Cuba as a national hero, was asked if he thought he would catch Berra's drive. "I dunno," he replied, grinning. "I just run like hell."

Amoros played in Brooklyn for two more years.

OCTOBER 4, 1955								
Brooklyn	ab	r	h	rbi	New York	ab	r	h	rbi
Gilliam, lf-2b	4	0	1	0	Rizzuto, ss	3	0	1	0
Reese, ss	4	1	1	0	Martin, 2b	3	0	1	0
Snider, cf	3	0	0	0	McDougald, 3b	4	0	3	0
Campanella, c	3	1	1	0	Berra, c	4	0	1	0
Furillo, rf	3	0	0	0	Bauer, rf	4	0	0	0
Hodges, 1b	2	0	1	2	Skowron, 1b	4	0	1	0
Hoak, 3b	3	0	1	0	Cerv, cf	4	0	0	0
Zimmer, 2b	2	0	0	0	Howard, lf	4	0	1	0
Shuba, ph	1	0	0	0	Byrne, p	2	0	0	0
Amoros, lf	0	0	0	0	Grim, p	0	0	0	0
Podres, p	4	0	0	0	Mantle, ph	1	0	0	0
					Turley, p	0	0	0	0
Totals	29	2	5	2	Totals	33	0	8	0

Brooklyn .... 0 0 0   1 0 1   0 0 0—2
New York .... 0 0 0   0 0 0   0 0 0—0

Brooklyn	IP	H	R	ER	BB	SO
Podres (W)	9	8	0	0	2	4
New York	IP	H	R	ER	BB	SO
Byrne (L)	5⅓	3	2	1	3	2
Grim	1⅔	1	0	0	1	1
Turley	2	1	0	0	1	1

E—Skowron. DP—Brooklyn 1. LOB—Brooklyn 8, New York 8. 2B—Skowron, Campanella, Berra. SH—Snider, Campanella. SF—Hodges. WP—Grim. T—2:44. A—62,465.

He spent most of the 1958 and '59 seasons playing for Montreal of the International League. He appeared in nine games with the Los Angeles Dodgers in 1960 before being traded to the Detroit Tigers and eventually drifting to the Mexican League.

He returned to Cuba in 1962 as a prelude to bringing his wife and daughter to the United States. Permission was denied. Fidel Castro offered Sandy a contract to manage the Cuban national team, but Amoros didn't want to work for the new government and turned down the offer. That refusal made him an enemy of the government, which confiscated almost everything he owned, including his 20-acre farm, his car and a bank account of approximately $40,000. He was not allowed to leave the country. To squeeze out a bare subsistence, Sandy worked as an auto mechanic or on road gangs—anything to earn a few pesos.

After five years of virtual imprisonment in his native country, Amoros returned to the United States on a Freedom Flight in 1967. A suit and two changes of clothes represented his entire wealth. At 140 pounds, he was 30 pounds under his playing weight.

Apprised by the commissioner's office that Sandy needed only seven days to become a five-year player, which would qualify him for a $250 monthly pension at the age of 50, the Dodgers signed their former World Series hero on May 5, 1967. He was released May 16 without having played in a game.

Dodger Manager Walter Alston (right) and Owner Walter O'Malley celebrate Brooklyn's first World Series championship in eight tries.

1924 Series Has Rocky Finish

Residents of Washington, D.C., were accustomed to great soul-stirring events, be they political, military or social. But this was an extraordinary occasion, unprecedented and with powerful national impact.

The capital's professional baseball team, after 12 seasons in the National League and 24 in the American, had captured its first pennant. Moreover, Walter Perry Johnson, the modest hero of a lost cause since 1907, finally would have an opportunity to pitch in a World Series. From coast to coast, the 36-year-old righthander was the chief topic of conversation among folks who embraced the national pastime.

No longer could vaudeville comedians evoke guf-

Former Giants third baseman Fred Lindstrom, twice a victim of a mysterious pebble in Game 7 of the 1924 Series, re-enacted the drama in 1951 with a more visible piece of the rock.

A Comedy of Errors

With the bases loaded (Leibold at third, Ruel at second and Shirley at first) and two out in the eighth inning, Harris hits a grounder to third base. The ball takes a crazy bounce over Lindstrom's head for a two-run single, tying the score.

Fate again aids the Senators in the 12th inning. With one out, Ruel lifts a fly ball between third base and home plate, but in chasing down the ball, Giants catcher Gowdy trips over his mask. Given a second chance, Ruel doubles.

Pitcher Johnson then reaches safely on shortstop Jackson's error, as Ruel holds second.

McNeely hits another grounder to third, but just like Harris' ball in the eighth, this one suddenly takes a crazy bounce over Lindstrom's head, scoring Ruel with the Series-winning run.

faws with their line about Washington—"first in war, first in peace and last in the American League." In 1924 they were league champions, deposers of the three-time champion Yankees and opponents of the New York Giants in the World Series.

The Giants were in their ninth Series under John McGraw, the crusty, 51-year-old Little Napoleon. The Senators were managed by Stanley Raymond (Bucky) Harris, the 27-year-old Boy Wonder who also played second base as well as anyone in the league.

Offensively, the Senators were led by Goose Goslin. The left fielder batted .344 and led the league in runs batted in with 129 that year. Sam Rice, the right fielder, was not far behind with a .334 average and a league-leading 216 hits.

The Giants had no 20-game winners such as Johnson, whose 23 victories, 2.72 earned-run average, six shutouts and 158 strikeouts (all league highs) earned him the A.L. Most Valuable Player award. But they had batted .300 as a team, compared with .294 for the Senators, and they knew how to win.

After a wild reception at the railroad station following the team's pennant-clinching victory in Boston and a subsequent motorcade down Pennsylvania Avenue, the capital made ready for the foremost sports extravaganza of many a lifetime. When the classic opened October 4, Griffith Stadium overflowed with 35,760 partisans, including President Calvin Coolidge and the First Lady, the first President-and-wife tandem ever to attend a Series opener. Surrounded by Secret Servicemen and celebrities of every persuasion, Silent Cal watched intently as Johnson and shortstop Roger Peckinpaugh were presented sleek new automobiles by admirers. He took in all the pregame pageantry and then lobbed the ceremonial first pitch from his front-row box.

Though most baseball fans across the nation were pulling for Johnson and the underdog Senators, Sir Walter proved no mystery to the Giants. He yielded 14 hits, compared with 10 by his opponent, lefthander Art Nehf. But he might have hurled a 2-0 shutout had it not been for temporary bleachers erected in left field.

In the second inning, Giants center fielder George Kelly's drive landed in the planked seats. Two innings later, a high fly by New York first baseman Bill Terry dropped into the same sector. If not for the temporary bleachers, Goslin almost certainly could have handled both fly balls. Instead, the Giants had a 2-0 lead.

The Senators later tied the score with a run in the sixth and another in the ninth, but the Giants scored twice in the 12th, offsetting Washington's one-run rally in the home half of the inning, and Johnson lost the opener, 4-3.

With lefthander Tom Zachary scattering six New York hits, the Senators reversed the 4-3 score the next day. Goslin and Harris smashed home runs to stake Washington to an early 3-0 lead, and Peckinpaugh doubled in the winning run in the bottom of the ninth.

When the Series transferred to New York's newly enlarged Polo Grounds on October 6, the Giants rewarded a record crowd of 47,608 fans with a 6-4 victory. Each manager employed four pitchers, with righthander Hugh McQuillan gaining the victory over righthander Fred Marberry.

The throng was even larger for the fourth contest as 49,243 fans saw George Mogridge pull the Senators even again with a 7-4 triumph. Goslin highlighted Washington's 13-hit attack against righthander Virgil Barnes and two other New York hurlers with four hits (including a home run) and four runs batted in.

Johnson was Harris' choice to work the fifth game, but the Big Train was roughed up again, 6-2. He yielded 13 hits, including four by Fred Lindstrom, the Giants' 18-year-old third baseman, and two (one a homer) by his pitching rival, Jack Bentley. The victory gave New York a three-games-to-two lead as the Series returned to Washington.

Harris assigned the sixth game to Zachary, the winner of the second contest. The lefthander allowed seven hits, three more than the Senators collected off Nehf, but Zachary squeezed out a 2-1 victory to force a seventh game. Harris' two-run single in the fifth inning was the difference.

The Boy Wonder's major concern on the eve of Game 7 was Terry, the Giants' 25-year-old first baseman. Playing against righthanded starters only (plus one unsuccessful pinch-hitting appearance against a lefty), Memphis Bill was batting .500 (six hits in 12 at-bats) in the Series. If the Senators were to win, Harris believed, Terry's potent bat would have to be eliminated from the lineup, or at least silenced.

Toward that end, Harris hatched a plot that he presented to Clark Griffith for approval. The club president listened as Harris outlined his strategy. He would start a righthander in the seventh game—any righthander would do—and then, having lured McGraw into starting Terry, he would switch to a lefthander whenever conditions were ripe. McGraw then could lift Terry or let him face the Washington southpaw.

Griffith liked the idea. In the days when he wore a uniform as a pitcher and manager, he was nicknamed the "Old Fox" for just such a reason as Harris was demonstrating.

The young skipper's strategy elicited surprise, if not shock, from the 31,667 fans who crowded into the Florida Avenue ball park October 10. The Washington pitcher was a righthander, Curly

Shortstop
Travis Jackson

Catcher
Hank Gowdy

Third Baseman
Fred Lindstrom

The Goats

Ogden, a winner of nine games against eight losses in a mediocre season divided between the Athletics and the Senators.

Ogden started impressively enough, striking out Lindstrom. He walked second baseman Frank Frisch, however, and then took a stroll himself. From his position at second base, Harris ambled to the mound, relieved Ogden of the baseball and beckoned to the far reaches of the grandstand. From a runway emerged Mogridge, the lefthander in Bucky's master scheme who had been warming up under the grandstand, out of sight.

McGraw stuck with Terry through two unproductive at-bats. After grounding out and striking out, Terry was removed for a pinch-hitter in the sixth inning. The Senators had seen the last of their tormentor. As was his custom against lefthanded pitching, McGraw switched Kelly from center field to first base, moved Hack Wilson from left to center and inserted Emil (Irish) Meusel in left.

Meusel, Terry's pinch-hitter, promptly drove in the Giants' first run of the game with a sacrifice fly off Marberry, who had relieved Mogridge when Meusel was announced. Wilson followed with a single, sending Kelly (who had singled) to third. Kelly and Wilson later scored when first baseman Joe Judge and shortstop Ossie Bluege committed errors on balls hit by two consecutive batters. The Giants had three runs, two more than the Senators, who had dented the scoreboard on Harris' solo homer in the fourth. New York starter Barnes had only 12 more outs to go to give McGraw his fourth world championship.

But the Senators weren't ready to quit. Pinch-hit-

ter Nemo Leibold socked a double to left with one out in the last of the eighth inning, and Washington loyalists started to stir—until they realized that the next batter was Muddy Ruel, who was yet to collect his first Series hit. The catcher chose this spot to break the spell. Ruel's single and a walk to pinch-hitter Bennie Tate loaded the bases.

Center fielder Earl McNeely's fly to left failed to advance a runner, leaving the bases full with two out. It appeared that the Giants were out of the inning with their 3-1 lead intact when the next batter, Harris, hit a routine grounder toward third base. But to the amazement of everyone at Griffith Stadium, the ball took an erratic bounce at the last second and jumped over Lindstrom's head. Leibold and Ruel scored to knot the game at 3-3. Nehf replaced Barnes on the mound for the Giants and retired Rice to end the inning, but the damage had been done.

Marberry had been lifted for a pinch-hitter during that eighth-inning rally, so Harris had to summon his fourth pitcher of the game. There was no question about whom the fans preferred. Cries of "We want Johnson" greeted Harris, followed by a deafening roar when the long-armed Kansan trudged to the mound.

For the third time in the Series, the Big Train was no particular puzzle to the Giants. They greeted him warmly. With one out in the ninth, Frisch tripled to deep center field. Outfielder Ross Youngs, another lefthanded batter, was next, and Harris ordered an intentional walk. No other Giants reached base, however, as Kelly struck out on three pitches and Meusel grounded out to third. One can only wonder how fervently McGraw wished at this spot that he had not removed Terry for Meusel.

After the ninth inning, Johnson fell into a groove that virtually silenced the New York bats. A leadoff walk to Wilson in the 10th went for naught, as did leadoff singles by pinch-hitter Heinie Groh in the 11th and Meusel in the 12th.

The Senators also mounted threats without scoring. In the ninth, a single by Judge and an error placed two runners aboard with one out and moved McGraw to summon McQuillan from the bullpen to replace Nehf. McQuillan immediately doused the flames with a double play. Two innings later, Goslin tagged Bentley, the fourth New York pitcher, for a two-out double and Judge coaxed a walk. Bluege's grounder, however, snuffed out that threat.

How much longer could Johnson go on? Sir Walter had pitched eight innings two days previously and four already in Game 7. He no longer was the young fireballer who once pitched three shutouts in four days. Weariness was a growing concern on the Washington bench.

But before Harris could entertain serious thoughts about pulling his ace pitcher, a bizarre set of circumstances took place in the bottom of the 12th inning. It started with one out when Ruel popped a foul fly down the third-base line.

"I could have caught it," Lindstrom said, "but (Hank) Gowdy called me off."

As he had done hundreds of times, Gowdy sighted the ball and then tossed his mask aside. Inexplicably, the mask bounced into the New York catcher's path, directly underfoot. Gowdy stumbled over the mask and was unable to make the play.

"I felt like a sinner forgiven," quipped Ruel, who redeemed himself by ripping a double to left field.

The odd occurrences continued when Johnson, who had hit a long fly in his first at-bat of the day, hit a grounder to shortstop that was fumbled by Travis Jackson. Ruel stayed at second and Johnson was safe at first.

McNeely was next. Earl smacked a ground ball toward third that had all the appearances of at least one out, perhaps an inning-ending double play. But just as Lindstrom braced to make the play, the ball struck a pebble or a clump of dirt and hopped high over his head. Poor Fred certainly must have felt an overwhelming sense of deja vu, having been similarly victimized four innings before, as slow-moving Ruel chugged home easily. The Washington Senators won, 4-3, thus climaxing a magnificent season with an incredible World Series victory. Sweetest of all for Washington fans was the fact that Johnson had won a Series game at last—and the decisive one at that. The excited throng in the nation's capital toasted the aging warrior in an all-night orgy, dowagers celebrating with schoolgirls, politicos with

bootblacks.

For the Giants, consolation was impossible. On the train ride home, McGraw sat stunned and impassive, muttering blasphemies against Gowdy's mask, the pebble and all else that had conspired against him.

At last the spell was broken when Bentley, the losing pitcher in that heartbreaking final game, addressed his teammates. "Cheer up, boys," he said. "It looks as though the good Lord couldn't stand seeing Walter Johnson lose again."

Even McGraw's black mood changed. All things considered, it had been a fine year, he realized, so why not toast the good and forget the evil.

"All you fellows who have wives in New York," he informed the players, "wire them to meet us at the Commodore Hotel. We're going to have a party."

The rush for telegram forms was on. Washington, with all its sad memories, was falling ever farther behind with each turn of the train's wheels. New York and all its pleasant associations lay just ahead.

The party, like all that were hosted by McGraw, was one never to be forgotten. One who was privileged to attend wrote: "Art Nehf played 'On the Banks of the Wabash' as his wife and father led the company in singing. The song caught on. The candlelight still shone through the sycamores at five o'clock in the morning."

OCTOBER 10, 1924									
New York	ab	r	h	rbi	Washington	ab	r	h	rbi
Lindstrom, 3b	5	0	1	0	McNeely, cf	6	0	1	1
Frisch, 2b	5	0	2	0	Harris, 2b	5	1	3	3
Youngs, rf-lf	2	1	0	0	Rice, rf	5	0	0	0
Kelly, cf-1b	6	1	1	0	Goslin, lf	5	0	2	0
Terry, 1b	2	0	0	0	Judge, 1b	4	0	1	0
Meusel, ph-lf-rf	3	0	1	1	Bluege, ss	5	0	0	0
Wilson, lf-cf	5	1	1	0	Taylor, 3b	2	0	0	0
Jackson, ss	6	0	0	0	Leibold, ph	1	1	1	0
Gowdy, c	6	0	1	0	Miller, 3b	2	0	0	0
Barnes, p	4	0	0	0	Ruel, c	5	2	2	0
Nehf, p	0	0	0	0	Ogden, p	0	0	0	0
McQuillan, p	0	0	0	0	Mogridge, p	1	0	0	0
Groh, ph	1	0	1	0	Marberry, p	1	0	0	0
Southworth, pr	0	0	0	0	Tate, ph	0	0	0	0
Bentley, p	0	0	0	0	Shirley, pr	0	0	0	0
					Johnson, p	2	0	0	0
Totals	45	3	8	1	Totals	44	4	10	4

New York..............0 0 0   0 0 3   0 0 0   0 0 0—3
Washington..........0 0 0   1 0 0   0 2 0   0 0 1—4
One out when winning run scored.

New York	IP	H	R	ER	BB	SO
Barnes	7⅓	6	3	3	1	6
Nehf	⅔	1	0	0	0	0
McQuillan	1⅔	0	0	0	0	1
Bentley (L)	1⅓	3	1	1	1	0
Washington	IP	H	R	ER	BB	SO
Ogden	⅓	0	0	0	1	1
Mogridge	4⅔ *	4	2	1	1	3
Marberry	3	1	1	0	1	3
Johnson (W)	4	3	0	0	3	5

*Pitched to two batters in sixth.

E—Jackson 2, Gowdy, Judge, Bluege 2, Taylor. DP—New York 2, Washington 1. LOB—New York 14, Washington 8. 2B—Lindstrom, Leibold, Ruel, Goslin, McNeely. 3B—Frisch. HR—Harris. SB—Youngs. SH—Meusel, Lindstrom. T—3:00. A—31,667.

1912 Red Sox Slay the Giants

Thirty years after the event, nationally known sportswriter Hugh Fullerton reported: "Everything, seemingly, that can happen in baseball happened in the World Series of 1912, which is declared by many who witnessed the eight battles between the Boston Red Sox and the New York Giants to have been the greatest ever played."

John B. Foster, editor of the Spalding Baseball Guide, declared, "It was a Series crammed with thrills and gulps, cheers and gasps, pity and hysteria, dejection and wild exultation, recrimination and adoration, excuse and condemnation, and therefore it was what may cheerfully be called 'ripping good' baseball."

Journalistic giants that they were and perhaps more inclined to superlatives than their counterparts of a latter day, Fullerton and Foster may, nevertheless, be excused for their flights of rhetoric. The Series, climaxed by the bizarre performance of the Giants in the deciding contest at Fenway Park on October 16, was indeed extraordinary.

The pennant races in both leagues featured remarkable pitching accomplishments. Lefthander Rube Marquard set a modern major league record by winning 19 consecutive games for the Giants, who won the National League flag by 10 games over

Pittsburgh. The Giants also had Christy Mathewson, a 23-game winner that year. Righthander Smokey Joe Wood, en route to a 34-5 season mark, reeled off 16 straight wins for the Red Sox, who took over first place in June and finished 14 lengths ahead of Washington in the American League.

In the first Series game, played October 8 at the Polo Grounds before 35,730 fans, Wood was matched against rookie Jeff Tesreau, who had gone 17-7 with a 1.96 earned-run average during the regular season. On this day, however, he could not control the Red Sox, who carried a 4-2 lead into the last half of the ninth inning. But one-out singles by first baseman Fred Merkle, third baseman Buck Herzog and catcher Chief Meyers produced one run against Wood. Meyers took second on the throw to the plate, giving New York runners at second and third. A base hit could win the game, but Wood struck out shortstop Art Fletcher and reliever Otis Crandall, one of the game's better pinch-hitters, to give Boston the early edge in the Series.

Mathewson pitched well enough to win the second game, which was played the next day under overcast skies in Boston, but five errors (including three by Fletcher) kept the Red Sox in contention. Boston tallied an unearned run in the eighth inning to tie the score, 5-5, and the game eventually went into overtime. In the 10th, Giants pinch-hitter Moose McCormick lofted a fly ball to left field that scored Merkle, who had tripled. That gave Mathewson a chance to close out the victory and even the Series at one game apiece, but in the bottom of the 10th, Red Sox center fielder Tris Speaker clouted a drive to deep center. As Speaker rounded third base, Herzog bumped him, apparently on purpose. The Gray Eagle continued to the plate and was safe when catcher Art Wilson dropped a perfect relay. After 11 innings, with the teams deadlocked, 6-6, the game was called because of darkness, although, Fullerton wrote, "it was lighter 40 minutes after the game was stopped than it had been in the fifth inning."

The next day a Boston crowd of 34,624 watched Marquard outduel Red Sox righthander Bucky O'Brien, 2-1, although the Giants would have fallen two games behind the A.L. champions if not for a defensive gem that ended the contest. With two

OCTOBER 16, 1912

New York	ab	r	h	rbi	Boston	ab	r	h	rbi
Devore, rf	3	1	1	0	Hooper, rf	5	0	0	0
Doyle, 2b	5	0	0	0	Yerkes, 2b	4	1	1	0
Snodgrass, cf	4	0	1	0	Speaker, cf	4	0	2	1
Murray, lf	5	1	2	1	Lewis, lf	4	0	0	0
Merkle, 1b	5	0	1	1	Gardner, 3b	3	0	1	1
Herzog, 3b	5	0	2	0	Stahl, 1b	4	1	2	0
Meyers, c	3	0	0	0	Wagner, ss	3	0	1	0
Fletcher, ss	3	0	1	0	Cady, c	4	0	0	0
McCormick, ph	1	0	0	0	Bedient, p	2	0	0	0
Shafer, ss	0	0	0	0	Henriksen, ph	1	0	1	1
Mathewson, p	4	0	1	0	Wood, p	0	0	0	0
					Engle, ph	1	1	0	0
Totals	38	2	9	2	Totals	35	3	8	3

New York .... 0 0 1   0 0 0   0 0 0 1—2
Boston .... 0 0 0   0 0 0   1 0 0 2—3
Two out when winning run scored.

New York	IP	H	R	ER	BB	SO
Mathewson (L)	9⅔	8	3	1	5	4

Boston	IP	H	R	ER	BB	SO
Bedient	7	6	1	1	3	2
Wood (W)	3	3	1	1	1	2

E—Doyle, Snodgrass, Speaker, Gardner 2, Stahl, Wagner. LOB—New York 11, Boston 9. 2B—Murray 2, Herzog, Gardner, Stahl, Henriksen. SB—Devore. SH—Meyers. SF—Gardner. T—2:39. A—17,034.

runners aboard and two out in the bottom of the ninth, Boston catcher Forrest Cady knocked a drive to deep right-center field. Red Sox fans went crazy as the ball sailed over right fielder Josh Devore's head and the two baserunners headed for home. But in the misty semi-darkness, Devore raced back and caught the ball on a dead run, preserving the Giants' victory.

Gray skies and a muddy, rain-soaked field greeted the teams when the Series returned to New York one day later. The first-game pitchers hooked up once more, and again Wood outpitched Tesreau, this time 3-1. Wood frequently was in trouble, but eight strikeouts and good defensive support helped him quash the New York threats.

A crowd of 34,683 turned out on Columbus Day when the Series went back to Boston. The Red Sox won again, taking a three-games-to-one lead, as righthander Hugh Bedient, a rookie 20-game winner, defeated Mathewson. Back-to-back triples by right fielder Harry Hooper and second baseman Steve Yerkes, plus an error by Giants second baseman Larry Doyle, produced two Boston runs in the third inning. Mathewson did not permit a single baserunner thereafter, but Bedient allowed only three hits to capture the 2-1 decision.

After a Sunday recess, the Series returned to New York on October 14. Garland (Jake) Stahl, Boston's manager-first baseman, had planned to start Wood, and the righthander already had begun warming up when he was ordered to stop. Club President Jim McAleer, a former player, had urged Stahl to start O'Brien as a reward for his fine work in the third game. Besides, McAleer said, Wood would be ready the next day if the Red Sox lost. Stahl yielded and Wood was furious.

Wood got even madder when O'Brien got rocked in the first inning. With two out and runners on first and third base, Bucky committed a balk. The Giants added to that 1-0 lead with a barrage of base hits that, mixed with a double steal, netted five runs.

When O'Brien returned to the bench, Wood made an incendiary remark that ignited a scuffle between the two pitchers. After order was restored, lefty Ray Collins pitched the last eight innings for Boston, and even though he held the Giants scoreless, the damage had been done. New York triumphed, 5-2, behind Marquard.

The Boston players did not conceal their bitterness as they returned home. They knew that Wood had been their manager's choice to start the sixth game and directed their hostility toward O'Brien, who sported a black eye, the souvenir of Paul Wood, who had wagered $100 on the Red Sox in anticipation of his brother hurling the game as advertised.

New York's Fred Snodgrass was branded forever for his $30,000 muff.

Chief Meyers couldn't catch up to the foul pop...

Wood drew the starting assignment for the October 15 contest at Fenway Park. Before the players left their clubhouse, however, the animosity between Wood and O'Brien flared again in fisticuffs, with several teammates joining in. When an armistice finally was arranged, Wood began his warmups. But, Fullerton recorded, he was upset and pitched "as if wild to fight the whole crowd (and) went to the slab white around the mouth from anger."

Joe's troubles, however, were only beginning. As

he prepared to deliver the first pitch, a group of fans surged onto the field. Known as the Royal Rooters, this crew of noisy enthusiasts pledged its eternal allegiance to the Red Sox. The Rooters had occupied the same section of seats in the left-field stands for quite some time, including the first three Boston contests of the Series. But because of the second-game tie, it became necessary to conduct another sale prior to the seventh game. A thoughtless front-office official had sold the Rooters' tickets, unbeknownst to them, on a general-admission basis, and when the Rooters paraded onto the field behind their band, and thence to their accustomed seats, they discovered them already occupied. They displayed their wrath by swarming onto the field and parading back and forth, and city policemen, many of them mounted, spent 30 minutes clearing the premises.

While the disturbance was being settled on this cold and blustery Tuesday afternoon, Wood looked on furiously. By the time he went out to the mound, his anger knew no limits. He was mad, and on top of that, his arm had stiffened during the long delay. Six singles, a double by Fred Snodgrass, a sacrifice, an error, a fielder's choice and a double steal added up to six runs against Wood in the first inning. Charlie (Sea Lion) Hall, Wood's successor, was little better. The righthander permitted five more runs, including two on a home run by Doyle, as the Giants and Tesreau triumphed, 11-4, to tie the Series at three victories apiece.

The game's only bright spot for Boston fans was an unassisted double play by Speaker. With Wilson on second base in the ninth inning, Spoke sprinted in for Fletcher's fly to short center and beat Wilson to second base to register the only such feat by an outfielder in Series play.

Because of the ticket faux pas, the Royal Rooters stayed away from Fenway Park for the decisive eighth game, which had been awarded to Boston by a flip of the coin. Only 17,034 fans were on hand when Bedient took the mound for the A.L. champions. His opponent was the frustrated Mathewson, a celebrated pitcher who was making his third start but was yet to win a game.

Matty was furnished a one-run lead in the third inning when left fielder Red Murray doubled home Devore. Hooper prevented a second New York run in the fifth inning when he made a spectacular catch of Doyle's bid for a home run. Racing toward the temporary bleachers in right-center field, Hooper hurled himself backward over a low railing and caught the ball. Though many questioned the legality of the catch, the out stood and the Giants' lead remained 1-0.

The Red Sox tied the score in the seventh inning on the first of a series of improbable events that made this classic forever memorable. With one out, Stahl hit a fly to short left-center field that could have been caught easily by any one of three players — Murray, Snodgrass or, most likely, Fletcher. All, however, backed off at the last moment, and the ball dropped untouched. Stahl was credited with a single.

Shortstop Heinie Wagner was walked, advancing Stahl to second. After Cady, the eighth-place batter, popped out, the situation dictated a pinch-hitter for Bedient. Stahl selected Olaf Henriksen, a part-time outfielder. It was an inspired move. Olaf swung at the first pitch from Matty and missed, then took the second for a called strike. The third delivery was high. Henriksen swung and sliced the ball toward third base. Herzog, playing wide of the bag for the lefthanded batter, flung himself at the ball, which struck the bag and bounced away as Stahl galloped home with the tying run.

Wood, who followed Bedient to the mound for the Red Sox, came into the game with a chance to either atone for his disaster of the previous day or allow the Giants to take the lead and earn a come-from-behind world championship. Wood appeared headed on the latter course when he gave up a run in the top of the 10th inning as Murray doubled and scored on Merkle's single, giving the Giants a 2-1 advantage. Additional scoring was averted when Wood barehanded a vicious smash by Meyers and threw him out.

The Red Sox were out of the inning and only three outs from extinction. The masterful Mathewson still was in control as the Giants were on the verge of a tremendous comeback from a three-games-to-one deficit.

Wood was scheduled to bat first in the home half of the inning. He was a good hitter, sufficiently good to switch to the outfield when his arm went lame some years later. In fielding Meyers' drive, however, he had injured his hand and was unable to swing a bat properly. A pinch-hitter was required. This time Stahl chose Clyde Engle, who swung at a Mathewson pitch and lifted a soft fly to center field. Snodgrass drifted a few steps, perhaps 10 feet, and raised his glove. The ball struck the leather — and then trickled to the ground. Engle pulled into second base, grateful to be aboard because of Snodgrass' blunder.

Snodgrass, three days shy of his 25th birthday, was an excellent fly-chaser, and he demonstrated his skills a moment later when he sprinted to deep center field to haul down Hooper's prodigious clout. Only two outs remained before the Red Sox would expire and Giants Manager John McGraw would have his second world championship, which he had missed the preceding year when the Giants lost to the Philadelphia Athletics.

But Yerkes refused to offer at Mathewson's tanta-

. . .after seeing Fred Merkle was out of the play.

lizing serves and drew a walk, bringing up Speaker, Boston's leading hitter. Spoke's first effort was a pop foul between home plate and first base, a routine play for either catcher Meyers or first baseman Merkle. Merkle, however, scarcely budged from his position, although the play really was his to make. Belatedly, the slow-footed Meyers sized up the situation and made a dash for the ball. It fell near the first-base coaches box and Speaker had another chance, which was all he needed. His single to right field drove in Engle and sent Yerkes to third. In

Smokey Joe Wood fought with teammates throughout the Series, but still recorded three victories. Tris

Speaker, given a new life by the Giants, got the key
hit that set up Boston's title-winning victory.

desperation, McGraw ordered an intentional pass
to left fielder Duffy Lewis to set up a force play at
every base. It didn't work. The next batter, third
baseman Larry Gardner, hit a long fly to right field,
too deep for Devore to nail Yerkes as he sped home
with the title-clinching run. With the 3-2 decision,
Wood had his third Series victory while Mathewson, despite three strong outings, had his second
loss.

While the Red Sox celebrated their first world
championship since their conquest of the Pirates in
the inaugural World Series of 1903, the Giants took
a funereal train ride back to New York. Snodgrass,
an instant goat of the Series for his "$30,000 muff"
—the approximate difference between the winning
and losing clubs' shares—sat alone, his gaze glued to
a window. Mathewson delivered a few pungent ob-
servations about his sieve-like support, then joined

a card game. McGraw, meanwhile, refused to censure Snodgrass. He recommended a raise for the
outfielder the following year. But he was critical of
Fletcher, the shortstop who had failed in the seventh inning to catch Stahl's fly ball, which set up
Henriksen's game-tying double.

After four more seasons in the game, Snodgrass
returned to his native California, where he became
a successful rancher-businessman. He died in 1974
at the age of 86, but for years prior to that, he was
constantly reminded of his World Series blunder.

"Hardly a day in my life, hardly an hour," Snodgrass said in a 1942 interview, "that in some manner
or other the dropping of that fly doesn't come up,
and after 30 years. On the street, in my store, at my
home, in Oxnard or Ventura, it's all the same. They
might choke up before they ask me and they hesi-
tate—but they always ask."

Somebody Has to Lose

Addie Joss had to be perfect to beat the White Sox on October 2, 1908.

From the earliest days, there was little question that the rangy righthander from Wisconsin eventually would gain recognition as a master of the pitching craft.

At 6-foot-3 and 185 pounds, he fired a devastating fastball like "it came out of his hip pocket," befuddled batters insisted. His delivery consisted of a complete pivot and a quick swing of the arms, after which the ball catapulted out of a weird tangle of arms and legs.

Adrian (Addie) Joss was 20 years old when a peddler who had seen him pitch for the University of Wisconsin and on various semipro teams around Juneau, Wis., recommended him to a scout for the Toledo club of the Inter-State League. Joss won 19 games as a professional rookie in 1900. The next season, still with Toledo but now in the Western Association, Addie posted a 25-15 record with four shutouts.

His record was sufficiently impressive to catch the eye of baseball officials in Cleveland. The American League club snatched up the phenom despite the howls of anguish from Toledo interests. Their protests brought $500 in compensation, hardly adequate for the quality of the merchandise.

Joss broke into the majors on a remarkable note. Pitching against the St. Louis Browns on April 26, 1902, the sidearmer allowed only one hit in hurling a 3-0 shutout. The lone safety was credited to Jesse Burkett, whose soft fly to right field was ruled a hit despite the vigorous squawks of Zaza Harvey, who argued to no avail that he had made the catch. Joss finished his rookie season with five shutouts, tops in the young major league, and 17 victories.

Starting in 1905, Joss won 20 or more games in four consecutive seasons. His high mark was 27 in 1907, but his most notable accomplishment occurred in 1908, when he accounted for 24 victories. So effective was the 28-year-old righthander that a Cleveland newspaper echoed the sentiments of every Indians fan with a headline that shouted, "Oh, for a Few More Like Joss."

Throughout the season, Joss crafted a number of games that foretold a supreme effort in the closing

LAST YEAR
NOT ONE
MAJOR
LEAGUE
PITCHER
WORKED
IN 300
INNINGS –

ED. WALSH
IN 1908 WITH
THE WHITE SOX,
PITCHED 66
GAMES, 464
INNINGS AND
WON 40 GAMES –

A. DEMAREE

This early-century sketch of Chicago's Ed Walsh
portrays him as one of baseball's classic iron men.

days. On May 12 he hurled a three-hit shutout against New York. Four days later he threw another three-hitter against Boston. He allowed only three hits to New York again August 17, and then he grew even more penurious. On September 1 he limited the Tigers to one hit in a 1-0 shutout, and he blanked the White Sox on two hits September 7. He was on the threshhold of his most glittering performance, which was observed by 10,598 fans October 2 at League Park in Cleveland.

More than the outcome of a ball game rode on every pitch. The Indians, who also were known as the Naps in tribute to Manager Napoleon Lajoie, were engaged in a tight pennant race with the Tigers, who were in front by only half a game. The White Sox, the visiting team on this Friday afternoon, were only 1½ games out of first place.

Before the game, Joss was asked for a prediction on the outcome. "They ain't gonna have no score," was Addie's alleged ungrammatical response.

The White Sox would have been justified in making a similar boast, considering that Ed Walsh would be on the mound for the visitors. Walsh, a 27-year-old righthander and a master of the spitball, was enjoying his finest season. Just three days earlier, Walsh had earned complete-game victories by working both ends of a doubleheader against the

Red Sox. Appearing in 66 games, Big Ed worked 465 innings and posted 40 victories by season's end.

It is doubtful that any crowd ever was rewarded as handsomely as the one that watched Joss and Walsh come to grips four days before the close of the season. Many years later, competent observers continued to insist that it was the most stupendous pitching duel of all time.

Walsh, despite having pitched 18 innings three days before, showed no signs of fatigue. He set the first six Cleveland batters down in order before surrendering a leadoff single in the third inning to center fielder Joe Birmingham, whose hit plopped in right field, just beyond the reach of Ed Hahn. The game's first baserunner took a big lead and made several feints toward second. That activity drew a throw from Walsh, whose pickoff move either caught Birmingham napping or provided the runner just the opportunity he wanted. Either way, Birmingham broke for second. First baseman Frank Isbell took Walsh's throw and fired toward second, but the ball struck Birmy on the head and rolled to the outfield, allowing the runner to sprint to third with none out.

Birmingham remained glued to the bag as rookie George Perring grounded to shortstop Freddy Parent, who glanced over at third before throwing the ball to Isbell for the first out. Walsh struck out Joss for out No. 2, and it looked as if the Indians were going to strand Birmingham. Next up was Cleveland's leadoff man, right fielder Wilbur Good. Walsh got two strikes on Good and looked to catcher Ossee Schreckengost for a sign. Big Ed nodded his assent, but as soon as he threw it was obvious there had been a mixup. Schreckengost attempted to snare the ball barehanded, but it ripped through his hand and rolled toward the grandstand as Birmingham raced home. Walsh was charged with a wild pitch, although he claimed it should have been a passed ball. Big Ed struck out Good to end the inning, but thanks to a single, Isbell's throwing error and Walsh's wild pitch, Cleveland had a 1-0 lead.

Joss, in the meantime, had retired nine batters in a row, and he continued to send them back to the dugout in clocklike precision. He fanned only a few, but White Sox batters could do little but beat the ball into the dirt. Second baseman Lajoie was the busiest man on the field, repeatedly charging forward and sideways to scoop up grounders. Joss also fielded a number of dribblers himself. At first base, George Stovall skipped adroitly from one side to the other to snatch off-target throws.

"Now it was the seventh inning," one historian chronicled, "and the crowd became suddenly still and silent. Even in those early days of the sport, superstition was acknowledged, and no one mentioned, other than in an aside to his neighbor, that the White Sox hadn't been able to get a runner to first."

The second Chicago batter in the seventh was Fielder Jones, the club's manager and center fielder. Jones worked the count to 3-and-2. Joss wound up again and fired his best sidearm pitch, known in later years as a sinker. Jones followed the flight of the ball. When it smacked into the catcher's mitt, he dropped his bat and started toward first base. He was brought up short, however, when umpire Tom Connolly called strike three and then turned a deaf ear to Jones' entreaties. Many who were there said it was a borderline strike at best, but it didn't matter. Jones was out, as were all 19 of the batters who had preceded him.

The Indians threatened to extend their lead in the eighth inning. Birmingham and Perring opened the frame with back-to-back singles and then executed a double steal to put runners at second and third with none out. But the momentary scare subsided as Joss and Good fanned and third baseman Bill Bradley grounded out.

Down to his last three outs, Jones sent up three pinch-hitters. The first was Doc White, a good-hitting pitcher who grounded to Lajoie. The next was Jiggs Donahue, a utility first baseman. He swung feebly at three pitches and became Joss' third strikeout victim when catcher Nig Clarke squeezed the ball tightly in his glove.

As Joss stood behind the mound awaiting the 27th batter, umpire Connolly turned toward the grandstand and announced: "Anderson now batting for Walsh."

John Anderson, a .262 hitter that season, was a big, strong Norwegian. The crowd held its collective breath. The stillness was oppressive. One reporter noted: "A mouse working his way along the grandstand floor would have sounded like a shovel scraping over concrete."

Joss decided to pitch low and inside to Anderson, but his first delivery was too high. Nor was it as far inside as Joss wished. Anderson swung and drove a liner to left field. It fell foul by inches.

Again the big righthander threw. Again Anderson swung. This time he grounded it toward third base. Bradley had been idle all afternoon with nary a fielding chance, partly because White Sox batters, respecting Bill's fielding talent, refused to bunt. But here Bradley was, poised to record the biggest assist of the day.

What happened on the play was debated for years. Bradley's throw to first base was low, and some reported that Stovall dropped the ball—some said he did it twice—before picking it up securely and tagging the base. Whether Stovall did so before Anderson arrived at first was questionable.

"There have been many stories about that play," Bradley later recalled, "but there was nothing unusual about it until I threw the ball. I knew something about John Anderson. He was a powerful man who played in the outfield and at first base. . . . He was a pull-hitter, and so when he came up in Addie's big game, I moved over closer to the base. John hit his grounder rather sharply over the bag. I was playing deep and I took the ball in back of the cushion. I threw to Stovall, but I threw low. George made a fine pickup of the ball out of the dirt."

From his position near the bag, colorful arbiter Silk O'Loughlin waved the batter out. Anderson thought differently, but fans swarming onto the field to congratulate Joss made a protest futile.

Addie Joss had his perfect game. He had fanned only three batters, but he had denied the other 24 who made contact with the ball. He had remarkable support defensively, although most of his outfielders basically enjoyed a day off. Left fielder Bill Hinchman provided three of the team's four outfield putouts that day.

"I never could have done it without Larry's (Lajoie's) and Stovall's fielding and without Birmingham's baserunning," the modest pitcher said.

Walsh, meanwhile, pitched almost as well as Joss but was saddled with the loss. Big Ed allowed only four hits, one unearned run and one walk while striking out 15 batters—Good four times, Clarke and Joss three times each, Lajoie twice and Birmingham, Bradley and Hinchman once each. Walsh's pitches were breaking so hard that his catcher, Schreckengost, broke his finger late in the game trying to flag one down. He never played in the majors again.

The victory was a key one for the Indians, although they didn't gain any ground on the Tigers, who also won that day. With the A.L. pennant race hotter than ever, 20,729 Indians fans, then the largest crowd in club history, flocked to League Park the next day for what they hoped would be an

OCTOBER 2, 1908								
Chicago	ab	r	h	rbi	Cleveland	ab	r	h	rbi
Hahn, rf	3	0	0	0	Good, rf	4	0	0	0
Jones, cf	3	0	0	0	Bradley, 3b	4	0	0	0
Isbell, 1b	3	0	0	0	Hinchman, lf	3	0	0	0
Dougherty, lf	3	0	0	0	Lajoie, 2b	3	0	1	0
Davis, 2b	3	0	0	0	Stovall, 1b	3	0	0	0
Parent, ss	3	0	0	0	Clarke, c	3	0	0	0
Schreckengost, c	2	0	0	0	Birmingham, cf	4	1	2	0
Tannehill, 3b	2	0	0	0	Perring, ss	2	0	1	0
Donahue, ph	1	0	0	0	Joss, p	3	0	0	0
Walsh, p	2	0	0	0					
Anderson, ph	1	0	0	0					
Shaw, c	0	0	0	0					
White, ph	1	0	0	0					
Totals	27	0	0	0	Totals	29	1	4	0

Chicago	0	0	0	0	0	0	0	0	0—0
Cleveland	0	0	1	0	0	0	0	0	x—1

Chicago	IP	H	R	ER	BB	SO
Walsh (L)	8	4	1	0	1	15

Cleveland	IP	H	R	ER	BB	SO
Joss (W)	9	0	0	0	0	3

E—Isbell. LOB—Chicago 4, Cleveland 0. SB—Birmingham 2, Lajoie, Perring. WP—Walsh. T—1:40.

equally tense engagement with the White Sox. While they were denied a no-hitter, they were treated to another thrilling game.

After 6½ innings, Chicago led, 3-1. In the bottom of the seventh, the Indians filled the bases with one out, prompting Jones to remove pitcher Frank Smith from the game. The Chicago manager waved to the bullpen and forthwith strutted the familiar figure of Ed Walsh, tireless and ever willing.

The first batter Walsh faced was Hinchman, who smacked a grounder to third base. Lee Tannehill fielded the ball and threw home for the forceout. Next up was the mighty Lajoie.

The count went to 2-and-2. Lajoie stepped out of the box; Walsh retreated off the mound. The battle of wits was on. Would Walsh throw his famous spitter, or would he dare to fire a fastball to a batter who feasted on the hummer?

Lajoie concluded that the moist delivery, or maybe a waste pitch, was Big Ed's logical choice. Perhaps, but Walsh was one step ahead of him. Lajoie's bat never wiggled as he stood transfixed, watching a fastball cut the plate. The Indians lost the game, 3-2, and finished the race four percentage points (half a game) behind the Tigers.

"That was the high spot of my career, fanning Larry in the clutch and without him swinging," Walsh said.

Walsh pitched a 5-0 no-hitter against Boston in 1911, the first of two consecutive years in which he won 27 games.

Joss, on the other hand, never won 20 games again. He registered 14 victories in 1909, then injured his arm the next season and saw his record dwindle to 5-5. One of his 1910 wins, however, was another 1-0 no-hitter over the White Sox, although not a perfect game. Three Chicago batters reached base, one on an error and two on walks.

Addie was hopeful of a comeback in the spring of 1911 when he fainted on the bench while the Indians were in Chattanooga for an exhibition game. He rejoined the team a few days later and apologized for having "pulled a baby trick."

When the team reached Cincinnati, however, Joss was too ill to continue. He returned to his home in Toledo, where he died April 14, two days after his 31st birthday, of tubercular meningitis. The Cleveland players were among the hundreds of mourners who jammed the Masonic Temple in Toledo for the funeral service. The sermon was preached by Billy Sunday, a former major leaguer turned evangelist.

After his retirement, Ed Walsh became an American League umpire.

Chicago iron man Ed Walsh wasted one of his finest performances on a day
when Addie Joss and the Cleveland Indians were perfect.

BASEBALL'S

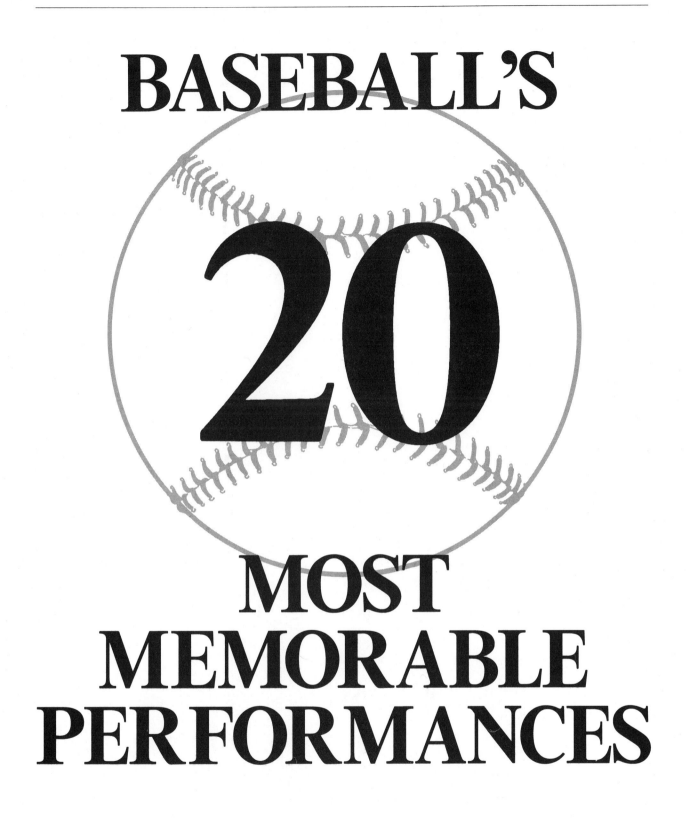

20

MOST
MEMORABLE
PERFORMANCES

The Man Who Would Be King

Traditionally, a major league baseball scout is the epitome of moderation, disinclined to flights of rhetoric or rhapsodies over an 18-year-old youth after only one tour of inspection. But Dewey Griggs threw tradition to the wind after obtaining a glimpse of the shortstop for the Indianapolis Clowns of the Negro American League on a rainy night in Buffalo in 1952.

Griggs' report to the Boston Braves was partly noncommittal, partly complimentary and totally incredible in its magnitude. The scout offered to purchase the youth with his own funds if the Braves did not.

The report read: "They played in the rain and I can't tell you what kind of fielder he is. The ground was slippery. I can't tell you anything about his range, either, but the guy can hit.

"I saw the guy in a doubleheader and he went 7-for-9. His arm looked strong enough. I really like the guy's bat. I don't know what it would take to get him, but I'd pay it out of my own pocket."

Griggs' unqualified endorsement of the teenager's hitting ability led to his acquisition by the Braves. For a down payment of $2,500 on a total investment of $10,000, Henry Louis Aaron became the property of the National League club on June 14, 1952.

The slender native of Mobile, Ala., broke into Organized Ball later that same year. He was not especially dazzling on defense but, confirming Griggs' evaluation, he batted .336 for Eau Claire of the Class-C Northern League.

Aaron leaped to the Class-A South Atlantic League in 1953, playing second base for the Jacksonville Braves. He led the league in virtually every offensive department, including batting average (.362) and runs batted in (125). The 6-foot, 190-pound

His swing completed, Hank Aaron watches homer No. 715 sail toward the left-field bullpen.

Career home run king Hank Aaron is joined in his triumphant trot by a couple of exuberant young Braves fans.

prospect was an overwhelming choice as the league's Most Valuable Player.

Such a remarkable performance merited a promotion, of course, but to what level? Aaron was slated to play for Atlanta of the Double-A Southern Association until outfielder Bobby Thomson broke his ankle during spring training, thus opening a roster spot on the parent club. The Braves, who had relocated to Milwaukee, introduced Aaron to County Stadium patrons as the regular left fielder in 1954.

The season was only 11 days old when Hank Aaron, just two years out of semipro ball, celebrated a significant event. The date was April 23, the place Busch Stadium in St. Louis, the opposing pitcher Vic Raschi. In the fourth inning, Aaron clouted his first major league home run, a feat he would perform more than 750 times over the next 23 years.

Hank whacked 13 homers in his freshman season, then 27 in 1955 and 26 in 1956. His round-tripper total soared to a league-leading 44 in 1957, a year in which he also tallied 132 RBIs and was named the N.L. MVP. Three more times in his illustrious career he poled 44 homers, matching his uniform number, and once he slugged 47 homers in a season. His homer tally never dropped below 20 until after 1974, when his playing days were ebbing fast.

The righthanded slugger reached the 100 mark in

Hank Aaron is greeted at home plate by the biggest reception committee of
his record-setting career.

home runs on August 15, 1957, against Cincinnati's Don Gross. He rapped Nos. 199 and 200 off Ron Kline of St. Louis on July 3, 1960, and breezed past 300 on April 19, 1963, against Roger Craig of the New York Mets. Ray Culp and Bo Belinsky of Philadelphia yielded Nos. 399 and 400, respectively, on April 20, 1966, by which time the Braves were calling Atlanta their home.

On July 14, 1968, Aaron reached the 500-homer plateau. The milestone hit, a three-run wallop off San Francisco's Mike McCormick, put Hammerin' Hank in a class with Babe Ruth, Willie Mays, Jimmie Foxx, Mel Ott, Ted Williams, Mickey Mantle and Eddie Mathews as sluggers with more than 500 home runs.

Almost without notice or public acclaim, Henry Aaron had emerged as one of the game's greatest sluggers. He was 34, in excellent health. His only concession to advancing years was an occasional trick as a first baseman.

The home runs continued to fly. The 600 mark was attained April 27, 1971. It produced two runs against Gaylord Perry of San Francisco and set tongues to speculating on Aaron's chances of overhauling Ruth's sacrosanct career record of 714 homers. Since the Bambino's retirement in 1935, that mark had stood supreme and supposedly inviolable against future assailants.

Exactly when the countdown to Ruth started is unrecorded, but it may have been June 27, 1971, when he connected against the Reds' Gary Nolan and Wayne Granger for Nos. 613 and 614, respectively. Aaron was in his final ascent, only 100 homers away from the summit and standing alongside the Babe.

At the close of the 1971 campaign, Aaron had slammed 639 homers, at which point the blow-by-blow reports started in earnest. He smacked 34 homers in 1972 to raise his total to 673—41 shy of Ruth's mark. He was 39 when the 1973 campaign opened, but the pace never slackened. The veteran outfielder tagged Philadelphia's Ken Brett for his 700th homer July 21, and on 39 other occasions he knocked the ball out of the park, marking the eighth time that he had clubbed two score or more in one season. By year's end, Aaron had accumulated 713 career homers.

As Hank's total climbed in 1973, so did the volume of hate mail and phone calls he received. To many, there was only one home run king. He was the ex-waterfront waif from Baltimore whose mighty bludgeon had purified the baseball atmosphere after the Black Sox stench a few years before. Anyone who would presume to dethrone the Babe, Henry was told, was an impostor, a fraud, a mountebank—or something worse. Much of the abuse he

Atlanta relief pitcher Tom House, who was in the right spot at the right time, returns the record-setting home run ball to Hank Aaron.

endured was racially oriented.

Others applauded Aaron for both his talent and his courage. He tried to forget the ill-conceived denunciations and to listen to the notes of encouragement from his supporters.

"I decided that the best way to shut up the kind of people who wrote those (derogatory) letters," Aaron said, "was to have a good year. The letters, I would say, inspired me."

The pressure, meanwhile, was inescapable. With each passing day, with every booming home run, the burden grew heavier. Aaron's pursuit of Ruth was captivating a nation—and sending the nation's media into a frenzy. Wherever he looked, Hank saw dozens of microphones, tilted note pads, searing klieg lights. He was on stage constantly as reporters fired tiresome questions at a weary athlete.

To preserve Henry's sanity and spare him mental anguish, a thoughtful club executive devised a novel scheme when the Braves went on the road. At every hotel he reserved two rooms, one under the name of Henry Aaron, which remained vacant, and the other under a fictitious name. Hank occupied the latter suite, where his serenity was undisturbed save by room service at mealtime.

Even tighter security measures were adopted when the Braves started spring training at West Palm Beach, Fla., in 1974. Hank was quartered in a

private home. "I can't give out the address," reported Don Davidson, the club's traveling secretary, "and even if I did, you couldn't get very close to him. There'll be an Atlanta detective on the premises—and at his elbow every second. . . . He's licensed to carry a gun and knows how to use it."

The Braves launched their 1974 season in Cincinnati amid a swarm of media people. Representatives of the print and electronic media from hither and yon demanded first-person accounts of "The Home Run," whenever and wherever it occurred.

For obvious financial reasons, the Braves wanted it to occur in Atlanta. But a three-game series with the Reds preceded the club's home opener, and there was much speculation that Aaron would not play until the Braves returned home.

Before the season started, Bowie Kuhn nixed that idea. The commissioner told Manager Eddie Mathews that he should play Aaron in at least two of the three games at Riverfront Stadium. Many observers believed that Kuhn had no business telling the manager how to arrange his lineup, but on opening day, Mathews penciled in Aaron as his starting left fielder.

A capacity crowd of 52,154 packed the Reds' park April 4 with the intention of witnessing history in the making. Aaron did not keep the fans in suspense for long. On his first official swing of the sea-

One of the first orders of business for the new home run king was a long hug
from one of his favorite ladies—his mother.

son, he deposited a 3-and-1 pitch from Jack Billingham over the left-center-field wall for a three-run homer. Babe Ruth had a partner.

"That's a load off my back," Henry said when the din subsided sufficiently for his voice to be heard. But the joy of his accomplishment was tainted, he said, by the Braves' 7-6 loss in 11 innings.

Aaron, who had gone hitless in his last three plate appearances, sat out the second game at Cincinnati, another Braves loss, but played in the third, a 5-3 Atlanta victory. Twice he was struck out by Clay Kirby and once he grounded out before leaving the game after seven innings. To intimations that he had exerted less than full effort, Hank snapped, "I have never stepped on a field but what I did not do my level best."

The final hurdle lay just over the horizon. If all went well, it would fall in Atlanta-Fulton County Stadium during the Braves' opening series with Los Angeles.

By that time, network television had joined the media menagerie. Camera crews were posted at every conceivable location. Atlanta had not been publicized so thoroughly since Gen. William T. Sherman applied a torch to the city more than a century before.

A carnival atmosphere prevailed April 8 as 53,775 loyal subjects, many of whom were forced to stand, paid allegiance to the new home run monarch. The hoopla surrounding Aaron was so pervasive that the identity of the Braves' starting pitcher, righthander Ron Reed, was largely overlooked. It was well known, however, that Al Downing, a veteran lefthander, had been named by Dodgers Manager Walter Alston to hold Aaron in check. The former American Leaguer had defeated the Braves twice without a loss in 1973 but had yielded two home runs to the Hammer, Nos. 676 and 693.

Henry had no opportunity to swing his bat on his initial try and drew a walk in the second inning. Aaron came around to score the first run of the game when Dusty Baker doubled and left fielder Bill Buckner bobbled the ball. When Hank crossed home plate for the 2,063rd time in his career, he surpassed Mays as the National League's all-time leading scorer.

The Dodgers had taken a 3-1 lead when Aaron strode to the plate in the fourth inning. Third baseman Darrell Evans, the beneficiary of an error by shortstop Bill Russell, was on first. Aaron took Downing's first delivery for ball one. But on his second pitch, the lefty tried to slip a fastball past the Braves' cleanup hitter. The moment

that everyone had waited for was at hand. Hank swung, and at 9:07 p.m. the ball took flight, stopping only when it smacked into relief pitcher Tom House's glove in the Atlanta bullpen in left field. The stadium erupted into pandemonium as countless normally composed individuals were transformed into screeching jumping jacks.

For the 715th time since that memorable day in April 1954, Henry Aaron circled the bases leisurely. Even though the long, sometimes painful climb was over and he stood alone at the summit, he displayed no signs of emotion, no leaps of jubilation, no hands thrust upward in triumph. "I just wanted to make sure," he said later, "I touched them (the bases)."

Between second base and third base, two teen-age volunteers who had raced out of the stands served as Aaron's escort. After Hank stepped on home plate, an elderly lady threw her arms around the 40-year-old destroyer. She appeared reluctant to relax her embrace for a long time. "I never knew," Aaron cracked later, "that my mother was so strong."

APRIL 8, 1974								
Los Angeles	ab	r	h	rbi	Atlanta	ab	r	h	rbi
Lopes, 2b	2	1	0	0	Garr, rf-lf	3	0	0	1
Lacy, ph-2b	1	0	0	0	Lum, 1b	5	0	0	1
Buckner, lf	3	0	1	0	Evans, 3b	4	1	0	0
Wynn, cf	4	0	1	2	Aaron, lf	3	2	1	2
Ferguson, c	4	0	0	0	Office, cf	0	0	0	0
Crawford, rf	4	1	1	0	Baker, cf-rf	2	1	1	0
Cey, 3b	4	0	1	1	Johnson, 2b	3	1	1	0
Garvey, 1b	4	1	1	0	Foster, 2b	0	0	0	0
Russell, ss	4	0	1	0	Correll, c	4	1	0	0
Downing, p	1	1	1	1	Robinson, ss	0	0	0	0
Marshall, p	1	0	0	0	Tepedino, ph	0	0	0	1
Joshua, ph	1	0	0	0	Perez, ss	2	1	1	0
Hough, p	0	0	0	0	Reed, p	2	0	0	0
Mota, ph	1	0	0	0	Oates, ph	1	0	0	1
					Capra, p	0	0	0	0
Totals	34	4	7	4	Totals	29	7	4	6

Los Angeles .... 0　0　3　0　0　1　0　0　0—4
Atlanta .... 0　1　0　4　0　2　0　0　x—7

Los Angeles	IP	H	R	ER	BB	SO
Downing (L)	3*	2	5	2	4	2
Marshall...........................	3	2	2	1	1	1
Hough..............................	2	0	0	0	2	1
Atlanta	IP	H	R	ER	BB	SO
Reed (W).........................	6	7	4	4	1	4
Capra (S)	3	0	0	0	1	6

*Pitched to four batters in fourth.

E—Buckner, Cey, Russell 2, Lopes, Ferguson. LOB—Los Angeles 5, Atlanta 7. 2B—Baker, Russell, Wynn. HR—Aaron. SH—Garr. SF—Garr. WP—Reed. PB—Ferguson. T—2:27. A—53,775.

Hank Aaron matched the Babe's career home run total with an April 4 blast against Cincinnati and pitcher Jack Billingham.

When Hank Aaron connected for home run No. 714 on April 4, 1974, Cincinnati catcher Johnny Bench joined the reception committee at home plate.

The game was held up for 10 minutes while the delirious crowd continued to shower cheers on the new home run champ. Hall of Famer Monte Irvin, an aide to Kuhn, presented Aaron a $3,000 watch on behalf of the commissioner, who could not attend the game because of a prior commitment. The mention of Kuhn's name brought a chorus of boos from the fans, who still were annoyed that he had forced Mathews to use Aaron in the Cincinnati series.

When the noise finally abated and the game resumed, few on hand were interested in the proceedings. The Braves ultimately won, 7-4, but for most of those in attendance—as well as the 30 million fans watching on television—everything after the fourth inning was a blur. Nothing could match the thrill that they experienced when Hammerin' Hank blazed past the Babe.

After the game, congratulatory messages enve-loped Aaron from every hand, starting with a phone call and an invitation to the White House from President Richard Nixon. In the days that followed, Kuhn took time to write, as did Ted Williams, Roy Campanella, Joe Louis, Bill Cosby and Sammy Davis Jr. All told, more than 2,000 expressions of praise poured in.

Hank smacked 18 more homers in 1974, after which he was traded to Milwaukee, now in the American League, in exchange for two players. After wearing a Brewers uniform for two seasons, he terminated his playing days in 1976 with 755 home runs listed among his other impressive statistics.

In October 1976, Aaron returned to Atlanta as the Braves' director of player development. Five years later, in his first year of eligibility, he was elected to the Hall of Fame, drawing 406 of 415 votes.

HANK AARON'S MILESTONE HOMERS

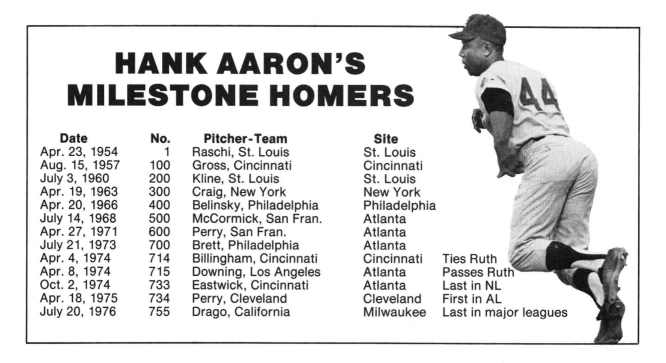

Date	No.	Pitcher-Team	Site	
Apr. 23, 1954	1	Raschi, St. Louis	St. Louis	
Aug. 15, 1957	100	Gross, Cincinnati	Cincinnati	
July 3, 1960	200	Kline, St. Louis	St. Louis	
Apr. 19, 1963	300	Craig, New York	New York	
Apr. 20, 1966	400	Belinsky, Philadelphia	Philadelphia	
July 14, 1968	500	McCormick, San Fran.	Atlanta	
Apr. 27, 1971	600	Perry, San Fran.	Atlanta	
July 21, 1973	700	Brett, Philadelphia	Atlanta	
Apr. 4, 1974	714	Billingham, Cincinnati	Cincinnati	Ties Ruth
Apr. 8, 1974	715	Downing, Los Angeles	Atlanta	Passes Ruth
Oct. 2, 1974	733	Eastwick, Cincinnati	Atlanta	Last in NL
Apr. 18, 1975	734	Perry, Cleveland	Cleveland	First in AL
July 20, 1976	755	Drago, California	Milwaukee	Last in major leagues

No. 61: Maris Passes the Babe

Roger Maris connects and watches home run No. 61 sail toward the right-field stands at Yankee Stadium on October 1, 1961.

To those who knew him, Roger Eugene Maris embodied most of life's admirable qualities. He was decent, honest, unselfish, devout and modest.

To those who saw him only in the postgame clubhouse, however, the New York Yankees' 6-foot, 205-pound slugger was surly, choleric, morose and petulant.

There was no middle ground of opinion on the native of Hibbing, Minn. There was no gray, only black and white. He was either a monster or a martyr, depending on one's perspective, in that turbulent season of 1961 when, by virtue of his explosive bat, he toppled Babe Ruth from his throne as baseball's most formidable home run hitter in a single season.

Maris might well have been an outstanding college football player. During his high school years in Fargo, N.D., he was a four-sport athlete who won all-state honors in football. The young halfback was offered a football scholarship by the University of Oklahoma after spending two weeks at a school-sponsored camp, but he turned it down, went home and later signed a contract to play baseball in the Cleveland Indians' farm system. In 1953, his first year as a professional, Maris batted .325 for Fargo-Moorhead of the Class-C Northern League.

By 1957 he was playing the outfield for the Indians. In June 1958 he was traded to the Kansas City Athletics, who then swapped him to the Yankees in December 1959.

Boston righthander Tracy Stallard was the victim of Roger Maris' historic blow.

The ruggedly handsome athlete with the sharply chiseled features and crew cut—he would have made an ideal model for a Marine Corps recruiting poster—did not turn handsprings or shout hosannas upon receiving word of the second trade. In fact, there had been so much speculation about a possible transaction beforehand that when a stranger mentioned the trade—before Roger even knew about it himself—he thought the man was kidding. "I'm not sure I want to go to New York," Maris responded. "They'll have to pay me a lot more money because I like it here in Kansas City."

Roger's remarks were misinterpreted in New York. It didn't sound like it, but he was quite willing to play for the Yankees, although he preferred to stay in Kansas City. He and his wife, Pat, and their growing family had just moved into a new home in the suburbs, which provided the small-town atmosphere he cherished. "He's not interested in bright lights," a Kansas City club executive said. "He prefers country life and barbecue pits."

Nor was his comment on a substantial pay increase out of line. Virtually any player moving from a second-division team to a contender had every right to expect a boost in salary. But to New York fans, Maris was just a greedy, thankless prima donna.

Nevertheless, Roger's first year in New York was impressive. He showed few signs of the batter about whom A's Manager Harry Craft had once said, "He's a very confused young ball player when he's

not hitting."

Maris did not dispute the statement. "I don't know how confused I was then," he admitted, "but I do know that when I'm not hitting, my wife could pitch and get me out."

Although he hammered 39 home runs, led the American League in runs batted in with 112 and was named the league's Most Valuable Player in 1960, he was not accorded the warmth that a player with such statistics ordinarily receives. He was not as adept at handling the press as, say, teammate Mickey Mantle, a nine-year Yankee veteran and the most beloved of the Bronx Bombers. While Mantle, already a Triple Crown winner and a two-time MVP, generally got along well with reporters, Maris did not. He quickly got tired of answering the same questions repeatedly, and his blunt, brutally honest responses never came across as well in print as they did in person. The result was a public perception of Maris as impolite, insensitive and inconsiderate.

So, Maris wasn't exactly the fans' favorite entering his second season with the Yankees. Still, there was no hint of impending turmoil when the 1961 campaign got under way. Although he did not find the home run range immediately, Roger was back in right field and earning new respect from baserunners with his powerful right arm. The Yanks were playing their 11th game when Roger connected against Paul Foytack of Detroit on April 26 for his first homer of the year. In the same contest, Mantle smacked a pair of home runs, giving him seven for the young season.

When Maris found his groove, though, the race was on. At the end of May, Roger had 12 home runs, Mickey 14. By the end of June, Maris had edged in front, 27 to 25. On July 31, the score was 40 for Maris, 39 for Mantle.

With two months of the season remaining and a new record a distinct possibility, Commissioner Ford Frick was prodded into a pronouncement. Folks were wondering whether the league's new 162-game schedule, which was brought about by the addition of two teams to the circuit that year, would have any bearing on Ruth's season home run record. The Bambino had hit 60 homers in 1927, when the league had a 154-game schedule. But in 1961, Maris and Mantle would have eight more games in which to reach Ruth's total. That didn't seem right to many reporters and fans, especially those who considered the Babe's record sacred.

Frick issued his ruling in late July. The onetime newspaperman and ghostwriter for Ruth declared that a player who sought to displace the Bambino in the record book would have to hit his 61st home run before his team played its 155th complete game of the season. If, however, a player hit No. 61 after game No. 154, the Ruth mark would stand and the

Sal Durante, the Brooklyn teen-ager who caught Roger Maris' 61st home run, displays his prize possession.

new player's accomplishment would receive secondary billing in the record book. Frick's decision came to be known as the "asterisk" ruling, although he never used that expression to indicate a separate category.

The dictum generated a flood of controversy. Many who didn't want to see Ruth's record broken in a longer season applauded Frick's ruling, but others lambasted it, maintaining that a season is a season, regardless of length.

Meanwhile, the M&M twins, Mantle and Maris, continued to drive balls out of ball parks from coast to coast. But Maris' mental anguish mushroomed. Media representatives, the majority just lately assigned to the Yankees from outlying newspaper or radio-TV outlets, bombarded Roger daily with absurd queries and comments. The question repeated most often was, of course, "Roger, do

you think you can break the record?" The interviewer invariably would be met with a cold stare. "Don't ask me about that damn record," Maris would say. "I don't want to talk about the record. All I'm interested in is winning the pennant."

The sincere assertion was repeated countless times, but nobody paid attention. How could he remain oblivious to the record he was assailing, people wondered, when it was the consuming thought of everyone who read the box scores daily?

As August drew to a close, Maris had 51 home runs, Mantle 48. But the Mick fell ill in September, and the pursuit of Ruth's mark eventually fell to one man: Roger Eugene Maris.

The last four weeks of the season were the most intense for the lefthanded slugger. Privacy was gone. He was constantly in range of someone's camera lens or notebook. The walls of the fishbowl in which he lived were closing in upon him. Out of uniform, he was a target for the jostling public. A fan would shove a slip of paper in front of his nose and demand, "Gimme your John Hancock." Sometimes, the paper would be returned bearing just what the fan requested, the forged signature of John Hancock.

"I just want to be left alone," he blurted time and again. But solitude was not forthcoming.

"Even the Yankee clubhouse attendants think I'm tough to live with," he admitted. "I guess they're right. I'm miffed most of the time regardless of how I'm doing. But regardless of my faults, I'll never take abuse from anybody—big or small, im-portant or unimportant—if I think it's undeserved."

Although the Yankees were doing well and marching toward their first pennant under Manager Ralph Houk, Maris found no way to ease the tension. The interminable asinine questions mingled with gossip column allegations that he was cheating on his wife. The only respite, he reported grimly, came when he visited the men's room or walked on the playing field. And even the diamond did not always offer sanctuary. He was the target of a garbage shower in Detroit, and no matter where he played he heard boos from those who idolized the Babe.

Whatever he did at the plate failed to satisfy him. Once he rapped four home runs in a doubleheader against the White Sox, then popped up while trying for a fifth. "Roger was mad as hell," a teammate said. "He reacted like a guy who'd gone 0 for 20."

"Maybe I'm a lot of things people say I am," Roger conceded. "I just don't like to lose. When I think I'm not doing the best I can, I get steamed."

Adding to Roger's misery was the widely circulated report that New York club officials were pulling for Mantle to win the home run title. If the Babe's record were to fall, the story went, executives preferred that Mickey, a Yankee from the start and a popular local hero, be the one to do it. There was no rift between Mickey and Roger, but it hurt Maris to think that his own team's executives might be rooting against him.

At the height of his harassment, Maris' wife arrived from Kansas City for a visit in New York. She took a look at the bare spots on the back of her husband's head and said, "You look like a molting bird." The never-ending pressure had caused some of his hair to fall out.

Maris tagged Detroit's Terry Fox for his 58th homer September 17. That was New York's 152nd game of the year, so if the record were to be broken in 154 games (not including ties) as prescribed by Frick, it would have to be done in an upcoming series at Baltimore.

Maris hit no home runs in a doubleheader September 19, but because of an early-season tie he had the benefit of a 155th game, just as Ruth had in 1927. He needed two homers in one contest to tie the Babe.

On September 20, the day of the decisive game, Maris ate dinner with Orioles outfielder Whitey Herzog, a teammate from their days in Kansas City.

Yankee bombers Roger Maris (left) and Mickey Mantle talk before the 1961 World Series.

The two did not discuss the record until they arrived at the park. "Well, Roger," Whitey said, "I hope you hit three homers and we beat you, 4-3."

Milt Pappas, a hard-throwing young righthander, was Manager Luman Harris' selection to stop Maris. On Roger's first at-bat, he flied deep to right field. A strong breeze helped keep the ball in the park.

In the third inning, Roger swung at a 2-and-1 pitch from Pappas and lined the ball to right field. "I knew it was gone as soon as I hit it," he reported. As he ran the bases he mused: "That's 59. Now I'm going to get up maybe three more times."

Maris struck out on a high pitch from reliever Dick Hall in the fourth inning. Hall still was on the mound for the Orioles when Roger batted in the seventh inning. The Yankee took a strike, then cut viciously at the second delivery. "It gave the crowd a thrill, but not me," Roger said. "I could see right away it was going to land on the wrong side of the foul pole."

On the next pitch he made solid contact, but again the wind caught it. The ball dropped into right fielder Earl Robinson's glove, 20 feet short of the fence.

One more chance remained. When the Yankees came up in the ninth, still another pitcher was working for Baltimore. He was, Maris said, "absolutely the last guy in the world I wanted to see"—Hoyt Wilhelm, a knuckleball artist who had fanned Maris the night before. The first pitch, Roger explained, hit his bat for a foul. The second butterfly delivery did the same on Maris' check swing, resulting in a meek dribbler down the first-base line. Wilhelm fielded the ball and tagged the batter for the out. The Yanks clinched the pennant with a 4-2 victory that day, but Maris fell one short of tying Ruth's record in 154 games.

Still the season was not over. Maris connected for homer No. 60 against Jack Fisher of Baltimore at Yankee Stadium on September 26. Maris went without a homer in the next three contests, however, and the season dwindled down to one final game.

Ordinarily, a team that had wrapped up the pennant nearly two weeks before would not draw a tremendous crowd for its season finale. But 1961 should have been different. Fans could come watch Roger Maris try to hit his 61st home run of the season, an unprecedented feat in major league annals. But Frick's ruling, which in effect downgraded anything Roger might accomplish in the last eight games of the season, severely diminished the public's interest after the 154th game. So it was that on October 1, a warm Sunday afternoon in the Bronx, only 23,154 spectators were on hand at Yankee Stadium to witness Maris' last-ditch effort.

The man whom Red Sox Manager Pinky Higgins

assigned to keep Maris in check that day was Tracy Stallard, a righthander in his first full major league season. Stallard got the 27-year-old outfielder to fly to left fielder Carl Yastrzemski in the first inning.

After 3½ innings, both Stallard and his opponent, righthander Bill Stafford, had prevented either team from scoring. There was one out and nobody on base when Maris came to the plate in the fourth inning. Neither of Stallard's first two deliveries were in the strike zone and Roger let them go by for balls. But on the third pitch, the 24-year-old hurler unleashed a fastball that was about waist-high and over the plate—right up Roger's alley. A roar went up as Maris connected, depositing the ball about 15 rows deep in the right-field seats. Sal Durante, a teen-ager from Brooklyn, caught the historic baseball and later sold it to a restaurateur in Sacramento for $5,000.

"I don't know what I was thinking of as I rounded the bases," said Maris, whose teammates did not allow him to enter the Yankee dugout while the crowd gave him a standing ovation for five minutes. "My mind was a blank."

And so was the rest of the game. Neither team scored again, so Roger's hit gave the Yankees a 1-0 victory. It also gave him the league RBI title for the second consecutive year as his total of 142 edged Baltimore's Jim Gentile by one RBI.

Stallard, the losing pitcher that day despite seven strong innings, did not appear upset that Maris had tagged him for homer No. 61. "I don't feel badly about it at all," he told reporters afterward. "Why should I? The guy hit 60 home runs off a bunch of other pitchers in the league before he got me today. . . . I gave him what I feel was my best fastball and

OCTOBER 1, 1961

Boston	ab	r	h	rbi	New York	ab	r	h	rbi
Schilling, 2b	4	0	1	0	Richardson, 2b	4	0	0	0
Geiger, cf	4	0	0	0	Kubek, ss	4	0	2	0
Yastrzemski, lf	4	0	1	0	Maris, cf	4	1	1	1
Malzone, 3b	4	0	0	0	Berra, lf	2	0	0	0
Clinton, rf	4	0	0	0	Lopez, lf-rf	1	0	0	0
Runnels, 1b	3	0	0	0	Blanchard, rf-c	3	0	0	0
Gile, 1b	0	0	0	0	Howard, c	2	0	0	0
Nixon, c	3	0	2	0	Reed, lf	1	0	1	0
Green, ss	2	0	0	0	Skowron, 1b	2	0	0	0
Stallard, p	1	0	0	0	Hale, 1b	1	0	1	0
Jensen, ph	1	0	0	0	Boyer, 3b	2	0	0	0
Nichols, p	0	0	0	0	Stafford, p	2	0	0	0
					Reniff, p	0	0	0	0
					Tresh, ph	1	0	0	0
					Arroyo, p	0	0	0	0
Totals	30	0	4	0	Totals	29	1	5	1

Boston	0	0	0	0	0	0	0	0	0—0
New York	0	0	0	1	0	0	0	0	x—1

Boston	IP	H	R	ER	BB	SO
Stallard (L)	7	5	1	1	1	5
Nichols	1	0	0	0	0	0

New York	IP	H	R	ER	BB	SO
Stafford (W)	6	3	0	0	1	7
Reniff	1	1	0	0	0	1
Arroyo	2	1	0	0	0	1

LOB—Boston 5, New York 5. 3B—Nixon. HR—Maris. SB—Geiger. SH—Stallard. WP—Stallard. PB—Nixon. T—1:57. A—23,154.

Roger Maris connects for home run No. 62, one of his two hits against Cincinnati in the 1961 World Series.

Roger Maris' 61-Homer Pace

SUN	MON	TUES	WED	THUR	FRI	SAT
APRIL						1
2	3	4	5	6	7	8
9	10	11	12	13	14	15
16	17	18	19	20	21	22
23 / 30	24	25	1 26	27	28	29

SUN	MON	TUES	WED	THUR	FRI	SAT
	1	2	2 3	4	5	3 6
7	8	9	10	11	12	13
14	15	16	4 17	18	5 19	6 20
7 21	22	23	8 24	25	26	27
9 28	29	10 30 11	12 31	MAY		

SUN	MON	TUES	WED	THUR	FRI	SAT
JUNE				1	13 2	14 3
15 4	5	16 6	17 7	8	18 9	10
19 11 20	12	21 13	22 14	15	16	23 17
24 18	25 19	26 20	21	27	23	24
25	26	27	28	29	30	

SUN	MON	TUES	WED	THUR	FRI	SAT
JULY						28 1
29 2 30	3	31 4	32 5	6	7	8
33 9	10	11	12	34 13	14	35 15
16	17	18	19	20	36 21	22
23 / 30	24 31	37 25 38	39	26 40	27	28	29

SUN	MON	TUES	WED	THUR	FRI	SAT
AUG		1	2	3	41 4	5
6	7	8	9	10	42 11	43 12
44 13 45	14	46 15	47 16 48	17	18	19
49 20	21	50 22	23	24	25	51 26
27	28	29	30	31		

SUN	MON	TUES	WED	THUR	FRI	SAT
SEPT					1	52 2 53
3	4	5	54 6	55 7	8	56 9
10	11	12	13	14	15	57 16
58 17	18	59 20	20	21	22	23
24 / Oct. 61	25	60 26	27	28	29	30

Roger Maris is greeted at home plate for the final time in 1961 after hitting a home run against Cincinnati in the World Series.

he hit it."

Maris, who struck out against Stallard and popped out against reliever Chet Nichols in his last two plate appearances, was named the league's MVP for the second year in a row. And though he had only two hits in 19 at-bats in the World Series against Cincinnati, one was a game-winning home run in the third contest. The Yankees wound up defeating the Reds in five games.

Maris never came close to hitting 61 homers in a season again. He pounded 33 in 1962, 23 in 1963, 26 in 1964, eight in 1965 and 13 in 1966 before being traded to the St. Louis Cardinals. He played on two more pennant-winners, then retired after the 1968 season. During his 12-year major league career he smacked 275 home runs, 22 percent of them in one unforgettable season.

Except for the time he spent in St. Louis, Maris' later years in baseball were no more happy than

1961 had been. He never did learn how to pacify journalists, who continued to sling darts in his direction in their columns and game reports. So, an embittered Maris vowed never to return to Yankee Stadium, a promise he kept for nearly a decade before relenting and beginning to show up at Old-Timers Day events. He appeared at the Yankees' 1985 home opener, when his uniform No. 9 was retired. "The fans stood and applauded for a good 15 minutes," Yankees Owner George Steinbrenner said of that occasion. "That did a lot for him."

Maris, who operated a beer distributorship in Gainesville, Fla., after leaving baseball, had developed lymphatic cancer by the time he was honored at Yankee Stadium, although official word of his condition did not escape until months later. He finally succumbed to the disease December 14, 1985, at the age of 51. About 1,000 friends, relatives and baseball fans attended his funeral in Fargo.

Carl Hubbell's All-Star Magic

It could have been Ty Cobb. Or perhaps George Moriarty. Or, if not them, maybe it was a coach for the Detroit Tigers. Whoever it was, he goofed.

The Tigers were in spring training in the mid-1920s when a club official beckoned to a lefthanded pitcher who was trying to become a major leaguer. "Lay off that crazy pitch you've been working on," the official ordered. "Forget about it. It will only ruin your arm."

That much is known. Whether it was Cobb who said it as manager of the Tigers in 1926, or Moriarty, the former umpire and Cobb's successor, in 1927, or even one of their assistants in either of those years, well, the records aren't too clear. But it is a fact that someone in the Detroit organization told Carl Owen Hubbell to dispense with the screwball for the sake of his career.

Carl followed orders and tried to get by without the butterfly pitch while toiling in the minor leagues. But the results were not impressive, and the Tigers released Hubbell outright to Beaumont of the Class-A Texas League in 1928. There Carl found a manager, Claude Robertson, who was not averse to his use of the screwball. All of a sudden, the pieces started to fall in place for the young lefthander.

In July 1928, the Beaumont club visited Houston for a series with the Buffaloes shortly after the Democratic national convention had been held in that same city. Such events ordinarily would be mutually exclusive, but in this case the presence of a delegate from Illinois was significant. Dick Kinsella, who doubled as a scout for the New York Giants, still was in Houston when he took the opportunity July 5 to watch the local minor league team. Hubbell caught the scout's eye by paralyzing the Buffs, 2-1, on a three-hitter.

That evening Kinsella telephoned John McGraw and informed the Giants' manager of his discovery.

An effective screwball helped lefthander Carl Hubbell gain fame as the Giants' 'Meal Ticket.'

Before the 1934 All-Star Game, National Leaguers gathered to watch Carl Hubbell being honored as the league's 1933 Most Valuable Player.

"Why did Detroit let him go?" the Little Napoleon wondered.

"They thought the screwball would ruin his arm," the scout explained.

"Nonsense!" McGraw snorted. "Christy Mathewson threw that pitch for years when it was known as the fadeaway and it never damaged his arm."

On the advice of the highly regarded scout, the National League club purchased Carl Hubbell for $30,000. By midsummer the Carthage, Mo., native was a starter for the Giants, for whom he won 10 games that season.

In 1929 Hubbell won 18 games, including an 11-0 no-hitter against Pittsburgh. Seasons of 17, 14 and 18 victories followed. He gained the cognomen of "King Carl," a title he fully justified on July 2, 1933, when he defeated St. Louis, 1-0, in an 18-inning marathon in which he allowed only six hits and issued no walks. That same year he also spun 10 shutouts and 46 consecutive scoreless innings.

In the major leagues' first All-Star Game, played July 6, 1933, at Comiskey Park in Chicago, Hubbell hurled two innings of scoreless relief in the National League's 4-2 loss. He registered 23 victories and a 1.66 earned-run average for the pennant-winning Giants and climaxed the season with a pair of victories in New York's five-game triumph over Washington in the World Series. He was a popular selection for the league's Most Valuable Player award.

By that time, Hubbell had acquired a second nickname. He was widely known as the "Meal Ticket," an appropriate moniker at a time when the Depression-racked nation read daily reports of bread lines in large cities.

When major league magnates gave their reluctant approval to the first All-Star Game, it was perceived as a onetime event to be played as a feature of Chicago's Century of Progress Exposition. The public's enthusiastic acceptance, however, convinced some moguls that an annual midsummer extravaganza had definite fiscal and promotional value. So, a second contest was scheduled at the Polo Grounds in New York on July 10, 1934. That inspired decision created the setting for one of baseball's most cherished episodes.

The fan response was incredible at a time when sellouts existed only in fancy. New Yorkers stormed the Harlem horseshoe on the day of the game, and thousands were locked out 15 minutes before the first pitch was thrown. Spectators jammed aisles and stood obediently in crannies for a chance to glimpse the cream of both leagues' crop. Officially, the paid attendance was 48,363. Unofficially, the crowd was estimated at more than 50,000.

The pregame ceremonies were brief. In one, Hubbell was presented his MVP award. In another, a memorial tablet to McGraw was unveiled in center field. The longtime New York skipper had died the previous February.

Bill Terry, an automatic choice to manage the

The Victims

Babe Ruth   Lou Gehrig   Jimmie Foxx   Al Simmons   Joe Cronin

N.L. team in the second classic because the Giants had won the 1933 flag, did not deliberate long in choosing his starting pitcher. In the home of the Giants, before a crowd consisting chiefly of New Yorkers, it had to be Hubbell.

Hubbell's start was uncharacteristically rocky. He gave up a leadoff single to Detroit second baseman Charlie Gehringer, who took second on Braves center fielder Wally Berger's error, and then walked left fielder Heinie Manush of Washington. From the packed stands came the clarion call, "Take him out!"

A conference on the mound was in order. From first base came Terry, from second Frank Frisch of the Cardinals, from shortstop Travis Jackson of the Giants, from third Pie Traynor of the Pirates.

"You all right?" they asked.

"I'm OK," Hubbell replied.

Before the game, Hubbell and catcher Gabby Hartnett had reviewed the American League lineup and concluded that there wasn't a solitary weakness in the first eight batters. "We'll waste everything except the screwball," the Chicago catcher advised. "Get that over, but keep your fastball and hook outside. We can't let 'em hit in the air."

Gabby's words of wisdom rang clear at this critical moment because instant devastation loomed at home plate in the person of right fielder Babe Ruth. On deck knelt Lou Gehrig, who was headed toward 49 home runs and 165 runs batted in that season. Beyond Gehrig was Jimmie Foxx, who had won the league's MVP award in 1933 with 48 homers and 163 RBIs.

Perhaps the least ruffled among the masses was Hubbell himself. Recalling Hartnett's advice, King Carl wasted one fastball and threw two screwballs, one of which Ruth swung at and missed and the other he took for a strike. Then, figuring that Hubbell would waste another pitch, the Bambino watched another screwball cut the outside corner of the plate.

"I can still see him looking at the umpire," Hubbell recalled years later. "He wasn't mad. He just

didn't believe it."

A big grin creased Hartnett's tomato face as he whipped the ball to Traynor and prepared to flash a sign for the first pitch to Gehrig. One pitch was wasted. The Iron Horse swung at and missed the second. Two balls and a swinging strike followed. As the Yankee first baseman swung and missed for the third time, Gehringer and Manush pulled a double steal.

On his way back to the dugout, Gehrig muttered to Foxx, "You might as well swing . . . they won't get any better."

Hubbell had not tried to fan the Yankees' big guns, but with two gone, he wanted a third victim. Hartnett called for screwballs only and the Philadelphia slugger, heeding Gehrig's suggestion, swung mightily three times, reaping only a foul for his efforts. Foxx, too, struck out.

Head down, Hubbell walked off the mound, seemingly deaf to the cacophony that exploded about him. The crowd that moments before had screamed for his ouster was cheering with delight after seeing King Carl fan three of the best hitters the junior circuit had to offer.

After Frisch lined a fastball from Lefty Gomez of the Yankees into the upper tier of the right-field stands to give the National League a 1-0 lead in the home half of the first, King Carl returned to the mound. The first batter was White Sox outfielder Al Simmons, who was en route to a season batting average of .344. Simmons looked at a ball, then swung willfully three times to become Hubbell's fourth successive strikeout victim.

Joe Cronin was next. The Washington shortstop-manager, who was directing the A.L. forces by virtue of the Senators' 1933 pennant-winning season, offered Hubbell no relief from the onslaught of sluggers he was facing. By year's end, Cronin's statistics would show 101 RBIs. But a ball and then three swinging strikes disposed of him. King Carl had whiffed five straight batters.

Bill Dickey, who was in the midst of his sixth consecutive .300-or-better season, came to the plate as the Polo Grounds rocked with appreciation for Hubbell. The Yankee catcher, a lefthanded batter, worked the count to 1-and-2 before slapping a single to left field. The blow proved inconsequential, however, as Gomez went down on strikes. Six strikeouts in two innings.

Hubbell didn't fan anyone in the third inning, but Ruth, who walked, was the only batter who reached base. After hurling his third shutout frame, Hubbell retired to the center-field clubhouse, his work done for the day, amid a standing ovation.

As the Nationals left the field for the home half of the third, Hartnett turned to the A.L. dugout and shouted, "We have to look at that all season."

Frisch, then 35, fell in behind Terry and quipped: "I could play 15 more years behind that guy. He doesn't need any help. He does it all by himself."

The National League took a 4-0 lead in the third inning when Cardinals left fielder Joe Medwick blasted a three-run homer, but the advantage evaporated when the American League scored two runs in the fourth and six in the fifth. The junior circuit's 9-7 victory was credited to Cleveland righthander Mel Harder, who allowed only one hit in five innings of relief.

The National League's loss was forgotten in the years that followed, but Hubbell's achievement gained luster with time. The feat of fanning five consecutive future Hall of Famers grew more impressive with each passing classic, making King Carl the crown prince of All-Star Game history.

Still more notable accomplishments awaited Hubbell after that famous July afternoon. Twice more he led the league in victories and ERA and once in strikeouts. From July 17, 1936, until the close of the season, Hubbell linked together 16 straight victories to highlight another pennant-winning campaign and earn a second MVP citation. He split two decisions against the Yankees in the World Series of both 1936 and '37 before completing his major league career in 1943 with 253 victories and 154 losses, all as a member of the Giants. Hubbell was elected to the Hall of Fame in 1947, by which time he was the director of the Giants' farm system.

Incidentally, the least remembered of Hubbell's six strikeout victims in the 1934 All-Star Game—Lefty Gomez, the batter who did not fit into the consecutive string—eventually earned a number of spots in the record book himself and was admitted to Cooperstown in 1972. But back in 1934, Gomez was afraid that he had missed out on his one chance to merit a place in baseball lore.

"I could punch you in the nose," Lefty said to Dickey after the game.

"Why?" his teammate asked in surprise.

"For getting that hit," the pitcher explained. "If you had struck out, I would have gotten my name in the book, too."

JULY 10, 1934

Americans	ab	r	h	rbi	Nationals	ab	r	h	rbi
Gehringer, 2b	3	0	2	0	Frisch, 2b	3	3	2	1
Manush, lf	2	0	0	0	Herman, ph-2b	2	0	1	0
Ruffing, p	1	0	1	2	Traynor, 3b	5	2	2	1
Harder, p	2	0	0	0	Medwick, lf	2	1	1	3
Ruth, rf	2	1	0	0	Klein, ph-lf	3	0	1	1
Chapman, rf	2	0	1	0	Cuyler, rf	2	0	0	0
Gehrig, 1b	4	1	0	0	Ott, ph-rf	2	0	0	0
Foxx, 3b	5	1	2	1	Berger, cf	2	0	0	0
Simmons, cf-lf	5	3	3	1	P. Waner, ph-cf	2	0	0	0
Cronin, ss	5	1	2	2	Terry, 1b	3	0	1	0
Dickey, c	2	1	1	0	Jackson, ss	2	0	0	0
Cochrane, pr-c	1	0	0	0	Vaughan, ph-ss	2	0	0	0
Gomez, p	1	0	0	0	Hartnett, c	2	0	0	0
Averill, cf	4	1	2	3	Lopez, c	2	0	0	0
West, cf	0	0	0	0	Hubbell, p	0	0	0	0
					Warneke, p	0	0	0	0
					Mungo, p	0	0	0	0
					Martin, ph	0	1	0	0
					J. Dean, p	1	0	0	0
					Frankhouse, p	1	0	0	0
Totals	39	9	14	9	Totals	36	7	8	6

American League .... 0 0 0 2 6 1 0 0 0—9
National League .... 1 0 3 0 3 0 0 0 0—7

Americans	IP	H	R	ER	BB	SO
Gomez	3	3	4	4	1	3
Ruffing	1†	4	3	3	1	1
Harder (W)	5	1	0	0	1	2
Nationals	IP	H	R	ER	BB	SO
Hubbell	3	2	0	0	2	6
Warneke	1*	3	4	4	3	1
Mungo (L)	1	4	4	4	2	1
Dean	3	5	1	1	1	4
Frankhouse	1	0	0	0	1	0

*Pitched to two batters in fifth.
†Pitched to four batters in fifth.

aPinch hit for Hubbell in third but was permitted to replace Frisch in seventh. E—Gehrig, Berger. DP—Nationals 1. LOB—Americans 12, Nationals 5. 2B—Foxx, Simmons 2, Cronin, Averill, Herman. 3B—Chapman, Averill. HR—Frisch, Medwick. SB—Gehringer, Manush, Traynor, Ott. T—2:44. A—48,363.

By the mid-1930s, Carl Hubbell was a favorite subject of baseball cartoonists.

Wambsganss Has Moment in the Sun

William Adolph Wambsganss, the son of a Lutheran minister, was in the midst of his own theological studies in 1912 when he felt the need for some diversion.

Laying aside his textbooks at Concordia College in Fort Wayne, Ind., he sauntered to the ball park, where the local Central League team was to play an exhibition game with the Cleveland team of the American League.

For the Concordia shortstop-ministerial student, it was a religious experience.

"There were all the great names—Manager Joe Birmingham, Terry Turner, Napoleon Lajoie—and some of the younger players, Steve O'Neill, Jack Graney, Ray Chapman, Joe Jackson and others," he remembered years later. "I had never thought about playing professionally, but from that moment on Lajoie became my idol."

A year later, Wambsganss was pursuing his courses in St. Louis when a fellow seminarian who had had a brief taste of professional baseball requested permission to recommend Wambsganss to the Cedar Rapids club, which was seeking a shortstop. Bill, who by this time was having serious doubts about his future as a clergyman, gave ready approval. He batted .244 in 67 games for the Class-D Central Association team that summer.

In 1914, after teaching school in North Dakota as part of his pastoral training, which he had not yet given up, Wambsganss returned to Cedar Rapids and batted .317 in 84 games. In August he was purchased by Cleveland for $1,250. He played 43 games for the A.L. club the remainder of the season, batting .217 for the eighth-place team, and decided to make baseball his full-time vocation.

One of the first people Bill encountered in Cleveland was a printer with a problem. The newcomer's 10-letter name, it was discovered, was too long for the allotted space in the box scores. Rather than risk typographical mayhem, Bill agreed to be known as "Bill Wamby" in the newspapers, although he always preferred his legal name.

After Lajoie's move to Philadelphia in January

Bill Wambsganss was Cleveland's solid, if unspectacular, regular second baseman for nine years.

Cleveland's Bill Wambsganss wheels around after stepping on second base and tags Brooklyn's Otto Miller to complete his unassisted triple play in Game 5 of the 1920 World Series.

1915, Wambsganss was installed as the Indians' regular second baseman. He remained there for nine years, reaching his peak batting mark of .295 in 1918. But the baseball community relished the memory of the former divinity student not because of his hitting or his fielding, both of which were entirely adequate, but because of a split-second incident in 1920 that, he always maintained, was merely the result of "being in the right place at the right time."

The Indians won their first pennant that year. Led by Tris Speaker, their .388-hitting center fielder-manager, and righthanded pitchers Jim (Sarge) Bagby, who recorded 31 victories, and Stan Coveleski, who won 24, the Tribe squeezed past the Chicago White Sox by two games. In 153 games, Wamby's contributions included a .244 batting average and 55 runs batted in.

The Brooklyn Dodgers, under Wilbert Robinson, earned the right to oppose the Indians in the World

Series by beating out the New York Giants in the National League race by seven games. The best-of-nine Series was to have opened in Cleveland, but because of the tardy installation of temporary bleachers at League Park, it began in Brooklyn on October 5. The Indians won the first game, 3-1, as Coveleski threw a five-hitter.

Burleigh Grimes, like Coveleski a spitballer, helped the Dodgers even the Series the next day with a 3-0 victory over Bagby. A distinct lack of offense continued to mark the Series as the Indians bowed, 2-1, to the three-hit pitching of lefthander Sherry Smith.

At this point, the Series moved from Ebbets Field to League Park. The Dodgers apparently left their bats behind when they traveled to Cleveland because, as it developed, the Dodgers did not win another game, scoring only two runs in the last four contests combined. Their offensive problems began in Game 4, in which Coveleski again held the visitors to five hits and one run. The righthander was aided in his 5-1 victory by two hits and two runs apiece from Wambsganss, who had gone hitless in the first three games of the Series, and Speaker. Joe Sewell, a young shortstop who had been promoted from the minor leagues shortly after Ray Chapman was killed by a pitched ball the previous August, also collected two hits.

The game—and the event—that were to memorialize Wamby for all time occurred October 10, 1920. The fifth contest attracted 26,884 fans to League Park on a Sunday afternoon that would long be remembered for its many unprecedented feats.

Grimes, Brooklyn's starting pitcher, quickly discovered that his second Series outing would not be as smooth as his first. Singles by left fielder Charlie Jamieson, Wambsganss and Speaker (the last a bunt) loaded the bases with none out in the bottom of the first inning. The fourth Cleveland batter was Elmer Smith. The angular right fielder, who had hit 12 home runs in the regular season, had two strikes against him when the Dodger righthander unleashed a spitter that failed to break. The lefthanded batter swung vigorously. From the moment of contact, there was no question about the destination of the baseball. It cleared the temporary bleachers in right field, sailed over the screen above the wall and landed across the street, atop a roof crowded with spectators. The Indians suddenly led, 4-0, and Smith owned the distinction of being the first player to hit a grand-slam homer in a World Series.

Robinson permitted Grimes to stay in the game. The 23-game winner shut out the Indians in the next two innings, but he encountered more trouble in the fourth. First baseman Doc Johnston led off with a single, then moved to second on Otto Miller's passed ball and to third on Sewell's infield out. Catcher Steve O'Neill was walked purposely, bringing up Bagby. The pitcher was not particularly imposing at the plate, although he had batted .252 and rapped one home run during the season.

Before the game, Bagby had squinted at the temporary bleachers. "Ah think Ah'll bust one out to those wooden seats," he had said to Speaker in his best Georgia drawl. "They seem just about right for me to hit."

It turned out that Sarge was a pretty good judge of his own ability. Grimes, who perhaps forgot that the pitcher could take advantage of closer fences, did not pitch carefully to Bagby. What happened after Sarge made contact was described in Spalding's Official Baseball Record: "The ball fell safely in a temporary stand, which had been built within playing space, and under ground rules went for a home run. (Hy) Myers was under it and could have caught it but for the barrier."

The editor of the Reach Guide added this comment on the three-run shot: "Bagby's homer was merely a piece of luck as the ball fell just inside the temporary bleachers in right-center, which should not have been permitted to encroach upon the playing field."

Luck or not, Bagby was credited with the first World Series home run by a pitcher and the Indians had a 7-0 lead.

But the most pulsating of all events on this day of historic achievements was still to come. It happened in the fifth inning as the Dodgers were beginning to rally against Bagby.

Pete Kilduff launched the frame with a single. The Brooklyn second baseman advanced on Miller's single to center field, but Speaker's strong throw held him at second.

The next batter was Clarence Mitchell, who had replaced Grimes on the mound. The lefthander had batted .234 during the season, and he was capable of hitting the ball hard.

With a commanding lead, the Cleveland infielders were not thinking of a double play. "I was playing deep, back on the grass," Wamby recalled in one of the hundreds of explanations of what happened next. The 26-year-old second baseman just wanted to prevent the ball from reaching

Game 5 of the 1920 World Series also featured the first Series grand-slam homer, by Cleveland outfielder Elmer Smith (left), and the first Series home run by a pitcher, by Cleveland's Jim Bagby (right).

the outfield.

"Mitchell hit a line drive to my right," he said. "I guess everybody (the runners) thought it was headed for center field. I took a step to my right and jumped. The ball stuck in my glove and my momentum carried me to second base.

"Kilduff, who took off for third when the ball was hit, was easy. All I had to do was touch second. . . . Miller apparently didn't see what happened because I looked to first base and saw him within five feet of me. He stopped running and just stood there, so I tagged him. . . . Before I tagged him, he said, 'Where'd you get that ball?' I said, 'Well, I've got it and you're out Number 3.' Then I trotted off the field."

The triple play occurred so fast that many spectators were bewildered. "They had to stop and figure out how many were out," Wamby related. "So there was a dead silence for a few seconds. Then, as I approached the dugout, it began to dawn on them what they had just seen, and the cheering started and quickly got louder and louder and louder. By the time I got to the bench it was bedlam, straw hats flying onto the field, people yelling themselves hoarse, my teammates pounding me on the back."

The incredible play may have saved Bagby. The Dodgers shelled him for 13 hits that day, one more than the Indians collected, but he still won, 8-1, thanks to his teammates' solid defensive performances. In addition to Wamby's triple play, the Indians turned three double plays. Mitchell hit into one of those, giving him the unenviable distinction of hitting into five outs in two at-bats that day.

Cleveland scored its last run in the fifth on third baseman Larry Gardner's run-scoring single, while Brooklyn tallied its only run in the ninth when first baseman Ed Konetchy singled off Johnston's chest,

allowing left fielder Zack Wheat to score.

When the joyful Indians stomped into the clubhouse, they found Bagby in tears. "If Johnston had got that ball," the pitcher sobbed, "I'd have had a shutout." Years later, Wambsganss and his teammates would laugh at the recollection of a winning pitcher crying because he had lost a shutout after giving up 13 hits.

Wamby's triple play was the talk of the baseball world, but one observer who was not particularly impressed was John Heydler. "What was so wonderful about it?" the N.L. president asked a gurgling reporter later that night. "I could have caught the ball myself if I had been out there."

On the day of his memorable feat, Wambsganss was interviewed by only one newspaperman. "He asked me how it felt," Wamby recalled, "and I said it was the chance of a lifetime. Later, Elmer Smith said we could have made a lot of money if we had capitalized on what we had done."

The landmark achievements of Wambsganss and Smith were recognized before the next day's game. Each received a diamond-studded medal depicting his significant accomplishment in the fifth contest. Local sportsmen footed the bill and craftsmen worked all night to produce the mementos.

The Series never returned to Brooklyn as the Indians won the next two games, 1-0 and 3-0, to wrap up their first world championship. Wamby did not stand out in either of those games, but it didn't matter. He'd already carved his indelible niche in baseball history.

After three more seasons with Cleveland, Wambsganss was sent to Boston in a multiplayer trade in 1924. He batted .275 and .231 in two seasons with the Red Sox before being sold to Philadelphia. With the A's, Bill performed capably as a shortstop and pinch-hitter. In 1926, his only season under Connie Mack, Wamby appeared in 54 games and batted .352, his highest average as a major leaguer.

He played with Kansas City and Louisville of the American Association and New Orleans (Southern) in the years that followed. He managed Springfield (Three-I) in 1931, then returned to the town that had spawned his interest in professional baseball 20 years before. As playing manager at Fort Wayne in 1932, Wamby batted .270 in 19 pinch-hitting appearances.

After retiring from Organized Baseball, Wambsganss managed Cleveland sandlot teams and a girls softball team. He also worked in industrial plants and for other Cleveland-area businesses.

When Wamby retired to the tranquility of his home in suburban Lakewood, O., he spent hours answering the never-ending stream of correspondence from fans who sought his autograph and just one more account of his unassisted triple play. He died December 8, 1985, at the age of 91.

OCTOBER 10, 1920									
Brooklyn	ab	r	h	rbi	Cleveland	ab	r	h	rbi
Olson, ss	4	0	2	0	Jamieson, lf	4	1	2	0
Sheehan, 3b	3	0	1	0	Graney, ph-lf	1	0	0	0
Griffith, rf	4	0	0	0	Wambsganss, 2b	5	1	1	0
Wheat, lf	4	1	2	0	Speaker, cf	3	2	1	0
Myers, cf	4	0	2	0	E. Smith, rf	4	1	3	4
Konetchy, 1b	4	0	2	1	Gardner, 3b	4	0	1	1
Kilduff, 2b	4	0	1	0	W. Johnston, 1b	3	1	2	0
Miller, c	2	0	2	0	Sewell, ss	3	0	0	0
Krueger, c	2	0	1	0	O'Neill, c	2	1	0	0
Grimes, p	1	0	0	0	Thomas, c	0	0	0	0
Mitchell, p	2	0	0	0	Bagby, p	4	1	2	3
Totals	34	1	13	1	Totals	33	8	12	8

```
Brooklyn.............................0  0  0   0  0  0   0  0  1—1
Cleveland ...........................4  0  0   3  1  0   0  0  x—8
```

Brooklyn	IP	H	R	ER	BB	SO
Grimes (L)	3⅓	9	7	7	1	0
Mitchell	4⅔	3	1	0	3	1
Cleveland	IP	H	R	ER	BB	SO
Bagby (W)	9	13	1	1	0	3

E—Sheehan, Gardner, O'Neill. DP—Brooklyn 1, Cleveland 3. TP—Cleveland 1. LOB—Brooklyn 7, Cleveland 6. 3B—Konetchy, E. Smith. HR—E. Smith, Bagby. SH—Sheehan, W. Johnson. WP—Bagby. PB—Miller. T—1:49. A—26,884.

4,192: Rose
Hits the Jackpot

Pete Rose takes his record-breaking swing at an Eric Show pitch during a September 11, 1985, game in Cincinnati.

Wave after wave of thunderous applause tumbled out of the stands at Riverfront Stadium and billowed toward first base, where red-hatted Cincinnati players were converging on their player-manager.

For seven minutes the roars ebbed and flowed. The 44-year-old first baseman was surrounded by his subordinates, who slapped him on the back, pumped his hand and shouted congratulations in his ears. The players returned to their dugout, but still the cheers cascaded on the skipper, a solitary figure pawing the dirt around the base. He didn't know what to do.

A tear welled in the eye of Peter Edward Rose. He blotted it out. Then he looked skyward and beheld a vision that proved more than he could handle. There was his father in the front row of the celestial box seats, and right behind him sat Ty Cobb. Tears coursed down the cheeks of old No. 14.

It was shortly after 8 p.m. on September 11, 1985, and Pete Rose, a hardened campaigner of 23 years who was most noted for his base-line collisions and belly-flop slides, had just banged out his 4,192nd major league base hit, converting Cobb's 57-year-old record into a runner-up.

"I felt like a man looking for a hole to jump into," Pete said later. "I looked around for somebody to talk to and there wasn't anyone."

In Pete's lonesomeness, his thoughts gravitated naturally to his late father, who had been his counselor, coach and inspiration since childhood, and to Cobb, whose challenging image had lured him on. Pete doesn't remember the day when he first heard of the Georgia Peach. It may have been when, as a tender youth, he accompanied his dad to Crosley Field in his hometown of Cincinnati to watch the Reds perform. From their bleacher seats, father and son admired the skills of Ted Kluszewski, Wally Post, Johnny Temple and others while Harry Rose preached the gospel of baseball to his eager audience of one.

"His father is the reason he has been such a great player," said Rose's mother, LaVerne. "He just kept pushing him, but at the same time he made playing sports fun. I know that is why Peter has maintained the enthusiasm all these years."

Pete Rose listened and learned at the knee of his dad, a fine athlete who played semipro football into his 40s. He complied willingly with his father's demands, which included swinging a weighted bat nightly, first righthanded and then lefthanded, before going to bed. And no opportunity to play the game ever was overlooked.

When he was 19 and weighed 155 pounds, Rose obtained a chance to turn professional. He signed with the Reds' organization in 1960 for $7,000, plus an additional $5,000 when and if he stayed with the

Pete Rose celebrated his record-tying hit with a tip of the cap to fans at Chicago's Wrigley Field.

Reds for 30 days.

Less than three years of minor league apprenticeship—at Geneva (New York-Pennsylvania), Tampa (Florida State) and Macon (South Atlantic)—put the finishing touches on the crew-cut second baseman. In his own mind, brash and cocky Pete knew he was ready. The opinion was shared by Fred Hutchinson, although the Cincinnati manager questioned his own fortitude more than Pete's talent. "If I had any guts," Hutch said when the 1963 season still was months away, "I'd stick the kid on second base and forget him."

In time, the Cincinnati native edged Don Blasingame off second base. National League fans quickly discovered a new and refreshing personality, a

Another tip of the cap was required when Pete Rose broke the hit record in a game at Cincinnati.

breed apart from the typical player. To Pete, a base on balls was not a walk. It was a sprint from home plate to first base, and when he became known as "Charlie Hustle" because of that practice, he accepted the nickname as a supreme compliment, one that made his father proud. The habit endured into superstardom.

Pete carried off N.L. Rookie of the Year honors in 1963 and two years later was named to the N.L. squad for the All-Star Game. As situations changed through the years, so did Pete's position. He became a third baseman, an outfielder and eventually a first baseman. He handled whatever job he was given in superb fashion, and he was selected an All-Star at every spot.

He performed in 16 midsummer classics, the most memorable of which was played at Cincinnati in 1970. In the 12th inning, Pete crashed full force into Ray Fosse at home plate to score the winning run. Both Rose and the Cleveland catcher felt the effects of that collision for the next few days.

Later that season, Rose played in his first League Championship Series and World Series. Rose was a vital cog in Cincinnati's Big Red Machine, which won four pennants and two world championships from 1970-76.

As one season blended into another and his career statistics climbed steadily, it became increasingly apparent that no record was secure as long as Rose remained mobile. He captured three batting titles. Ten times he rapped 200 or more hits in a season. Five times he led the league in doubles. He was named the N.L. Most Valuable Player in 1973 and was The Sporting News' choice for Player of the Decade in the 1970s.

One of Pete's most remarkable seasons in a Cincinnati uniform was 1978. He collected his 3,000th hit, a single off Steve Rogers of Montreal, on May 5. Later he hit safely in 44 consecutive games for a modern N.L. record.

Just when it appeared that the Rose-Reds union would be permanent, difficulties developed. When the two parties were unable to agree on a new contract, Pete declared his free agency. He negotiated with several other clubs before signing a lucrative four-year contract with Philadelphia. He picked the Phillies, he explained, because the club fielded a contender regularly and because he wished to remain in the National League, where he could pursue certain objectives.

His first goal was Stan Musial's 3,630 hits. Rose shattered that N.L. record in his third year with the Phils, a year after leading the club to the world championship over Kansas City. On June 10, 1981, he tied the mark with a single against Houston's Nolan Ryan. He then sat out a 50-day recess as management and labor resolved their differences during baseball's first midseason players strike.

When the schedule resumed August 10 at Veterans Stadium, the Phils' park was packed with 60,561 fans, all eager for a peek at history in the making. Rose failed in his first three tries to set a new record. In the eighth inning, however, he slapped an inside fastball from Mark Littell of the Cardinals to left field for a single. As 3,631 colored balloons drifted skyward, Stan the Man himself leaped from his box seat and trotted to first base to offer congratulations to his 40-year-old successor. A phone call from President Ronald Reagan climaxed the historic night.

Rose later took time to discuss his next objective, Cobb's all-time major league record of 4,191 hits, a mark that had stood since the Georgia Peach retired in 1928.

"People are worried I may not have a chance to break that because I missed 55 games during the strike," he said. "Well, if I get that close, I think I will find a way to get it. I'm not going to think back and worry about the strike. After all, I could have missed 55 games with an injury."

Rose was a .245 hitter in 151 games in the Phils' pennant-winning season of 1983, and though he batted .313 in the team's World Series loss to Baltimore, he was released afterward. The Phillies wanted to make him a part-time player, but Rose wouldn't accept that. So, approaching his 43rd birthday, Rose was a free agent again. Though fewer teams were calling than five years earlier, Rose ultimately signed a one-year contract with the Montreal Expos.

"We want someone who is accustomed to winning, a player who can provide leadership," explained John McHale, the club's chief executive officer. "We're tired of losing pennants in the last month."

Pete was 10 hits shy of 4,000 when the 1984 campaign began. The number was down to five when the Expos moved into Cincinnati on April 9 for the start of a three-game series. Two hits that day and a pair the next raised him to 3,999. One more and Pete Rose would join Ty Cobb as the only major leaguers with 4,000 hits to their credit.

But Pete had little opportunity to get his hit in the last game of the Cincinnati series. Rose, who had gotten married (his second) that morning, was walked four times and grounded out in his other trip to the plate. He finally got hit No. 4,000 two days later—on Friday, April 13—in the Expos' home opener against the Phillies. A fourth-inning double off Jerry Koosman hoisted Rose into Cobb's exclusive club.

By midseason, Pete's course took another dramatic turn. The Reds, languishing near the bottom of the N.L. West Division, were on the hunt for a manager to replace Vern Rapp. Rose, who was playing less than he had hoped for Montreal, meanwhile was looking for another team that would increase his playing time. Eventually, Rose and Reds President Bob Howsam made connections, and on August 16, 1984, Rose was traded for infielder Tom Lawless. The seemingly ageless man-boy was a player-manager at an age when most professional athletes are retired.

When he changed uniforms, Rose had 72 hits for the season. He needed only 129 more to tie Cobb. That figure dwindled by one on Pete's first at-bat as a recycled Red. Giving 35,038 partisans a chance to exercise their vocal cords, Rose rapped a run-scoring single and, thanks to Cubs center fielder Bob Dernier's throwing error, lumbered around to third base, where he was safe on a headfirst slide. It was like old times and Cincinnati loved it. Pete was home again.

The player-pilot batted .365 (35 for 96) in 26 games before the season ended. His total of 107 hits for the year left him with 4,097 for his career—95 short of breaking Cobb's record.

When the 1985 season started, Rose was amusing skeptical sportswriters by predicting that the Reds, who had finished no higher than fifth in the division the previous three

ROSE'S MILESTONE HITS

No.	Date	Type	Pitcher	Opponent
1	4-13-63	Triple	Bob Friend	Pittsburgh
500	9-16-65	Single	Al Jackson	at New York
1,000	6-26-68	Single	Dick Selma	New York
1,500	8-29-70	Single	Carl Morton	at Montreal
2,000	6-19-73	Single	Ron Bryant	at San Francisco
2,500	8-17-75	Single	Bruce Kison	Pittsburgh
3,000	5- 5-78	Single	Steve Rogers	Montreal
3,500	8-15-80	Single	Tom Hausman	at New York
3,631	8-10-81	Single	Mark Littell	St. Louis
4,000	4-13-84	Double	Jerry Koosman	Philadelphia
4,191	9- 8-85	Single	Reggie Patterson	at Chicago
4,192	9-11-85	Single	Eric Show	San Diego

seasons, would contend for the N.L. West title. The scribes chuckled, but under Rose's leadership, the Reds made a spirited challenge that lasted until the last week of the season. They finished second with an 89-72 record—19½ games better than the year before—and only 5½ games behind Los Angeles. Rose had proven himself a talented manager.

Meanwhile, the skipper was drawing ever closer to Cobb's record. With each productive swing of the bat, Rose's media entourage grew larger. Pete, never one to shy away from publicity, handled his position in the spotlight well. He was especially adept at fielding questions from those who intimated that Cobb was a much better player than he was because, at the start of the season, he already had collected nearly 2,000 more at-bats than the Georgia Peach did in his career.

"I will never say I was a better baseball player than Cobb," Rose explained. "All I'll say is I got more hits than he did."

The hit that matched Cobb's total was delivered September 8 in Chicago. It was a single on a 3-and-2 pitch from Cubs righthander Reggie Patterson in the fifth inning. The 28,269 fans gave the visitor a five-minute standing ovation. Rose's Ty-tying hit keyed a three-run inning, but the game was halted by darkness after nine innings with the teams dead-locked, 5-5.

The Reds returned to Cin-

A hug from son Petey was one of many emotional highs that Pete Rose experienced after breaking Ty Cobb's all-time career hit record.

SEPTEMBER 11, 1985									
San Diego	ab	r	h	rbi	Cincinnati	ab	r	h	rbi
Templeton, ss	4	0	0	0	Milner, cf	5	0	0	0
Royster, 2b	4	0	1	0	Rose, 1b	3	2	2	0
Gwynn, rf	4	0	1	0	Parker, rf	1	0	1	0
Garvey, 1b	4	0	0	0	Esasky, lf	3	0	0	2
Martinez, lf	3	0	0	0	Venable, lf	0	0	0	0
McReynolds, cf	3	0	1	0	Bell, 3b	4	0	1	0
Bochy, c	3	0	1	0	Concepcion, ss	4	0	1	0
Bevacqua, 3b	3	0	1	0	Diaz, c	3	0	1	0
Show, p	2	0	0	0	Redus, pr	0	0	0	0
Davis, ph	1	0	0	0	Van Gorder, c	0	0	0	0
Jackson, p	0	0	0	0	Oester, 2b	3	0	1	0
Walter, p	0	0	0	0	Browning, p	4	0	1	0
					Franco, p	0	0	0	0
					Power, p	0	0	0	0
Totals	31	0	5	0	Totals	30	2	8	2

```
San Diego.............................0  0  0   0  0  0   0  0  0—0
Cincinnati............................0  0  1   0  0  0   1  0  x—2
```

San Diego	IP	H	R	ER	BB	SO
Show (L)	7	7	2	2	5	1
Jackson	⅓	1	0	0	1	0
Walter	⅔	0	0	0	0	2
Cincinnati	IP	H	R	ER	BB	SO
Browning (W)	8⅓	5	0	0	0	6
Franco	⅓	0	0	0	0	0
Power (S)	⅓	0	0	0	0	0

Game-winning RBI—Esasky.
E—Show. DP—San Diego 1, Cincinnati 1. LOB—San Diego 4, Cincinnati 11. 2B—Browning, Diaz, Bell. 3B—Rose. SB—Gwynn. SF—Esasky. T—2:17. A—47,237.

Even Cincinnati Reds Owner Marge Schott couldn't resist a congratulatory hug.

cinnati for a series with San Diego the next day, much to the delight of the thousands of fans who wanted to see Rose break the record at home. But Pete did not play in the first game of the series and was held hitless in the second, a 3-2 loss to the Padres. It seemed inevitable that Pete would get his "big knock," as he called it, the next night, and 47,237 confident spectators showed up to watch.

On Wednesday, September 11, Rose wrote his name in the starting lineup again. The date carried special significance. Precisely 57 years earlier, on September 11, 1928, Tyrus Raymond Cobb concluded his major league career, which had been spent mostly in Detroit, as an outfielder with the Philadelphia Athletics.

Center fielder Eddie Milner fouled out leading off the first inning for the Reds, bringing Peter Edward Rose to the plate. With righthander Eric Show on the mound for the Padres, Pete went into his crouch from the left side of the plate. He took the first pitch for a ball, fouled off the second and then looked at another ball. The fourth pitch was a slider . . . and then the long, grueling haul ended in the form of a line single to left-center field.

From the Cincinnati dugout burst a uniformed contingent led by Rose's 15-year-old son, Petey. Several members of the San Diego club, including Show briefly, joined the party at first base. Among the Padres who went over to congratulate Rose was shortstop Garry Templeton, who had successfully outmaneuvered third baseman Kurt Bevacqua in order to take the cutoff throw from left fielder Carmelo Martinez and personally present the ball to baseball's all-time hits champion.

"It was a moment without words," said Bevacqua, who later watched Rose triple, walk and score both runs in the Reds' 2-0 victory. "It's the first time I've ever seen Pete break down."

The parade of players eventually dissipated, leaving the newest national hero alone with his thoughts— and his tears.

The Catch: Mays' Miracle

In the long history of professional sports, and baseball in particular, never did so many competent journalists strain for superlatives the way they did on the afternoon of September 29, 1954.

Marvelous, magnificent and miraculous failed to describe the play that ever since has been recognized as simply The Catch. This play, for which Willie Howard Mays Jr. will be remembered long after most feats by hitters and pitchers are obscured by time, was incredible, incomparable, insuperable —and even those adjectives don't do the play justice.

The Catch, made in the first game of the World Series, surpassed any defensive play before or since,

according to those whose recollections are long and reliable. Individually, it capped the best season to date by the 23-year-old center fielder and future Hall of Famer. Collectively, it changed the complexion of the Series for the New York Giants and their effervescent manager, Leo Durocher.

"Say Hey" Willie was absent when the Giants assembled for training in Phoenix in the spring of 1954. He was completing almost two years of military service, during which the Giants, minus their National League Rookie of the Year of 1951, finished second and fifth. But Willie arrived before spring training was over and again infected his teammates with his good-natured enthusiasm. As

The above sequence shows Willie Mays making The Catch during Game 1 of the 1954 World Series against Cleveland.

before, when the Giants won the N.L. pennant in his rookie year, Willie's exuberance was contagious. With his boundless energy and limitless talent, Mays was an inspiration, the spark that galvanized a good team into a superior one.

The season still was in its infancy when Willie started flexing muscles that had matured during his years in the U.S. Army. By late July, Mays already had smacked 36 home runs, putting him on a pace to endanger Babe Ruth's record of 60 in one season. But with two months of the season remaining, he received an extraordinary request from Durocher.

"Stop hitting homers," the Lip said.

The Alabama native was incredulous. But Durocher had been Willie's most vocal supporter from the start, so he listened.

"You're hitting .316 now," the manager explained. "If you stop swinging for the fences, you can add 30 points to your average before the end of the season."

"What do you want me to do?" asked Mays, who still was skeptical.

"Start going to right field," Durocher replied.

"Why?"

"You can get on base more," Durocher said. "You can run. You can spread the defense. There are hitters coming up behind you who can get you around. It means more runs for us. That's why I'm asking it."

The Lip's logic convinced Willie to try it. The righthanded slugger started hitting to the opposite field. He ran with his blinding speed and he scored runs, as the skipper had predicted. And his already-impressive batting average shot up.

As the Giants prepared to close out their season September 26 in Philadelphia, Mays was batting .3422. Center fielder Duke Snider of the Brooklyn Dodgers was hitting .3425, while right fielder Don Mueller, also of the Giants, was barely ahead at .3426. Facing Robin Roberts, a 23-game winner for the Phillies, in the finale was not conducive to fattening a batting average, but Willie went 3 for 4 against the righthander. His mark for the season rose to .345, compared with .342 for Mueller, who went 2 for 6, and .341 for Snider, who went 0 for 3 against Jake Thies of Pittsburgh. Mays had won the first and only batting title of his distinguished career.

By adopting Durocher's suggestion, however, Mays smacked only five home runs in the last two months of the season, finishing with 41. But the Giants were pennant-winners, beating out the Dodgers by five games.

Mays and Mueller, of course, were not the only factors in the Giants' 97 victories. Shortstop Alvin Dark batted .293 and drove in 70 runs. First baseman Whitey Lockman and left fielder Monte Irvin also were big contributors. And James Lamar (Dusty) Rhodes was a positive sensation as a part-time outfielder and pinch-hitter. In 82 games, Dusty belted 15 homers with 50 runs batted in. In all, 10 homers sailed off the bats of New York pinch-hitters in 1954.

The Giants also benefited from several strong pitching performances. Led by lefthander Johnny Antonelli (21-7) and righthanders Ruben Gomez (17-9) and Sal Maglie (14-6), the staff hurled 19 shutouts and compiled a 3.09 earned-run average, the lowest in the league.

By comparison, the Cleveland Indians tallied an American League-record 111 victories in winning the flag. Manager Al Lopez's club boasted the league's batting champion, second baseman Bobby Avila (.341), and a slugging third baseman, Al Rosen, who hit .300 with 24 homers and 102 RBIs. The Cleveland pitching staff was fearsome, too, as evidenced by its league-best 2.78 ERA. The Indians' top hurlers were righthanders Bob Lemon (23-7), Early Wynn (23-11) and Mike Garcia (19-8). The Indians, the better team statistically, were installed as 8-to-5 favorites entering the World Series.

The starting pitchers for the September 29 opener at the Polo Grounds were Lemon and Maglie, but the game didn't start out like a pitching duel. The Indians cuffed Maglie for two runs in the first inning on a hit batsman, a single by Avila and a two-out triple off the right-field wall by first baseman Vic Wertz. Lemon then surrendered a pair of runs in the third inning as the Giants knotted the score. Lockman led off with a single and advanced to third on Dark's single. Mueller forced Dark to

SEPTEMBER 29, 1954									
Cleveland	ab	r	h	rbi	New York	ab	r	h	rbi
Smith, lf	4	1	1	0	Lockman, 1b	5	1	1	0
Avila, 2b	5	1	1	0	Dark, ss	4	0	2	0
Doby, cf	3	0	1	0	Mueller, rf	5	1	2	1
Rosen, 3b	5	0	1	0	Mays, cf	3	1	0	0
Wertz, 1b	5	0	4	2	Thompson, 3b	3	1	1	1
Regalado, pr	0	0	0	0	Irvin, lf	3	0	0	0
Grasso, c	0	0	0	0	Rhodes, ph	1	1	1	3
Philley, rf	3	0	0	0	Williams, 2b	4	0	0	0
Majeski, ph	0	0	0	0	Westrum, c	4	0	2	0
Mitchell, ph	0	0	0	0	Maglie, p	3	0	0	0
Dente, ss	0	0	0	0	Liddle, p	0	0	0	0
Strickland, ss	3	0	0	0	Grissom, p	1	0	0	0
Pope, ph-rf	1	0	0	0					
Hegan, c	4	0	0	0					
Glynn, ph-1b	1	0	0	0					
Lemon, p	4	0	0	0					
Totals	38	2	8	2	Totals	36	5	9	5

Cleveland ....2 0 0   0 0 0   0 0 0 — 2
New York ....0 0 2   0 0 0   0 0 3 — 5
One out when winning run scored.

Cleveland	IP	H	R	ER	BB	SO
Lemon (L)	9	9	5	5	5	6
New York	IP	H	R	ER	BB	SO
Maglie	7*	7	2	2	2	2
Liddle	⅓	0	0	0	0	0
Grissom (W)	2⅔	1	0	0	3	2

*Pitched to two batters in eighth.

E—Mueller 2, Irvin. LOB—Cleveland 13, New York 9. 2B—Wertz. 3B—Wertz. HR—Rhodes. SB—Mays. SH—Irvin, Dente. HBP—By Maglie (Smith). WP—Lemon. T—3:11. A—52,751.

drive in Lockman, and after Mays walked on four pitches, third baseman Hank Thompson singled to drive in Mueller.

Neither team threatened seriously again until the eighth inning, when the Indians started a rally. Center fielder Larry Doby walked and Rosen singled. The Tribe had runners at first and second with nobody out.

At that point, Durocher decided to pull Maglie in favor of a fresh pitcher. Don Liddle, a little left-hander, was the Lip's choice to pitch to Wertz, a lefthanded swinger. What happened next was described by Charles Einstein, Mays' biographer:

"Wertz swung . . . and there it went on a rising, soaring line toward deepest center field, just to the right of dead center. To be seated in the press section back of home plate, in the imperceptible flash of time it took to focus from the swing to the horizon beyond, was to encounter a sight: the number 24 on the back of Willie Mays' uniform, already in full flight toward the wall."

That account describes The Pursuit that preceded The Catch. Another view of The Catch was provided by a writer who was sitting in the bleachers that day. In his book, "A Day in the Bleachers," Arnold Hano wrote:

"This ball did not alarm me because it was hit to dead center field—Mays' territory—and not between the fielders, into those dread alleys in left-center and right-center which lead to the bullpens.

"And this was not a terribly high drive. It was a long low fly or a high liner, whichever you wish. This ball was hit not nearly so high as the triple Wertz struck earlier in the day, so I may have assumed that it would soon start to break and dip and come down to Mays, not too far from his normal position.

"Then I looked at Willie and alarm raced through me, peril flaring against my heart. To my utter astonishment . . . the inimitable Mays, most skilled of outfielders, unique for his ability to scent the length and direction of any drive and then turn and move to the final destination of the ball, was turned full around, head down, running as hard as he could, straight toward the runway between the two bleacher sections.

"I knew then that I had underestimated—badly underestimated—the length of Wertz's blow.

"I wrenched my eyes from Mays and took another look at the ball, winging its way along, undipping, unbreaking, 40 feet higher than Mays' head, rushing along like a locomotive, nearing Mays, and I thought then: It will beat him to the wall.

". . . For the briefest piece of time . . . Mays started to raise his head and turn it to his left, as though he were about to look behind him.

"Then he thought better of it, and continued the swift race with the ball that hovered quite close to

Cleveland's Vic Wertz was victimized by what many observers regard as the greatest catch of all time.

him now, 30 feet high and coming down (yes, finally coming down) and again—for the second time—I knew Mays would make the catch.

". . . He simply slowed down to avoid running into the wall, put his hands up in cuplike fashion over his left shoulder and caught the ball much like a football player catching leading passes in the end zone. . . .

"Mays caught the ball and then whirled and threw, like some olden statue of a Greek javelin hurler, his head twisted away to the left as his right arm swept out and around. But Mays is no classic

Willie Mays (left) and Dusty Rhodes enjoy a light moment after helping the Giants to a Game 1 victory over Cleveland in the 1954 World Series.

study for the simple reason that at the peak of his activity, his baseball cap flies off. And as he turned, or as he threw . . . off came the cap, and then Mays himself continued to spin around after the gigantic effort of returning the ball whence it came, and he went down flat on his belly, and out of sight.

"But the throw! What an astonishing throw, to make all other throws ever before it . . . appear (like) the flings of teen-age girls. This was the throw of a giant, the throw of a howitzer made human, arriving at second base . . . just as Doby was pulling into third, and as Rosen was scampering back to first."

While others raptured over The Catch, Mays himself regarded it as rather routine.

"Any ball you go a long way for," he wrote in his autobiography, "is exciting to the fans in the stands because they're not looking at you when you get your jump on it—at that moment they're looking at the hitter. But I'd gotten the good jump, and I had running room, and the ball stayed up for me. I didn't have to pick it off the grass, I didn't have to avoid another fielder, I didn't have to crash the wall, I didn't have to jump in the air, I didn't have to gauge the wind (there was none) or some eccentric thing the ball itself did (it didn't rise, fall, curve, swerve or bend too much). I doubt there's a day goes by in the big leagues but some outfielder

doesn't make a more difficult play."

Mays' modesty is commendable, but few observers shared his opinion that The Catch was routine. And there is no denying that it saved the Giants that day. Had Willie not caught the ball, two runs would have scored and Wertz would have been in scoring position with none out.

But he did, much to the relief of Liddle, who promptly was replaced on the mound by Marv Grissom. The righthander walked pinch-hitter Dale Mitchell to load the bases but preserved the 2-2 tie by striking out pinch-hitter Dave Pope and retiring catcher Jim Hegan on a fly ball to Irvin.

Neither team scored again by the end of the ninth inning, sending the game into overtime. Grissom survived a leadoff double by Wertz (his fourth hit of the day), a sacrifice and an intentional walk in the top of the 10th to give the Giants a chance to win the game in the home half of the frame. With one out, Mays walked and stole second. Lemon then walked Thompson on purpose, bringing up Irvin. But Durocher decided it was time to bring out his ace in the hole, Rhodes, to pinch hit. Dusty responded beautifully. He lofted Lemon's first pitch down the right-field line and into the outfield seats, barely 260 feet from home plate, for a home run. The Giants won, 5-2.

Rhodes was a deserving hero that day, but it was

Though robbed of a possible game-winning extra-base hit by Willie Mays' catch, former Cleveland star Vic Wertz earned his niche in baseball history.

Mays' unbelievable defensive gem that had everyone abuzz after the game. The Catch was the turning point of the game and, as it turned out, the Series. It prevented the Indians from winning by at least a 4-2 margin in regulation time and helped propel the Giants to a four-game sweep.

Mays played 19 more seasons in the majors before concluding his career with the New York Mets in 1973, by which time he had hit 660 home runs and compiled a .302 lifetime average. He accumulated numerous awards and distinctions at almost every step along his illustrious path and was recognized by The Sporting News as the Player of the Decade for the 1960s. He was elected to the Hall of Fame in 1979.

Wertz, the victim of Willie's wizardry, was stricken with polio in 1955 but overcame the disease and played in the majors through 1963. In addition to the Indians, he saw service with the Tigers, Browns, Orioles, Red Sox and Twins in his 17-year major league career.

For years he operated a successful beer distributorship in suburban Detroit. Wertz was 58 when he died in a Detroit hospital July 7, 1983, while undergoing heart surgery.

Though Vic had 266 home runs and a .469 slugging average to his credit for his major league career, it was the out he made in Game 1 of the 1954 World Series that people remembered.

"I'm very proud that I'm remembered in connection with it," Wertz had said in a 1979 interview. "I look at it this way: If it had been a home run or a triple, would people have remembered it? Not very likely."

Ted Williams Steals the Show

By common consent, Walter O. Briggs was unsurpassed as a host for the All-Star Game. The owner of the Detroit Tigers practiced hospitality in its grandest style and spared no expense in tossing out the welcome mat for visitors to the Motor City on July 8, 1941.

Briggs Stadium, which had grown a trifle dowdy over the years, was brightened with a $15,000 coat of paint. Reporters covering the game were treated to an abundance of viands and victuals that would have delighted a gourmet's palate. For the first time at a major league event other than the World Series, snazzy identification buttons were presented to media members. Without question, magnates hosting future midsummer classics would be hard-pressed to match Briggs' lavishness.

Such largesse, it was agreed, deserved a memorable contest, one that equaled in drama Briggs' lofty standards of graciousness. It would be fitting if the ninth annual extravaganza produced pitching heroics such as Carl Hubbell achieved in 1934, or perhaps home run feats as performed by Babe Ruth, Lou Gehrig and Jimmie Foxx in other years.

Those who wished along such lines were compensated more generously than they ever could have imagined. Of all the midsummer rivalries, none was as memorable as the 1941 contest, which was decided with two out in the ninth inning when Ted Williams unleashed a titanic home run that converted imminent defeat into incredible victory.

Williams, not yet 23, already was one of the game's superstars. As a rookie with the Red Sox in 1939, Ted led the American League in runs batted in with 145. The next year he led in runs scored with 134. By the All-Star break in 1941, the Splendid Splinter was on another meteoric course, batting an amazing .405 to lead the loop.

Bunting festooned the historic old park at Michigan and Trumbull avenues when Al Schacht, a former major league pitcher and the Clown Prince of Baseball, started to entertain early arrivals with his pantomimes. And necks craned when a figure wearing the home uniform of the Yankees stepped into the batting cage to take some practice swings. He was Joe DiMaggio, who already had established a major league record by hitting safely in 48 consecutive games and would hit in eight more before seeing his streak snapped.

Bob Feller, a 22-year-old righthander already in his sixth major league season, drew the starting pitching assignment for the Americans and put on a show worthy of baseball's most heralded hurler. The Cleveland fireballer, who brought his own trainer as well as his own special soap to the game, faced only nine National League batters in his three-inning term. He struck out four and allowed only one hit, a single by Reds second baseman Lonny Frey, who was promptly picked off base.

Tigers Manager Del Baker, who was piloting the A.L. team that day, plotted his pitchers for three innings each. His N.L. counterpart, Bill McKechnie of Cincinnati, favored four stints of two innings each, with a fresh reliever working the ninth. The system had paid dividends the year before when the Nationals posted a 4-0 victory, and Deacon Bill indicated he would follow the same pattern, calling on Brooklyn's Whitlow Wyatt, Cincinnati's Paul Derringer and Bucky Walters and Chicago's Claude Passeau. The final inning of work would come from an undesignated pitcher—perhaps Hubbell, who had wrapped up the victory in 1940.

Wyatt and Derringer matched Feller's scoreless pitching for three innings before the Americans scored a fourth-inning run through no particular fault of Derringer. Senators third baseman Cecil Travis got the first A.L. hit of the day when he doubled with one out. Travis advanced to third on DiMaggio's fly ball and scored when Bob Elliott slipped while fielding Williams' line drive, which went over the Pittsburgh right fielder's head for a double.

White Sox lefthander Thornton Lee was on the mound when the Nationals tied the score, 1-1, in the sixth inning. A leadoff double by Walters was followed by a sacrifice by Cubs third baseman Stan Hack and a long fly to left by Terry Moore of the Cardinals.

Walters, who had pitched a scoreless fifth while allowing two hits and fanning a pair, apparently was winded by his baserunning exertions. In the bottom of the sixth, the righthander surrendered walks to DiMaggio and Indians outfielder Jeff Heath and a two-out, run-scoring single by Heath's teammate, shortstop Lou Boudreau. Again the

Ted Williams gets a warm greeting from Joe DiMaggio (5) after hitting his 1941 All-Star Game-winning home run.

Americans led by a run.

Sid Hudson, just two years out of a Class-D league, took over the A.L. pitching duties in the seventh inning. The Washington righthander encountered instant difficulty. Cardinals right fielder Enos Slaughter led off with a single to left and took second when Williams fumbled the ball. But the error was rendered meaningless when Pirates shortstop Arky Vaughan pulled a drive into the upper deck of the right-field stands. Despite surrendering a double to the next batter, Billy Herman of Brooklyn, Hudson avoided further damage, but the senior circuit had its first lead of the game, 3-2.

Passeau took over for Walters in the bottom of that frame and retired the Americans in order. The righthander then gazed on gratefully in the top of the eighth when the N.L. lead grew to 5-2. Cardinals first baseman John Mize touched lefthander Edgar Smith of the White Sox for a double off the right-field screen and Vaughan duplicated his feat of the previous inning by walloping another homer into the right-field upper deck. With his team boasting a three-run advantage and only six A.L. outs to go, Vaughan loomed as the definite All-Star hero.

The junior circuit retrieved one run in the last of the eighth when DiMaggio doubled and his kid brother Dom of the Red Sox singled, making the score 5-3. When Boudreau sent Dom DiMaggio to third with his second single and took second on an error by Brooklyn's Pete Reiser, prospects brightened for even more runs as Boston's Jimmie Foxx stalked to the plate with two out. But Double X, who was not quite as fearsome as in earlier years, fanned on three Passeau pitches.

As matters developed, the strikeout might have been the Americans' best break of the game. Convinced that Passeau had lost nothing from his assortment of pitches, McKechnie junked his original format and let the righthander hurl the ninth frame, despite the fact that he could have had a pinch-hitter bat for Passeau, who was scheduled to lead off the next inning. Smith made quick work of the pitcher and the other two N.L. batters in the top of the ninth, and Passeau trudged back to the mound for the third time.

The 30-year-old hurler retired A's catcher Frank Hayes on a pop fly to Herman to open the home half of the ninth. Pinch-hitter Ken Keltner of Cleveland followed with a scratch single off the glove of Braves shortstop Eddie Miller, however, and when Yankees second baseman Joe Gordon singled and Travis walked, the bases were jammed. Even worse for Passeau, the next batter was Joe DiMaggio.

But Passeau appeared to be in luck. The Yankee Clipper hit sharply to Miller for what figured to be a game-ending double play. The shortstop's throw to Herman forced Travis for the second out, but Travis' bold baserunning forced Billy to make a hurried throw that pulled Reds first baseman Frank McCormick off the bag. DiMaggio was safe

Cubs pitcher Claude Passeau was the victim of Ted Williams' 1941 blast.

and Keltner scored, cutting the N.L. lead to 5-4. A.L. hopes still flickered.

McKechnie called for a conference on the mound, where he discussed his options with Passeau and several of the N.L. players and coaches. He could summon help from the bullpen, but the logical choice, lefty Hubbell, had not yet warmed up. He could have Passeau intentionally walk Williams, a lefthanded batter, and pitch to righthanded swinger Dom DiMaggio, but that would put the winning run on second base. Or, McKechnie explained, he could let Passeau take his chances with Williams. He chose the third option.

Meanwhile, Williams, who had been called out on strikes in the eighth inning, was getting himself primed for the duel. "I stood back and sort of gave myself a fight talk," he recalled. "I said: 'Listen, you lug. He outguessed you last time and you got caught with your bat on your shoulder for a called third strike. You were swinging late when you fouled one off, too. Let's swing and swing a little earlier this time and see if we can connect.'"

Williams took the first pitch for a ball. He fouled off the second, then watched the third sail outside the strike zone. "Passeau pitched to me pretty carefully," Ted said. "I . . . had him in the hole and (knew) the next one would be in there. I was cocked when he let go."

The fourth pitch was a chest-high fastball. The Splendid Splinter swung maliciously and lined the

Ted Williams received a postgame hug from American League Manager Del Baker.

JULY 8, 1941

Nationals	ab	r	h	rbi	Americans	ab	r	h	rbi
Hack, 3b	2	0	1	0	Doerr, 2b	3	0	0	0
Lavagetto, ph-3b	1	0	0	0	Gordon, 2b	2	1	1	0
T. Moore, lf	5	0	0	1	Travis, 3b	4	1	1	0
Reiser, cf	4	0	0	0	J. DiMaggio, cf	4	3	1	1
Mize, 1b	4	1	1	0	Willams, lf	4	1	2	4
F. McCormick, 1b	0	0	0	0	Heath, rf	2	0	0	0
Nicholson, rf	1	0	0	0	D. DiMaggio, rf	1	0	1	1
Elliott, rf	1	0	0	0	Cronin, ss	2	0	0	0
Slaughter, rf	2	1	1	0	Boudreau, ss	2	0	2	1
Vaughan, ss	4	2	3	4	York, 1b	3	0	1	0
Miller, ss	0	0	0	0	Foxx, 1b	1	0	0	0
Frey, 2b	1	0	1	0	W. Dickey, c	3	0	1	0
Herman, ph-2b	3	0	2	0	Hayes, c	1	0	0	0
Owen, c	1	0	0	0	Feller, p	0	0	0	0
Lopez, c	1	0	0	0	Cullenbine, ph	1	0	0	0
Danning, c	1	0	0	0	Lee, p	1	0	0	0
Wyatt, p	0	0	0	0	Hudson, p	0	0	0	0
Ott, ph	1	0	0	0	Keller, ph	1	0	0	0
Derringer, p	0	0	0	0	E. Smith, p	0	0	0	0
Walters, p	1	1	1	0	Keltner, ph	1	1	1	0
Medwick, ph	1	0	0	0					
Passeau, p	1	0	0	0					
Totals	35	5	10	5	Totals	36	7	11	7

```
National League.................0  0  0   0  0  1   2  2  0—5
American League ...............0  0  0   1  0  1   0  1  4—7
```
Two out when winning run scored.

Nationals	IP	H	R	ER	BB	SO
Wyatt	2	0	0	0	1	0
Derringer	2	2	1	1	0	1
Walters	2	3	1	1	2	2
Passeau (L)	2⅔	6	5	5	1	3

Americans	IP	H	R	ER	BB	SO
Feller	3	1	0	0	0	0
Lee	3	4	1	1	0	0
Hudson	1	3	2	2	1	1
Smith (W)	2	2	2	2	0	2

E—Reiser 2, Williams, Heath, Smith. DP—Nationals 1, Americans 1. LOB—Nationals 6, Americans 7. 2B—Travis, Williams, Walters, Herman, Mize, J. DiMaggio. HR—Vaughan 2, Williams. SH—Hack, Lopez. T—2:23. A—54,674.

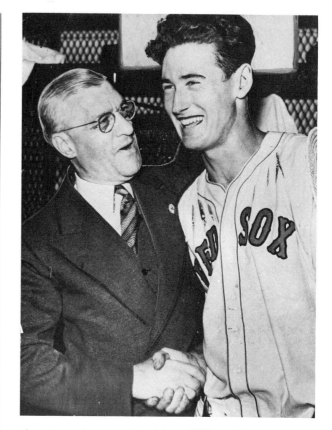

American League President William Harridge took an active part in the postgame celebration.

ball to right field. About 450 feet from home plate, the ball struck the facade of the upper tier of seats and fell to the ground, where Slaughter left it for a souvenir hunter as he ambled off the field. Briggs Stadium erupted with raucous applause as the largely pro-A.L. crowd of 54,674 celebrated the junior loop's stunning 7-5 victory.

"That's the best hit I ever made," an excited Williams told reporters afterward.

Gordon and DiMaggio crossed the plate as Williams, displaying all the exuberance of youth, loped around the bases. When he reached home, the entire A.L. team converged on the young hero to slap him on the back or shake his hand.

"What a beating I took after I touched the plate!" Ted recalled. "I got pounded from all sides, and my own boss gave it to me the worst. (Red Sox executive) Eddie Collins had come running out of the stands and he gave me a belt, too. When I got into the clubhouse . . . they gave it to me again."

Williams was the last player to leave Briggs Stadium, but when he arrived at the players' gate he found "a trillion people" waiting for him. He retreated and exited by another gate. He was trying to

All-Star Game-Ending Hits

July 8, 1941—Ted Williams' 3-run homer in 9th wins game, 7-5.
July 12, 1955—Stan Musial's solo homer in 12th wins game, 6-5.
July 11, 1961—Roberto Clemente singles in Willie Mays in 10th to win game, 5-4.
July 7, 1964—Johnny Callison's 3-run homer in 9th wins game, 7-4.
July 12, 1966—Maury Wills singles in Tim McCarver in 10th to win game, 2-1.
July 14, 1970—Jim Hickman singles in Pete Rose in 12th to win game, 5-4.
July 25, 1972—Joe Morgan singles in Nate Colbert in 10th to win game, 4-3.

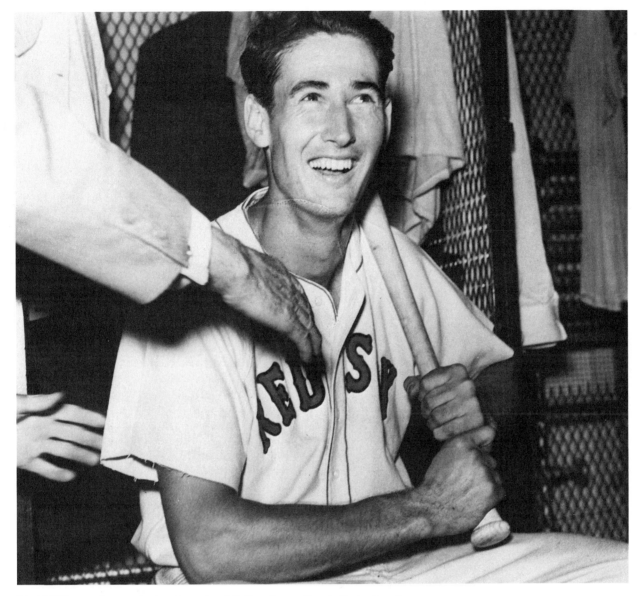

Ted Williams demonstrates how he hit the dramatic ninth-inning home run that ended the 1941 All-Star Game.

hail a cab when a motorist stopped and offered him a lift. En route to Williams' hotel, the kindly driver exulted over the dramatic climax, unaware that his passenger was the man of the hour himself. Ted finally identified himself when he got out of the car and thanked the man for the ride.

Williams went on to lead the league with a .406 batting average, 37 homers and 135 runs scored in 1941. His average dropped 50 points the next season, but he still won the league batting title, plus the first of two Triple Crowns.

With World War II in progress, Williams spent the seasons of 1943-44-45 in military service. He also missed most of the 1952 and '53 seasons due to service as a Marine pilot in the Korean War. He won the last of his six batting titles in 1958 when, at age 40, he batted .328. He closed out his spectacular career in style, socking a home run on his final at-bat in 1960, a year in which he still was good enough to clout 29 home runs and bat .316 for the Red Sox. Williams, The Sporting News' selection as Player of the Decade in the 1950s, compiled a lifetime batting mark of .344 and was elected to the Hall of Fame in 1966.

Passeau, the pitcher who surrendered Williams' memorable wallop, remained with the Cubs for six more seasons and enjoyed his finest hour on October 5, 1945, when he faced only 28 batters while defeating the Detroit Tigers on one hit in the World Series. After leaving the majors, he managed briefly in the minors and then retired to his home in Lucedale, Miss., where he ran a farmers' supply business.

Babe Ruth Hits Baseball Jackpot

Babe Ruth greeted the arrival of the 1927 season with his customary gusto. With his arms widespread and a translucent smile creasing his regal puss, he itched to start kicking the starch out of American League pitchers.

The 1926 campaign had been a good one. He had wiped out the memories of a wretched performance in 1925 with a .372 batting average and league-leading totals in home runs (47), runs batted in (145) and runs scored (139). Although the Yankees lost the World Series to the Cardinals, the Bambino clouted four home runs, including three in one game.

For 12 weeks in the off-season, the game's foremost slugger made a tour of vaudeville theaters from Minneapolis to Southern California, for which he received $65,000. He later spent 22 days in Hollywood making a film with Anna Q. Nilsson titled "The Babe Comes Home." The bright lights of Tinseltown ordinarily would have had a deleterious effect on baseball's most notorious playboy, but this time was different. He was accompanied by his trainer, Artie McGovern, who made certain that the Sultan of Swat ran five miles daily and got to bed nightly at 9 p.m. in order to be on the set at 6 a.m.

Because of the austere regimen, the Babe's waistline shrank a couple of inches by the time he returned to New York and signed a three-year contract calling for $70,000 annually. He was happy about both his salary and his physical condition. The Babe's euphoria extended through spring training before striking a snag on opening day at Yankee Stadium. Facing Lefty Grove of the Athletics, Ruth struck out twice and popped out once to the disappointment of a packed house. "Get me outta there," he told Manager Miller Huggins in utter disgust. Hug complied and Ben Paschal, a reserve outfielder, pinch hit for the Babe on his next scheduled at-bat.

Three games later, Ruth finally delighted the fans at Yankee Stadium with his first homer of the season. The solo shot in the first inning came off Philadelphia righthander Howard Ehmke on April 15. It

By 1927, the amazing Babe Ruth was primed for an assault on the home run record he already owned.

was another seven games before he connected off A's lefthander Rube Walberg for his second round-tripper, and by the end of the month Ruth had only four homers in the Yankees' first 15 games.

Ruth caught fire in May, socking 12 homers to raise his season total to 16. He blasted a pair of homers off righthander John Picus Quinn and Walberg in a May Day game against the A's. And home run No. 10, which came May 22 off Indians righthander Ben (Baldy) Karr, reportedly was a 600-foot smash—300 feet up and 300 feet down—that barely cleared the right-field wall in Cleveland's Dunn Field.

The Bambino's pace slackened in June, when he hit only nine homers. But he enjoyed a couple of two-homer games, against Indians lefthander Garland Buckeye on June 11 and Red Sox lefty Hal (Whitey) Wiltse on June 22. Ruth launched his July cannonading with a monstrous drive off Senators righthander Hod Lisenbee on July 3. The smash, which landed in the back section of the center-field bleachers at Griffith Stadium, tied Ruth for the A.L. lead with 26, the same number hit by teammate Lou Gehrig, who also was leading the league in batting with a .390 average.

As in June, the Babe slugged nine homers in both July and August. The former month featured two more two-in-one games—on July 9 against righthander Ken Holloway of Detroit and on July 26 against righthander Milt Gaston of St. Louis. The outfielder's most significant wallop of August was delivered at Chicago's Comiskey Park on the 16th.

Swinging on a pitch from righthander Tommy Thomas, a 19-game winner that year, Ruth cleared the right-field stands, thus becoming the first player to accomplish that feat since the outfield pavilion was double-decked before the '27 season.

At that point, the Bambino still trailed Gehrig by one in the home run derby. If he hoped to surpass his teammate and perhaps challenge the major league record for homers in one season—59, set in 1921 by a slugger named George Herman (Babe) Ruth—he would have to accelerate his pace dramatically.

Ruth did just that, finishing the season in a blaze of glory that left fans nationwide spellbound. He had 43 homers, two more than Gehrig, by the end of August, and when the first baseman's production fell off in September, the pursuit of Ruth's own record fell to the Babe himself.

He started the final month dramatically by tagging Walberg for the 400th circuit clout of his career. It was the fourth time the Philadelphia lefty had been victimized by Ruth in 1927.

The lefthanded slugger teed off on four Red Sox righthanders for five home runs September 6 and 7. Two came off Tony Welzer in the first game of a doubleheader, another off Jack Russell in the second game and one each off Danny MacFayden and Slim Harriss the next day. The Fenway Park spree boosted his total to 49, leaving him 11 short of a new record with 21 games to play.

Six days later, the Yankees swept a doubleheader from Cleveland by identical 5-3 scores to clinch

Babe Ruth watches the flight of his record-setting 60th home run (left) and then is greeted at the plate by teammate Lou Gehrig.

their fifth A.L. flag in seven years. Ruth contributed one homer to each victory, the first off righthander Willis Hudlin and the other off lefthander Joe Shaute.

With the pennant race no longer in doubt, baseball followers focused their complete attention on the Babe's race with the calendar. Could Ruth, by that time with 52 homers, hit eight more in 15 games to reach that magic No. 60? The nation watched and waited.

Ruth kept up a steady pursuit. The 32-year-old Baltimore native went two games without a homer before smacking No. 53 off righthander Ted Blankenship of Chicago. Then three games went by before righthander Ted Lyons, also of the White Sox, surrendered No. 54. Ruth poled a homer in each of the next two games as Detroit's Sam Gibson and Holloway gave up Nos. 55 and 56, respectively. After being held without a round-tripper in the Yanks' next two outings, Ruth had four more games in which to hit as many home runs.

The Babe earned a measure of revenge when the Yankees hosted the A's on September 27. Facing Grove, the pitcher who had rendered him helpless on opening day, Ruth blasted a grand-slam homer that provided the margin of victory in the Yanks' 7-4 triumph. It was his first bases-loaded clout of the year, and with just three games against Washington remaining, it also figured to be his last.

It wasn't. In New York's next contest, Ruth produced his eighth two-homer game of the season as the Yanks crushed the Senators, 15-4, at Yankee Stadium. He smashed a two-strike curve from Lisenbee over the wall in right-center field with the bases empty in the first inning, then tripled home a

run in the second. The Babe flied out in his next at-bat, but with the bases crammed in the fifth, Ruth drove a 3-and-2 pitch from righthander Paul Hopkins into the right-field bleachers for his record-tying 59th home run of the year. There were only about 5,000 fans on hand that day, but they gave Ruth a standing ovation that lasted several minutes.

That blast constituted the Babe's 16th homer in September, which already had become the best home run month of his career. Because of that splurge, Ruth had two more games, both at home, in which to hit one ball out of the park and set a new standard.

In the first of those contests, played September 30 in front of about 10,000 enthusiastic fans, Yankees righthander George Pipgras was scheduled to face Tom Zachary, a lean lefthander who had started the season with the St. Louis Browns. In fact, Zachary had surrendered Ruth's 22nd homer June 16, when he was a Brown, as well as his 36th August 10, by which time he was a Senator.

Pipgras, who later became an A.L. umpire after his pitching days were over, held the Senators scoreless until the fourth inning, when catcher Muddy Ruel and third baseman Ossie Bluege each singled in one run apiece. The Yanks then halved Washington's 2-0 lead in the home half of the fourth when Ruth, who had walked in his first plate appearance, singled to right field, took third on Gehrig's single to center and scored on left fielder Bob Meusel's long fly ball to Goose Goslin.

New York tied the score, 2-2, in the sixth, and again it was Ruth who tallied for the Yankees. The Babe started the two-out rally with a single and

Babe Ruth's 60-Homer Pace

then came around to score on singles by Gehrig and Meusel. Lefthander Herb Pennock then took over for Pipgras and blanked the Nats on one hit and one walk over the last three innings.

Zachary, however, still was on the mound when the Yankees came to bat in the home half of the eighth. The lefthander retired center fielder Earle Combs to start the inning, but shortstop Mark Koenig followed with a triple to left. The Babe was next. This was the propitious moment for baseball's leading thespian.

The Senators could have walked Ruth to set up a double play, but with Gehrig on deck a double play wasn't likely, and they decided against it. Zachary's first pitch was a fastball that the Bambino took for a strike. The second, according to umpire Bill Dinneen, was high. The third was a curve—"a little low," Zachary recalled—but it was close enough to

Senators lefthander Tom Zachary was Babe Ruth's record-setting victim.

tempt the batter. "I don't say it was the best curve anybody ever threw," Zachary said years later, "but it was as good as any I ever threw."

Ruth swung, and the crack of the bat was unmistakable. The ball sailed toward the right-field bleachers.

"It was not necessary to follow the course of the ball," John Drebinger wrote in the New York Times. "The boys in the bleachers indicated the route of the record homer . . . a fitting wallop to top the Babe's record of 59 in 1921.

"While the crowd cheered and the Yankee players roared their greetings, the Babe made his triumphant, almost regal tour of the paths. He jogged around slowly, touched each bag firmly and carefully, and when he imbedded his spikes into the rubber dish . . . hats were tossed into the air, papers were torn up and tossed liberally and the spirit of celebration permeated the place."

Citing Dinneen and Ruel as his authority, Drebinger added: "The ball traveled on a line and landed a foot inside fair territory about halfway to the top of the bleachers. But when the ball reached the bleacher barrier it was about 10 feet fair and curving rapidly to the right.

"The ball . . . was caught by Joe Forner of 1937 First Avenue, Manhattan. He is about 40 years old and has been following baseball for 35, according to his own admission. He was far from modest, and as soon as the game was over (he) rushed to the dressing room to let the Babe know who had the ball."

The audience continued to cheer uproariously as the New York players beat bats against the wooden floor of the dugout. Third-base coach Charley O'Leary, forgetting momentarily his embarrassment over his bald pate, flung his cap skyward and danced wildly. At the plate, with a broad grin and an extended hand, waited Gehrig, who wound up

with 47 homers himself that season.

When Ruth went out to right field for the start of the ninth inning, the fans in the bleachers greeted their hero with another deafening ovation. The Bambino responded with a brisk military march and a series of snappy salutes. The crowd ate it up.

Pitching great Walter Johnson, closing out his major league career with a pinch-hitting appearance, made one of the Senators' three outs in the ninth inning as the game ended with the score still 4-2. It was fitting that Ruth's momentous home run was the game-winner. And it mattered not that Ruth was held hitless the next day in the season finale. No one expected him to improve on what already was being touted as an unbreakable record.

In the World Series, however, Ruth batted .400 with two homers and seven RBIs. His performance sparked the '27 Yankees, perhaps the greatest baseball team ever, to a four-game rout of the Pittsburgh Pirates.

Ruth, who spent seven more seasons with the Yankees before winding up his Hall of Fame career with the Boston Braves in 1935, always cherished his 60-homer season. But he never forgot the contributions of his easygoing teammate, Gehrig, who for a while appeared capable of beating Ruth to the home run title that year.

"I don't think I ever would have established my home run record of 60 if it hadn't been for Lou," he wrote in his autobiography. "He was really getting his beef behind the ball that season. . . . Pitchers began pitching to me because if they passed me, they still had Lou to contend with."

As for the pitcher who had served up the Bambino's landmark homer, Zachary himself was a member of the Yankees by August 1928. He won the only World Series game in which he appeared that year as the Yankees swept the Cardinals. He went 12-0 for the Yanks in 1929, thus posting the best record ever by an undefeated pitcher.

Zachary later pitched for the Braves, Dodgers and Phillies and finished his career in 1936 with 186 victories. He then retired to Graham, N.C., where he was a successful tobacco farmer for many years.

In 1960, nine years before his death at the age of 72, a reporter asked Zachary about his encounter with Ruth.

"I didn't want him to put it into the seats," the grizzled farmer recalled. "I'd hardly won any games that season and I thought it would be right smart of me to win one. I wasn't working for Ruth. You should've heard his ripe language when I walked him once!"

When asked whether he wished he had thrown a different pitch to the slugger, Zachary replied: "I reckon it might have been safer to throw behind him. I don't guess Ruth hit those behind his head much better than the next guy."

SEPTEMBER 30, 1927

Washington	ab	r	h	rbi	New York	ab	r	h	rbi
Rice, rf	3	0	1	0	Combs, cf	4	0	0	0
Harris, 2b	3	0	0	0	Koenig, ss	4	1	1	0
Ganzel, cf	4	0	1	0	Ruth, rf	3	3	3	2
Goslin, lf	4	1	1	0	Gehrig, 1b	4	0	2	0
Judge, 1b	4	0	0	0	Meusel, lf	3	0	1	2
Ruel, c	2	1	1	1	Lazzeri, 2b	3	0	0	0
Bluege, 3b	3	0	1	1	Dugan, 3b	3	0	1	0
Gillis, ss	4	0	0	0	Bengough, c	3	0	1	0
Zachary, p	2	0	0	0	Pipgras, p	2	0	0	0
Johnson, ph	1	0	0	0	Pennock, p	1	0	0	0
Totals	30	2	5	2	Totals	30	4	9	4

```
Washington.................0  0  0   2  0  0   0  0  0—2
New York...................0  0  0   1  0  1   0  2  x—4
```

Washington	IP	H	R	ER	BB	SO
Zachary (L)	8	9	4	4	1	1

New York	IP	H	R	ER	BB	SO
Pipgras	6	4	2	2	5	0
Pennock (W)	3	1	0	0	1	0

E—Gehrig. DP—Washington 2. LOB—Washington 7, New York 4. 2B—Rice. 3B—Koenig. HR—Ruth. SB—Ruel, Bluege, Rice. SH—Meusel. HBP—By Pipgras (Rice). T—1:38.

Veeck's 65-Pound Birthday Present

Because birthday parties adhere to no prescribed pattern and can range from intimate cake-and-candle affairs to gigantic public functions attended by thousands, no one was certain what Bill Veeck might offer on August 19, 1951, as a means of celebrating the 50th anniversary of the American League.

The daily papers hinted that the owner of the St. Louis Browns had something extravagant in mind for that day's doubleheader with Detroit. Some surmised that Veeck's plan would exceed anything he had ever done at Milwaukee or Cleveland, where he had amused untold multitudes with colorful and wacky capers that not only entertained spectators, but also endeared him to fans as the premier showman of baseball.

More than 20,000 curious customers (18,369 paid) clicked the turnstiles at Sportsman's Park to view the latest manifestation of the Veeck genius. It's safe to say that none went home disappointed. Sportshirt Bill's observance of the golden anniversary was a bright chapter in the history of baseball, one that was remembered long after the principals had quit the scene.

The celebration started in traditional style, with plenty of cake and ice cream available for all the patrons upon their arrival at the historic old park. During the first game, comedian-contortionist Max Patkin, who had just been signed to a coaching contract, delighted the crowd with his comical antics along the first-base line. After two innings, however, umpire Art Passarella decided the silliness had gone far enough, and he ordered Patkin, who was lying down in the coaching box, to stand up.

The star attraction of Bill Veeck's 1951 American League birthday celebration was midget Eddie Gaedel, who popped out of a cake.

The opener resulted in a 5-2 St. Louis defeat, which came as no surprise to the followers of a team that was headed toward yet another second-division finish. But the loss didn't detract from the festivities between games, which began with a parade of performers streaming onto the field. It was a three-ring circus as each base featured a different act. At first base was a hand-balancer, at second a trampoline troupe and at third a juggling exhibition. Patkin, wearing a Browns uniform with a "?" on it, danced by himself on the mound, then grabbed a pretty girl from the crowd and swung into a jitterbug dance.

The intermission entertainment also featured the music of an oddly attired group of troubadours, a parade of old bicycles and classic cars, plus aerial bombs that released miniature American flags, which floated down on the field. In addition, a Brownie band consisting of pitchers Satchel Paige and Al Widmar and coaches Johnny Berardino and Ed Redys rendered three snappy numbers at home plate.

At the height of the show, a 7-foot papier-mache cake was wheeled onto the field. On a prearranged signal, a tiny figure in a Browns uniform leaped through the make-believe frosting and scurried into the St. Louis dugout.

This finale to the 30-minute program amused the spectators, who laughed, applauded and sat back to enjoy the second game. Veeck truly had come through with a unique birthday party, although some in attendance wondered whether it had lived up to its advance billing.

Oh well, they thought, let the second game begin. Perhaps the Browns could erase the sting of the first-game loss and defeat lefthander Bob Cain in the Sunday nightcap.

After Browns righthander Duane Pillette retired the Tigers without a run in the top of the first inning, the fans checked their scorecards. Right fielder Frank Saucier, who had led the Texas League in batting in 1950, was scheduled to lead off. Maybe he could start something.

Suddenly, the field announcer's voice echoed through the park: "Batting for Frank Saucier, number one-eighth, Eddie Gaedel."

The throng was stunned. A pinch-hitter for the home team's first batter of the game? Why? Who was Eddie Gaedel? What was his record? Could he hit? Or throw? Or run? What was going on?

In a moment, the crowd knew. A roar of laughter billowed out of the stands.

Approaching the plate and vigorously swinging three toy bats was the 3-foot-7-inch, 65-pound Brownie from the cake. Eddie Gaedel was a midget, and Bill Veeck wanted him to play. For the first time, a midget was appearing in a major league game.

Ed Hurley, umpiring at the plate, and Passarella had to uphold the dignity of the national pastime. Hurley scowled in the direction of the St. Louis dugout and summoned Manager Zack Taylor to a conference. What was Veeck up to now?

Bill had anticipated just such an occurrence. Taylor trotted toward the plate and thrust an official A.L. contract, duly signed by both parties, into Hurley's hands. All was in order, the arbiter determined, and there was nothing he or Tigers Manager Red Rolfe could do about it. The midget could bat.

Batting righthanded, Gaedel went into his crouch, which thus constituted his natural stance and created a strike zone that was "just about visible to the naked eye," Veeck said. "I picked up a ruler (before the game) and measured it for posterity. It was 1½ inches."

On the mound, Cain and his catcher, Bob Swift, went into a huddle. Cain saw the humor in the situation and suggested that he lob the ball underhand. Swift said that would be illegal, as would his sitting down to catch, and so he assumed a kneeling position while Cain just tried to pitch low.

The neophyte batter, a native of Chicago who had never played a game of baseball in his life, did not have to look over his shoulder for signals from a coach. Gaedel's strict instructions already had come from Veeck. "If you swing at a pitch," the owner warned, "I'll kill you." The temptation was great, but Eddie's bat never twitched as Cain missed the strike zone with four consecutive pitches.

Gaedel dropped his bat and waddled to first base, where he gave way to pinch-runner Jim Delsing. As the midget slowly returned to the bench, the park rocked with applause unlike anything heard since the team won its first and only pennant in 1944.

Delsing worked his way to third base as the Browns filled the bases, but he failed to score and St. Louis ultimately lost, 6-2. It was one of 102 defeats the club suffered that year, finishing in last place, 46 games behind the pennant-winning Yankees.

The Sportsman's Park crowd enjoyed Veeck's latest crowd pleaser, and for the most part, so did the rest of the country. The "Barnum of baseball" was not hailed universally, however, especially on South Michigan Boulevard in Chicago. A.L. President Will Harridge was not amused by the latest antic of the game's archmaverick. Late the day after the game, Harridge issued a statement expressing his displeasure and ordering Veeck to cease and desist. To wit:

"The American League office does not approve the contract submitted by the St. Louis American League club for the services of Edward Gaedel on the basis that his participation in American League championship games, in our judgment, is not in the best interest of baseball."

Harridge's edict did not totally surprise Veeck, but the owner said he would have appreciated a delay until he signed another player for one of the team's roster vacancies. The player, he said with tongue in cheek, was an Englishman standing 9-foot-3½.

Still, a protest was in order. "I have examined the rules of Organized Ball," Veeck told reporters, "and can't find a single paragraph which states how tall or how small a player must be to be eligible to play. . . . I suppose Mr. Harridge has banned Gaedel because he's so small—on the grounds that he's so tough to pitch to that he presents an unfair advantage for the Browns over our opponents.

"Well, if that's the case, I want to protest right now that visiting clubs that play such (tall) men as Larry Doby and Ted Williams present an unfair advantage over us. . . . Gaedel drew a base on balls, good for one base, while fellows like Doby and Williams hit homers against us."

But Veeck's pleas for justice were to no avail. Gaedel's name was stricken from the official statistics, although the Baseball Encyclopedia lists Gaedel as a righthanded batter and lefthanded thrower who played in one game. At the same time, the base on balls was permitted to remain on Cain's record and Delsing was credited with an appearance as a pinch-runner.

As Veeck stewed under the Harridge ruling, Gaedel, unaware that his career was over, exulted in Chicago. "Mr. Veeck wants me back and told me he'd have plenty of work for me the rest of the season," the nation's tiniest new hero told a Chicago scribe the day after the game.

Referring to his confinement in the papier-mache cake, Gaedel said: "It was hot and stuffy inside that cake and I thought I'd suffocate before I got out. This may have weakened me or perhaps I'd have reached up and slugged one of Cain's high pitches for a solid base hit."

As news of the midget episode spread, it came out that Veeck did not dream up the plan all by him-

Eddie Gaedel, the 3-foot-7 testimonial to Bill Veeck's promotional genius, takes a Bob Cain pitch high as umpire Ed Hurley looks over the shoulder of Detroit catcher Bob Swift.

Before his historic appearance, Eddie Gaedel received an assist from Browns Manager Zack Taylor.

AUGUST 19, 1951									
Detroit	ab	r	h	rbi	St. Louis	ab	r	h	rbi
Priddy, 2b	5	1	1	1	Saucier, rf	0	0	0	0
Kryhoski, 1b	4	1	1	0	Gaedel, ph	0	0	0	0
Kell, 3b	4	1	3	0	Delsing, pr-cf	3	0	1	0
Wertz, rf	2	0	0	0	Young, 2b	4	0	1	0
Keller, rf	2	0	1	2	Mapes, cf-rf	5	0	2	0
Mullin, cf	5	1	3	2	Lollar, c	5	1	0	0
Souchock, lf	4	0	1	1	Wood, lf	3	0	2	1
Swift, c	4	0	1	0	Arft, 1b	4	0	0	0
Lipon, pr	0	1	0	0	Marsh, 3b	4	1	1	0
Ginsberg, c	0	0	0	0	Jennings, ss	4	0	0	0
Berry, ss	4	0	0	0	Pillette, p	2	0	0	0
Cain, p	2	1	0	0	Suchecki, p	0	0	0	0
Trout, p	0	0	0	0	Maguire, ph	1	0	0	0
Totals	36	6	11	6	Totals	35	2	7	1

```
Detroit ................... 0  0  0   1  0  1   3  1  0—6
St. Louis ................ 0  0  0   0  0  2   0  0  0—2
```

Detroit	IP	H	R	ER	BB	SO
Cain (W)	8⅓	7	2	0	5	1
Trout	⅔	0	0	0	0	1
St. Louis	IP	H	R	ER	BB	SO
Pillette (L)	6⅔	9	5	5	4	3
Suchecki	2⅓	2	1	0	0	0

E—Kell 2, Berry, Young. DP—Detroit 1. LOB—Detroit 9, St. Louis 11. 2B—Mullin 2, Delsing, Wood, Marsh. HR—Priddy. SH—Cain, Keller. PB—Lollar. T—2:34. A—18,369.

self. The idea had germinated a couple of years before when Veeck picked up a copy of the Saturday Evening Post and read an article titled "You Could Look It Up." In the story, James Thurber recounted the adventures of a midget who, contrary to orders, swung on a 3-and-0 pitch with the bases loaded and two out in the ninth inning. He dribbled the ball down the third-base line. Although several infielders sprawled on the turf in their efforts to field the ball and one fired wildly into the outfield, the ball was retrieved and thrown to first base for the putout while the midget still was 15 feet from the bag.

The story appealed to Veeck's sense of the bizarre, and he filed it away mentally for future use. When he finally decided the time was ripe to introduce the majors' first midget, he hatched his scheme in secrecy, tipping off only those who had to know what he was planning.

Years later, Bob Fishel, the Browns' public relations director in 1951, recalled the difficulties he encountered in obtaining the right person for the lead role.

"The agent kept trying to send us dwarfs—grotesque gnomes you couldn't present in a baseball uniform," Fishel said. "Veeck held out for his midget and we finally got Eddie Gaedel, a nice-looking little guy. The uniform was no problem. The 7-year-old son of Bill DeWitt, our vice president, had one hanging in the clubhouse. We swiped it and had the number '⅛' sewn on the back."

Gaedel, 26, was an office worker and errand boy for a daily publication in Chicago when he signed a contract that guaranteed him $100 for every game in which he appeared. But it took a little convincing to get him to go along with the plan.

"Eddie, you'll be the only midget in the history of the game," Veeck explained. "You'll be appearing before thousands of people. Your name will go into the record books for all time. You'll be famous."

It wasn't too much longer before Gaedel, who "had more than a little ham in him," according to Veeck, agreed to become a Brownie.

While awaiting his introduction to the national spotlight, Eddie was hidden in a hotel several blocks from the ball park. He then was driven to the park, where he dressed in Taylor's office. As curtain time approached, Gaedel was stricken with a case of pregame jitters and was unable to tie his shoes. Gallantly, the manager came to his rescue.

By the time it was over, however, Eddie was full of bravado. "I felt like Babe Ruth at the plate," he cracked. "Now I want to face Bob Feller." That ambition foundered, of course, but because of his one fleeting appearance on the baseball scene, his name now is almost as memorable as Williams, DiMaggio and all the other superstars.

Gaedel returned to his old job in Chicago and was largely unheard from until almost 10 years later. On opening day of the 1961 season, Eddie and seven other midgets were hired as vendors at Comiskey Park. Veeck employed them, he explained, "so they wouldn't obstruct the view of the spectators."

Gaedel was not disappointed about his one-day employment. "That was all my feet could stand," he said.

About two months later, Gaedel was mugged and beaten on a Chicago street somewhere between his home and a bar. He crawled home and fell into bed, where his lifeless form was discovered by his widowed mother.

Among those who attended Gaedel's funeral was Bob Cain, who flew in from his home in Cleveland. The former pitcher explained that, as a public relations representative of a major food chain, "I've

Midget Eddie Gaedel probably ranks as master promoter Bill Veeck's top publicity stunt.

been a good-will man and speaker for all these years and the midget was my best story. I owed him that one."

Veeck operated the Browns through the 1953 season. When the financially troubled franchise was transferred to Baltimore, he retired from the game. The premier showman resurfaced in 1959 as the head of the White Sox, who promptly won the A.L. pennant to end a four-year Yankee domination. But ill health forced him into retirement again in 1961. By late 1975 he was well enough to return to the game, so he headed a syndicate that acquired the White Sox. He was unable to compete with affluent clubs in the free-agent market, however, and he bowed out in 1980. He was 71 when he died January 2, 1986, of cardiac arrest in a Chicago hospital.

Ruth's Called Shot: Fact or Fiction?

On a warm, clear and windy autumn afternoon on the North Side of Chicago, a legend was born. Some swore it was based on fact, while others maintained it was pure myth. Because of that disagreement, a controversy has raged for decades. It may never be resolved to universal satisfaction.

There were about 50,000 people at the third World Series game in 1932, but that abundance of eyewitnesses did little to help solve the dilemma. Some reporters chose to ignore it altogether. Even the players on the competing teams differed in their opinions of whether Babe Ruth truly "called" his home run on Saturday afternoon, October 1, at Wrigley Field.

The 1932 season had been most remarkable for the 37-year-old Sultan of Swat. Injuries limited him to only 133 games, but he still slugged 41 home runs, drove in 137 runs and batted .341 as the New York Yankees cantered to an easy American League pennant, winning by 13 games over the three-time defending champion Philadelphia Athletics.

Ruth gave the Yankees quite a scare in September. Citing severe stomach cramps, the slugger rushed home from Detroit to be examined. Doctors feared appendicitis, but after packing him in ice and bringing his fever down they eventually vetoed surgery. He was confined to bed for 10 days, however, during which time the Yanks clinched the pennant. When the big fellow finally was well enough to work out at Yankee Stadium, he was so weak that he failed to drive a ball out of the park in one hour of batting practice against an amateur pitcher. Ruth was back in the lineup a few days later, but the Yanks were justifiably concerned that the Babe might not be 100 percent recovered in time for the World Series against the Cubs, particularly when he hit safely only three times in 16 at-bats during the five games he played before the end of the regular schedule.

When the Series started in New York, however, Ruth was beginning to return to form. In the first two games at Yankee Stadium, the Babe collected two singles and one run batted in as the home team won both contests handily, prevailing 12-6 behind Red Ruffing and 5-2 behind Lefty Gomez.

Bitterness between the combatants flared early, born of the Cubs' alleged parsimony in dividing their share of the Series pot. Shortstop Mark Koenig, a member of earlier Yankee championship teams, had been acquired in August from the Pacific Coast League and sparked the Cubs to the National League pennant, for which he was voted only half a share by his teammates. The Yankees considered that decision unconscionable, and they never let the Chicagoans forget it. They showered their adversaries with all forms of verbal abuse, starting with "cheapskates" and working downward. The Cubs, in turn, taunted Ruth about his age and his reported desire to manage the Yankees.

The Yankees discovered open hostility when they arrived in Chicago for the third game. In order to enter their hotel, the players and wives had to run a gauntlet of two lines of howling women who, Ruth said, greeted them with "some words that even I had never heard." All this, plus a shower of spit, much of which landed on Ruth's wife, Claire.

Pregame drills at Wrigley Field took the form of a clouting carnival. Ruth socked nine baseballs out of the park, first baseman Lou Gehrig seven. When the Babe worked out in left field—he played that position to avoid the sun's glare in his customary right-field spot—he was assaulted with catcalls as well as lemons. Showman that he was, he tossed back the lemons and carried on a running conversation with the hecklers.

Yankees Manager Joe McCarthy, who had been fired as manager of the Cubs two years earlier because of his supposed inability to win a world championship, was pondering the sweet taste of revenge when he chose righthander George Pipgras, a 16-game winner that year, to start Game 3. Charlie Grimm, the Cubs' first baseman-manager, selected righthander Charlie Root, a victor in 15 decisions.

Root found himself in a bind in the first inning. Center fielder Earle Combs led off with a grounder to shortstop. In his haste, Billy Jurges fired the ball into the Yankee dugout and Combs wound up on second base. A walk to third baseman Joe Sewell followed. As Ruth approached the plate, he was greeted by a storm of epithets that died abruptly when the Bambino hammered a 2-and-0 pitch deep into the temporary seats in right-center field.

A run-scoring double by Cubs right fielder Kiki Cuyler in the bottom of the first cut New York's

The Babe is greeted at home plate by teammate Lou Gehrig as Cubs catcher Gabby Hartnett watches after Ruth's called-shot homer.

lead to 3-1, but the Yanks got that run back when Gehrig led off the third inning with a home run. The Cubs bounced back, however, to tie the score, 4-4, with two runs in the third (one on a homer by Cuyler) and another in the fourth. Ruth's unsuccessful attempt at a shoestring catch on a hit by Jurges in the fourth gave the fans even more incentive to ridicule the Babe.

The fifth inning began innocently enough with Sewell going out on a grounder to shortstop. Ruth was next, and once more the hail of invective pelted down from the stands. The Chicago players rose to the top step of the dugout and joined the fusillade. Everyone in the stadium, it seemed, was screaming insults at the big guy.

A lemon sailed out of the stands and rolled toward the Babe. Ruth's response, John Drebinger wrote in the New York Times, was a signal "that the nature of his retaliation would be a wallop right out of the confines of the park."

The first pitch from Root caught the strike zone. Ruth held up one finger in accordance with the call. The next two pitches were wide of the mark, but the fourth was another called strike. Again Ruth ac-

knowledged the call with his hand. By that time the park had become a cacophony of insults, including a few from Ruth to his tormentors. "I'm going to knock the next pitch right down your goddamn throat," Gehrig later quoted Ruth as yelling to Root. And to many in attendance that day, it appeared as if Ruth pointed directly toward the center-field bleachers.

Root fired again, and Babe unfurled his most savage cut. "As I hit the ball," he later said, "every muscle in my system, every sense I had, told me that I had never hit a better one, that as long as I lived nothing would ever feel as good as this."

In center field, Johnny Moore took a few steps and gazed skyward. Far overhead, the ball streaked toward the bleachers and disappeared near the base of the flagpole. The homer, said by some to be the longest ever clouted in the park, was the Babe's 15th and last in 10 World Series.

As Ruth passed first base on his home run trot, he said something to Grimm. At second he made a remark to Billy Herman. Rounding third, he clasped his hands overhead like a victorious pugilist. As he stepped on home plate and proceeded to

ROBERT THOM

a joyous Yankee dugout, a bespectacled gentleman seated near the field threw back his head and laughed. The spectator was the governor of New York, Franklin Delano Roosevelt, who was elected a few weeks later to his first of four terms as President.

The huge throng, Drebinger wrote, was "suddenly unmindful of everything save that it had just witnessed an epic feat (and) hailed the Babe with a salvo of applause."

Root faced one more batter. Gehrig followed Ruth with his second homer of the day, finishing off Root and giving New York a 6-4 lead. The Yankees went on to win, 7-5. They wrapped up their fourth world championship the next day with a 13-6 crusher as second baseman Tony Lazzeri cracked two homers and a single and drove in four runs.

Immediately after the third game, disputes arose over whether Babe Ruth had called his home run shot by pointing to center field beforehand. Among the dissenters, the most vociferous was Root. "If he had," the pitcher fumed, "I would have knocked him down with the next pitch." Root, who died in 1970, never wavered in his opinion in the years following the incident.

Many of Root's teammates backed him. Pitcher Burleigh Grimes asserted that Ruth had brandished two fingers as if to tell the Cubs, "I've still got the big one left." And Gabby Hartnett, the Chicago catcher who was situated directly behind Ruth during the slugger's memorable at-bat, had this explanation: "Looking at our dugout and not at center field, he held up the index finger of his left hand, though pointing to the outfield. This is what he said: 'It only takes one to hit it.'"

New York players were divided in their opinions. Sewell thought Ruth had pointed to the Cubs' bench, not the center-field bleachers. Right fielder Ben Chapman thought the Babe had gestured toward the pitcher. Chapman said that upon his return to the bench, the Bambino told him that he had called Root "everything I could think of."

The editors of the annual baseball guides treated the incident differently. John B. Foster of the Spald-

Reproductions from movie film taken by Matt M. Kandle of Chicago seem to show Babe Ruth calling his home run in a 1932 World Series game at Wrigley Field. Ruth (above right) has his arm extended, hits the ball (center right) and then rounds first base after his blast. An entry from Kandle's journal confirms his presence at the game and refers to a movie of 'Babe Ruth slamming out one of his famous home runs.' The artist's conception of the called shot (left) differs from the movie film in both the positioning of the catcher and the absence of the temporary bleachers in right field.

ing Guide ignored the episode. Jimmy Isaminger of the Reach Guide wrote that Ruth hit "a tremendous drive—after indicating by pantomime to his hostile admirers what he purposed to do—and did!"

Frederick G. Lieb, a veteran New York scribe, entertained no doubts about the validity of the called shot. Writing in "The Story of the World Series," Lieb reported that some New York writers visited Ruth in the clubhouse after the game. "Suppose, Babe, you hadn't connected?" one remarked. "I never thought of that," Ruth replied. "I'd surely (have) looked like an awful ass, wouldn't I?"

That evening Lieb dined with Gehrig, who marveled at the audacity of his teammate. "What do you think of the nerve of that big monkey," he said, "calling his shot and getting away with it?"

In "The Babe Ruth Story," an autobiography transcribed by Bob Considine, the Bambino is quoted as saying, "While he (Root) was making up his mind to pitch to me (after the second strike) I stepped back again and pointed my finger at those bleachers, which only caused the mob to howl that much more."

Ruth said that after swinging, "I didn't have to look. But I did. That ball just went on and on and on and hit far up in the center-field bleachers in exactly the spot I had pointed to. To me, it was the funniest, proudest moment I had ever had in baseball."

Another player who was convinced that Ruth had delivered on his promise was Ruffing. The New York pitcher offered this version: "I don't care what anybody else says, I was sitting right there. I saw it.

"I was going to pitch the next day if there was a fifth game, so I sat as close as I could to the (Chicago) hitters, at the edge of the bench right by the steps leading to the plate. I had a perfect angle when Ruth came up.

"I saw him point with his fingers. In my mind there was no doubt. He was pointing to center field as if to say he was going to hit one there."

Forty years after the "called shot" event, Robert W. Creamer researched the subject thoroughly for his Ruth biography, "Babe, The Legend Comes to Life." Creamer discovered that only one account printed right after the game mentioned specifically that Ruth had pointed to the fence. The story, written by Joe Williams of the Scripps-Howard newspapers, ran in the afternoon editions of October 1, the day of the game. The New York World-Telegram carried the story under the headline, "Ruth Calls Shot as He Puts Homer No. 2 in Side Pocket."

"In the fifth," Williams' account read, "with the Cubs riding him unmercifully from the bench, Ruth pointed to center and punched a screaming liner to a spot were no ball had ever been hit before."

Creamer also included this passage in his excellent volume: "Westbrook Pegler, who wrote a column but not a running account of the game, said: '(Cubs pitcher Guy) Bush pushed back his big ears, funneled his hands at his mouth and yelled raspingly at the great man to upset him. The Babe laughed derisively and gestured at him—wait, mugg, I'm going to hit one out of the yard. Root threw a strike past him and he held up a finger to Bush, whose ears flapped excitedly as he renewed his insults. Another strike passed him and Bush crawled almost out of the hole to extend his remarks. The Babe held up two fingers this time. . . . Then with a warning gesture of his hand to Bush he sent the signal for the customers to see. Now, it said, this is the one, look. And that one went riding on the longest home run ever hit in the park. . . . Many a hitter may make two home runs, possibly three, in World Series play in years to come, but not the way Ruth hit these two. Nor will you ever see an artist call his shot before hitting one of the longest drives . . . laughing at and mocking the enemy, two strikes gone.'"

Perhaps Ruth captured the essence of the incident in this explanation to Chicago sportswriter John Carmichael: "I didn't exactly point to any spot. All I wanted to do was give that thing a ride out of the park, anywhere. I used to pop off a lot about hitting homers, but mostly among the Yankees. Combs and Lazzeri and (coach Art) Fletcher used to yell, 'Come on, Babe, hit one.' So, I'd come back, 'OK, you bums, I'll hit one.' Sometimes I did. Sometimes I didn't. Hell, it was fun."

OCTOBER 1, 1932

New York	ab	r	h	rbi	Chicago	ab	r	h	rbi
Combs, cf	5	1	0	0	Herman, 2b	4	1	0	0
Sewell, 3b	2	1	0	0	English, 3b	4	0	0	0
Ruth, lf	4	2	2	4	Cuyler, rf	4	1	3	2
Gehrig, 1b	5	2	2	2	Stephenson, lf	4	0	1	0
Lazzeri, 2b	4	1	0	0	Moore, cf	3	1	0	0
Dickey, c	4	0	1	0	Grimm, 1b	4	0	1	1
Chapman, rf	4	0	2	1	Hartnett, c	4	1	1	1
Crosetti, ss	4	0	1	0	Jurges, ss	4	1	3	0
Pipgras, p	5	0	0	0	Root, p	2	0	0	0
Pennock, p	0	0	0	0	Malone, p	0	0	0	0
					Gudat, ph	1	0	0	0
					May, p	0	0	0	0
					Tinning, p	0	0	0	0
					Koenig, ph	0	0	0	0
					Hemsley, ph	1	0	0	0
Totals	37	7	8	7	Totals	35	5	9	4

New York	3	0	1	0	2	0	0	0	1—7
Chicago	1	0	2	1	0	0	0	0	1—5

New York	IP	H	R	ER	BB	SO
Pipgras (W)	8*	9	5	4	3	1
Pennock	1	0	0	0	0	1

Chicago	IP	H	R	ER	BB	SO
Root (L)	4 1/3	6	6	5	3	4
Malone	2 2/3	1	0	0	1	4
May	1 1/3	1	1	0	0	1
Tinning	2/3	0	0	0	0	1

*Pitched to two batters in ninth.

E—Lazzeri, Herman, Hartnett, Jurges 2. DP—New York 1, Chicago 1. LOB—New York 11, Chicago 6. 2B—Chapman, Cuyler, Jurges, Grimm. HR—Ruth 2, Gehrig 2, Cuyler, Hartnett. SB—Jurges. HBP—By May (Sewell). T—2:11. A—49,986.

Seaver Fans Strikeout Flames

Major league strikeout artists had practiced their craft for nearly 100 years, but none of them—not Walter Johnson, nor Bob Feller, nor Sandy Koufax—attained the bewildering proficiency that was demonstrated by a 25-year-old righthander on the sunny and clear afternoon of April 22, 1970.

From the day he burst upon the national scene, Tom Seaver was a singular individual. A native of Fresno, Calif., he had earned all-city honors in high school baseball and basketball circles. He had starred at Fresno City College and then gone on to the University of Southern California. One summer, pitching for the Alaska Goldpanners semipro team, he excelled in the National Baseball Congress tournament at Wichita, Kan.

Seaver, a 6-foot-1, 210-pounder, was a prospect of rare quality and the Los Angeles Dodgers selected him in the player draft of 1965, only to discover that they could not satisfy Tom's bonus demands. The player's name was returned to the list of draft eligibles and he was chosen by the Atlanta Braves in January 1966 after he had posted a 10-2 record for Southern Cal in '65.

Several weeks later, Atlanta's West Coast scout obtained Seaver's signature on a contract of the Richmond club of the International League, the top farm team of the Braves. The terms included a bonus of $40,000.

All details of the agreement appeared in order until it was disclosed that the signing ceremony took place after Southern Cal had played two games, a distinct violation of the agreement between organized baseball and the colleges. The contract was voided.

Because of the signing, Seaver also was ineligible to play college ball, a situation that prompted him to write to Commissioner William D. Eckert. "I told him this wasn't fair to me," Tom explained, "and that I was being victimized by circumstances."

Eckert agreed. A bulletin was issued from the commissioner's New York office, notifying all clubs (with the exception of Atlanta) who were interested in matching the Braves' $40,000 bonus to inform Eckert accordingly. On April 4, Eckert added, a drawing would be held to determine which organization received negotiation rights to the young pitcher.

A youthful Tom Seaver holds the Cy Young Award that he was presented prior to his incredible 1970 strikeout performance.

"I did it for the interest of the boy and the public," Eckert said. "It was not his fault that the contract (with Atlanta) was later invalidated."

The Philadelphia Phillies, Cleveland Indians and New York Mets signified their interest in signing Seaver. The Dodgers fully intended to join in the bidding, too. Buzzie Bavasi, the team's chief executive officer, composed a telegram to that effect, but in the frenzy of negotiating contracts with the team's pitching aces, Sandy Koufax and Don Drysdale, he neglected to send the wire.

The Mets' name was drawn from the hat, and no organization fared more handsomely with less effort. Almost everything good that befell the club in the next decade stemmed from the strong right arm of the poised, articulate and skillful young athlete.

Seaver made his professional debut with Jacksonville of the Class AAA International League in 1966. He registered a 12-12 record and led the league in games started with 32.

Seaver joined the Mets in 1967 and earned Rookie of the Year honors with his 16 victories and 2.76 earned-run average. In the All-Star Game at Anaheim, he pitched a scoreless inning of relief that capped the National League's 2-1 victory in 15 innings.

By 1969, Seaver was a superstar. He won his first of three Cy Young Awards that year with 25 victories and climaxed the season by splitting two decisions in the Mets' stunning upset of the Baltimore Orioles in the World Series.

Tom, who completed the '69 regular season with 10 straight victories, won his first two decisions in 1970 as well. But the defending World Series champions were playing so-so ball in the early going of '70 when Seaver took the mound at Shea Stadium on April 22 for a weekday afternoon game against San Diego. The Mets needed a lift, and Seaver provided it in a most remarkable manner.

With 14,197 fans in the seats at six-year-old Shea Stadium, Seaver held the Padres to two hits—a home run by Al Ferrara in the second inning and a single by Dave Campbell in the fourth.

In the meantime, the Mets pushed over two runs. A first-inning single by Bud Harrelson and a double by Ken Boswell netted one; a single by Tommie Agee and a triple by Harrelson produced another in the third.

The game moved into the sixth inning. Seaver was pitching effectively, although not spectacularly, while protecting his 2-1 lead. Throwing fastballs, sliders and curves, he had fanned nine batters before Ferrara came

San Diego's Al Ferrara swings and misses, becoming Tom Seaver's 10th straight strikeout victim in a 1970 game in New York.

up with two outs in the sixth. The left fielder looked at a third strike and became victim No. 10.

In the seventh inning, Nate Colbert went down swinging, Campbell and Jerry Morales were called out on strikes and Seaver's strikeout total climbed to 13.

Bob Barton led off the San Diego eighth and took a third strike. Ramon Webster, pinch-hitting for pitcher Mike Corkins, swung at a third strike and Seaver had tied the club strikeout record of 15, set four days earlier by Nolan Ryan. When the information was flashed on the message board, Seaver redoubled his efforts. "I tried for 16," he reported. Ivan Murrell batted next, pinch-hitting for shortstop Jose Arcia. He went down swinging. The Mets' record belonged to Seaver.

By this time, Tom was on an emotional high. He could hardly wait for the start of the ninth inning and almost raced to the mound when the moment arrived. Three fastballs to Van Kelly accounted for strikeout No. 17 and Seaver's eighth in a row. Only four other major leaguers had ever fanned eight consecutive batters: Max Surkont, Johnny Podres, Jim Maloney and Don Wilson.

Clarence Gaston became the ninth successive victim by looking at a third strike. Ferrara was next and now Seaver was deeply concerned. "I was still worried I'd make a mistake and Ferrara might hit it out," he said.

"I knew he was going to give me his heat," Ferrara noted later. "It was his best shot against my best shot."

Seaver's first pitch was a slider on the outside of the plate. He got the call from umpire Harry Wendelstedt. The second delivery was called a ball and the crowd protested mildly. The righthanded batter cut on the third pitch, a fastball, and Seaver stood on the threshold of a most remarkable achievement.

He remembered, though, how Steve Carlton of the St. Louis Cardinals had fanned 19 Mets the previous year, establishing a big-league strikeout record for a nine-inning game, but lost, 4-3, because of two mistakes that Ron Swoboda hit for home runs.

"I might have thrown him (Ferrara) a different pitch," Seaver said. "The pitch probably should have been a slider outside. But I decided to challenge Ferrara. I was close and I wanted it. I just let the fastball rip."

Seaver fired . . . and Ferrara swung and missed. Tom Terrific had struck out a record 10 straight batters and fanned a record-tying 19 overall.

One of the witnesses to the extraordinary performance was Podres. Pitching coach for the San Diego farm system at the time, Podres marveled at Seaver's achievement. "There was no doubt in my mind he would break the record," Johnny said. "He had perfect rhythm. As hard as he was throwing, he was still hitting the spots. If you didn't swing, it was still a strike."

"Actually, he wasn't that strong in the early innings," Mets catcher Jerry Grote said of Seaver. "He just kept building up as the game went on. The cool weather helped and by the end of the game he was stronger than ever."

In the opinion of teammates, Seaver received a big break when Murrell was sent up to bat for

APRIL 22, 1970								
San Diego	ab	r	h	rbi	New York	ab	r	h	rbi
Arcia, ss	3	0	0	0	Agee, cf	3	1	1	0
Murrell, ph	1	0	0	0	Harrelson, ss	3	1	2	1
Roberts, p	0	0	0	0	Boswell, 2b	4	0	1	1
Kelly, 3b	4	0	0	0	Jones, lf	4	0	0	0
Gaston, cf	4	0	0	0	Shamsky, rf	2	0	0	0
Ferrara, lf	3	1	1	1	Swoboda, rf	1	0	0	0
Colbert, 1b	3	0	0	0	Foy, 3b	2	0	0	0
Campbell, 2b	3	0	1	0	Kranepool, 1b	2	0	0	0
Morales, rf	3	0	0	0	Grote, c	3	0	0	0
Barton, c	2	0	0	0	Seaver, p	3	0	0	0
Corkins, p	2	0	0	0					
Webster, ph	1	0	0	0					
Slocum, ss	0	0	0	0					
Totals	29	1	2	1	Totals	27	2	4	2

```
San Diego.............................0  1  0   0  0  0   0  0  0—1
New York..............................1  0  1   0  0  0   0  0  x—2
```

San Diego	IP	H	R	ER	BB	SO
Corkins (L)	7	4	2	2	5	5
Roberts	1	0	0	0	0	2
New York	IP	H	R	ER	BB	SO
Seaver (W)	9	2	1	1	2	19

LOB—San Diego 3, New York 6. 2B—Boswell. 3B—Harrelson. HR—Ferrara. SB—Agee. T—2:14. A—14,197.

Tom Seaver gets a victory kiss from wife Nancy after his record-tying 19-strikeout performance against the Padres.

Arcia. "Arcia doesn't swing hard enough to strike out," Boswell said.

"He was like a machine those last few innings," declared New York first baseman Ed Kranepool. "Whomp, whomp, whomp."

Seaver made 136 pitches in subduing the Padres —81 fastballs, 34 sliders, 19 curves and two change-ups. Of all the pitches, Tom remembered one to Webster in the eighth inning. "It was just an inch or two below the strike zone," he said. "I told Harry (Wendelstedt) that would have been a strike two years ago before they changed the strike zone."

The arbiter replied, "Yeah, so what?"

To which the pitcher responded, "I'm glad to see you're obeying the rules."

Seaver led the league in 1970 with 283 strikeouts and a 2.81 ERA. He remained with the New York club until mid-1977, winning 20 or more games in 1971, 1972 and 1975 and pitching in the 1973 World Series against Oakland. On June 15, 1977, while sporting a 7-3 record, Seaver was traded to Cincinnati for Doug Flynn, Pat Zachry, Dan Norman and Steve Henderson. He went 14-3 for the Reds in the remainder of '77, thus achieving his fifth 20-victory season in the majors.

As a Red, Seaver twice posted the best winning percentage in the league and he pitched a no-hitter against the Cardinals on June 16, 1978.

After the 1982 season, in which he compiled a 5-13 record, Seaver was dealt back to the Mets for three players. This time he remained only one year. In January 1984 he was selected by the Chicago White Sox in the player compensation draft (after the Mets surprisingly left him unprotected), and he won 31 games and lost 22 for the Sox in the next two years. In the same span, he raised his career victory total to 304 and his lifetime strikeout figure to 3,537.

Joseph Durso (right) and Red Foley present Tom Seaver with an enlarged copy of his 19-strikeout box score.

Gibson Makes Series History

Once, when both were retired as players, Joe Torre was asked to evaluate Bob Gibson, whom he had observed fearfully as an opponent and admiringly as a teammate.

"To describe Gibby," began Torre, then manager of the New York Mets, "try pride, intensity, talent, respect and dedication. You need them all."

Towering rage and seething hatred might have been added to those qualities. At least those were the emotions imparted to batters as they stood quaking at home plate.

This malevolence on the part of the St. Louis righthander, when mixed with a blazing fastball and a curveball that, some maintained, broke as much as eight inches, sent 268 National League batters slinking back to the dugout in 1968 muttering imprecations about this Lucifer incarnate.

Robert Gibson, born on November 9, 1935, in an Omaha ghetto, exhibited an unbridled ferocity every time he took the mound. With number 45 emblazoned on his shirt and his long arms encased in Cardinal red down to his wrists, Gibby let no one question his battle plan as he threw with startling marksmanship, frequently close to an adversary's torso. Red Schoendienst, the pitcher's manager for many years, knew Gibson as well as anyone. "I never saw Gibby smile on the days he was scheduled to pitch," Schoendienst said.

Detroit's Norm Cash swings and misses, becoming Bob Gibson's 16th strikeout en route to 17 in the first game of the 1968 World Series.

On the firing line, Gibson was like a sophisticated automaton. Rapidity was his trademark. With almost imperceptible halts, he snatched at the baseball as it was returned by the catcher, peered in for the sign and started his delivery. It behooved the batter to stay alert.

The 6-foot-1, 193-pound Gibson was the youngest of seven children of a widowed mother. He attended Creighton University in his native city, where he starred in baseball and basketball. Signed by the Cardinals in 1957, he progressed through the farm system, with three stops at Omaha (American Association), one at Columbus (South Atlantic) and two at Rochester (International) before joining the Redbirds to stay in 1961.

When Gibson retired 14 years later, nearing his 40th birthday and having spent his entire big-league career with St. Louis, a host of records trailed after his name.

By 1964, the Nebraskan was a World Series pitcher. Appearing in three games, Bob won two and lost one as the Cardinals upset the Yankees in seven games.

Gibby won 20 games in 1965 and 21 in 1966 and was on a similar course in 1967 when he was sidelined on July 15 after a line drive off the bat of Pittsburgh's Roberto Clemente struck the pitcher on the leg. Competitor that he was, Gibson tried to continue pitching that day. Excruciating pain and a buckling ankle convinced him to retire to the clubhouse, where it was discovered he had suffered a fracture. He was out of action until September 7. He won three of four decisions after returning to the rotation, finishing with a 13-7 mark, and then tied a record against the Boston Red Sox by winning three times in a seven-game World Series.

Undoubtedly, the 1968 season was Gibson's finest. In the opinion of some, it may have been the most brilliant year in the history of pitching.

Gibson won 22 games, threw 13 shutouts, pitched 28 complete games and never was relieved during an inning. In 305 innings, he fanned 268 batters and walked only 62, including six intentionally. He allowed just 198 hits, including 11 home runs, and only 38 earned runs. From June 2 through August 19, the Redbird won 15 straight games and in one span of 95 innings permitted only two runs, one on a wild pitch. His earned-run average for the year was 1.12, a National League record for pitchers in at least 200 innings. The old mark of 1.22 was set by Grover Cleveland Alexander of the Philadelphia Phillies in 1915.

As a result of his phenomenal performance, Gibby was the unanimous choice for the Cy Young Award in the National League. He also was acclaimed the league's Most Valuable Player, beating out Pete Rose of Cincinnati.

Gibson's counterpart in the American League was Detroit's Denny McLain, a 24-year-old right-hander whose 31 victories in '68 were the most of any big-league pitcher since 1931 when Lefty Grove of the Philadelphia A's accounted for a like number.

When it was announced that Gibson and McLain would square off in the first game of the World Series on October 2 at St. Louis, folks with a promotional flair immediately labeled it "the pitching duel of the century." McLain, an accomplished organist who entertained at a lounge in a downtown hotel on the eve of the Series, heaped additional fuel on the matchup by declaring publicly that "I don't want only to defeat the Cardinals, I want to humiliate them."

The quotation found a prominent spot on the bulletin board in the Cardinals' clubhouse.

The pitching pairing was not applauded univer-

Cardinals catcher Tim McCarver greets a victorious Bob Gibson.

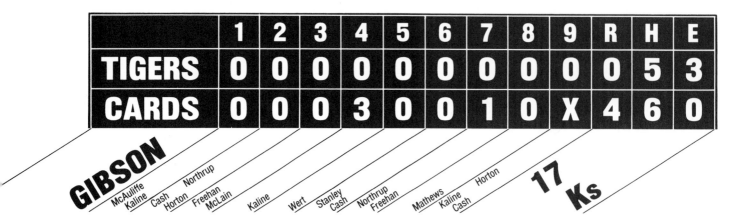

	1	2	3	4	5	6	7	8	9	R	H	E
TIGERS	0	0	0	0	0	0	0	0	0	0	5	3
CARDS	0	0	0	3	0	0	1	0	X	4	6	0

GIBSON

McAuliffe · Kaline · Cash · Northrup · Horton · Freehan · McLain · Kaline · Wert · Stanley · Cash · Northrup · Freehan · Mathews · Kaline · Cash · Horton

17 Ks

Bob Gibson is pictured in various stages of his delivery during his record-setting Game 1 outing in the 1968 World Series.

sally. "If I know Gibson," former Dodger great Sandy Koufax said, "he'll eat 'em alive."

Others suggested that Detroit Manager Mayo Smith would have been more prudent to nominate a lesser pitcher to sacrifice to Gibson and save his ace for the second game.

As it developed, the selection of the Detroit pitcher mattered not a whit. On this summery Wednesday afternoon, the Nebraskan was invincible. He opened the game by striking out Dick McAuliffe. Mickey Stanley slapped a single to left field, but was caught stealing on the first pitch to Al Kaline, who went down swinging.

Norm Cash, Willie Horton and Jim Northrup were strikeout victims in the second inning and when Gibson fanned Bill Freehan and McLain (who bunted foul on a third strike) in the third frame, his statistics showed seven strikeouts on the first trip through the Detroit batting order.

Kaline became victim No. 8 in the fourth inning, and the Cardinals then broke through against McLain. The Tiger pitcher, who had issued only 63 bases on balls in 336 innings during the regular season, opened the home half of the fourth by walking Roger Maris. One out later, Tim McCarver walked on four pitches. Mike Shannon singled home one

Cardinals players offer congratulations to Bob Gibson after the big righthander's shutout victory over the Tigers.

run and when Horton misplayed the ball in left field, McCarver advanced to third and Shannon to second, from where they scored on Julian Javier's single to right field. Lou Brock's 400-foot homer to right-center field produced the last St. Louis run in the seventh inning.

McLain departed after five innings, yielding three hits, three runs (two earned) and three walks. Gibson, meanwhile, continued at full tilt. In the fifth, he made Don Wert his ninth strikeout victim. Stanley (No. 10) and Cash (No. 11) joined the growing list in the sixth, followed by Northrup (No. 12) and Freehan (No. 13) in the seventh and pinch-hitter Eddie Mathews (No. 14) in the eighth.

Stanley collected his second single, and fifth Detroit hit, to open the ninth inning. To those fans acquainted with the Tigers' penchant for coming from behind during the '68 season, the hit could have been interpreted as a harbinger of success. The notion was quickly quashed, however, when Kaline went down swinging for strikeout No. 15.

On the illuminated message board in right-center, spectators were informed that Gibson had equaled a World Series strikeout record set by Sandy Koufax of the Dodgers in 1963 against the New York Yan-

kees.

Gibson was unaware of what was transpiring behind his back. "Throw me the damn ball," he demanded, snarling at McCarver. Tim hesitated, then gestured with his mitt toward center field. Reluctantly, Gibson stole a peek before he understood why he was being given a standing ovation. When the roar showed no sign of subsiding, he pawed the dirt and tipped his hat. "I hate such things," he said afterward.

Cash followed Kaline into the batter's box. His luck was no better. After running the count to 2 and 2 and fouling off a couple of pitches, Norm cut and missed. No. 16. Now the record belonged to Gibson exclusively.

With Stanley still anchored at first base, Horton took his stance. The producer of 36 homers in '68, Horton built the count to 2 and 2 and, like Cash, fouled off several pitches. Gibby's last pitch of the game, a slider, was a wicked breaking ball that left the batter flinching slightly. Horton watched helplessly as the ball streaked toward him, dipped abruptly and smacked into McCarver's glove, which was held on the inside corner of the plate.

Umpire Tom Gorman let Horton know that he

Bob Gibson (right) and Lou Brock, Game 1 heroes.

had been had. The game was over. With his 141 pitches, 91 of them fastballs, Gibson had fanned Kaline and Cash three times each, Horton, Northrup and Freehan twice, and McAuliffe, Stanley, Wert, McLain and Mathews once.

"I've never seen such overpowering pitching," Kaline said of the Tiger tamer.

"I was awed," McAuliffe exclaimed. Had he ever seen anyone to compare with Gibson? "He stands by himself," replied the second baseman.

Shannon, who played third base for the Cardinals without a fielding chance, called Gibson's performance "frightening." Years later, he said, "I've never seen major league hitters overmatched that way. It was like watching a major league pitcher against Little League batters."

McCarver also had vivid recollections of the game. When he was a broadcaster for the Phillies, the former catcher remarked, "I can still see that last pitch and I bet Willie Horton still thinks the ball hit him."

Aside from the 17 strikeouts, Gibson's proficiency was reflected in the box score that showed only two assists for the Cardinals. One was credited to McCarver, on his first-inning throw that caught Stanley trying to steal. The other went to Orlando Cepeda, who tossed to Gibson covering first base after fielding pinch-hitter Tom Matchick's grounder in the sixth inning.

Gibson also pitched Game 4 of the Series at Detroit on October 6. After warming up, he was forced to take a 35-minute rest because of rain. A 74-minute rain interruption in the third inning sent the pitcher to the bench again and required a third warmup. Nevertheless, he won the game, 10-1, aided by his own homer. It was his seventh consecutive

World Series victory, a record.

When he attempted to make it eight straight in the finale, Gibson bowed, 4-1. He went the distance in Game 7, but was betrayed by a misplay in the outfield that led to three seventh-inning runs.

Gibson won 20 games in 1969 and tied for the league lead with 23 victories in 1970. He hurled his only no-hitter on August 14, 1971, when he beat the Pirates, 11-0. He closed out his career in 1975 with 251 victories and 3,117 strikeouts. He tried his hand briefly as a network television broadcaster, later served as a pitching coach for the Mets and Atlanta Braves and then turned to radio work.

Gibby was elected to the Hall of Fame in 1981.

OCTOBER 2, 1968

Detroit	ab	r	h	rbi	St. Louis	ab	r	h	rbi
McAuliffe, 2b	4	0	1	0	Brock, lf	4	1	1	1
Stanley, ss	4	0	2	0	Flood, cf	4	0	1	0
Kaline, rf	4	0	1	0	Maris, rf	3	1	0	0
Cash, 1b	4	0	0	0	Cepeda, 1b	4	0	0	0
Horton, lf	4	0	0	0	McCarver, c	3	1	1	0
Northrup, cf	3	0	0	0	Shannon, 3b	4	1	2	1
Freehan, c	2	0	0	0	Javier, 2b	3	0	1	2
Wert, 3b	2	0	1	0	Maxvill, ss	2	0	0	0
Mathews, ph	1	0	0	0	Gibson, p	2	0	0	0
Tracewski, 3b	0	0	0	0					
McLain, p	1	0	0	0					
Matchick, ph	1	0	0	0					
Dobson, p	0	0	0	0					
Brown, ph	1	0	0	0					
McMahon, p	0	0	0	0					
Totals	31	0	5	0	Totals	29	4	6	4

Detroit	0	0	0	0	0	0	0	0	0—0
St. Louis	0	0	0	3	0	0	1	0	x—4

Detroit	IP	H	R	ER	BB	SO
McLain (L)	5	3	3	2	3	3
Dobson	2	2	1	1	1	0
McMahon	1	1	0	0	0	0
St. Louis	IP	H	R	ER	BB	SO
Gibson (W)	9	5	0	0	1	17

E—Cash, Horton, Freehan. LOB—Detroit 5, St. Louis 6. 2B—Kaline. 3B—McCarver. HR—Brock. SB—Brock, Javier, Flood. SH—Gibson. T—2:29. A—54,692.

A Fatal Day In New York

Life was at its crest for the occupants of an automobile as it rolled toward the Cleveland railroad terminal on Sunday evening, August 15, 1920.

One of the passengers was Raymond Johnson Chapman, the brilliant shortstop of the Indians. A few hours earlier, Cleveland had shut out the St. Louis Browns, 5-0, to retain its grip on first place in the American League.

The son of an Illinois coal miner and himself familiar with the back-breaking toil underground, Chapman was a nine-year major league veteran. He was 29 years old, hitting above .300 and fielding as spectacularly as ever. What more could anyone ask?

By his side was his wife of a year. The former Kathleen Daly, the daughter of a utility company executive, was an expectant mother.

The two other members of the party were Jack Graney, a Cleveland outfielder and Chapman's roommate on the road, and Kathleen's brother, Dan.

Fond farewells were exchanged at the depot. This was to be Chapman's last extended absence from his wife. He planned to retire, enter business in Cleveland and settle down in the luxury home now under construction as a wedding gift from his father-in-law.

With spirits high, Chapman boarded a train bound for New York and the start of the Indians' final tour of the Eastern cities.

Ray was a particular favorite among Cleveland players. Catcher Steve O'Neill once said of him: "I don't think I ever knew a ball player with more likable or admirable qualities. He was lighthearted, loved to sing, wore the finest clothes, was a good dancer and had a grand sense of humor. On top of all that, he was a brilliant ball player, the best shortstop in the business."

After checking into their New York hotel, the Cleveland players hopped on the elevated train for their ride to the Polo Grounds, where they were scheduled to meet the Yankees. En route, Chappie entertained the players with his rich tenor voice, stopping only long enough to quip: "(Carl) Mays is pitching for the Yankees today, so I'll do the fielding and you fellows do the hitting."

Although Chapman had batted .300 on occasion,

he was better known for his glove. Several times he led league shortstops in putouts and once in assists. He also was an adept bunter. In 1917, Ray set a record with 67 sacrifices and in 1919 he sacrificed four times in one game.

Mays, who did not hold special appeal for Chappie, was a 26-year-old righthander who, like Ray, was a native of Kentucky. He entered the majors in 1915 and, before his acquisition by New York in July 1919, had pitched for the Red Sox. Mays twice posted 20 victories in a season for Boston, and he climaxed the 1918 campaign by defeating the Chicago Cubs twice in Boston's triumphant World Series.

In 1920, Mays would win 26 games, baffling batters with his unorthodox style in which he released the ball from the vicinity of his shoetops.

A light fog hung over New York when Mays and the Indians' Stanley Coveleski started to warm up on August 16. By the fifth inning, a light drizzle was falling and the Indians—on the way to a 4-3 victory—were in control, 3-0, with one run coming on a homer by O'Neill.

Chapman, hitless in one official at-bat, led off the fifth inning. As was his custom, the righthanded batter crowded the plate, with his head draped into the strike zone. Because of his extreme speed—he once circled the bases in 14 seconds during a field day in Boston—pitchers liked to work Chapman inside. Otherwise, he would push a bunt down the base line for a sure hit.

"If he had been a lefthanded batter," Mays once remarked, "he would have dragged pitchers to desperation."

Chapman worked the count to 1 and 1. "My next pitch," Mays related, "was to have been a low fastball in the strike zone. But just as my arm reached the farthest point of my backswing, I saw Ray shift his back foot into the position he took for a running bunt, a push bunt. So, at the last split second before hurling the ball, I changed to a high and tight strike pitch."

What ensued was described by a press-box eyewitness.

"Chapman seemed rooted to the spot," wrote Joe Vila of the New York Sun. "He made no move either with his head or feet to get out of the way and the ball, pitched with all of Mays' strength, struck him squarely on the left temple. The impact sounded as if the ball had hit the bat, but as it rolled back toward Mays, who threw it to Pipp (first baseman Wally Pipp), Chapman crumpled up and slowly went down on his knees, never uttering a sound, and in that position he was unconscious."

Players from both teams rushed to Chapman's side. Umpire Tom Connolly asked that a physician be called from the stands. After first-aid treatment, Chapman was lifted to his feet and, with blood trickling from his ears, started to walk toward the clubhouse in center field. In the middle of the diamond, however, he collapsed again and had to be carried the rest of the way.

While the game went on (Harry Lunte took over for Chapman), an ambulance was summoned to the Polo Grounds. As he was being placed on a stretcher, Chapman mumbled, "Tell Kate I'm all right." And the stricken player asked for—and received—a diamond ring, a gift from his wife. The ring had been in custody of the team trainer.

At St. Lawrence Hospital, Chapman underwent X-ray examinations that revealed a depressed fracture of the skull 3½ inches long. In the operation, which began at 12:29 a.m. Tuesday, surgeons removed a piece of skull about 1½ inches square and found that the brain had been so severely damaged that blood clots had formed.

After the operation, which was completed at 1:44 a.m., Chapman breathed more easily and teammates, who had maintained an all-night vigil, returned to the hotel confident that the worst was over. When they awoke, they learned that the popular shortstop had died at 4:40 a.m.

For Mays, the tragedy revived memories of a spring exhibition game in which his teammate, Chick Fewster, was struck on the head by a pitch thrown by Brooklyn's Jeff Pfeffer. Like Chapman, Fewster suffered a depressed fracture.

But unlike Chapman, Fewster was kept still after being beaned. And Fewster was carefully hoisted aboard a refrigerated freight car and rushed by train to the hospital, where a metal plate was inserted in his head. He returned to action late in the season and remained in the majors until 1927.

"I firmly believe," Mays said, "that if they had done for Chapman what was done for Fewster, Ray would have recovered."

Lefty O'Doul, a Mays teammate, also was critical of the way the Chapman situation was handled. He noted that while Fewster was not moved, Chapman "was permitted to walk" from home plate toward the center-field clubhouse. Besides the possible harmful effects of Chapman's attempted walk, as

In 1920, Cleveland's Ray Chapman became the only player in major league history to die of injuries incurred when struck by a pitch.

pointed out by O'Doul, Mays also said there was laxity in getting the Cleveland player to the hospital (although newspaper accounts didn't indicate any such delay).

Mrs. Chapman, who had been apprised of the accident immediately, arrived with her brother at 10 a.m. Tuesday, a little more than five hours after her husband's death. She was met at the station by a priest, a friend of the family, who had rushed from Philadelphia on learning of the tragedy. She was escorted to a hotel where, learning the sad news, she collapsed.

That evening, as the body was borne through Grand Central Station, hundreds of fans stood silently with bared heads in tribute to the deceased player. Accompanying the widow and her brother were Tris Speaker and Joe Wood of the Indians.

When the funeral car arrived in Cleveland, all flags were flying at half-staff and citizens were in profound mourning. The funeral service on Friday was held in St. John's Cathedral, the huge midtown edifice with accommodations for 2,000 persons. Even so, it was inadequate. An estimated 3,000 stood outside the church, blocking traffic in all directions and unable to hear the chancellor of the diocese extoll Chapman as a man and a player.

One of the floral tributes to Chapman measured nine feet by six feet and contained more than 20,000 flowers. It was purchased through a fund raised by a local newspaper at 10 cents a person.

Duffy Lewis, Ernie Shore and Wally Pipp represented the Yankees at the funeral. With two exceptions, all of the Indians attended. The absentees were Speaker, the playing manager, and Graney. Their grief was too profound for them to stand the extra burden.

The tragedy aroused instant indignation among players of other clubs. Members of the league's Boston, Detroit and St. Louis teams circulated a petition demanding that Mays be barred from baseball. The movement foundered, however, when more rational individuals interceded.

Mays learned of Chapman's death about the same time Mrs. Chapman did when a front-office official of the Yankees arrived at the pitcher's hotel apartment. Later, Mays declined the offer of a police guard, little dreaming of the flood of crank calls

Yankee righthander Carl Mays threw the pitch that resulted in Ray Chapman's death.

Carl Mays looks through a baseball scrapbook with his wife many years after his fateful encounter with Ray Chapman.

and letters that would inundate him. At the suggestion of friends on the police force, Mays visited the district attorney's office, where he gave his version of the accident. He was absolved of any blame, but thoughtless fans continued to remind him of his role in the only fatal beaning in major league history.

The Indians overcame the tragedy and, sparked in part by Chapman's eventual replacement, Joe Sewell (brought up from New Orleans), went on to win the pennant and the World Series.

Mays remained with the Yankees through 1923 and then was sold to the Cincinnati Reds, for whom he compiled a 20-9 record in 1924. He also pitched for the Giants, winning seven games and losing two in 1929, before drifting into the minors for the final two seasons of his career.

For a number of years, Mays engaged in ranching in Oregon. He abandoned that vocation following a heart attack and devoted his latter years to coaching young players and scouting the Northwest for, ironically, the Cleveland Indians.

He died in El Cajon, Calif., on April 4, 1971, at age 77.

For Kathleen Daly Chapman, the end was as tragic as that of her husband. After giving birth to a daughter, Rae-Marie, in 1921—the child lived only

eight years—Mrs. Chapman married a California oilman. She was living in Los Angeles when she suffered a nervous breakdown. She died on April 20, 1928, at age 34. According to the coroner, she died from "a self-administered poisonous acid." Like her first husband, she was buried in Lakeview Cemetery, Cleveland.

AUGUST 16, 1920

Cleveland	ab	r	h	rbi	New York	ab	r	h	rbi
Jamieson, lf	5	0	2	0	Ward, 3b	4	0	0	0
Chapman, ss	1	0	0	0	Peckinpaugh, ss	4	0	0	0
Lunte, pr-ss	1	0	0	0	Ruth, rf	4	1	1	0
Speaker, cf	4	1	0	0	Pratt, 2b	3	1	1	0
Smith, rf	4	0	0	0	Lewis, lf	4	0	0	0
Gardner, 3b	3	1	1	0	Pipp, 1b	3	0	0	0
O'Neill, c	4	2	3	2	Bodie, cf	4	1	2	2
Johnston, 1b	4	0	1	0	Ruel, c	3	0	2	1
Wambsganss, 2b	4	0	0	0	Mays, p	2	0	0	0
Coveleski, p	3	0	0	1	Vick, ph	1	0	1	0
					Thormahlen, p	0	0	0	0
					O'Doul, ph	1	0	0	0
Totals	33	4	7	3	Totals	33	3	7	3

```
Cleveland .............................0  1  0  2  1  0    0  0—4
New York...............................0  0  0  0  0  0    0  0  3—3
```

Cleveland	IP	H	R	ER	BB	SO
Coveleski (W)	9	7	3	3	2	4

New York	IP	H	R	ER	BB	SO
Mays (L)	8	7	4	2	1	3
Thormahlen	1	0	0	0	0	0

E—Ward, Ruel. DP—New York 1. LOB—Cleveland 6, New York 6. 2B—Bodie. HR—O'Neill. SH—Chapman, Ruel, Coveleski. HBP—By Mays (Chapman). T—1:55.

Jim Bottomley Drives In 12 Runs

Manager Wilbert Robinson shifted uneasily in the Brooklyn dugout, sorely disturbed by St. Louis base-hits that were rattling around Ebbets Field before a single batter was retired in the first inning.

Up to this moment, the season of 1924 had been a surprise to many, a shocker to others because the Robins—named for the manager—had not been expected to figure in the pennant race. On paper, they had not been improved substantially over the team that finished sixth in 1923, yet here they were two weeks before the close of the season within striking distance of first place.

A victory over the Cardinals on this Tuesday afternoon, September 16 would lift the Robins within one-half game of the first-place New York Giants. It was not inconceivable that they might pull out the pennant, as they had done in 1916 and 1920.

Uncle Robbie's pitching choice to nudge the Robins a bit closer to the top was Welton Claude (Rube) Ehrhardt, a 29-year-old rookie who boasted a modest five-game winning streak. True, the righthander was not to be confused with Dazzy Vance and Burleigh Grimes, the team's pitching stars, but neither was he to be discounted.

His mound opponent was Willie Sherdel, a diminutive lefthander who was on his way to an 8-9 record. With that mark, Sherdel was one of the more effective members of a Cardinals staff that numbered only one 10-game winner, Allan Sothoron.

Whatever mastery Ehrhardt exhibited in his five previous decisions was absent on this day in Flatbush. He started by issuing a base on balls to Heinie Mueller, then yielded an infield single to Taylor Douthit. Rogers Hornsby's safe bunt, one of 227 hits that the Rajah registered in a season during which he batted .424, loaded the bases.

Jim Bottomley, the 24-year-old first baseman whose perpetual smile belied the evil in his bat, was next. Sunny Jim rapped a single, driving in two runs, and Chick Hafey's triple added another pair.

Uncle Robbie had seen enough. Down four runs and with a possible pennant riding on every pitch, he waved Ehrhardt to the showers and beckoned John (Bonnie) Hollingsworth, another righthander, who retired the Redbirds in the first without further scoring.

Hollingsworth surrendered a fifth St. Louis run in the second inning, however, on two walks and Bottomley's double.

The Robins retrieved one of the runs in the last of the second, but the hopes of the 8,000 spectators were dashed further in the fourth when the Cardinals erupted for four more runs. The assault was launched by Sherdel's double. When Mueller drew a walk, his second, Hollingsworth was excused. He was replaced by another righthander, Art Decatur. Douthit greeted the third Brooklyn pitcher with a sacrifice, which forced Robinson into a critical decision. With first base open, the 60-year-old skipper could (1) pitch to Hornsby or (2) walk the Rajah intentionally and take his chances with Bottomley.

Robinson chose the second option, probably on the belief that Sunny Jim already had his quota of RBIs for the game. Bottomley showed him the error of his ways, however, by smacking a grand slam over the right-field wall, giving the Cardinals a 9-1 lead. Bottomley now had seven runs batted in.

As though the complexion of the game were not sufficient cause for concern, Robinson now faced another growing worry. For 32 years he had cherished the memory of his performance on June 10, 1892. As a member of the hard-bitten Baltimore Orioles of the National League, the stocky catcher had rapped seven hits in seven at-bats and driven in 11 runs, both major league records, against St. Louis. Now, a member of the latter-day Cards was seriously threatening his RBI mark.

Decatur still was on the mound when St. Louis broke loose again in the sixth inning. A walk to Douthit ignited another four-run spurt and one out later Bottomley whacked another home run into Bedford Avenue. Sunny Jim was within two of Robbie's all-time RBI record.

A single by Hafey, a triple by Mike Gonzalez and a single by Jimmy Cooney produced two more runs before Decatur retired the side.

Gomer (Tex) Wilson, a lefthander appearing in his second and last major league game, was pitching in the seventh when Bottomley singled home two runs, raising his RBI total for the game to 11.

Sunny Jim was active again in the ninth when the Cards scored their 17th run. After Hornsby tripled off righthander Jim Roberts, Bottomley singled him

Jim Bottomley was a 24-year-old first baseman when he made a lasting imprint on baseball history.

home to cap a 6-for-6 day (the first of two such performances he had in the majors). Although Wilbert Robinson's 7-for-7 record was secure, his RBI mark was reduced to runner-up status.

On the day after his record-setting feat, Bottomley stopped by the Brooklyn dugout to tap Robinson's bountiful supply of chewing tobacco as he had done in times past.

"You'll get no more chews from me," snorted Uncle Robbie, whose Robins went on to finish the season a game and a half behind the Giants. "You chased me right out of the record book. Get outta here."

James Leroy Bottomley was in his second full big-league season when he established his record. He was born in Oglesby, Ill., on April 23, 1900, and, as a child, moved with his parents to the coal-mining town of Nokomis, Ill.

After quitting school at age 16, he clerked in a grocery store, drove a truck and worked for the New York Central Railroad. The 6-foot, 175-pounder was a blacksmith's helper working above ground for the Mason Coal Co. when his boss walked through the shop door one afternoon and announced, "We'll shut down for the day. There's been two men killed down in the mine shaft. One of them was a young fellow."

Fearful of what the superintendent's answer would be, Jim nevertheless asked, "Was it my brother?"

"Yes," was the reply. "There must have been 50 tons of rock that fell from the roof and killed him and his buddy."

It was to have been the younger Bottomley's last day as a miner. He was scheduled to leave for college the following day.

Sunny Jim's baseball talents surfaced early. At 12, he played with adults, eventually graduating to a team that paid him $5 a game. On Labor Day of 1919, Bottomley blasted two homers and three triples for the Witt, Ill., semipro team and found his course irrevocably altered.

Among the spectators was an off-duty St. Louis policeman known only as "Mr. King." On his return home, King notified Branch Rickey of the teen-age phenom. The Cardinals' manager dispatched the club's chief—and only—scout, Charles Barrett, to check out the young first baseman, who was signed to play for the Sioux City (Western) team in 1920 for $150 a month.

After six games—and one hit in 14 at-bats—Bottomley was released by Sioux City. "The manager said I was too dumb for his team," related Sunny Jim. Without awaiting instructions from St. Louis, Bottomley headed for Mitchell, S.D., whose team, he had heard, was seeking a first baseman.

Bottomley was virtually forgotten by Cardinal brass until it was discovered that he was batting

Jim Bottomley's Big Game

1st inning—single, 2 RBIs
2nd inning—double, 1 RBI
4th inning—grand slam, 4 RBIs
6th inning—home run, 2 RBIs
7th inning—single, 2 RBIs
9th inning—single, 1 RBI

over .300 in the South Dakota State League. Not unexpectedly, Barrett arrived and declared, "This is a helluva league for you to be playing in. I'm going to send you to a good league next year."

The "good league" was the Texas League, where Bottomley encountered a series of mishaps. He suffered injuries to his leg, ankle and hip while sliding and batted only .227 in 130 games. "Nobody made a single suggestion about my hitting or fielding," Bottomley reported, "and the manager told the Cardinals that he would not take me back under any circumstances."

Jim nevertheless advanced to Syracuse of the International League in 1922 and was batting .348 after 119 games when he was promoted to the Cardinals.

At age 22, Bottomley was the prototype of a greenhorn. Arriving at Union Station in St. Louis, he stepped into a cab and asked to be taken to Sportsman's Park. The driver spotted Jim as a rustic and took a circuitous route before depositing him at the club office. The fare was $5.10, much more than if Jim had found a responsible cabbie.

Bottomley had given other evidence of his vernal nature three years earlier, when he first tried out with the Cardinals. Examining the team bats, each bearing the name of its owner, Jim found a thin-handled, lightweight stick. "Hey," he called out, "who's this guy named Fungo?"

Word of the blooper circulated when Bottomley reached the majors, and for years bench jockeys around the league took delight in reminding him of the incident.

In 1925 and 1926, Bottomley led the National League in doubles. In '26, when the Cardinals captured their first pennant, he topped the league in runs batted in with 120. He climaxed the season with 10 hits and a .345 batting average in St. Louis' spectacular World Series conquest of the Yankees.

A .325 batting average, 31 home runs (which tied Hack Wilson for the N.L. lead) and league-high figures in triples (20) and RBIs (136) earned Most Valuable Player honors for Sunny Jim in 1928. He also appeared in the World Series of 1928, 1930 and 1931.

At the close of each season bachelor Jim returned to his parents' home in Nokomis, where he spent months hunting and socializing with old cronies. In recognition of their famous neighbor, the town fathers erected a sign at the city limits proclaiming: "Nokomis, Home of Jim Bottomley."

After batting .296 in 1932, Bottomley was traded to Cincinnati to give James (Rip) Collins, another product of the Cardinals' far-flung farm system, the regular first-base job.

The coal miner's son spent three years in a Reds uniform, batting .284 one season and driving home 83 runs in another. When Larry MacPhail was in-

formed that Bottomley was considering retirement, the general manager rasped, "He can't afford to retire."

The comment was relayed to Bottomley, who had invested his earnings, which included four World Series checks, wisely. "I'll bet him $50,000 I can," retorted Sunny Jim, exuding all the confidence of a Wall Street banker.

The aging first baseman returned to St. Louis in 1936 as a member of the American League's Browns. At 36, he still was able to bat .298 in 140 games and drive in 95 runs for St. Louis, managed by Jim's old Cardinal buddy, Rogers Hornsby.

Released after the 1937 campaign, in which he managed the Browns for the last half of the season, Bottomley managed Syracuse the next year. Having married in 1933, Bottomley retired to his 120-acre farm near Sullivan, Mo., in 1939.

In 1957, he scouted for the Cubs. In the middle of the year, when the Cubs' Appalachian League farm club at Pulaski needed a manager, Sunny Jim stepped in. A heart attack forced him to relinquish the reins after two games.

Bottomley and his wife were in St. Louis on a Christmas gift-buying trip on December 11, 1959, when he suffered a fatal heart attack while sitting in his car on a downtown parking lot. Fifteen years later, the man who compiled a .310 lifetime batting average in the majors—and drove in 111 or more runs in six consecutive seasons—was named to the Hall of Fame.

SEPTEMBER 16, 1924									
St. Louis	ab	r	h	rbi	Brooklyn	ab	r	h	rbi
Mueller, rf-1b	3	3	2	1	High, 2b	4	0	2	0
Douthit, cf	3	3	1	0	Mitchell, ss	4	0	1	1
Hornsby, 2b	4	2	2	0	Wheat, lf	4	0	0	0
Blades, 2b	0	1	0	0	Fournier, 1b	2	1	0	0
Bottomley, 1b	6	3	6	12	Loftus, 1b	1	0	1	0
Smith, rf	0	0	0	0	Brown, cf	4	0	1	0
Hafey, lf	6	1	2	2	Stock, 3b	3	1	1	0
Gonzalez, c	4	1	1	1	Griffith, rf	2	0	0	0
Clemons, c	2	0	0	0	DeBerry, c	3	0	1	1
Toporcer, 3b	1	0	0	0	Ehrhardt, p	0	0	0	0
Cooney, 3b	4	0	1	1	Hollingsworth, p	1	0	0	0
Thevenow, ss	5	0	0	0	Decatur, p	0	0	0	0
Sherdel, p	4	3	3	0	Johnston, ph	1	0	1	0
Rhem, p	0	0	0	0	Wilson, p	0	0	0	0
					Taylor, ph	1	1	1	0
					Roberts, p	0	0	0	0
					Hargreaves, ph	1	0	0	0
Totals	42	17	18	17	Totals	31	3	9	2

St. Louis	4	1	0	4	0	4	2	1	1—17
Brooklyn	0	1	0	0	0	0	0	1	1— 3

St. Louis	IP	H	R	ER	BB	SO
Sherdel (W)	8	8	2	2	2	1
Rhem	1	1	1	0	3	0

Brooklyn	IP	H	R	ER	BB	SO
Ehrhardt (L)	0	4	4	4	1	0
Hollingsworth	3	2	3	3	3	2
Decatur	3	5	6	5	2	0
Wilson	2	4	3	3	0	1
Roberts	1	2	1	1	0	0

E—Fournier. DP—St. Louis 3. LOB—St. Louis 7, Brooklyn 6. 2B —Bottomley, Sherdel. 3B—Mueller, Hornsby, Hafey, Gonzalez. HR —Bottomley 2. SB—Douthit, Cooney. SH—Douthit 2, Hornsby. WP —Decatur, Rhem. PB—Clemons. T—1:55.

192

Reggie Puts On a Show

It had been a most distressful year for Reggie Jackson, a season of valleys broad and deep with only an occasional peak to disturb the emotional landscape.

Jackson, who had slugged 254 home runs in eight-plus seasons with the A's and 27 in one year

with the Orioles, was a member of the Yankees in 1977. Granted his free agency in November 1976, he shopped his talents widely for a couple of weeks. His most lucrative offer was tendered by the Montreal Expos, but Jackson felt he should play in the United States. And where better than in New York,

the media capital of the world where his transcendent talents could be exploited to the fullest?

On November 29, 1976, as a nation watched through the wonders of countless television replays, Reginald Martinez Jackson signed a Yankee contract that paid him $2.96 million over five years. Few people doubted that the Yankees, with Reggie on their roster, would soon capture the World Series championship that had been denied them in '76 by the Reds' four-game sweep.

Yankees Owner George Steinbrenner regarded the acquisition of Jackson as a personal triumph. Manager Billy Martin and some of Reggie's new teammates didn't share the club owner's excitement.

Martin, according to one of the team's coaches,

resented Jackson because of the large amount of attention he was certain to divert from the skipper, who coveted the spotlight.

Among the players, team captain Thurman Munson found Reggie's presence distasteful, particularly since it meant that the catcher was no longer the team's highest-paid player. Others who were inclined to monosyllabic interviews saw only embarrassment in the presence of the voluble son of a Philadelphia tailor.

An awkward situation greeted Jackson when he reported for spring training at Fort Lauderdale, Fla., in March 1977. A definite chill was in the air, totally unrelated to the temperature on the east coast of Florida. To many, Reggie was an intruder unacquainted with Yankee tradition that had been building for more than 50 years. He was not invited to join in the earthy clubhouse banter. When he engaged in workouts or played in exhibition games, bleacherites pelted him with all manner of opprobrium.

Added to Reggie's woes was an interview he granted reluctantly to a writer for a national sports monthly. When the article appeared, Jackson was horrified to read the quotations attributed to him. He said he had been misquoted flagrantly, charging that the writer made him appear to be a super egocentric who viewed his new teammates from an Olympian pedestal. Veteran New York players also read the article, and their chill turned to ice.

As Reggie chattered on, the Yankees seethed until pitcher Jim (Catfish) Hunter spoke up. The pitcher and outfielder had starred on three straight World Series title teams at Oakland. Hunter knew Jackson well and suggested that the Yanks treat the outfielder's blatherings just as the A's had done—ignore them.

Relations between Jackson and Martin were strained well into the season. A cleanup hitter most of his career, Reggie batted as low as sixth in the Martin system. Constant shifts in the batting order were considered degrading by Reggie; Billy, meanwhile, looked upon them as his managerial prerogative.

The smoldering resentment between the two erupted into open warfare at Boston during a nationally televised game in June. The contest was in the middle innings when a blooper to right field by Jim Rice fell in front of Jackson for a double. As cameras recorded every move, Martin strolled to the mound and changed pitchers. Then he ordered Paul Blair to replace Jackson.

Yankees slugger Reggie Jackson, Dodgers catcher Steve Yeager and umpire John McSherry watch the flight of one of Jackson's three Game 6 home runs.

Reggie Jackson is greeted at the plate by teammate Chris Chambliss (left)
after his third home run of the game.

Reggie Jackson homer victims Burt Hooton (left), Elias Sosa (center) and Charlie Hough.

In consuming rage, Jackson ran to the dugout, laid down his glove and sunglasses and accosted Martin. Angry shouts were exchanged, each man accusing the other of trying to show him up. The 205-pound player was eager to swap punches with the 170-pound manager, but teammates kept them apart.

The next day, the principals were summoned to the hotel room of Gabe Paul, where the club executive negotiated an armistice. It was a shallow peace at best and for many weeks the two continued on their separate ways.

The first signs of a thaw in the Jackson-Martin relations occurred on August 10 when Billy penciled Reggie's name in the fourth spot of the batting order. Jackson was overjoyed. From that date through September 28, when the Yankees clinched a tie for the American League East title, Reggie drove in 48 runs and clouted 13 homers. The Yanks won 39 of 49 games in that span.

One of the home runs was a dramatic wallop on September 14 when the Yanks, leading second-place Boston by 2½ games, played the Red Sox at Yankee Stadium. For 8½ innings, New York's Ed Figueroa and Boston's Reggie Cleveland matched pitch for pitch. It was a scoreless deadlock when Munson and Jackson stood beside each other in the on-deck circle as Cleveland threw his preliminary pitches in the ninth.

Munson, whose antagonism toward Jackson had moderated in the intervening months, turned to Reggie. "I'll single through shortstop," the catcher said, "then you drive me in."

"It's a deal," said Reggie, who forthwith watched his teammate rap a base hit between the third baseman and shortstop. The count on Jackson went to 3 and 2. Cleveland fired a fastball. It was low, very

likely out of the strike zone, but Reggie liked his chances. A purposeful cut sent the ball streaking on its way. It disappeared into the seats in right-center field, approximately 430 feet away. "I never hit a ball harder," Jackson declared later.

When Reggie arrived at the plate, Munson was waiting. "You done good," he shouted above the crowd's roar.

"Just following orders," Jackson countered.

The game-winning smash went far toward bringing Jackson into the inner circle of the clubhouse, although his relations with Martin continued sullen.

When the race ended and the Yankees prepared to meet the Kansas City Royals in the A.L. Championship Series, statistics showed that Jackson had batted .286 with 32 home runs, 39 doubles and 110 runs batted in. He had performed precisely as Steinbrenner had predicted the previous November when he signed Reggie.

But one more embarrassment remained. It happened in the final game of the playoffs at Royals Stadium. The outfielder collected only one hit in 14 at-bats in the first four contests, yet his sterling performance in the closing weeks of the season left him unprepared for the shock that awaited him when he arrived at the park for Game 5.

Catcher Fran Healy, who understood Reggie better than the rest, informed him that Blair was to start in right field. For seven innings, the disconsolate slugger squirmed in his unaccustomed bench role and watched Paul Splittorff hold the Yanks to one run while the Royals scored three times. In the eighth, however, Jackson was called upon as a pinch-hitter and delivered a run-scoring single off reliever Doug Bird that brought the Yankees within 3-2.

Tommy Lasorda, whose Dodgers were victimized by Reggie Jackson's three-
home run performance, enjoys a locker-room chat with the Yankee slugger.

Three more runs in the ninth gave New York a
5-3 victory and the American League pennant.

After four games of the World Series, the Yankees led the Dodgers three games to one. In 13 trips
to the plate, Reggie had four hits, including a home
run and a double. The Dodgers captured Game 5 at
Dodger Stadium, 10-4, with Jackson contributing a
home run on his final at-bat in a losing cause.

The teams resumed the Series at Yankee Stadium
on October 18. It was a 51-degree evening, with
56,407 howling partisans in the south Bronx ball
park. Jackson, ever the showman, gave the fans ex-

actly what they came for.

In batting practice, he drilled baseballs to distant
sectors. He estimated 20 balls had sailed out of the
playing field. "Save some of those for the game,"
Yankees second baseman Willie Randolph pleaded.

"There are more where those came from," Jackson shot back.

Burt Hooton, the righthander who had handcuffed the Yanks on five hits in Game 2, was Los
Angeles Manager Tom Lasorda's choice to square
the Series.

This time, however, he was no mystery to the

Yanks—or to Reggie Jackson.

On his first at-bat, Reggie never moved the bat from his shoulder, walking on four pitches.

Munson opened the Yanks' fourth inning with a single and Jackson, expecting high and inside pitches—which was the way all pitchers worked on him—was surprised when the first delivery came in high and across the heart of the plate. With New York trailing, 3-2, Jackson jumped on the pitch.

The crack of the bat informed the multitude that the man wearing number 44 had made solid contact. There was only one question in Reggie's mind: Would the ball stay up long enough to clear the barrier in right field? It did. The Yankees now led, 4-3, and Jackson had his second home run on as many swings, dating to his last at-bat in the previous game. "Mr. October" was gradually taking shape.

When Jackson batted again in the fifth inning, New York was ahead, 5-3, one Yankee was on base and Elias Sosa was in his second inning of work for the Dodgers. The righthander's first offering was a fastball. Again, the lefthanded swinger took a cut. Once more the crash of bat on ball portended good fortune for the home team.

It was a line drive toward right field. Reggie feared the ball might dip before it found the mark. Again his worries were groundless. His second home run of the game and third homer on as many consecutive swings raised the Yanks' lead to 7-3. What more could the fans, or his teammates—or Billy Martin—expect from this superlative thespian? A few more innings would tell.

Jackson led off the last half of the eighth, the final at-bat of the year for New York. Still another pitcher was on the mound for the Dodgers. He was Charlie Hough, a knuckleballer who had saved 22 games for the National League champions. Jackson was not intimidated by the butterfly pitch. Years before, while playing winter ball in the Caribbean, he had been taught how to hit the unpredictable pitch by his manager, Frank Robinson.

Hough's initial pitch was a knuckler—that failed to break. Jackson took another savage cut and the ball rocketed into the center-field seats, more than 450 feet from the plate. Four homers on four consecutive swings!

Jackson's loyal subjects shrieked, "REG-gie, REG-gie, REG-gie." As the slugger rounded first base, Los Angeles' Steve Garvey greeted him with a smile. Jax reciprocated with a grin. The historic stadium rocked as seldom before.

The Dodgers tagged Mike Torrez for a nuisance run in the top of the ninth before bowing, 8-4. As Torrez gloved Lee Lacy's pop fly for the final out, Jackson sprinted from his right-field post, snaking through undisciplined fans who sought to bowl him over.

In the clubhouse, Lasorda, Garvey and Dodgers pitcher Don Sutton elbowed through a cordon of newsmen to extend their congratulations to the game's latest colossus. "Greatest performance I've ever seen," Lasorda yelled. Nobody disagreed.

Reggie's performance was extraordinary. While Babe Ruth had socked three homers in a game in the World Series of 1926 and 1928, Jackson's feat seemed particularly special in light of the season-long strife Reggie endured, the first-pitch dramatics that marked the achievement and the fact that the onslaught helped the Yankees win their first World Series title in 15 years (and do so before the home fans). Reggie established Series records for homers (five), runs (10) and total bases (25).

Jackson helped the Yankees win another pennant in 1978 with 27 homers and 97 RBIs. As a designated hitter, he aided the Yanks as they again beat the Dodgers in the World Series. He hit two homers and knocked in eight runs.

After a banner season in 1980 (41 homers, 111 RBIs and a .300 average), Jackson played 94 games in strike-torn 1981 and saw his home runs drop to 15, his RBIs to 54 and his average to .237.

Granted his free agency after the '81 season, he signed a four-year, $3.6 million contract with the California Angels. At 36, Reggie enjoyed a renaissance in 1982, tying for the league lead in home runs with 39, driving in 101 runs and batting .275.

On September 17, 1984, Jackson became the 13th big-league player to hit 500 career home runs. He connected against Bud Black of Kansas City in a 10-1 defeat.

OCTOBER 18, 1977

Los Angeles	ab	r	h	rbi	New York	ab	r	h	rbi
Lopes, 2b	4	0	1	0	Rivers, cf	4	0	2	0
Russell, ss	3	0	0	0	Randolph, 2b	4	1	0	0
Smith, rf	4	2	1	1	Munson, c	4	1	1	0
Cey, 3b	3	1	1	0	Jackson, rf	3	4	3	5
Garvey, 1b	4	1	2	2	Chambliss, 1b	4	2	2	2
Baker, lf	4	0	1	0	Nettles, 3b	4	0	0	0
Monday, cf	4	0	1	0	Piniella, lf	3	0	0	1
Yeager, c	3	0	1	0	Dent, ss	2	0	0	0
Davalillo, ph	1	0	1	1	Torrez, p	3	0	0	0
Hooton, p	2	0	0	0					
Sosa, p	0	0	0	0					
Rau, p	0	0	0	0					
Goodson, ph	1	0	0	0					
Hough, p	0	0	0	0					
Lacy, ph	1	0	0	0					
Totals	34	4	9	4	Totals	31	8	8	8

Los Angeles ....2 0 1 0 0 0 0 0 1—4
New York ....0 2 0 3 2 0 0 1 x—8

Los Angeles	IP	H	R	ER	BB	SO
Hooton (L)	3*	3	4	4	1	1
Sosa	1⅔	3	3	3	1	0
Rau	1⅓	0	0	0	0	1
Hough	2	2	1	1	0	3
New York	IP	H	R	ER	BB	SO
Torrez (W)	9	9	4	2	2	6

*Pitched to three batters in fourth.

E—Dent. DP—New York 2. LOB—Los Angeles 5, New York 2. 2B—Chambliss. 3B—Garvey. HR—Chambliss, Smith, Jackson 3. SF—Piniella. PB—Munson. T—2:18. A—56,407.

McLain Becomes 30-Game Winner

Detroit's Denny McLain, attempting to become the first 30-game winner in 34 years, delivers a pitch in a September game against Oakland.

For 34 years the major leagues awaited the arrival of the next 30-game winner, a pitcher who could rank with the mound masters of earlier days when such a victory total was a fairly common achievement.

Several times in the years after Dizzy Dean won 30 games for the Cardinals in 1934, a strong-armed pitcher threatened to attain that magic figure, only to fall short as the season drew to a close.

Dean himself made a swipe at 30 in 1935, but finished at 28. Hal Newhouser of the Tigers gave it a strong bid in 1944. The lefthander was stopped at 29. A third assault was launched by Robin Roberts in 1952. Though he won 21 of his last 23 decisions, the Phillies' righthander was hampered by a sluggish start and closed out at 28-7.

After Roberts' extraordinary performance, the most serious challenges to the 30-victory circle were mounted by two Dodgers, Don Newcombe in 1956 and Sandy Koufax in 1966. Both registered 27 victories.

Two years after an arthritic elbow forced Koufax into retirement, another figure emerged as a serious candidate for the elusive 30. He was Dennis Dale McLain, and from the very start of his career it was apparent that he was a most remarkable individual.

The graduate of Mount Carmel High School in Chicago would have preferred to sign with his favorite team, the Cubs, but when they expressed no interest in him, he accepted a bonus of $17,500 from the White Sox, who assigned him to Harlan of the rookie Appalachian League in 1962.

Unawed by the mystique of professional baseball, the 18-year-old fireballer threw a no-hitter against Salem in his first trip to the mound. After two games with Harlan (in which he struck out 32 batters in 18 innings), Denny was promoted to Clinton of the Midwest League. At Clinton, McLain posted a disappointing 4-7 record.

McLain was fully prepared to pay his dues in the White Sox system in his quest to reach the majors. However, his career took an abrupt turn on April 8, 1963, when he was claimed on first-year waivers by the Detroit Tigers and assigned to Duluth-Superior of the Class A Northern League. When he won 13 of 15 decisions there, Denny was hustled off to Class AA Knoxville, where he won five and lost four. Called up by the Tigers for the final days of the American League season, Denny won two of three decisions.

Detroit management discovered quickly that free-spirited Denny was not a conventional rookie. While he possessed blinding speed, he could not throw a curve. That came later. He also had an unquenchable thirst—for Pepsi-Cola. He quaffed two bottles of the soft drink before a game, five afterward, one before dinner and three while watching television. In a week's time, he might consume 100 bottles.

After a brief stay with Syracuse (International) in 1964, McLain rejoined the Tigers, winning four of nine decisions the rest of the season.

He also acquired a nickname. Teammates determined that the 20-year-old was a "fish" at card games and christened him "Dolph," as in "Dolphin."

In his first three full seasons as a Tiger, Denny

Willie Horton's game-winning hit prompted this burst of excitement from teammates Al Kaline (left) and Denny McLain.

compiled victory totals of 16, 20 and 17, figures that he surpassed dramatically in 1968 when he catapulted into national focus.

Slowed by no-decisions in his first two starts of '68, McLain won only twice in April. He beat Chicago, 4-2, and shut out New York, 7-0.

In May, he won six games and lost one, a 10-8 setback to Baltimore. At the end of June, Denny's record was 14-2. His only setback in June was a 2-0 loss to Cleveland.

The Chicagoan compiled seven victories in July while suffering only one defeat, 5-3, to the Orioles. With a record of 21-3 and two months of the season remaining, the 24-year-old McLain was clearly on a 30-victory course. Speculation sprouted almost daily that, after more than three decades of concern, the 30-win species was not extinct.

At the end of August, Denny had won 26 games and lost five. His losses during that month were to Chicago, 10-2, and New York, 2-1.

On September 1, McLain beat Baltimore, 7-3. No. 27.

On September 6, Minnesota fell, 8-3. No. 28.

On September 10, California succumbed, 7-2. No. 29.

At this juncture, Denny's 1968 record against other American League clubs broke down to: Baltimore, 2-2; Boston, 3-0; California, 5-0; Chicago, 3-1; Cleveland, 3-1; Minnesota, 6-0; New York, 1-1; Oakland, 3-0; Washington, 3-0.

McLain's 38th start of the season was scheduled for September 14 against Oakland at Tiger Stadium. The contest was a natural selection by NBC as its nationally televised "Game of the Week" and was viewed by millions. In addition, a paid crowd of 33,688 (and more than 44,000 fans overall) witnessed the game at the historic ball park. Resplendent in his 10-gallon hat and engaging personality, Dizzy Dean himself was on hand. Ol' Diz declaimed expertly to all who inquired that Denny McLain reminded him of another pitcher of bygone days, a Gas House Gang member named Dean.

McLain slept "like a baby" for 11 hours in preparation for his date with destiny. If he felt undue pressure, it was concealed behind his wisecracks. If he should win 30 games, he announced, he certainly would demand at least $100,000 in salary for 1969.

One of the first sights Denny spotted when he stepped on the field revealed that he was not alone in attacking a goal on this Saturday afternoon. Across the way, catcher Jim Pagliaroni of the A's brandished a sign reading: "Chuck Dobson Goes for No. 12 Today." The reference to Oakland's starting pitcher and his victory objective brought a chuckle from the Tiger.

The Bengals, comfortably ensconced in first place, and the A's, 18½ games back in the sixth spot, played three scoreless innings before McLain yielded a two-run homer in the fourth to Reggie Jackson, who was playing his first full season in the majors.

That 2-0 Oakland advantage disappeared in the bottom of the fourth when Norm Cash hammered a three-run homer off Dobson.

A walk, sacrifice and Bert Campaneris' single enabled Oakland to tie the score in the fifth before Jackson clouted his second homer

Denny McLain poses with Dizzy Dean, who won 30 games for St. Louis in 1934.

McLAIN'S 31 VICTORIES

Game-by-Game Account of All His Decisions in 1968

Date	Opponent	Result	Score	Opp. Pitcher of Decision	Cum. Rec.
Apr. 21	At Chicago	W	4-2	Carlos	1-0
27	At New York	W	7-0	Peterson	2-0
May 1	Minnesota	W	3-2	Merritt	3-0
5	California	W	5-2	Brunet	4-0
10	At Washington	W	12-1	Moore	5-0
15	Baltimore	L	8-10	Watt	5-1
20	At Minnesota	W	4-3*	Merritt	6-1
25	At Oakland	W	2-1	Krausse	7-1
29	At California	W	3-0	McGlothlin	8-1
June 5	At Boston	W	5-4	Landis	9-1
9	Cleveland	L	0-2	Tiant	9-2
13	Minnesota	W	3-1	Merritt	10-2
16	At Chicago	W	6-1	Carlos	11-2
20	Boston	W	5-1	Ellsworth	12-2
24	At Cleveland	W	14-3	Paul	13-2
29	Chicago	W	5-2	Carlos	14-2
July 3	California	W	5-2	McGlothlin	15-2
7	Oakland	W	5-4	Sprague	16-2
12	At Minnesota	W	5-1	Kaat	17-2
16	At Oakland	W	4-0	Dobson	18-2
20	Baltimore	L	3-5	McNally	18-3
23	At Washington	W	6-4	Ortega	19-3
27	At Baltimore	W	9-0	Phoebus	20-3
31	Washington	W	4-0	Bertaina	21-3
Aug. 4	At Minnesota	W	2-1	Kaat	22-3
8	Cleveland	W	13-1	Siebert	23-3
12	At Cleveland	W	6-3	Romo	24-3
16	At Boston	W	4-0	Lonborg	25-3
20	Chicago	L	2-10	Peters	25-4
24	At New York	L	1-2	Stottlemyre	25-5
28	California	W	6-1	Burgmeier	26-5
Sept. 1	Baltimore	W	7-3	Hardin	27-5
6	Minnesota	W	8-3	Kaat	28-5
10	At California	W	7-2	Messersmith	29-5
14	Oakland	W	5-4	Segui	30-5
19	New York	W	6-2	Stottlemyre	31-5
23	At Baltimore	L	1-2	Nelson	31-6

* 10 innings.

of the day—and 28th of the season—to put the A's on top, 4-3, in the sixth. "It was a bad pitch, a changeup high," McLain disclosed later.

The Tigers mounted a threat in the eighth against reliever Diego Segui, placing two runners aboard with a walk and single. Two were out at the time,

Denny McLain struggled in the 1968 World Series, dropping two decisions to the Cardinals.

and Gates Brown, Detroit's standout pinch-hitter, was called upon to bat for Tigers third baseman Don Wert. Segui induced Brown to ground out.

The A's were retired in routine fashion in the top of the ninth, after which McLain was lifted for a pinch-hitter, Al Kaline, to open the Tigers' half of the inning.

The veteran outfielder worked the count to 3 and 2 and fouled off a couple pitches before drawing a base on balls. Dick McAuliffe attempted to sacrifice, but fouled out before Mickey Stanley singled up the middle, sending Kaline racing to third.

A's Manager Bob Kennedy visited the mound to discuss the situation and particularly the next batter, Jim Northrup, who posed a serious home run threat. Segui, a righthander, was allowed to face the lefthanded batter.

Northrup's best effort was a high bouncer to the right side, where first baseman Danny Cater fielded the ball and threw wildly to the plate. As A's catcher Dave Duncan chased the ball, Kaline scored the tying run and Stanley scurried to third. On the Detroit bench, McLain leaped up and shouted excitedly. He felt that Stanley should have attempted to score on Cater's overthrow.

"Calm down, calm down," Manager Mayo Smith counseled. Denny sat down.

Muscular Willie Horton, with 35 homers already to his credit, was up next. He ran the count to 2 and 2 before rifling a drive to left field. Jim Gosger had no chance to make the catch. The ball shot over his glove and Stanley scored the run that made the Tigers 5-4 winners and elevated Denny McLain into the 30-victory class.

McLain bolted from the dugout to congratulate those who had figured in the game-winning rally. Then he accepted a brief ride to the dugout on teammates' shoulders.

Many in the large crowd remained for fully 15 minutes, shouting, "We want Denny." The jubilant pitcher took a few curtain calls and waved to all sectors before retiring to an interview room, where he was pelted by questions from a press corps that was swelled substantially by the significance of the day.

Nearly two hours after the game, Denny and his wife headed for their car. "I'm glad it's over," he said with a touch of weariness.

Added his wife, "I feel like a balloon that's been blown up and now all the air's been let out."

Dizzy Dean also offered some comments: "Next year I'd like to bet he'll win 25 games. He's capable of winning 30 again . . . the league's gonna go to 12 teams and all the clubs will be weaker."

Denny won his 31st game of the year on September 19 when he defeated the Yankees, 6-2. With that victory, he joined Lefty Grove of the 1931 A's and Jim Bagby of the 1920 Indians as the only pitchers

Among Denny McLain's rewards for his big 1968 season was a license plate
with his initials and season record.

to win that many games in a season since Grover-Cleveland Alexander posted 33 victories for the Phillies in 1916.

In consequence of his magnificent season, which included a gaudy 1.96 earned-run average, McLain won Most Valuable Player and Cy Young Award honors in the American League. He dropped two decisions to Bob Gibson of the Cardinals in the World Series but won his third start, 13-1, in Game 6.

Denny wasn't quite as dominant in 1969, but he did win 24 games and shared the Cy Young Award with Mike Cuellar of Baltimore.

At age 25, Denny McLain enjoyed wealth and prestige. Prospects were bright for many years of productive pitching. It never happened.

He won only three games in 1970, a year in which he was suspended three times—for allegedly consorting with gamblers and participating in a bookmaking operation; for carrying a gun, and for pouring buckets of ice water on two sportswriters.

Traded to Washington on the eve of the 1970 World Series between Cincinnati and Baltimore, he won 10 games for the Senators in 1971 and led the league in defeats with 22. Traded to Oakland in March 1972, McLain started the season with the A's, was assigned to Birmingham (Southern) and finished the year with the Atlanta Braves.

McLain later pitched without distinction in the minor leagues, ran a minor league club and then, except for two bankruptcies, virtually sank from sight. He resurfaced in 1985. As his wife and two daughters wept in the rear of a Florida courtroom, the former pitching star was sentenced to a 23-year prison term for racketeering, conspiracy, extortion and attempted drug-dealing.

"I don't know how you get to where I am from where I was 17 years ago," said McLain, reflecting on his baseball acclaim and troubles with the law.

"I'll pay for my conviction the rest of my life. I've gone through a lot of shame and disgrace. The lessons I've learned . . . have prepared me for the rest of my life."

SEPTEMBER 14, 1968								
Oakland	ab	r	h	rbi	Detroit	ab	r	h	rbi
Campaneris, ss	4	0	1	1	McAuliffe, 2b	5	0	1	0
Monday, cf	4	0	1	0	Stanley, cf	5	1	2	0
Cater, 1b	4	1	2	0	Northrup, rf	4	1	0	0
Bando, 3b	3	0	0	0	Horton, lf	5	1	2	1
Jackson, rf	4	2	2	3	Cash, 1b	4	1	2	3
Green, 2b	4	0	0	0	Freehan, c	3	0	1	0
Keough, lf	3	0	0	0	Matchick, ss	4	0	1	0
Gosger, lf	0	0	0	0	Wert, 3b	2	0	0	0
Duncan, c	2	1	0	0	Brown, ph	1	0	0	0
Dobson, p	1	0	0	0	Tracewski, 3b	0	0	0	0
Aker, p	0	0	0	0	McLain, p	1	0	0	0
Lindblad, p	0	0	0	0	Kaline, ph	0	1	0	0
Donaldson, ph	0	0	0	0					
Segui, p	1	0	0	0					
Totals	30	4	6	4	Totals	34	5	9	4

```
Oakland.................................0  0  0   2  1  1   0  0  0—4
Detroit..................................0  0  0   3  0  0   0  0  2—5
   One out when winning run scored.
Oakland              IP      H     R    ER    BB    SO
Dobson............................ 3⅔     4     3     3     2     4
Aker............................... 0*      0     0     0     1     0
Lindblad ......................... ⅓       0     0     0     0     1
Segui (L) ........................ 4⅓     5     2     1     2     1
Detroit              IP      H     R    ER    BB    SO
McLain (W) ...................... 9        6     4     4     1    10
   *Pitched to one batter in fourth.
```

E—Bando, Cater, Matchick. DP—Detroit 1. LOB—Oakland 2, Detroit 10. HR—Jackson 2, Cash. SH—Bando, Donaldson, McLain. WP—Aker. T—3:00. A—33,688.

Drysdale String Is Finally Broken

He was a handsome specimen, a 6-foot-6, 208-pounder, but when he scowled from the additional height of the pitching mound, he transformed normally composed batters into quivering globs of protoplasm.

In the 14 seasons that he pitched for the Dodgers —both the Brooklyn and Los Angeles branches— the righthander sent countless batters sprawling in the dirt. If they lacked the necessary agility to leap out of harm's way, they became a statistic in the big fellow's "hit by pitcher" table. After all, this man holds the modern National League career record for hit batsmen, plunking 154.

They called him "Big D," which might have stood for demolition or destruction or devastation. It represented, however, the first and last initials of Donald Scott Drysdale, who wrung maximum benefits from his "purpose pitch."

While he stoutly maintained that he "never tried to hit a batter intentionally," Drysdale insisted that it was necessary to pitch high and tight to guarantee continued employment. Righthanded batters, in particular, felt the heat of Don's fastball, delivered in a sweeping, sidearm motion.

If the batter took pains to claw out a hole with his spikes in order to anchor his back foot, he could

Don Drysdale, one of baseball's brightest stars in 1968, is interviewed by a young-looking Howard Cosell.

expect the next pitch to come hurtling toward his head. In the parlance of the pitching fraternity, Don said, "If you're gonna dig a hole, make it big enough to crawl in."

Drysdale learned the pitching gospel at the knee of Sal Maglie, a sinister-looking character who was in the twilight of his career when he joined the Dodgers during Don's rookie season of 1956. Maglie, nicknamed "The Barber" because of his practice of giving batters a close shave with a baseball, found a willing disciple in the 19-year-old Drysdale. The youngster learned early the value of a "purpose pitch," first to catch the batter's attention, then to shake him up and render him vulnerable for a pitch on the outside edge of the plate.

A native of Van Nuys, Calif., where he was born July 23, 1936, Drysdale rejected scholarship offers from Stanford and Southern California to join the Dodger organization. He was given a $4,000 bonus and assigned to Bakersfield of the California League.

Life in the Class C circuit was acceptable to the professional rookie, although there was one serious drawback. For a youngster shooting upward, the lengthy bus rides were pure torture. He spent hours restoring circulation to his cramped legs.

Drysdale complained to his father about existence in a bus league. The elder Drysdale replied in a letter, "If you don't like the bus league, get out of it."

The kid accepted the counsel. He advanced to Montreal of the International League in 1955. His record of 11-11 in Class AAA competition earned him a second advancement in as many years, this

Don Drysdale is surrounded by teammates after shutting out Pittsburgh and stretching his scoreless-inning streak to 54.

time to the parent club of Reese, Hodges, Robinson, Snider, et al.

Though Drysdale pitched impressively in spot roles, his immature tongue caused occasional embarrassments. He was quick to complain publicly about personalities, even coaches on his team. When the club moved to Los Angeles in 1958 and played its home games in the Memorial Coliseum, the 22-year-old pitcher raged constantly about the 251-foot left-field foul line and the way lefthanded batters looped his best pitches over the barrier for cheap home runs.

After one particularly galling defeat, he cried, "I'll never win another game in this place. Trade me."

"Even to the Phillies?" inquired a newsman, referring to the National League's last-place team.

"Even to Cucamonga," Big D snapped.

Bench jockeys were quick to label the youngster "Crybaby" and "Busher" and, in response to his aggressive style, they called him "Headhunter" as well.

The combination of high-and-tight pitching and a low boiling point precipitated a number of brawls. In one instance, after Bill Bruton of Milwaukee had hit his second homer of a 1957 Braves-Dodgers game, Drysdale bounced a pitch off the next batter, Johnny Logan.

"Wait'll you get down to second base," the shortstop screamed.

"Why wait?" replied the pitcher, running to meet his adversary.

As players of both teams swarmed onto the field, Big D got in some telling blows. When order was restored, one witness awarded the bout to Don on points.

Early in his career, Drysdale hit Frank Robinson of Cincinnati on the hand with a pitch. Such an occurrence was not rare for the outfielder, who annually challenged for the league lead in being hit by pitches. But somehow the umpire detected malicious intent on Don's part. A $100 fine and a five-day suspension followed.

Personal failures ignited temper tantrums as rapidly as the behavior of opponents. Once, after making a putout at first base that ended a distressing inning, Don disgustedly fired the ball into the stands. "I was trying to hit my glove," he explained with a straight face.

Another time, he vented his displeasure by grabbing a stack of batting helmets and firing them wildly, one by one, around the dugout.

But for pure rage, nothing compared to his wrath

Philadelphia's Roberto Pena grounds out to lead off the inning in which Don Drysdale broke baseball's scoreless-inning record.

in Cincinnati after Big D was staked to a 5-0 lead in the second inning. By unanimous agreement, this storm was world class.

Showing signs of blowing the lead, Drysdale was removed from the game with none out in the Reds' second and stalked into the clubhouse. He stormed to his locker where, in meticulous manner, he fired all the contents to the floor, piece by piece.

That done, he peeled off his garments and stomped upon them. With no more apparel available to assuage his wrath, the terrible-tempered Mr. Drysdale spotted a bat bag. Why not!

He delivered a swift kick. The bag bounced a few inches, indicating that it was full of bats. A sharp pain in his foot confirmed the fact.

Drysdale picked up the recalcitrant bag and lugged it to the stairs, where he sent it clattering to the floor below. Still mad at himself, he retrieved the bag, filled it with the bats and toted it upstairs.

Finally, drained of all his anger, he collapsed on a stool and told himself, "You're a damn fool. You'll never get anywhere in this game without self-discipline."

In due course, the big righthander developed that quality to a satisfactory degree. Blinding rage was conquered, but not his competitive fire. As self control improved, so did his statistics. At age 23, he led the National League in strikeouts with 242 in 1959.

By 1962, the Californian was a 25-game winner, the league strikeout king for the third time and recipient of the Cy Young Award. Three years later, he posted 23 victories and compiled a 1-1 record in two World Series starts against Minnesota.

Big D was in his 13th, and penultimate, season when he etched his most enduring mark on the baseball books. When the 1968 campaign opened, the big fellow was three months short of his 32nd birthday and for the first five weeks he did little to augur well for the days ahead. He lost three of his first four decisions, beating only the Mets, 1-0.

On May 14, however, Drysdale shut out the Cubs, 1-0, on two hits. In his next outing, May 18, he blanked the Astros by the same 1-0 score, allowing five hits. Next, the Cardinals were whitewashed, 2-0, on May 22, also on five hits, and Houston was victimized by a six-hit, 5-0 shutout on May 26.

With four consecutive shutouts, Big D was just one short of the major league record set by Guy (Doc) White of the White Sox in 1904, long before the birth of the lively ball.

Drysdale's next assignment fell on May 31 against the Giants. For eight innings, Big D held the archrivals scoreless and Los Angeles built a 3-0 lead. Starting the ninth, however, he issued his first walk, to Willie McCovey, then gave up a single to Jim Ray

DRYSDALE'S STREAK

Here is a game-by-game breakdown of Don Drysdale's record 58 consecutive scoreless innings:

Date	Team	Score	AB	H	SO	BB
May 14	Cubs	1-0	29	2	7	3
May 18	Astros	1-0	32	5	6	2
May 22	at Cards	2-0	31	5	8	0
May 26	at Astros	5-0	31	6	6	2
May 31	Giants	3-0	34	6	7	2
June 4	Pirates	5-0	29	3	8	0
June 8*	Phillies	4-0	14	2	3	0
	Totals	21-0	200	29	45	9

Composite batting average of opponents—.145.

Extra-base hits—3 doubles (by Jim Wynn of Astros, Lou Brock of Cardinals and Gary Kolb of Pirates).

HITS BY INNINGS

May 14	(Cubs)	000	110	000—	2	
May 18	(Astros)	000	011	102—	5	
May 22	(Cards)	100	010	201—	5	
May 26	(Astros)	210	001	002—	6	
May 31	(Giants)	110	111	001—	6	
June 4	(Pirates)	000	011	001—	3	
June 8*	(Phillies)	101	0xx	xxx—	2	
Totals		521	254	307—	29	

*June 8 stats through first four innings only.

Among the many honors Don Drysdale earned in 1968 was baseball's Player
of the Month award for his May scoreless streak.

Hart and another pass to Dave Marshall to load the bases with none out.

Almost anything from Dick Dietz would produce a run and snap Drysdale's streak short of Doc White's ancient record. The count on the San Francisco catcher went to 2 and 2 and Don threw again. The ball grazed the batter's arm and three runners advanced a base, with McCovey crossing the plate.

But things were not what they seemed. Behind the plate, umpire Harry Wendelstedt gestured animately. Dietz, he ruled, had made no effort to avoid the pitch; in fact, he had thrust his arm into the path of the ball. The count was now 3 and 2 and Drysdale's record remained intact, however tenuously.

In the five-minute rhubarb that ensued, Drysdale collected his thoughts and assessed the situation. When play resumed, he was ready and retired Dietz on a fly to left field, too shallow for the runners to risk an advance. Ty Cline's best effort was a grounder to first baseman Wes Parker, whose throw to the plate forced McCovey. Jack Hiatt's pop fly accounted for the final out, and Drysdale stood alongside Doc White in the record book.

Don's next turn came on June 4. The struggling Pittsburgh Pirates were the opponents and they bowed meekly, 5-0, collecting only three hits.

Don Drysdale, the former redneck, was the monarch of the mound with six consecutive shutouts. Overall, his 54 straight scoreless innings—during which the opposition managed only 27 hits and a composite .145 batting average—were just two short of the all-time major league mark established by Walter Johnson of Washington in 1913. The chance to topple Johnson's lofty standard of 56 arrived on June 8 when more than 50,000 partisans packed Dodger Stadium to watch Don face the Phillies.

Big D matched the Big Train's listed record with scoreless pitching in the first two innings. He passed Sir Walter in the third, an inning in which leadoff batter Roberto Pena grounded out, pitcher Larry Jackson singled and Cookie Rojas and Johnny Briggs struck out. And Drysdale added another shutout frame in the fourth, giving him 58 consecutive shutout innings.

Tony Taylor and Clay Dalrymple solved Don for singles to open the fifth inning. With Taylor on third base, Dalrymple at first and no one out, Drysdale's streak seemed about to end. But the Dodger star struck out Pena and appeared to get a break

Philadelphia's Tony Taylor (left) scored to break Don Drysdale's streak on Howie Bedell's only RBI of the season.

when weak-hitting Howie Bedell was called upon as a pinch-hitter. Bedell, who appeared in only nine games the entire season, lifted a fly ball to left field and Taylor romped home with the run that snapped Drysdale's streak at 58⅔ innings. The sacrifice fly produced the only RBI of the year for Bedell, a .193 lifetime hitter.

The Dodgers went on to win, 5-3, and the victory was the seventh in a row for Big D after his 1-3 start. However, Don won only six more games the remainder of the season, finishing with a 14-12 record. The next season, he had a 5-4 mark in August when he decided to retire, at 33, because of chronic discomfort in his elbow. For 14 years in Dodger blue, his record was 209-166.

From the pitching mound, Drysdale stepped into the radio booth of the Montreal Expos and later handled similiar tasks with the Texas Rangers and the California Angels.

Drysdale, who has drawn choice ABC network television assignments, joined the announcing team of the Chicago White Sox in 1982 and added a second responsibility in 1986 when he was named a "pitching consultant" for the American League club.

Big D was elected to the Hall of Fame in 1984, about three years after his most notable accomplishment underwent a slight adjustment in the record books. Major league baseball's records committee, acting early in the decade, decided to eliminate from its compilations any fractional innings in instances where runs were scored at any point in *that* inning (on the basis that, logically, a "shutout inning" is free of runs—period).

Accordingly, the record-book entry for most consecutive scoreless innings pitched in the majors now reads: Don Drysdale, 58. Walter Johnson's figure also was reworked, to 55⅔.

JUNE 8, 1968									
Philadelphia	ab	r	h	rbi	Los Angeles	ab	r	h	rbi
Rojas, 2b	5	0	2	1	Parker, 1b	4	1	2	1
Briggs, cf	2	0	0	0	Davis, cf	4	1	0	0
Sutherland, ph	1	0	0	0	Gabrielson, lf	4	0	1	0
Farrell, p	0	0	0	0	Fairey, lf	0	0	0	0
Gonzalez, lf	4	0	0	0	Haller, c	3	1	3	0
Callison, rf	3	0	0	0	Boyer, 3b	4	1	2	1
White, 1b	4	1	1	1	Fairly, rf	4	1	1	1
Taylor, 3b	4	1	1	0	Popovich, 2b	4	0	1	0
Dalrymple, c	2	1	1	0	Versalles, ss	3	0	0	1
Allen, ph	1	0	0	0	Drysdale, p	2	0	0	0
Ryan, c	0	0	0	0	Aguirre, p	1	0	0	0
Pena, ss	4	0	0	0					
L. Jackson, p	1	0	1	0					
Bedell, ph	0	0	0	1					
G. Jackson, p	0	0	0	0					
Lock, ph-cf	2	0	0	0					
Totals	33	3	6	3	Totals	33	5	10	4

Philadelphia ....0 0 0 0 1 1 1 0 0—3
Los Angeles ....1 0 0 3 0 0 1 0 x—5

Philadelphia	IP	H	R	ER	BB	SO
L. Jackson (L)	4	5	4	3	1	1
G. Jackson	2	1	0	0	0	2
Farrell	2	4	1	1	0	1

Los Angeles	IP	H	R	ER	BB	SO
Drysdale (W)	6 ⅓	6	3	2	2	5
Aguirre	2 ⅔	0	0	0	1	2

E—Pena, Versalles, Fairly. DP—Philadelphia 1. LOB—Philadelphia 7, Los Angeles 6. 2B—Haller. HR—White, Parker. SB—Davis. SF—Bedell, Versalles. T—2:29. A—50,060.

Babe Adds Spice To Ruthian Legend

In the realm of human accomplishments, the New York Yankees of the 1920s were unexcelled in their profession as well as in all-night revelries.

Twice during that decade they won three successive pennants under Miller Huggins. How often they greeted the dawn behind red-rimmed eyes and with unsteady steps is unrecorded.

While ancient cultures roistered to the tempo of degenerate emperors, the Yankees gorged and guzzled to the call of their own sovereign, the incomparable George Herman (Babe) Ruth.

One of the Bambino's most notable bacchanalias took place in Detroit in late September of 1928 after the team had clinched its sixth pennant in the "Roaring Twenties."

The king of clout rented a number of adjoining rooms in a downtown hotel and arranged for waiters to deliver liquid and solid provisions throughout the night for his friends and their guests. Next, Babe requested a piano to accompany his carousers. When management pleaded inability to fulfill the order, Ruth peeled off a few bills and bought the item for immediate delivery.

Baseball's all-time champion bon vivant had much to celebrate in 1928 aside from a pennant, his ninth as a major leaguer. He had enjoyed a vintage season, tying for the American League lead in runs batted in (142) and topping the A.L. in home runs (54) and runs (163). And he remained the game's master showman. At age 33, he was still the foremost gate attraction with heroic feats and ebullient spirit.

The Yankees galloped away from the pack in the early part of the '28 season and led second-place Philadelphia by 12 games on July 4. In the next 10 weeks, however, the youthful A's rampaged past the Yanks, only to fall back when the New Yorkers took three of four games in a crucial series in the second week of September. The Yanks never relinquished first place thereafter.

As the Yankees prepared to meet the Cardinals in the World Series, the New York club was severely hampered by injuries. Herb Pennock, the stylish lefthander, was incapacitated by neuritis in his shoulder.

Earle Combs, the fleet center fielder, had suffered a badly bruised wrist in a collision with a fence and was available only for pinch-hitting duty.

Second baseman Tony Lazzeri was unable to throw overhand because of an ailing shoulder, and shortstop Mark Koenig was hobbled by a bad heel.

Even the Babe was not completely whole. A nagging leg problem forced him to limp when he ran.

As a result of the bumps and bruises, the American Leaguers were decided underdogs when the Series opened at Yankee Stadium on October 4.

The starting pitchers for the Thursday game, which attracted 61,425 fans, were Waite Hoyt (23-7 in the regular season) for the Yanks and Willie Sherdel (21-10) for the Cardinals.

The Yankees won the game, 4-1. Ruth hit two doubles and a single and scored two runs.

Yankees Manager Huggins selected George Pipgras (24-13) to start the second game, while St. Louis' Bill McKechnie nominated Grover Cleveland Alexander (16-9), New York's nemesis in the 1926 classic. It quickly became evident that Old Pete, at 41, was not the puzzle he had been two years before. He was knocked out of the game in the Yanks' four-run third inning and tagged with a 9-3 defeat. Ruth rapped a double and a single in the winners' eight-hit attack.

After a day off for travel, the Series resumed in St. Louis on Sunday, October 7. Tom Zachary (9-12), a late-season acquisition from Washington, started for New York against Jesse Haines (20-8). Though the Redbirds outhit their rivals, 9-7, two of the Yankees' hits were homers by Lou Gehrig. Ruth singled twice and scored two runs in the Yanks' 7-3 victory.

A heavy rain forced postponement of the fourth game until Tuesday, October 9, a balmy, summerlike day. The first-game starters were on the mound again, with Hoyt seeking his sixth World Series triumph and Sherdel looking for his first victory in four career postseason decisions.

Early arrivals in the crowd of 37,331 detected signs of an extraordinary day for Ruth, the Sultan of Swat. In time, some would call it the greatest game of his lengthy big-league career (which numbered more than 2,500 contests).

In batting practice, he rifled a vicious shot up the middle and smashed three balls over the pavilion in right field. Unquestionably, the Babe was ready.

After grounding into a double play in his first at-bat, Ruth homered to the pavilion roof in the fourth, tying the score, 1-1.

In the fifth, Babe grounded out. When he batted in the seventh, there was one out and the Yanks trailed, 2-1. Sherdel threw two slow curves that Ruth took for strikes. As Babe stepped out of the box, Sherdel fired again without taking his usual windup. The ball split the strike zone. Apparently, he was out and lusty shouts of approbation swirled out of the stands.

Almost instantly, however, the cheers subsided. Plate umpire Cy Pfirman of the National League voided the pitch. Sherdel had made a quick pitch, he ruled. While that was legal in the National League, it had been decided by Commissioner Kenesaw M. Landis in a pre-Series conference with the

After Babe Ruth hit three home runs in Game 4 of the 1926 World Series at
St. Louis' Sportsman's Park, the auto agency across Grand Avenue took note
of the spot where one of the Bambino's drives allegedly hit.

Ruth's Three - Homer Victims

1926 Series

Flint Rhem

Hi Bell

1928 Series

Grover Cleveland Alexander

Willie Sherdel

managers that the stratagem was illegal in October.

The Redbirds, led by McKechnie, Sherdel, catcher Earl Smith and second baseman Frank Frisch, protested vehemently, insisting that it was not a quick pitch in the strictest interpretation of the term. Pfirman was asked to consult fellow umpires. When they supported him, the disputants retired.

While the argument raged, Ruth stood close by, beaming broadly at the principals. When it ended, he applauded politely and prepared to bat again.

Words were exchanged between Ruth and Sherdel, who threw two pitches out of the strike zone. More comments. What, Ruth was asked later, had been the nature of their conversation?

"I said the National League is a hell of a league," Ruth reported.

What did Willie say?

"Oh, he said it sure was, or something like that."

What did the Bambino say then?

"I said put one right here and I'll knock it out of the park."

What happened then?

"He did, and I did," Ruth answered.

What Ruth did was smack the 2-and-2 pitch over the pavilion roof for his second homer that tied the score, 2-2.

As Babe rounded first base, he waved to the hostile throng, which hadn't known of the quick-pitch ban. At second base, he waved a salute to the left-field bleacherites who had been shocked into silence.

Gehrig stepped up next. Columbia Lou clouted a Sherdel delivery even farther than Babe's blast and the Yanks led, 3-2. A single by Bob Meusel chased Sherdel. Grover Cleveland Alexander took over, but Old Pete was no more effective than he had been in the second game and two more runs scored in the seventh before he retired the side.

Alexander yielded a leadoff homer in the eighth to center fielder Cedric Durst, who had entered the game defensively in the bottom of the seventh. One out later, he faced Ruth, with the same dismal luck. Babe whacked a pitch into the pavilion seats, equaling the Series record of three homers in one game that he had established in 1926 in the same ball park (and also in Game 4).

Later, when he took his position in left field—he did not play his normal right-field spot in St. Louis because of the sun—he was bombarded with missiles of all description, including a bottle. He retrieved the bottle, amid a chorus of jeers, and acted as if he'd toss it back at his tormentors. Then he grinned mischievously and threw the bottle off the field of play. The simple gesture converted enemies into admirers, and Ruth was given a rousing ovation. One writer called Babe's maneuver "a masterpiece of mob control." Another wrote, "First he cowed the crowd, then he won them over."

The Cardinals scored a run in the last of the ninth, cutting New York's lead to 7-3, and had two runners on base with two out when Frisch sliced a towering foul fly to left field. The ball appeared headed for the seats, but Ruth, disregarding his gimpy leg and a hail of scorecards and other debris from spectators, dashed to the railing of the temporary box seats and plucked the ball out of the stands. Without breaking stride and holding the ball aloft in a triumphant manner, he sprinted to the New York dugout and out of sight.

In New York's four-game sweep, Ruth had batted .625, an all-time World Series record, with 10 hits in 16 at-bats.

The club's third World Series championship was a signal for another night of unrestrained indulgence and who better to promote such a celebration than the master organizer of orgies, the Babe himself.

Before the Yankee Special departed for New York, he supervised the loading of illicit potables, spareribs and other viands to suit his gargantuan appetite. Before the train left the station, the party was in full flower and, from all accounts, there never was another like it.

With Ruth and Gehrig leading the way and followed closely by sportswriter Ford Frick, later the commissioner of baseball, the carousers marched through the cars, stopping only to rip shirts off backs or to gulp another mouthful of their favorite beverage.

When they knocked on the door of the compartment occupied by Colonel Jake Ruppert, the club owner ordered them to move on. He wanted to sleep.

"This is no time for sleeping," Babe bellowed. With Gehrig's assistance, he shattered the panel of the door, reached inside and unlocked the door and proceeded to exact a prize trophy from his boss—the top of his custom-made pajamas.

Through Illinois and Indiana, the train sped on. At various stops, villagers congregated on the station platforms to hail the conquering heroes. They shouted for the Bambino, who did not disappoint his subjects. Partly clothed and brandishing a drink and a sparerib, he acknowledged their cheers in raspy monosyllables.

When the train arrived in New York the next day, the most pitiable passenger was Miller Huggins. Ordinarily, the little manager eschewed alcohol but, caught up in the spirit of the celebration, he had partaken liberally. As he roamed the aisles, he asked of all he met: "Have you seen my teeth?"

The Yankees' second Series sweep in as many years (New York had beaten Pittsburgh in four straight in 1927) inspired John B. Foster, editor of the Spalding Baseball Guide, to write: "It was incomprehensible . . . that any club of a major league could achieve such a thing twice in succession, and still more incomprehensible . . . that a team, presumably without its full strength, could defeat a team seemingly as strong as the St. Louis Nationals four times in as many trials, with such effectiveness that the National League champions appeared to be walking in a dream."

Sam Breadon, the Cardinals' owner, concurred. He blamed McKechnie for the debacle and demoted him to Rochester (International).

Ruth led the American League in home runs in the next two seasons with totals of 46 and 49 and shared the homer crown in 1931 with 46, but did not realize his oft-quoted ambition of playing in 10 World Series until 1932 when the Yankees dethroned the American League champion Athletics. Philadelphia had won three straight pennants.

The Yankees' Series opponents were the Cubs, who fared no better than the '27 Pirates or the '28 Cardinals. Ruth hammered two homers in New York's four-game breeze in '32, both coming in Game 3 in Wrigley Field and the second being the Bambino's "called shot."

After playing 125 games and hitting 22 homers in 1934, Babe was released by the Yankees. He was signed by the Boston Braves as a vice president and player, but appeared in only 28 games before calling it a career.

Ruth was among the first five players elected to the Hall of Fame in 1936. He died of cancer in New York City on August 16, 1948.

OCTOBER 9, 1928

New York	ab	r	h	rbi	St. Louis	ab	r	h	rbi
Paschal, cf	4	0	1	0	Orsatti, cf	5	1	2	0
Durst, cf	1	1	1	1	High, 3b	5	0	3	0
Koenig, ss	5	0	1	0	Frisch, 2b	4	0	0	1
Ruth, lf	5	3	3	3	Bottomley, 1b	3	0	0	0
Gehrig, 1b	2	1	1	1	Hafey, lf	3	0	1	0
Meusel, rf	5	1	1	0	Harper, rf	3	0	0	0
Lazzeri, 2b	4	1	3	0	Smith, c	4	0	3	0
Durocher, 2b	1	0	0	0	Martin, pr	0	0	0	0
Dugan, 3b	3	0	1	0	Maranville, ss	4	1	2	0
Rob'rts'n, ph-3b	2	0	0	1	Sherdel, p	3	0	0	0
Bengough, c	3	0	1	0	Alexander, p	0	0	0	0
Combs, ph	0	0	0	1	Holm, ph	1	0	0	1
Collins, c	1	0	1	0					
Hoyt, p	4	0	1	0					
Totals	40	7	15	7	Totals	35	3	11	2

New York	0 0 0	1 0 0	4 2 0—7
St. Louis	0 0 1	1 0 0	0 0 1—3

New York	IP	H	R	ER	BB	SO
Hoyt (W)	9	11	3	2	3	8

St. Louis	IP	H	R	ER	BB	SO
Sherdel (L)	6⅓	11	4	4	3	1
Alexander	2⅔	4	3	3	0	1

E—Koenig, Hoyt. DP—New York 1, St. Louis 1. LOB—New York 11, St. Louis 9. 2B—Lazzeri, Collins, Orsatti, High, Maranville. HR—Ruth 3, Durst, Gehrig. SB—Lazzeri, Maranville. SH—Hoyt. SF—Frisch, Combs. T—2:25. A—37,331.

Roger Clemens Strikes Out 20

Boston's Roger Clemens, pitching in the ninth inning of his incredible 1986 performance against Seattle, takes aim at record strikeout No. 20.

With the nine-inning strikeout record safely tucked away, Roger Clemens gestures triumphantly.

Long before the Hall of Fame sought his clothing, Roger Clemens was accumulating honors with astonishing regularity.

At Spring Woods High School in Houston, Clemens earned all-state baseball laurels as a pitcher-first baseman. He also led his American Legion team to the state championship, won three letters as a defensive end in football and two as a center in basketball.

The 6-foot-4, 215-pound righthander stayed home to attend junior college at nearby San Jacinto in Pasadena, Tex., where he gained All-America distinction as a pitcher in 1981 and was drafted by the New York Mets. The prodigy was not yet ready for the professional ranks, however, and he transferred his talents to the University of Texas instead. In two years at Austin, Clemens posted a 25-7 record with 241 strikeouts in 275 innings and was named an All-America twice. His final victory for the Longhorns was a 4-3 triumph over Alabama in the deciding game of the 1983 College World Series.

The Boston Red Sox made Clemens their first choice in the 1983 amateur draft. This time the pitcher signed a contract and was sent to Winter Haven of the Florida State League. He won three of four starts, compiled a 1.24 earned-run average and registered 36 strikeouts without a solitary base on balls in 29 innings, earning him a quick promotion to New Britain of the Double-A Eastern League. Clemens continued his spectacular efforts, going 4-1 with a 1.38 ERA and 59 strikeouts in 52 innings. He climaxed the season by allowing just one earned run in 17 innings as he defeated pennant-winner Reading and Lynn in the Eastern League playoffs. Indisputably, the native of Dayton, O., was one of Boston's top young prospects.

After training with the Red Sox as a non-roster player in 1984, Clemens opened the season with Pawtucket. Again his stay was relatively brief, just long enough for Roger to appear in seven International League games and compile a 1.93 ERA. He was recalled by the parent club in May.

Clemens posted his first major league victory on May 20, 1984, beating the Twins, 5-4. In late July and August he reeled off six consecutive victories and was acclaimed the American League Pitcher of the Month. In one of his August victories, Clemens struck out 15 Kansas City batters, the second-highest total ever by a Boston pitcher. The number matched feats of Smokey Joe Wood (1911) and Mickey McDermott (1951) and was overshadowed only by Bill Monbouquette's 17 in 1961.

Roger appeared headed for another exceptional performance August 31 when disaster crossed his path. Pitching against the Indians at Cleveland, he allowed only one hit and fanned seven in the first 3⅔ innings when, without warning, he walked off the mound with the first arm ailment of his career.

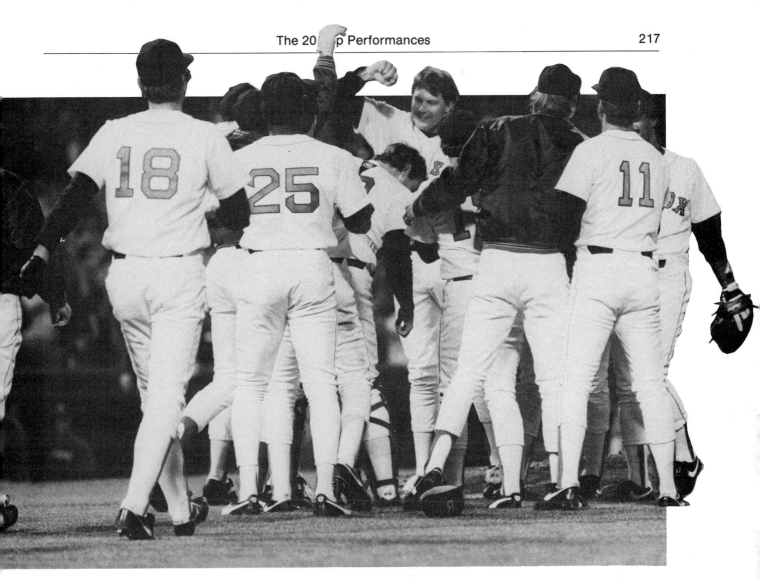

Happy Boston teammates mob Roger Clemens after the young righthander's
awesome 1986 strikeout performance against the frustrated Seattle
Mariners.

He hurled no more that season. He returned to Texas, where he spent the off-season letting the muscle strain in his right forearm mend.

The 1985 season signaled a new start for Clemens, but the arm problems began anew in May as pain became his constant companion. He made only five appearances after May 27, three after June 16 and none after August 11. He was on the disabled list twice, and on August 30 he underwent arthroscopic surgery to remove a small piece of cartilage from his right shoulder. James Andrews, the doctor who performed the operation, pronounced the ailment cured and wished the patient well.

The Red Sox were more hopeful than optimistic when Clemens reported to the team's 1986 training camp at Winter Haven, Fla. Damaged pitching arms do not always recuperate fully, despite the finest medical attention, and for weeks Manager John McNamara and his coaches handled the convalescent with special care, fearful that the smallest excess might reinjure the prized wing.

"We babied him along," Red Sox pitching coach Bill Fischer said.

When the season opened, the fireballer was ready. He made his initial appearance April 11 at Chicago and responded with a 7-2 decision over the White Sox. The needle on the Boston optimism meter leaped perceptibly.

His next time out, Clemens whipped the Royals, 6-2, and followed with a 6-4 verdict over the Tigers to raise his record to 3-0. In 24⅓ innings, the fellow nicknamed the Rocket showed 19 strikeouts, 10 walks and a 1.85 ERA.

Clemens was scheduled to face Kansas City in his fourth start, but a rainout and an open date provided him six days of rest before he took the mound April 29 against Seattle at Fenway Park.

A chilly New England night helped limit the crowd to 13,414. Countless Bostonians later would wish that they had donned a coat and headed down to Fenway, though, because Clemens gave the crowd plenty of reasons—20, to be precise—to forget about the temperature.

From the beginning, it was evident that Roger's

once-tender arm had healed nicely. His fastball, clocked at speeds up to 98 miles per hour, thundered into catcher Rich Gedman's mitt, while his curve, used sparingly, crackled. The first Mariner to encounter Clemens' blistering deliveries was shortstop Spike Owen, Roger's former Texas Longhorn teammate, who went down swinging on a 3-and-2 pitch. Left fielder Phil Bradley also ran the count to the limit and struck out swinging, as did first baseman Ken Phelps.

Pitching in only his 40th major league game, the Rocket retired designated hitter Gorman Thomas on a liner to Jim Rice in left field to open the second inning. Clemens did not miss the strike zone with either of the next two batters as third baseman Jim Presley and right fielder Ivan Calderon both were punched out by umpire Vic Voltaggio—Presley swinging, Calderon looking.

The crowd responded to Clemens' fifth strikeout with raucous applause. Though the game was young, those in attendance could sense something grand in the making.

"It was a small crowd," Clemens later would recall, "but it was a noisy one."

Center fielder Dave Henderson, who was called out on a 0-2 pitch, was Clemens' only strikeout victim in the third inning, but neither second baseman Danny Tartabull nor catcher Steve Yeager was able to reach base safely as Clemens kept his perfect game intact. But Roger's hitless streak was snapped in the fourth when the leadoff batter, old buddy Owen, singled to right field. Spike advanced no farther, however, as Bradley and Phelps both struck out on 2-2 pitches, bringing Thomas to the plate.

Thomas, a veteran who had overcome shoulder problems himself with an impressive '85 season, worked the count to 2-2 before lifting a pop foul outside first base. While no one could realize it at the moment, what followed was to become a significant part of the unfolding drama.

Don Baylor, ordinarily Boston's designated hitter, was playing first base because the regular custodian, Bill Buckner, was suffering from an ailing elbow and could not play in the field. Baylor circled under the foul ball, extended his glove and dropped it for an error.

Thomas had a new life at the plate, as did Roger Clemens in his pursuit of strikeout glory. After taking the next pitch for a ball, Thomas was waved out by Voltaggio.

With nine strikeouts after the first four innings, Clemens then really got on a roll. He set the Mariners down on called third strikes in the fifth—Presley and Tartabull on 2-2 counts, Calderon on 0-2. When Henderson went down swinging and Yeager was called out to open the sixth, Clemens had eight consecutive strikeouts to his credit, tying

an A.L. record. But any hopes the Rocket may have entertained of matching Tom Seaver's major league mark of 10 successive strikeouts were dashed when Owen ended the inning with a fly ball to center fielder Steve Lyons.

After fanning Bradley on a 1-2 delivery to open the seventh, Clemens walked off the mound and headed for the dugout. McNamara had his back to the field and was talking to Fischer when he saw a strange look come over the coach's face. "I turned to see what he was looking at," McNamara recalled, "and there was Roger crossing the foul line. My

heart jumped and I almost collapsed.

"(Trainer) Charlie (Moss) and I leaped up the dugout steps, and as I ran toward Clemens I said, 'Roger, my God, what's the matter?' "

Clemens shot a quizzical look at his boss. "Nothing," he said. "I just want something to clean the mud out of my spikes."

The manager let out a deep sigh. "When he said that," McNamara recalled, "I almost passed out from relief."

With his spikes unencumbered once more, Clemens returned to the mound and fanned Phelps, his

16th victim, on a 2-2 pitch.

By that time, the fans were on their feet and applauding wildly every gesture of Voltaggio's right arm. Their cheering grew even louder as the next batter, Thomas, fell behind in the count, 1-2. But Thomas shocked the crowd into silence with a high fly that dropped into the first row of the center-field seats.

The inning ended when Presley grounded out to first base. But for all his strikeout heroics, Roger now trailed the Mariners, 1-0, and was in danger of losing his first game of the year. That's because Seattle righthander Mike Moore also was pitching impressively, and though he was striking out fewer batters, he was keeping the Red Sox off the scoreboard.

"Moore was pitching a great game," Clemens said.

That continued into the home half of the seventh as Moore retired the first two Boston batters. Lyons then singled to left field, however, and shortstop Glenn Hoffman walked, inspiring some hope among the fans. After Ed Romero was inserted as a pinch-runner for Hoffman, right fielder Dwight Evans bounced a 1-0 pitch from Moore off the back wall in center field to give the Red Sox a 3-1 lead.

"After Dewey hit that home run," Clemens said, "it put about 10 more innings in my arm. There was nothing that was going to stop us then."

Indeed, the clout revived Clemens, who had been furious with himself for allowing Thomas' homer. With the count at 0-2, he got Calderon swinging to launch the eighth frame. After Tartabull singled, Clemens went to work on Henderson. The center fielder worked the count to 2-2, then went down swinging to become the Rocket's 18th victim. Clemens was one short of the nine-inning major league record established by Charlie Sweeney of Providence in 1884 and matched in modern times by Steve Carlton, Nolan Ryan and Seaver. Pinch-hitter Al Cowens accounted for the last out of the eighth with a fly to center.

When Clemens returned to the bench, puzzled about the excitement, he was met by Al Nipper. "You have a chance for the all-time record," said the Red Sox righthander, who had seen the information on the scoreboard. "Go for it."

Roger Clemens (right) and catcher Rich Gedman pose triumphantly in the locker room after Clemens' record-setting performance.

"I was tired," Clemens recalled, "but when I made the decision to play this game, I said I was going to give it everything I had. The ninth inning was all adrenaline. I was just out there throwing."

Adrenaline and a blistering fastball that belied symptoms of fatigue combined in Roger's favor as he toed the rubber for the last inning. Pesky old pal Owen led off for the Mariners. Twice on Roger's first three deliveries, the umpire's arm shot outward to signal strikes. On the fourth offering, Owen swung—and missed. Suddenly, Clemens stood shoulder to shoulder with Sweeney, Carlton, Ryan and Seaver.

Bradley, already a three-time strikeout victim, moved tentatively into the batter's box. The former all-conference quarterback at the University of Missouri took Roger's first two pitches for balls. The next two pitches caught the strike zone, evening the count. The cacophony was deafening as Roger fired again. Bradley stood helplessly as the ball shot across the plate and into Gedman's glove. Voltaggio's arm told the story of a new nine-inning record.

The mark for a single game—21 strikeouts by Tom Cheney of Washington in a 16-inning marathon on September 12, 1962—still was within the Rocket's reach. The record eluded the big right-hander, however, as Phelps grounded out to Romero to wrap up the three-hit, 3-1 victory.

"I almost had tears in my eyes," said Fischer, Boston's 55-year-old coach.

McNamara was similarly touched by Clemens' performance. "I've seen perfect games by Catfish Hunter (Oakland, 1968) and Mike Witt (California, 1984)," he said, "but I've never seen a pitching performance as awesome as that, and I don't think you will again in the history of baseball."

The history of baseball is filled with strange coincidences, and the Clemens episode was no exception. Consider this curious twist of circumstances: The Washington second baseman when Cheney established his record was Chuck Cottier, who was managing the Mariners when Clemens established his nine-inning record. More curious still was the fact that Cheney's 21st victim was Dick Williams, who succeeded Cottier as Seattle manager on May 9, just 10 days after the team's humbling experience in Boston.

In his masterpiece, Clemens made 138 pitches, 97 of them fastballs. Every Seattle starter fanned at least once, with Bradley going down four times. Eight batters looked at third strikes, while 12 swung. In the two-hour and 39-minute game, only two Mariners were able to pull the ball against Roger. He walked no one.

Thanks to Clemens' superior pitching, battery-mate Gedman set an A.L. record and equaled a major league mark by making 20 putouts in nine innings.

"The thing that amazed me the most was that they had so many swings and weren't even able to foul the ball," Gedman said. "It wasn't like he was trying to paint the corners or anything. He was challenging them and they weren't able to get a bat on the ball."

The Mariners didn't dispute that point.

"He was throwing really hard, mostly a sinking fastball," said Henderson, a three-time victim. "Everything was on the black of the plate. . . . You knew you didn't have much of a chance up there."

Added Thomas: "Anything you say is an understatement. Clemens was overbearing. I think we should all be happy we were here. We'll never see that again."

Voltaggio was unaware that Roger was on a record pace. "All I knew was that I was working the best pitching performance I'd ever seen," the 10-year veteran of the A.L. umpiring staff said. "I told the batboy that after the seventh inning."

Clemens was in a bit of a daze immediately after the game, but the onslaught of interview requests and calls from well-wishers that night kept his adrenaline pumping for hours afterward.

"I think I finally dozed off about 4:30 in the morning," he said. "I tossed and turned pretty much up until that time. I tried to count sheep and everything I was supposed to. Maybe I should have started to count Ks."

It wasn't until Clemens heard the Hall of Fame called that he fully comprehended the magnitude of his achievement. Officials in Cooperstown, N.Y., wanted to display his glove, cap, spikes and the ball he threw past Bradley for strikeout No. 20.

"I'm in the Hall of Fame," he said. "That's something nobody can take away from me."

April 29, 1986									
Seattle	ab	r	h	rbi	Boston	ab	r	h	rbi
Owen, ss	4	0	1	0	Evans, rf	4	1	2	3
Bradley, lf	4	0	0	0	Boggs, 3b	3	0	0	0
Phelps, 1b	4	0	0	0	Buckner, dh	4	0	2	0
G. Thomas, dh	3	1	1	1	Rice, lf	4	0	1	0
Presley, 3b	3	0	0	0	Baylor, 1b	3	0	1	0
Calderon, rf	3	0	0	0	Stapleton, 1b	0	0	0	0
Tartabull, 2b	3	0	1	0	Gedman, c	4	0	1	0
Henderson, cf	3	0	0	0	Barrett, 2b	3	0	0	0
Yeager, c	2	0	0	0	Lyons, cf	3	1	1	0
Cowens, ph	1	0	0	0	Hoffman, ss	2	0	0	0
Kearney, c	0	0	0	0	Romero, pr-ss	0	1	0	0
Totals	30	1	3	1	Totals	30	3	8	3

Seattle.......................0 0 0   0 0 0   1 0 0—1
Boston.........................0 0 0   0 0 0   3 0 x—3

Seattle	IP	H	R	ER	BB	SO
Moore (L. 1-2)	7⅓	8	3	3	4	4
Young	⅓	0	0	0	0	0
Best	⅓	0	0	0	0	1

Boston	IP	H	R	ER	BB	SO
Clemens (W. 4-0)	9	3	1	1	0	20

E—Baylor, Tartabull. DP—Seattle 1. LOB—Seattle 2, Boston 7. 2B—Buckner. HR—G. Thomas, Evans. T—2:39. A—13,414.

Cloninger's Bat Cuts Down Giants

Major league scouts swarmed about the farmhouse in Lincoln County, N.C., each offering fancy sums of money and lavish promises of opportunities for success if the teen-ager would only affix his signature to the contract thrust before his eyes.

Gradually, the scouts dropped out of the bidding until only four remained—agents for the Cubs, Braves, Reds and Giants. The Cincinnati representative withdrew and the San Francisco scout languished in the front yard, leaving agents of the Braves and Cubs to compete for the young pitching prize.

If odds had been quoted on the outcome, they would have favored the Cubs because their representative, Rube Wilson, lived in the area. But Wilson finished second. Gil English of the Braves captured the prospect with a bonus estimated at $100,000 and a convincing argument. He emphasized that the Braves' pitchers were showing signs of age and that chances of quick advancement in the Milwaukee system were considerably brighter than elsewhere.

When the Giants' scout, lolling under the shade of a front-yard tree, learned that he had definitely lost Tony Lee Cloninger, he hastened to Williamston, N.C., where he signed the other half of North Carolina's hot-shot twosome, Gaylord Perry.

Cloninger, a 6-foot, 210-pound pitcher, was well equipped for a career in professional baseball. In addition to a powerful right arm, he swung the bat forcefully and possessed desire seldom seen in one so young.

As a 14-year-old, Tony arose regularly at 6:30 a.m. during the baseball season and walked a mile to the home of a friend, who chauffeured him to Lincolnton, 12 miles away, where he worked. Here Tony visited the home of his coach until game time. After the game, he was transported back to the family farm near Iron Station by his driver of the morning.

Cloninger started out as a catcher, but discarded the mitt when his coach handed him a baseball and announced, "You're my pitcher."

Almost immediately the coach gained stature as a man of unusual perception. In an early relief appearance, Tony struck out 17 of 18 batters. Another time, as a starter, he fanned 12 batters and allowed only one hit, but an unearned run made him a 1-0 loser.

Lest the world fail to learn about the young phenom quickly enough, an umpire named Red Sherrill sent letters to major league clubs detailing the accomplishments of the righthander. The rush to rural Lincoln County followed.

When tranquility eventually returned to the Cloninger household, Tony invested his handsome bonus in (1) stocks, (2) a sizable pledge to the local Baptist church and (3) a 40-acre farm adjoining that of his parents. At 19, he married his high school sweetheart, Millie Ruth Dellinger.

Cloninger spent three-plus seasons in the minor leagues, with stops at Eau Claire, Wis., Midland, Tex., Cedar Rapids, Ia. (where his record was 0-9), Boise, Idaho, Jacksonville, Fla., Austin, Tex., and Louisville, Ky., where his 5-3 record earned him promotion to the Braves in June 1961.

The rookie made his first major league start on June 15 against the Giants, a team that would figure prominently in Tony's career. After easing through the first two innings, he tried to slip a fastball past Willie McCovey in the third inning and learned his first lesson as a big leaguer. McCovey drove the ball out of sight. The two-run home run gave San Francisco a 3-0 lead, and the Giants went on to win, 6-3.

In his second start, he coasted to a 13-4 victory over the Cubs and, at season's end, owned a record of 7-2.

By 1964, Tony was a 19-game winner and could have added a 20th victory if he had not been so highly principled. Two days before the close of the campaign, he defeated the Pirates, 3-2, in 10 innings for No. 19. On the final day, with the Braves out of pennant contention, Manager Bobby Bragan appointed third baseman Eddie Mathews as "Manager of the Day." Bob Sadowski started against the Pirates and quickly was provided a six-run lead.

Before the righthander completed the five innings necessary for a starter to receive credit for a victory, Mathews proposed to Cloninger that he take over the mound chores and possibly gain credit for an easy 20th victory, the goal of all pitchers.

"Thanks very much," Tony replied. "There's nothing I'd like more than being a 20-game winner. But when I make it I want to earn it on my own.

Pitching took a backseat to hitting for Tony Cloninger in one 1966 game.

Bob is pitching too well to take this one away from him."

It was the type of reaction expected of the unanimous choice for the annual Citizenship Award during his senior year in high school. It also gave additional substance to a comment by Whitlow Wyatt, the Braves' pitching coach, who said, "If I ever had another son, I'd want him to be just like Tony."

Even as a 19-game winner, Cloninger did not post an imposing earned-run average. Nevertheless, his mark of 3.56 was the second lowest figure in his 12-year major league career.

Bragan was not unduly alarmed by Tony's untidy pitching statistics. "In a game against the Cubs," the manager reported, "Tony threw 76 pitches in the first two innings. Some pitchers don't throw many more than that in a whole game. He was 3 and 2 on everybody, left the bases loaded both times and barely survived.

"He finally found his groove, though, and we won."

Cloninger gained his first victory of 1964 on April 29, downing the Pirates. It was a remarkable effort in which he held the Bucs hitless for 6⅔ innings. With two out in the seventh, Willie Stargell approached the plate. As the two faced each other from 60 feet, 6 inches away, their lines of reasoning evolved as follows:

Cloninger: "I've been throwing him curves all night. I got two strikes on him with curves and he

won't expect another."

Stargell: "He's been curving me all night. He knows I won't expect another. So he'll try to cross me up with another."

The curve broke in on Willie, who lined it to right field for a single, the only Pittsburgh hit in Tony's 1-0 victory.

Cloninger achieved the coveted 20-victory pinnacle in 1965. He won 24 games, second in the majors only to the 26 registered by the Dodgers' Sandy Koufax. Tony also shared the National League lead in bases on balls with 119 while striking out 211.

When the Braves, transplanted to Dixie, launched the 1966 campaign, Tony drew the pitching assignment before 50,671 fans in Atlanta. He battled the Pirates for 13 innings, only to lose, 3-2, as Stargell broke a 1-1 tie with a two-run homer. Joe

Torre rapped two homers for the Braves.

The overtime ordeal took its toll on Cloninger's arm. One journalist reported weeks later, "After 13 innings, they had to show him where his right arm was. It was so numb he couldn't find it. Ever since the long and tedious night, Tony has been trying to relocate the touch that won 24 games last season. Every time he pitches, it's a major crisis."

Though he tried constantly to "reach back for something extra" that was nowhere to be found, Cloninger continued to take his turn. Pitching from memory, he forced his record to 8-7 by the end of June. His next start was against the Giants at Candlestick Park on July 3. En route to San Francisco's wind-swept park, Tony recalled his debut there, when Giants catcher Ed Bailey asked him, "You a good hitter, kid?"

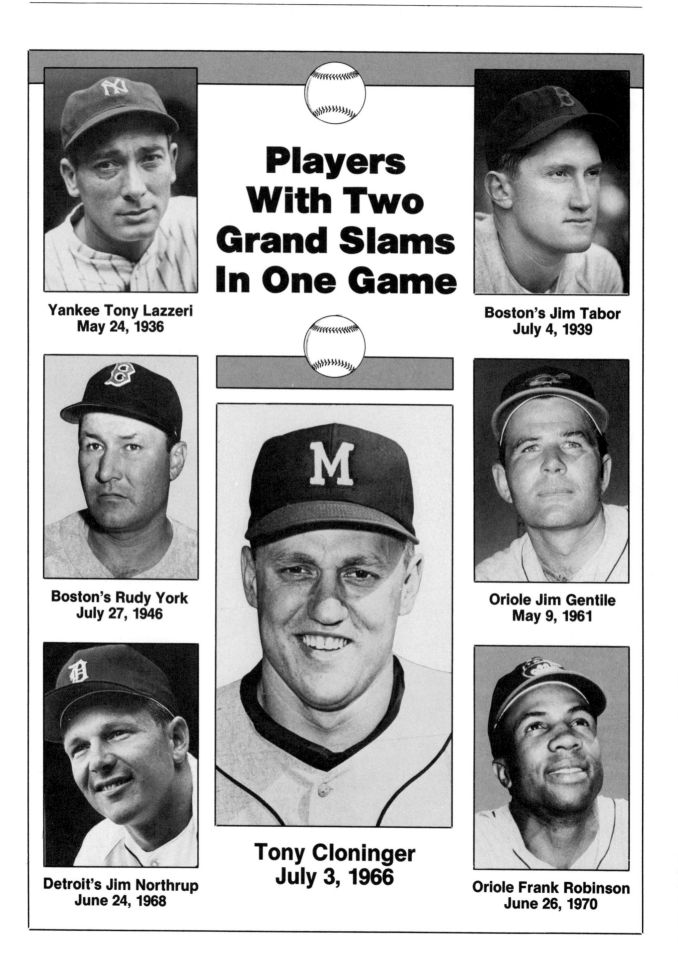

Players With Two Grand Slams In One Game

Yankee Tony Lazzeri
May 24, 1936

Boston's Jim Tabor
July 4, 1939

Boston's Rudy York
July 27, 1946

Oriole Jim Gentile
May 9, 1961

Tony Cloninger
July 3, 1966

Detroit's Jim Northrup
June 24, 1968

Oriole Frank Robinson
June 26, 1970

"No, not very much," Tony had replied before socking a pitch from Mike McCormick to deepest center field, where Willie Mays deprived him of a home run with a spectacular catch.

On this afternoon of July 3, however, no one, not even Willie Mays, would deny Cloninger's right to be called a slugger. Tony's mound opponent was Joe Gibbon, a lefthander with a 3-4 record. As 27,002 fans looked on, the Braves shelled Gibbon from the game after two-thirds of an inning.

With two out in the first inning and Hank Aaron on base after a forceout, Rico Carty hit a bloop single to right, sending Aaron to third. Joe Torre's homer to right-center, his 19th of the season, produced three runs.

When Frank Bolling and Woody Woodward rekindled the attack with singles, Gibbon was replaced by Bob Priddy. The righthander quickly worsened a bad situation by walking Denis Menke, loading the bases.

Cloninger followed and worked the count to 3 and 2 before pounding the payoff pitch over the center-field fence. The grand slam gave the visitors a 7-0 lead.

Cloninger was retired on his second at-bat, but in the fourth inning the Braves struck again, with the 25-year-old pitcher providing the big blow. With one out, Ray Sadecki, the Giants' third pitcher, walked Carty. Torre was safe on an error and Bolling's single drove in Carty. After Woodward popped out, Menke walked again to fill the bases.

As Cloninger stepped into the batter's box, Atlanta's third-base coach, Grover Resinger, turned toward Torre. "Tony's gonna hit another one and set an all-time record," Resinger predicted. "I feel it in my bones."

Torre was flabbergasted. "Go on," the Braves' catcher said. "I've never seen anyone come close to hitting two grand slams in one game."

Sadecki got a strike over before firing a fastball. Tony was ready. The ball set off on a high arc toward right-center field, where Mays and Jesus Alou gave chase. The pursuit was brief. They pulled up short as the ball easily cleared the wall.

As Braves baserunners circled the diamond, Resinger went into an impromptu war dance near third base. At home plate, Torre greeted Cloninger with an enthusiastic embrace that nearly swept Tony off his feet.

Cloninger had become the first National Leaguer —and, not surprisingly, the first big-league pitcher —to hit two grand slams in one game. The four American Leaguers who had accomplished the feat earlier were Tony Lazzeri of the Yankees (1936), Jim Tabor of the Red Sox (1939), Rudy York of the Red Sox (1946) and Jim Gentile of the Orioles (1961). And Cloninger had set an RBI record for major league pitchers, surpassing the mark of seven estab-lished by the Yankees' Vic Raschi in 1953.

Still, Tony's cartridge box was not empty. In the eighth inning, after Woodward doubled and advanced on a wild pitch, Tony collected his ninth RBI of the day by singling home the Braves' 15th run in their 17-3 victory.

In the wake of his historic bombardment, Cloninger commented wryly, "Funny thing, nobody asked me about my pitching."

Cloninger, in fact, was on a batting tear. In the five games he started from June 16 through July 3, he had collected nine hits in 21 at-bats, slugged four home runs and driven in 18 runs. He had begun the fireworks with a two-homer, five-RBI performance against the Mets.

The husky righthander won only 14 games in 1966, though, and topped the league in walks with 116.

He showed flashes of his old speed at the outset of the 1967 season. Then misfortune struck again in the form of a pulled muscle in his right shoulder, a troubling virus and a mysterious eye ailment. Cloninger finished the season with a 4-7 record.

On June 11, 1968, he was traded to Cincinnati in a six-player deal. Cloninger won 11 games for the Reds in 1969, but lost 17 and had an ERA of 5.02. The arm that once propelled a baseball at lightning speed had lost its firepower and Tony slipped steadily.

On March 24, 1972, he was traded to the Cardinals. After losing his only two decisions, he was released in July and never returned to the majors. The onetime phenom's final major league log showed 113 victories, 97 losses.

JULY 3, 1966									
Atlanta	ab	r	h	rbi	San Francisco	ab	r	h	rbi
F. Alou, 1b	3	0	0	0	J. Alou, rf	4	0	1	0
de la Hoz, 3b	2	0	0	0	Haller, c-1b	3	1	1	1
Jones, cf	6	1	3	0	Mays, cf	1	1	0	0
Aaron, rf	4	2	1	1	Landrum, cf	2	0	0	0
Geiger, rf	2	1	1	1	McCovey, 1b	1	0	0	0
Carty, lf	4	3	3	1	Dietz, c	3	0	0	0
Herrnstein, lf	1	0	0	0	Hart, 3b	3	0	1	0
Torre, c	6	2	3	3	Virgil, 3b	1	0	0	0
Bolling, 2b	5	2	2	2	Gabrielson, lf	4	0	1	1
Woodward, ss	6	2	4	0	Davenport, ss	1	0	0	0
Menke, 3b	3	2	0	0	Lanier 2b-ss	4	0	2	0
Cloninger, p	5	2	3	9	Mason, 2b	3	0	0	0
					Gibbon, p	0	0	0	0
					Priddy, p	0	0	0	0
					Sadecki, p	3	1	1	1
					Peterson, ph	1	0	0	0
Totals	47	17	20	17	Totals	34	3	7	3

Atlanta	7	1	0	5	1	0	0	1	2—17
San Francisco	0	0	0	1	1	0	0	1	0— 3

Atlanta	IP	H	R	ER	BB	SO
Cloninger (W)	9	7	3	3	2	5

San Francisco	IP	H	R	ER	BB	SO
Gibbon (L)	⅔	5	5	5	0	0
Priddy	2	4	3	3	2	0
Sadecki	6⅓	11	9	9	2	4

E—Cloninger, Hart, Lanier, Gabrielson. DP—Atlanta 1, San Francisco 1. LOB—Atlanta 8, San Francisco 6. 2B—Woodward 2, Jones, Geiger. HR—Torre, Cloninger 2, Carty, Aaron, Sadecki, Haller. SF—Bolling. WP—Cloninger, Sadecki. T—2:42. A—27,002.

BASEBALL'S

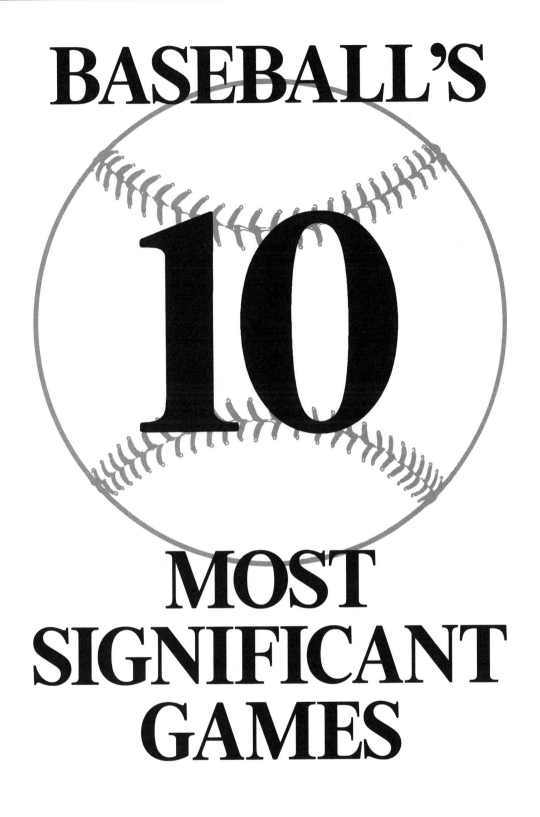

10

MOST
SIGNIFICANT
GAMES

Robinson Breaks Color Barrier

For more than 50 years professional baseball had been divided into two parts. One segment consisted of the major leagues and an assortment of minor leagues operating under the designation of Organized Baseball, and the other was made up of the Negro leagues, loosely knit alignments in which teams often performed at the whim of booking agents.

Teams in Organized Baseball were manned exclusively by white players and catered to a Caucasian clientele. Negro teams featured black athletes with a following composed almost entirely of fans from the same race.

In 1946, the system started to crumble due to the convergence of two iron-willed personalities, Branch Wesley Rickey and Jack Roosevelt Robinson.

The precise moment when Rickey decided to break the game's modern color line is unknown, but it may have occurred in 1943, shortly after the former general manager of the Cardinals signed a five-year contract to serve the Brooklyn Dodgers in a similar capacity.

World War II still was in progress, but the Mahatma of Montague Street was already formulating plans to assemble talent for the peacetime years. In a conversation with George V. McLaughlin, president of the Brooklyn Trust Co., which had been a financial bulwark of the Dodgers for many years, Rickey said:

"We are going to beat the bushes and take whatever comes out. And that might include a Negro player or two."

After a moment to ascertain the sincerity in Rickey's tone, McLaughlin said, "I don't see why not. You might come up with something."

Rickey quizzed club directors on the subject of black players. None took issue. Under his own roof, however, there was strong dissent.

Harold Parrott, traveling secretary of the Dodgers at the time, recalled years later that he learned his boss planned to recruit blacks for the Dodgers—and not, as thought, for the Brown Dodgers of a new Negro league—during a night of bridge at the Rickey home in 1945.

According to Parrott, Rickey sounded out the card players on their views of blacks playing for the

Jackie Robinson played for the Kansas City Monarchs before turning pioneer.

National League club. Mrs. Rickey, Parrott said, was aghast and said, "Why you? Haven't you taken enough abuse about being 'El Cheapo,' about the chain gang (a reference to the far-flung farm system that Rickey developed in St. Louis) and all that? This will just add more slander on your name."

Rickey's son, Branch Jr., also vetoed the idea, maintaining that blacks would ruin the team's scouting program in the South—particularly in the Carolinas, which had been a fertile field for talent in years past. Others in the room echoed the first opinions. Then Rickey turned to Parrott.

"I voted no," Parrott revealed, "because I thought we were strong enough to win without a black. I knew most of the problems would be mine if we brought in a black player. Ebbets Field would embrace a black . . . if he could drive in runs. But road games would bring up many headaches and (Manager Leo) Durocher and I were the only members of the official family who went on the road."

Having been outvoted seven to one, Rickey observed soberly, "The greatest untapped reservoir of raw talent in the history of the game is the black race. The Negroes will make us winners for years to come. And for that I will bear happily being called a bleeding heart and a do-gooder and all that humanitarian rot."

Maintaining the "Brown Dodger" illusion, Rickey assigned two scouts, George Sisler and Wid Matthews, to the Negro leagues. Essentially, their reports concurred. The best prospect was Jackie Robinson, a 26-year-old shortstop with the Kansas City Monarchs. The former four-sport star at UCLA and Army lieutenant in World War II had foot speed and could develop into a fine hitter, they said. Because of Robinson's limited arm strength, the scouts thought second base would be his best position.

Having digested the reports, Rickey dispatched a third scout to bring in the prospect. Clyde Sukeforth ushered Robinson into Rickey's office on the afternoon of August 28, 1945.

Among Rickey's first questions was: "Do you know why you are here?"

"Not exactly," the native of Cairo, Ga., replied. "I heard something about a colored team in Ebbets Field. That it?"

"No, that isn't it. You were brought here to play for the Brooklyn organization, perhaps on Montreal to start with."

Jackie was flabbergasted. "Me? Play for Montreal?" he stammered.

"If you can make it, yes," Rickey answered. "Later on, also if you can make it, you'll have a chance with the Brooklyn Dodgers."

The dialogue continued, in which Rickey lectured Robinson on the verbal abuse that would be rained upon him as a pioneer of racial integration. It was

Before breaking baseball's color barrier, Jackie Robinson served an apprenticeship with the Montreal Royals.

Jackie Robinson officially became a member of the Brooklyn Dodgers when he signed his 1947 contract with Branch Rickey looking on.

imperative, Rickey stressed, that Robinson don "the armor of humility" and also turn a deaf ear—as well as the other cheek—to blasphemous antagonists. Jackie assured Rickey he could stand up under the foulest invective.

The interview over, Robinson departed for points west. About two months later, he was instructed to fly to Montreal and to sign a contract to play for that city's International League club. The signing took place on Tuesday, October 23, 1945. Terms included a signing bonus of $3,500 and a monthly salary of $600.

Several weeks later, Rickey announced the signing of four more blacks. They included pitcher Don Newcombe ($1,000 bonus, $350 a month) and catcher Roy Campanella ($2,900 bonus, $185 a month). Both were prominent Dodgers within a few years.

Robinson, however, was the trailblazer, the pioneer who bore the major portion of the racial burden, who lived alone in cities that practiced segregation and ate meals of questionable quality in third-class restaurants.

Despite such demeaning conditions, however, and the added weight of learning to play second

base during spring training, Robinson was primed for the Montreal Royals' first game at Jersey City, where a capacity crowd welcomed the two teams on April 18, 1946.

Batting second, Robinson grounded out to shortstop on a 3-and-2 pitch on his first at-bat in Organized Baseball. Then matters improved.

In the third inning, Jackie hammered a three-run homer. In the fifth, he bunted for a base hit. He stole second, went to third on an infield out and then rattled the pitcher so badly he committed a balk, allowing Jackie to score.

Robinson laced a clean single in his next at-bat and later bunted safely again (and eventually scored on another balk).

After the final out in Montreal's 14-1 victory, in which Jackie went 4 for 5 and scored four runs, many of the 25,000 spectators rushed onto the field and delayed Robinson's exit for a full five minutes.

Robinson went on to have an outstanding season. He withstood a near nervous breakdown late in the season and led the league in batting with a .349 average, stole 40 bases and led second basemen in fielding percentage. Climaxing a remarkable profes-

Jackie Robinson is greeted at the plate after hitting his first major league home run in his third game as a Dodger.

sional debut, Robinson starred in the Royals' conquest of Louisville in the Junior World Series. At the conclusion of the sixth and deciding game, Jackie and his manager, Clay Hopper, were carried off the field by exuberant spectators.

Robinson remained the property of Montreal well into the 1947 training season. Again, he was learning the rudiments of a new position, first base, because he was told his chances of making the Dodgers were greatly enhanced at that spot.

Indignant, though obedient, Robbie mastered the intricacies of the job and displayed continued skill as a hitter. In seven exhibition games between Montreal and Brooklyn in Panama, he batted .625. Despite his performance, and a constant stream of queries to Rickey about Jackie's future, Robinson remained in a Montreal uniform as the touring clubs reached Brooklyn prior to the start of the National League season.

The long-awaited announcement was made at Ebbets Field on April 10, just as Robinson, playing for Montreal, bunted into a fifth-inning double play in an exhibition game against Brooklyn. Writers were handed a one-sentence release: "The Brooklyn Dodgers today purchased the contract of Jackie Robinson from the Montreal Royals."

On opening day, April 15, Jack Roosevelt Robinson walked into the clubhouse at Ebbets Field and searched for a locker bearing his name. He found none. He checked with John Griffin, the clubhouse custodian.

"Throw your clothes over a chair until a locker becomes available," he was instructed.

The Boston Braves furnished the opposition for the inaugural, and 25,623 of the Flatbush faithful — a disappointing crowd to the club executives — turned out to witness the debut of major league baseball's first black since Moses (Fleet) Walker played for the Toledo club of the American Association in the 1880s.

Batting behind leadoff man Eddie Stanky, Robinson went 0 for 3 but the Dodgers beat Johnny Sain, 5-3. "Every pitch was a curve," Jackie muttered afterward, "and it seemed that he (Sain) threw every one differently." The Braves also used two relievers.

On his first trip to the plate as a National Leaguer, Jackie grounded out to third base. However, with the Dodgers trailing, 3-2, in the seventh inning and Stanky on first as the result of a walk, Jackie laid down a bunt to the right of the mound. First baseman Earl Torgeson fielded the ball, but his hurried throw to nip the speeding Robinson struck the runner and caromed into right field. Both runners scored on a double by Pete Reiser, and Brooklyn went on to win, 5-3.

Hours later, a reporter dropped by Robinson's apartment in a Manhattan hotel and asked for his opinion on the historic event.

"I was comfortable on the field," Jackie said. "The Brooklyn players have been swell and they were encouraging all the way. I realize that to stay in the National League, I'll have to hit. Will I hit? I know I will."

Despite his unfamiliarity with the opposing pitchers, not to mention the impact of continued racial slurs and the threat of a player strike by the St. Louis Cardinals, Jackie performed impressively, sometimes brilliantly, as he remembered Rickey's earlier admonition for self-discipline.

Robinson collected his first major league hit, a bunt single, against Glenn Elliott of Boston in his second game. He socked his first home run against Dave Koslo of the Giants in the third contest.

He stole his first base in the fifth game, and a truly fulfilling theft it was. The Phillies, led by Alabama-born Manager Ben Chapman, were heaping all manner of revilement on Jackie, who offered not a word or a gesture in rebuttal.

As the flood of abuse crested, Stanky, a resident

of Mobile, Ala., but a native of Philadelphia, shouted, "Chapman, why don't you pick on somebody who can fight back?"

The Phillies' bench fell silent, and Jackie knew for certain that his teammates were solidly behind him.

Robinson did strike back against the Phillies, however, in a style that got Rickey's approval. With the Dodgers' Hal Gregg and Phils knuckleball ace Dutch Leonard engaged in a scoreless duel, Jackie singled in the eighth inning, stole second, took third on the catcher's overthrow and scored the only run of the game on Gene Hermanski's single.

Playing in 151 games during his freshman season, Jackie batted .297 and hit 12 home runs. In addition, he stole a league-high 29 bases for the pennant-winning Dodgers and was acclaimed Rookie of the Year by The Sporting News and the Baseball Writers' Association. In announcing his publication's selection, Publisher J.G. Taylor Spink of The Sporting News wrote: "That Robinson might have had more obstacles than his first-year competitors and that perhaps he had a harder fight to gain major league recognition, was no concern of this publication. The sociological experiment that Robinson represented, the trailblazing that he did, the barriers he broke down did not enter into the decision. He was rated and examined solely as a freshman player in the big leagues—on the basis of his hitting, his running, his defensive play, his team value."

With Robbie proving a huge gate attraction around the league in '47, the Dodgers drew 1,807,526 fans, an N.L. record at the time, into Ebbets Field and 1,863,542 on the road.

In the first of his six World Series, Jackie batted .259 in the Dodgers' seven-game loss to the Yankees.

With the arrival of Gil Hodges to play first base, Robbie returned to his favorite position, second base, in 1948. The next year, he won the N.L. batting championship with a .342 mark, drove in 124 runs and gained recognition as the Most Valuable Player in the National League.

In 10 years with the Dodgers, Robinson batted .311. In the 1952 World Series, he tied a record by drawing four walks in one game. And in the opening game of the 1955 Series, he stole home. While the Dodgers lost that game and Game 2 as well, Brooklyn rebounded to capture the only Series crown in the borough's history.

On December 13, 1956, he was traded to the Giants. Jackie, though, announced his retirement three weeks later (he was accepting an executive position with a restaurant chain) and the deal was canceled.

Robinson died of a heart attack on October 24, 1972, at his home in Stamford, Conn., one decade after his election to the Hall of Fame.

APRIL 15, 1947

Boston	ab	r	h	rbi	Brooklyn	ab	r	h	rbi
Culler, ss	3	0	0	0	Stanky, 2b	3	1	0	0
Sisti, ss	0	0	0	0	Robinson, 1b	3	1	0	0
Hopp, cf	5	0	1	1	Schultz, 1b	0	0	0	0
McCormick, rf	4	0	3	0	Reiser, cf	2	3	2	2
R. Elliott, 3b	2	0	1	0	Walker, rf	3	0	1	0
Litwhiler, lf	3	1	0	0	Tatum, rf	0	0	0	0
Rowell, lf	1	0	0	0	Vaughan, ph	1	0	0	0
Torgeson, 1b	4	1	0	0	Furillo, rf	0	0	0	0
Masi, c	3	0	0	0	Hermanski, lf	4	0	1	1
Ryan, 2b	4	1	3	2	Edwards, c	2	0	0	1
Sain, p	1	0	0	0	Rackley, pr	0	0	0	0
Cooper, p	0	0	0	0	Bragan, c	1	0	0	0
Neill, ph	0	0	0	0	Jorgensen, 3b	3	0	0	1
Lanfranconi, p	0	0	0	0	Reese, ss	3	0	1	0
Holmes, ph	1	0	0	0	Hatten, p	2	0	1	0
					Stevens, ph	1	0	0	0
					Gregg, p	1	0	0	0
					Casey, p	0	0	0	0
Totals	31	3	8	3	Totals	29	5	6	5

Boston.................................0 0 0 0 1 2 0 0 0—3
Brooklyn.............................0 0 0 1 0 1 3 0 x—5

Boston	IP	H	R	ER	BB	SO
Sain (L)	6	6	5	3	5	2
Cooper	1	0	0	0	0	0
Lanfranconi	1	0	0	0	0	2
Brooklyn	IP	H	R	ER	BB	SO
Hatten	6	6	3	1	3	3
Gregg (W)	2 1/3	2	0	0	2	2
Casey	2/3	0	0	0	0	1

E—Edwards, Torgeson. DP—Boston 1, Brooklyn 1. LOB—Boston 12, Brooklyn 7. 2B—Reese, Reiser. HBP—By Hatten (Litwhiler), by Sain (Edwards), by Gregg (Neill). WP—Hatten. A—25,623.

Though he did endure countless racial slights and slurs, Jackie Robinson had
supporters and signed his share of autographs.

Night Baseball Debuts in Cincinnati

Cincinnati Reds Owner Powel Crosley Jr. (left) and Larry MacPhail brought night baseball to the major leagues in 1935.

On an open date in the National League schedule of 1930, Sam Breadon, who delighted in conclaves of congenial souls, invited writers covering the Giants and Cardinals to an outing on his farm southwest of St. Louis.

After a vigorous baseball game and a pleasant interlude for food and drink, the Cardinals' owner was subjected to a crossfire of queries on all aspects of the national game.

The most popular topic was night baseball, which had been introduced in the minor leagues a few months earlier with encouraging results at the turnstiles. Asked if he thought lights would be installed in National League parks, Breadon replied:

"I certainly do and let me tell you, some of the owners who have been quoting themselves out on a limb will be looking at it from another angle before long. Wait until I give them some reports on the minors at the winter meeting . . . they'll change their tunes."

Revealing that Houston, a St. Louis farm club, and other Texas League franchises were enjoying remarkable attendance increases, Breadon exclaimed, "If I can get 15,000 to 18,000 out at night instead of 3,500 to 5,000 in the daytime, nobody is going to condemn me."

Of the 16 major league club owners, Sam Breadon was the first and most vocal to endorse afterdark play. Ironically, however, he was denied the honor of pioneering night ball in the majors.

At the time Sam was extolling the virtues of nocturnal play, the Cardinals were tenants of the

Major league baseball's first night game was preceded by a fireworks display
that heralded the trailblazing event.

Browns in Sportsman's Park. Before he could seriously consider the installation of lights, Breadon had to negotiate a deal with his landlords. His first offer was to split the cost between the National League and American League clubs. No deal.

Breadon tried again, proposing that he pay the entire cost of installation. The Browns acquiesced, with the stipulation that all the equipment, once installed, then belonged to the Browns.

Now it was Breadon's turn to say no, and on that point the matter foundered and died.

While Breadon and the Browns haggled, a young dynamo was attracting attention for his progressive operation in Columbus, O. In four seasons, Leland Stanford (Larry) MacPhail had taken a moribund American Association franchise and made it flourish.

Not too many miles to the south, a bank was operating the Cincinnati Reds for the estate of the late Sidney Weil. An imaginative and aggressive personality was sorely needed to pump vitality into the Reds' franchise. MacPhail was that man.

Arriving in Cincinnati after the 1933 season, Larry cast about for a civic-minded man of affluence to purchase controlling interest in the team. He found his angel in Powel Crosley Jr., who had accumulated a fortune in the manufacture of radios.

In one of their early conversations, Crosley congratulated MacPhail on his brilliant success at Columbus during a period when the nation was attempting to emerge from the Great Depression.

"Well, of course, we played under lights there," MacPhail replied modestly.

"Why not lights in the National League?" Crosley countered.

"Oh, they'd never let me do that," Larry answered.

"How do you know? You could try," Crosley responded.

At the National League meeting in the fall of 1934, MacPhail laid his proposal before the club owners and received the expected opposition. Well-to-do owners rejected the notion as a poor man's scheme to escape insolvency. Let the city that produced the first professional team in 1869 solve its own problems. Night ball was bush league. The fans would never support it. So ran the arguments. But the Reds' vice president could be as persistent as the hidebound reactionaries.

MacPhail refused to back down, and his persuasiveness ultimately drove a wedge in the opposition. He was granted, albeit grudging, the "privilege" of playing seven night contests in 1935, one against each league rival. However, if a team did not wish to participate, it could not be coerced into doing so.

Brash and brassy Larry had scored the first of his numerous major league victories. Returning to Cincinnati, he engaged General Electric engineers to illuminate Crosley Field for nighttime activity. The New York Giants flatly declined an invitation to play under the arcs, which was fine with Sam Breadon, whose Cardinals willingly accepted a second date.

As the Reds prepared for the historic occasion, American League executives looked on in haughty disdain. The Yankees' Edward G. Barrow declared unequivocally that night ball would never invade the sacred precincts of the House that Ruth Built.

In Washington, Clark Griffith was equally adamant. "There is no chance of night baseball ever becoming popular in bigger cities," the president of the Washington Senators predicted. "People there are educated to see the best there is and will stand for only the best. High-class baseball cannot be played at night under artificial lights. Furthermore, the benefits derived from attending the games are largely due to fresh air and sunshine, and electric lights are a poor substitute. . .The game was meant to be played in the Lord's own sunshine."

May 23, 1935, was chosen as the date for the great experiment in Cincinnati. But rain forced the nighttime inaugural to be postponed 24 hours. On May 24, the Reds and Phillies shared the distinction of playing the majors' first night contest.

Undoubtedly, chilly temperatures held down the crowd. Nevertheless, 20,422 Rhineland fans paid to witness the milestone event. Had the game been played on Friday afternoon, instead of Friday night, one journalist pointed out, it probably would have attracted about 2,000 persons.

To entertain the topcoat-clad fans, showman MacPhail hired four drum and bugle corps. Fireworks, featuring a huge "C" encompassing "Reds," together with aerial bombs gave the occasion a holiday flair.

President Franklin Delano Roosevelt pushed a

MAY 24, 1935

Philadelphia	ab	r	h	rbi	Cincinnati	ab	r	h	rbi
Chiozza, 2b	4	0	0	0	Myers, ss	3	1	1	0
Allen, cf	4	0	1	0	Riggs, 3b	4	0	0	0
Moore, rf	4	0	1	0	Goodman, rf	3	0	0	1
Camilli, 1b	4	0	1	0	Sullivan, 1b	3	1	2	0
Vergez, 3b	4	0	1	0	Pool, lf	3	0	1	0
Todd, c	3	1	1	0	Campbell, c	3	0	0	1
Watkins, lf	3	0	0	0	Byrd, cf	3	0	0	0
Haslin, ss	3	0	1	0	Kampouris, 2b	3	0	0	0
Bowman, p	2	0	0	1	Derringer, p	3	0	0	0
Wilson, ph	1	0	0	0					
Bivin, p	0	0	0	0					
Totals	32	1	6	1	Totals	28	2	4	2

Philadelphia	0	0	0	0	0	1	0	0	0	0—1
Cincinnati	1	0	0	1	0	0	0	0	x—2

Philadelphia	IP	H	R	ER	BB	SO
Bowman (L)	7	4	2	2	1	1
Bivin	1	0	0	0	0	1

Cincinnati	IP	H	R	ER	BB	SO
Derringer (W)	9	6	1	1	0	3

DP—Cincinnati 1. LOB—Philadelphia 4, Cincinnati 3. 2B—Myers. SB—Vergez, Myers, Bowman. T—1:55. A—20,422.

Baseball's first game under the lights was tougher on photographers than the players on the field.

button in the White House and, through the magic of electronics, Crosley Field was illuminated. It was, one witness attested, "the closest approach to daylight ever attained on an outdoor field."

Inasmuch as most of the players had never performed under lights, each team was allowed 12 minutes to practice under the unfamiliar conditions.

Bill Klem, the "Old Arbitrator," soon took his position behind home plate. His associates were Ziggy Sears and Babe Pinelli, allegedly chosen for this assignment because they had umpired under lights in the minor leagues.

Judge Kenesaw M. Landis had been designated to make the ceremonial first pitch, but the commissioner was confined to his Chicago home by illness and the honor was accorded Ford Frick, president of the National League. The ball was caught by Chuck Dressen, manager of the home team. After Paul Derringer, the Cincinnati starter, delivered one pitch to Lou Chiozza, the ball was relayed to

Frick for display among National League memorabilia.

After Derringer disposed of the Phillies in the top of the first inning, Billy Myers led off the bottom of the frame with a double that glanced off the glove of left fielder George Watkins. Infield outs by Lew Riggs and Ival Goodman produced the first run under major league lights. The pitching victim was the Phils' Joe Bowman.

A second Cincinnati run scored in the fourth when Billy Sullivan and Harlin Pool singled and Gilly Campbell grounded out.

The Phils solved Derringer for their only run in the fifth when Al Todd singled, went to third on Mickey Haslin's single to center and crossed the plate on Bowman's infield roller.

Immediately after the Reds' 2-1 victory, executives were besieged for their opinions of nighttime baseball. Frick was enthusiastic. "Now it's up to the fans," he commented. "There were many great fielding plays, especially in the outfield. I don't think there was any difficulty on the part of the hitter either."

Defensive gems were registered by Reds shortstop Myers, who drifted far into the outfield to catch a high pop fly; by Cincinnati center fielder Sammy Byrd, who crashed into the fence and snared a long drive by Dolph Camilli, and by first baseman Camilli, who made several dazzling pickups of errant throws by Phillies infielders.

American League President Will Harridge, though noncommital on the future of night ball, termed the game "the best spectacle I've seen in years. I enjoyed the game very much. Nothing is lost by playing at night."

The low-hit contest—there were six hits by the Phillies, four by the Reds—was not attributable to the lights, Phils Manager Jimmy Wilson said. "Both pitchers had all their stuff working," Wilson explained. "You can see that ball coming up to the plate just as well under those lights as you can in daytime."

Phils outfielder Watkins added, "It's my bread and butter and while I prefer daylight ball, I'm willing to do my best to help the game."

The 600-plus lamps, installed at a cost of more than $40,000, were hailed universally for transforming night into day. The system could not be faulted, customers maintained, for the limited visibility created by a passing locomotive that belched forth black smoke that settled over the field late in the game.

Though the Reds drew well for their six other nighttime attractions in 1935, the editor of the Spalding Guide still had reservations—to say the least.

"That it (night ball) will succeed depends upon whether it was made common or not," John B. Foster wrote. "An attendance of 20,000 followed by three 'crowds' of 3,000 on the next three days will not average very high. Then there may be another series, or two more, before another night game is played and the attendance will drop to 16,000 or less for eight games. The attendance, if games were played nightly, would drop steadily until it was no better than in the daytime, with the added expense made necessary by artificial lighting.

"Cincinnati has been a problem in attendance ever since its admission into the National League. Yet, in common with other cities in the circuit, attendance will pick up quickly once winning baseball becomes a steady diet."

For three seasons the Reds were the only major league club to boast of an illuminated park. Not until 1938, by which time Larry MacPhail was the chief executive officer of the Brooklyn Dodgers, was a second park equipped with lights. The Dodgers inaugurated night ball at Ebbets Field on June 15, 1938, and attracted 38,748 paying fans, who watched Johnny Vander Meer of the Reds pitch his second consecutive no-hitter in beating the Dodgers, 6-0.

Gradually, the stern resistance to night ball softened. There was no gainsaying the financial benefits to be reaped from increased attendance created by nocturnal play. On May 16, 1939, Connie Mack of the A's introduced after-dark play at Shibe Park in Philadelphia and two weeks later his tenants, the Phillies, became the third National League club to stage a night contest. The same season, the Indians and White Sox fell in line.

May 24, 1940, was a significant date in the annals of night play. The Giants, fiercely opposed to the novelty five years earlier, switched on the lights at the Polo Grounds while the Browns, Sam Breadon's adversaries of years before, joined the ranks on the same evening in St. Louis.

The lights went on at Forbes Field in Pittsburgh a week and a half later, the same evening (June 4) that the Cardinals played their first nighttime home game.

On May 28, 1941, Clark Griffith, forgetting about the "Lord's sunshine," added Washington to the swelling list of night-ball participants.

After World War II, the Braves and Yankees illuminated their parks (both doing so in 1946), followed by the Red Sox (1947) and Tigers (1948).

Only the Cubs remained out of step and, curiously, they were set to install lights for the 1942 season when international events intervened. Equipment had been delivered to Wrigley Field and installation was scheduled to start shortly when the Japanese attacked Pearl Harbor on December 7, 1941. With the outbreak of hostilities, the Cubs donated the material to the war effort and junked the idea of nighttime baseball.

Baseball Reaches For the Stars

Arch Ward (right), pictured with American League President Will Harridge, was the man behind baseball's All-Star Game.

Chicagoans lined up at the Comiskey Park gates in 1933 to purchase tickets for the 'Game of the Century.'

Baseball addicts had dreamed for years of a game between heroic figures of one major league against those of another, but because regulations provided for no such Olympian struggle, it remained pure fantasy, good only for whiling away rainy Sunday afternoons or drowsy hours in study hall.

Great pleasure was created by speculation on the result of a matchup of Christy Mathewson and Ty Cobb, Walter Johnson and Honus Wagner. As members of rival leagues, there was no hint to which would be the master and which the serf unless they met in a World Series, which they never did.

In truth, teams of select players had been assem-

bled on occasion, but they served only to whet the appetite of the fans. Once, after Addie Joss, the redoubtable Cleveland pitcher, died at the peak of his career, an American League all-star team was selected to play an exhibition against Cleveland to raise funds for the family of the deceased player.

Another time, when the American League schedule ended a week before that of the National, the A.L. champions played a team of stars chosen from the league's seven other clubs in "tuneup" competition preceding the World Series.

But these games did not satisfy the fans' thirst for a game of stars versus stars, the cream of one circuit against the cream of the other. Only a confrontation of the demigods would do.

The chances of such a supreme engagement were non-existent until the city fathers of Chicago drafted plans for the Century of Progress Exposition in 1933. To supplement the cultural and industrial exhibits—as well as the performance of a terpsichorean teaser named Sally Rand—a member of the committee suggested a gigantic sports extravaganza to focus the nation's attention on the Illinois metropolis.

Anybody have a suggestion on how to achieve this goal? Arch Ward, the 36-year-old sports editor of the Chicago Tribune, did.

Ward was a native of Irwin, Ill., and had attended St. Joseph's Academy in Dubuque, Ia., for two years before transferring to Notre Dame in 1919. While at South Bend, he had served as sports publicity director. He was sports editor of the Morning Star in Rockford, Ill., for several years before joining the Tribune sports staff in 1925. By 1930 he was sport editor, recognized widely as a fine administrator with progressive ideas.

Ward was invited into the inner councils of the World's Fair planners. From this confab evolved a rough blueprint for a baseball contest between the superstars of the American League and the National League. As a result of the fans' fantasizing for decades over just such a game, it would be heralded as the "Dream Game" or the "Game of the Century." Ward was empowered to work out the details.

The Tribune, it was determined, would underwrite the game, to be played at Comiskey Park on July 6, 1933, and would oversee the fans' balloting for the composition of both teams, aided by newspapers nationwide.

Major league executives, however, took a dim view of the proposed project. Some threw up their hands in horror. The idea was too preposterous, even though the concept was old. It required study, profound cerebrations, consultations, deliberations. The World Series, to be played for the 30th time in 1933, was a sufficient test of the relative strength of the two leagues.

Ward did not have time to argue or plead. He arranged a luncheon date with Will Harridge, the American League president. Harridge endorsed the idea, promising his wholehearted support in convincing his eight club owners that the colossal contest would stimulate interest in baseball during the financial panic of the time and generate volumes of publicity.

The sports editor's next stop was Wrigley Field, where he outlined his proposal to Bill Veeck Sr., president of the Cubs. Veeck, too, embraced the plan and recommended that Ward enlist the help of John A. Heydler, president of the National League.

Replying by letter, Heydler assured Ward that while he personally liked the idea, three unnamed

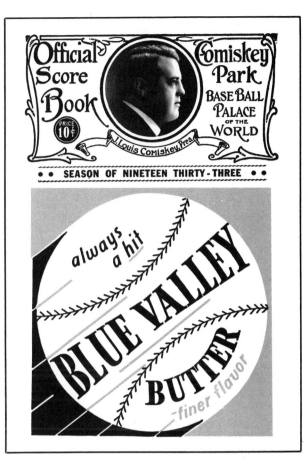

The game's scorebook pictured White Sox President J. Louis Comiskey and sold for 10 cents.

N.L. club owners opposed it. Which three, Arch wondered, and what were their objections? Did they oppose the game for personal reasons, or was it simply an aversion to change?

Eventually, the dissenters were identified as the New York Giants, Boston Braves and St. Louis Cardinals.

When the Giants arrived in Chicago for a series with the Cubs, Ward confronted Jim Tierney, seeking to ascertain from the traveling secretary the reasons for the New York club's posture.

Tierney had a plausible explanation. The Giants were scheduled to play a doubleheader in Boston on July 4. Moreover, an earlier rainout had created another doubleheader on July 5. Under those circumstances, New York players selected for the All-Star Game would be unable to reach Chicago in time the following day.

If the July 5 commitment could be changed, Ward wondered, would the Giants give their consent? Tierney thought they would.

To bring the Braves into line, Ward consulted Major Frederic McLaughlin, owner of the Chicago Black Hawks hockey team and a close friend of

First American League All-Star Team

The brightest stars of the American League gathered for a picture prior to
baseball's first All-Star Game.

First National League All-Star Team

National League stars gathered around acting Manager John McGraw for
their pregame picture.

Charles F. Adams, a major stockholder in the Boston Bruins of the National Hockey League and president of the Braves. Adams promised to recommend a schedule change to club executives, which was adopted.

Now only the Cardinals remained between Arch Ward and the "Dream Game." It seemed uncharacteristic for an imaginative club owner like Sam Breadon to stand in the way of progress. Ward conferred with the last holdout.

Breadon, it developed, feared that an interleague game in the middle of a season would establish a bad precedent, that other cities would start clamoring for a similar event and that newspapers would start competing for the right to conduct player balloting.

"They will want to only if the game is a success," Ward assured Breadon. "If the game goes over, the Tribune will turn back all rights and the two leagues can present the game as their affair."

Breadon was mollified and Ward was ecstatic. With all roadblocks eliminated, the "Game of the Century" would be a certainty.

Comiskey Park, which had not witnessed such excitement since the ill-fated White Sox of 1919 performed in the World Series, was festooned lavishly with the national colors when fans arrived on July 6, a warm and sunny Thursday afternoon. More than 47,500 wide-eyed customers gazed expectantly as warm-up drills revealed giants of the American League cavorting in their home uniforms, those of the senior circuit sporting special attire emblazoned with "National League" on the shirt front.

The managers for the monumental event were household names. Tall and spare and wearing a Panama hat was Connie Mack, venerable pilot of the Philadelphia Athletics. His counterpart, also in civilian attire but wearing a straw skimmer, was John McGraw, longtime skipper of the Giants who had retired

A's Manager Connie Mack handled the A.L. squad and longtime Giants Manager John McGraw came out of retirement to direct the National Leaguers.

slightly more than a year before. The two had matched wits three times in World Series play, but not since 1913 when the A's whipped the Giants and gave Mack a 2-1 edge over Little Napoleon.

The umpires, too, represented the best of their profession. Bill Dinneen of the American League started behind the plate, Bill Klem of the National League was at first base, Bill McGowan of the A.L. at second and Cy Rigler of the N.L. at third. After 4½ innings, the umpires moved one base clock-wise.

The starting-pitcher honor for the home team went to Lefty Gomez of the Yankees. Bill Hallahan of the Cardinals drew the assignment for the N.L. Each had pitched nine innings only two days earlier (Gomez actually worked 9⅓ innings), a fact that—as matters developed—was less damaging to the 24-year-old Gomez than to the 30-year-old Hallahan.

Gomez breezed through the first inning as Senators shortstop Joe Cronin threw out two batters and snared a line drive off the bat of the third. Hallahan issued a base on balls to Charley Gehringer (Tigers) in the bottom of the inning, but allowed no hits.

Singles by Chick Hafey (Reds) and Bill Terry (Giants) opened the second inning for the National League, but Wally Berger (Braves) grounded into a double play and Dick Bartell (Phillies) struck out to end the inning.

With one out in the home half of the second, Jimmie Dykes (White Sox) and Cronin drew walks from Hallahan. After Rick Ferrell (Red Sox) flied out, there appeared little likelihood that anything would come of the threat because the next batter

was Gomez, one of baseball's notoriously weak hitters (as evidenced by his .147 lifetime average). But, at this instant, the lefthander they called El Goofy stepped out of character. He lined a Hallahan pitch to center field for a run-scoring single and thereby gained distinction as the manufacturer of the first RBI in All-Star Game annals.

"Don't ask me what the pitch was," the self-deprecating Gomez cracked. "It could have been a fastball down the pike. With a bat in my hands, I couldn't tell a curve from a Cuban palm ball. I do recall that one of my eyes was closed when I swung."

The American Leaguers struck again in the third inning. Gehringer launched the uprising with his second walk. When Hallahan attempted to slip a pitch past Babe Ruth, the Yankee slugger drilled it to right field. The ball sailed into the lower pavilion just inside the foul pole, giving the junior league a 3-0 lead.

When Hallahan followed by walking Lou Gehrig (Yankees), he was removed in favor of Lon Warneke (Cubs), who retired the side without further damage.

With Alvin Crowder (Senators) on the mound for the Americans, the Nationals closed the gap in the sixth with a two-run outburst that was ignited by Warneke. The righthanded batter sliced a drive to right field that the aging Ruth played none too well. Before the Bambino could return the ball to the infield, Warneke was on third base with a triple. An infield grounder by Pepper Martin (Cardinals) produced the National League's first run. When Frank Frisch (Cardinals) followed with a clout into the right-field seats, the N.L. was within one run.

But that was as close as McGraw's team came. In the last of the sixth, the American League scored its fourth run on a single by Cronin, a sacrifice by Ferrell and a single by pinch-hitter Earl Averill (Indians).

Lefty Grove (A's) succeeded Crowder on the mound at the start of the seventh and quickly ran into trouble. A single by Terry, a forceout and a pinch double by Pie Traynor (Pirates) raised comeback hopes of N.L. partisans, but Grove extricated himself by striking out Gabby Hartnett (Cubs) and getting pinch-hitter Woody English (Cubs) to fly out.

The Nationals mounted a minor threat in the eighth when Frisch singled and, with two out, Hafey lifted a long fly to right field. For a second, the drive appeared headed for the stands, but Ruth backed to the wall and made the catch.

Grove disposed of the Nationals without disruption in the ninth, wrapping up the 4-2 triumph for Gomez, the first of three victories by the Yankee pitcher in five All-Star Game appearances.

JULY 6, 1933									
Nationals	ab	r	h	rbi	Americans	ab	r	h	rbi
Martin, 3b	4	0	0	1	Chapman, lf-rf	5	0	1	0
Frisch, 2b	4	1	2	1	Gehringer, 2b	3	1	0	0
Klein, rf	4	0	1	0	Ruth, rf	4	1	2	2
P. Waner, rf	0	0	0	0	West, cf	0	0	0	0
Hafey, lf	4	0	1	0	Gehrig, 1b	2	0	0	0
Terry, 1b	4	0	2	0	Simmons, cf-lf	4	0	1	0
Berger, cf	4	0	0	0	Dykes, 3b	3	1	0	0
Bartell, ss	2	0	0	0	Cronin, ss	3	1	1	0
Traynor, ph	1	0	1	0	R. Ferrell, c	3	0	0	0
Hubbell, p	0	0	0	0	Gomez, p	1	0	1	1
Cuccinello, ph	1	0	0	0	Crowder, p	1	0	0	0
Wilson, c	1	0	0	0	Averill, ph	1	0	1	1
O'Doul, ph	1	0	0	0	Grove, p	1	0	0	0
Hartnett, c	1	0	0	0					
Hallahan, p	1	0	0	0					
Warneke, p	1	1	1	0					
English, ph-ss	1	0	0	0					
Totals	34	2	8	2	Totals	31	4	9	4

National League	0	0 0	0 0 2	0 0	0—2
American League	0	1 2	0 0 1	0 0	x—4

Nationals	IP	H	R	ER	BB	SO
Hallahan (L)	2*	2	3	3	5	1
Warneke	4	6	1	1	0	2
Hubbell	2	1	0	0	1	1
Americans	IP	H	R	ER	BB	SO
Gomez (W)	3	2	0	0	0	1
Crowder	3	3	2	2	0	0
Grove	3	3	0	0	0	3

*Pitched to three batters in third.

E—Gehrig. DP—Nationals 1, Americans 1. LOB—Nationals 10, Americans 5. 2B—Traynor. 3B—Warneke. HR—Ruth, Frisch. SB—Gehringer. SH—Ferrell. T—2:05. A—47,595.

The immortal Babe Ruth marked his imprint on the historic occasion by hitting a two-run homer.

To win the 2-hour, 5-minute spectacle, Connie Mack called on 13 of his 18 players. In his pregame speech to the troops, the Tall Tactician said that if the A.L. jumped into the lead, he would stick with his starting eight "position" players. And, with the exception of a ninth-inning defensive switch that sent Sam West (Browns) into the outfield, Mack did just that. As a result, Jimmie Foxx (A's), Bill Dickey and Tony Lazzeri (both of the Yankees) and Wes Ferrell and Oral Hildebrand (both of the Indians) saw no action. John McGraw used all the National Leaguers except Hal Schumacher (Giants).

Because of the public's enthusiastic support of the first All-Star Game, a second interleague contest was scheduled in 1934 and the Giants were selected as the host club. The game became a fixture on the baseball calendar after the Giants' Carl Hubbell caught the public fancy by striking out five straight future Hall of Famers in the '34 classic.

Arch Ward, who orchestrated baseball's first All-Star Game, also founded the Chicago College All-Star football game in 1934 and was instrumental in the birth of the professional All-America Football Conference in 1946. He was 58 when, on July 9, 1955, he suffered a fatal heart attack. Funeral services were held July 12, the day that baseball's 22nd All-Star Game was played in Milwaukee.

In his memory, the major leagues subsequently inititated the Arch Ward Memorial Award for the outstanding player in the All-Star Game.

Baseball's First World Series

Boston fans swarm onto the field at Huntington Avenue Grounds after watching their A.L. club win the first World Series.

Several weeks before the close of the 1903 major league season, newspapers in Pittsburgh and Boston started to editorialize in favor of a postseason series between the league-leading teams representing those cities. The objective was to determine the baseball champion of the world.

The concept of such a series was not new, of course. In the 19th Century, teams from the National League and the American Association (also part of "big time" baseball in that era) had contended for best-in-the-world distinction. However, there had been no need for a championship tournament at the outset of the 20th Century. In 1900, the National League was the lone "major league"—as it had been for eight years. And when the American League came along in 1901 and fought on in 1902, the National League continued to regard itself as the sole major league. The fledgling A.L., a self-proclaimed "big league," was considered little more than an interloper.

The bitter two-year war between the leagues

ended in 1903, though, with the signing of a peace treaty. Now the leagues were equals, operating without fear of player raids and bound in comity by a National Agreement.

Talk of an interleague championship series horrified some club owners in the National League. The wounds from the vicious struggle still festered. A simple document, signed in Cincinnati, was no panacea.

One who differed from that posture was Barney Dreyfuss, a 125-pound scrapper who owned the Pittsburgh Pirates. At an early age, Barney emigrated from Germany to escape military conscription. He arrived in Paducah, Ky., home of some relatives, and went to work in a distillery cleaning out whiskey barrels.

Within a short time, he was head bookkeeper. When the distillery transferred its business operations to Louisville, Dreyfuss went along.

Through diligent application and an onerous work schedule, he made steady progress until his health, never robust, started to fail. He consulted a physician, who recommended an outdoor recreation to build up Barney's frail physique.

"Like what?" Dreyfuss asked.

"Like baseball," the doctor replied.

Until then, Barney had been so busy poring over ledgers there had been no time for the burgeoning national pastime. Now, however, he investigated the sport, learned the rules and mechanics and even formed his own semipro team. He found the game to be the perfect diversion. He acquired stock in the local professional club and by 1899 was president of the Louisville club of the National League.

When, at the end of that season, league executives voted to reduce membership from 12 to eight clubs, eliminating Louisville among others, Barney purchased controlling interest in the anemic Pittsburgh franchise. Taking along the cream of the Louisville roster—Honus Wagner, Fred Clarke, Tommy Leach and Charles (Deacon) Phillippe—Dreyfuss transformed the Pirates into instant contenders. In fact, Pittsburgh won pennants in 1901, 1902 and 1903 under Clarke, and both Barney and the Buccos were ready when the opportunity arose for a championship series against Boston's American League titlists, who had finished 14½ games ahead of the defending A.L. champion Philadelphia Athletics.

The American League pennant-winners were owned by Henry J. Killilea, a Milwaukee lawyer, who was invited to a conference by Dreyfuss to work out details of a championship series.

Before accepting, Killilea checked with Ban Johnson, the forceful onetime sportswriter who had muscled the American League into major status.

"Do you think you can beat 'em?" the A.L. president inquired.

"My manager thinks we can," Killilea answered.

"Then play 'em," said Johnson, fully cognizant that, as the neophyte, the American League had everything to gain and nothing to lose.

The two moguls—little Barney with the heavy Teutonic accent, and the urbane Killilea—hammered out an agreement providing:

"1. That the said clubs shall play a postseason series consisting of nine games, if it should be necessary to play that number of games before either club should win five games.

"2. Said games are to be played as follows:

"At Boston, October 1, 2, 3.

"At Pittsburgh, October 5, 6, 7, 8.

"At Boston, October 10 and 12.

"In the event of one postponement or more on account of bad weather, the clubs must remain in the city in which the games were scheduled until it shall be possible for them to complete the series. In other words, if one game of the first series be postponed, the clubs will not appear in Pittsburgh until October 6. If two games be prevented, the Pitts-

burgh series will not begin until October 7 and if three games be postponed, the opening in Pittsburgh will be delayed until Thursday, October 8. When the said clubs do begin the Pittsburgh series, they must remain in said city until the completion of the series of four games, or the number required to decide the championship. Should the entire series of nine games be necessary, the said clubs shall play the remaining two games in Boston.

"3. It is agreed that the umpires shall be Henry O'Day (of the National League) and Thomas Connolly (of the A.L.).

"4. No player shall participate who was not a regular member of either team on September 1, 1903. (A similar restriction has governed World Series competitors until the present day.)

"5. The respective captains shall confer with the umpires before the series begins and agree upon a uniform interpretation of the rules."

In relating the details of the agreement, the Pittsburgh correspondent for The Sportng News wrote: "As will be noted, nothing is said . . . as to the division of the receipts. The matter was amicably adjusted between the two moguls and will not be made public."

Another issue untouched was the payment of players. Dreyfuss had no immediate worries on that score because National League contracts extended until October 15. In the American League, however, contracts expired on September 30 and Boston players threatened to strike if they were not satisfied financially. Killilea won over the disgruntled athletes by granting them two extra weeks of pay while also throwing part of the club owner's share into the players' pool.

To swell the revenue, the clubs raised ticket prices.

As they prepared for the first modern World Se-

OCTOBER 1, 1903									
Pittsburgh	ab	r	h	rbi	Boston	ab	r	h	rbi
Beaumont, cf	5	1	0	0	Dougherty, lf	4	0	0	0
Clarke, lf	5	0	2	0	Collins, 3b	4	0	0	0
Leach, 3b	5	1	4	1	Stahl, cf	4	0	1	0
Wagner, ss	3	1	1	1	Freeman, rf	4	2	2	0
Bransfield, 1b	5	2	1	0	Parent, ss	4	1	2	1
Ritchey, 2b	4	1	0	0	LaChance, 1b	4	0	0	2
Sebring, rf	5	1	3	4	Ferris, 2b	3	0	1	0
Phelps, c	4	0	1	0	Criger, c	3	0	0	0
Phillippe, p	4	0	0	0	O'Brien, ph	1	0	0	0
					Young, p	3	0	0	0
					Farrell, ph	1	0	0	0
Totals	40	7	12	6	Totals	35	3	6	3

Pittsburgh ....4 0 1   1 0 0   1 0 0—7
Boston....................................0 0 0   0 0 0   2 0 1—3

Pittsburgh	IP	H	R	ER	BB	SO
Phillippe (W)	9	6	3	2	0	10
Boston	IP	H	R	ER	BB	SO
Young (L)	9	12	7	3	2	5

E—Ferris 2, Criger 2, Leach, Wagner. LOB—Pittsburgh 9, Boston 6. 3B—Freeman, Parent, Leach 2, Bransfield. HR—Sebring. SB—Wagner, Bransfield, Ritchey. HBP—By Phillippe (Ferris). PB—Criger. T—1:55. A—16,242.

A.L. President Ban Johnson (left) knew his league had nothing to lose by playing Barney Dreyfuss' Pittsburgh team in a World Series.

ries, the Pirates were handicapped badly by injuries. Honus Wagner, their extraordinary shortstop, was limping on a severely wrenched knee.

Sam Leever, whose 25-7 record produced the National League's best winning percentage (.781) in 1903, was suffering from a sore shoulder, the result of a trapshooting accident. Moreover, Ed Doheny, a lefthander who had contributed 16 victories in the Pirates' flag triumph, was hospitalized with mental problems.

Arriving in Boston the day before the start of the Series, the Pirates checked into the Vendome Hotel and then engaged in a brisk two-hour workout at the Huntington Avenue Grounds.

Back at the Vendome, the Pirates ran the gamut of verbal abuse. Leather-lunged Boston partisans subjected the visitors to sharp ridicule. Coarse epithets flew across the lobby and bodily threats were not uncommon.

Gamblers were plentiful, too. One journalist reported that "about $10,000 was wagered on the outcome of the first game and the Series."

Manager Fred Clarke nominated Deacon Phillippe, a 6-foot righthander who had won 24 games in 1903, as the starting pitcher for the Pirates in Game 1. Jimmy Collins, Boston's slick-fielding third baseman and manager, chose Cy Young, who had prevailed in 28 decisions in the A.L. that season and, at that point, had won 378 games in his big-league

career. Phillippe was 31 years old, Young 36.

The opening contest drew "a tremendous crowd of 16,242," many of whom camped on the foul lines or behind ropes in the outfield. Also on hand, and much in evidence, were the Royal Rooters, a large group of Boston zealots who paraded behind their own band and sang uproariously a popular tune of the day, "Tessie," whenever they hoped to inspire a home-club rally.

Barney Dreyfuss also was in the throng, and he was in a foul mood. The club owner and his guests were required to pay their way into the park. But Barney had little cause to grouse. The Boston business manager treated his own club officials in like manner.

Dreyfuss' mood changed abruptly in the first inning when the Pirates scored four runs off Young. Cy retired the first two batters before Tommy Leach drove a ball into the roped-off outfield crowd for a triple. He scored on Wagner's single.

Honus stole second. Kitty Bransfield grounded to the right side, and second baseman Hobe Ferris misplayed the ball. The batter was safe and Wagner took third. Ferris' jitters proved contagious. As Bransfield stole second on a delayed double steal, catcher Lou Criger threw the ball into the outfield, permitting Wagner to score and Bransfield to move to third.

Claude Ritchey coaxed a walk from Young and

New York Giants Owner John T. Brush (in carriage) and Manager John McGraw refused to play a World Series in 1904.

promptly stole second. Jimmy Sebring then singled to left field, driving in Bransfield and Ritchey.

Bransfield's triple and Sebring's single produced the Pirates' fifth run in the third inning and Pittsburgh added a sixth in the fourth when Ginger Beaumont, safe on Ferris' second ground-ball error, moved around on singles by Clarke and Leach.

The National Leaguers concluded their scoring in the seventh when Sebring blasted a home run to center field. It was his third hit and fourth RBI of the afternoon.

Boston broke through against Phillippe for two runs in the seventh on triples by Buck Freeman and Freddie Parent and a fly ball. The American Leaguers pushed across their last run in the ninth when Freeman reached base on Wagner's error, Parent singled to left and Candy LaChance delivered his second run-scoring fly ball of the day. Pittsburgh had won, 7-3.

Boston tied the Series the next day when Bill Dinneen tossed a 3-0 shutout, but Pittsburgh's Phillippe, pitching again after only one day of rest, turned in another remarkable game on Saturday, October 3. He yielded four hits and triumphed, 4-2.

The largest crowd of the Series, 18,801, had overflowed onto the playing field for the Saturday game and hundreds stood 20 deep behind ropes in the outfield. After the start of the game, the standees grew unruly. They flatly refused to make way for Pittsburgh outfielders chasing fly balls, but eagerly opened gaps in their ranks for Boston players on similar pursuit. Still, the National Leaguers collected five automatic doubles on drives into the roped-off area, the Americans two.

Game 4, scheduled for Exposition Park in Pittsburgh on October 5, was postponed a day because of rain. Only 7,600 turned out for the game that matched Phillippe against Dinneen. Neither pitcher was as sharp as in earlier play—the Deacon yielded nine hits, Bill gave up 12—as the Pirates won, 5-4.

Boston then ran off four consecutive victories—11-2, 6-3 and 7-3 in Pittsburgh, and 3-0 behind Dinneen back home—and clinched the first modern World Series, five games to three.

Hours after the last out, after the final defeat in the Series that had begun so auspiciously for his team, Barney Dreyfuss hosted a midnight dinner for the Pittsburgh players and their guests. In his broken English, Barney paid tribute to his athletes and then drew a roar of applause by announcing that he would toss the club owner's share of the proceeds into the players' pool.

As a result, each losing Pirate received $1,316, each winning Boston player $1,182.

Boston repeated as the American League champion in 1904 and invited the New York Giants, pennant-winners in the National, to another postseason series. The offer was declined by Giants Owner John T. Brush and Manager John McGraw, both of whom were still nursing old sores that were opened by the interleague strife.

Provisions for a World Series under the auspices of the National Commission, the game's ruling authority, were enacted in 1905. Curiously, the rules for the Series were drafted by Brush himself, who gained added satisfaction when his Giants dominated the Philadelphia Athletics that fall, four games to one, with each contest being a shutout.

Baseball's Newest Wonder

While waiting for the completion of baseball's first domed stadium, the Houston Colt .45s played in Colt Stadium, next door to the new facility.

If the muse of history is to be trusted, a Texas tourist in Rome heard a guide explain that in ancient times the Colosseum featured a "velarium," a type of awning operated by slaves and machinery that protected emperors and patricians from the broiling sun as they cheered themselves hoarse for a favorite entry in the "Man Vs. Beast" competition.

As he gazed in awesome wonder, the traveler was struck by a sudden inspiration. If the ancients could combat the sun so effectively, why couldn't moderns erect an enclosed stadium to neutralize the heat and humidity that held Houston in its midsummer clutches?

From that point forward, Roy Mark Hofheinz, familiarly known as "Judge," directed his energies toward the construction of an enclosed arena in which spectators could enjoy a spectacle free from sinister elements.

To many non-Texans, the suggestion of a roofed-over stadium smacked of Lone Star hyperbole. A major sports event indoors was anathema to those who believed that baseball fans were meant to endure summer's heat and football fans were supposed to freeze in late autumn's cold.

Arguments against the futuristic project were loud and persistent. They also were blithely dismissed by Texans, who equated huge dreams with huge accomplishments.

Plans for a domed stadium received their first major impetus in October 1960 when Houston and New York were awarded National League expansion franchises starting in 1962. "There can be no question about building the stadium for the 1962 opening," asserted the chairman of the county board of commissioners. All portents appeared favorable in late January 1961 when the voters of Harris County, in which Houston is located, approved a $22 million bond issue, $18 million earmarked for the stadium and $4 million going for access roads and bridges.

Hofheinz and other members of the Houston Sports Association, which had been awarded the National League franchise, were jubilant over the outcome of the election.

"Dirt will fly on South Main Street immediately," enthused Hofheinz, a former mayor of Houston. "From now on our motto is going to be 'full speed ahead.' "

But agonizing delays intervened before work could begin. Months passed. On October 30, 1961, when bids for the excavation work were to be opened, it was discovered that only one contractor

This panoramic view of the Astrodome in the spring of 1965 shows the playing surface dwarfed by the imposing dome.

out of 13 who obtained specifications submitted a bid. It was $857,769. The figure was exorbitant, snapped one official, who insisted the job could be done for $500,000. Two months later, the contract was awarded for $430,311, with the stipulation that the work be completed within 120 working days. Based on estimates that 12 to 14 months would be required for the stadium construction, Houstonians fully expected to watch baseball under cover by midseason of 1963.

That hope, too, was extravagant. A half-dozen lawsuits had to be settled first. A labor strike upset the timetable further. When funds ran low, the Houston Sports Association went back to the voters and asked for $9.6 million to complete the project. The proposition was approved by 6,801 votes.

As the stadium took shape on what once had been swamp land, visitors to the site denigrated the structure with phrases like "pompous pimple," "blustering blister" and "great carbuncle." Texans paid such slurs no heed. To them, it was the "Eighth Wonder of the World."

Hofheinz never doubted the wisdom of his ways. "We are building something that nobody in the world has or ever will have for years to come, something that will set the pattern for the 21st Century,"

Even New York Mets Manager
Casey Stengel was awed by the
Astrodome, baseball's newest
wonder.

he said. "It will antiquate every other structure of this type in the world. It will be an Eiffel Tower in its field."

Still more problems arose as construction progressed. Initially, a green tint was applied to the 4,596 plastic skylights. To the horror of everyone, it was discovered that sunlight cast a bilious glow over spectators, so a cream-white tint was substituted.

With one problem corrected, another sprouted. How could grass thrive without benefit of direct sunlight? The problem was referred to Texas A&M University, which was awarded a grant to develop a new strain that met the peculiar needs of the enclosed arena. At the time, a "grass bank" was established at College Station, 90 miles away, to furnish replacement turf as needed.

During its first three seasons, the Houston team was known as the Colt .45s. While awaiting completion of the domed stadium, Houston played in 32,000-seat Colt Stadium. When the firearms company protested the use of its name by a baseball club, the team was rechristened the Astros in honor of the nearby space center. The enclosed stadium, while known officially as the Harris County Domed Stadium, became known generally as the Astrodome.

To guarantee the utmost in creature comfort, a 6,600-ton air conditioning system was installed in the "rain or shine" structure. Every minute, it was pointed out proudly, two million cubic feet of air circulated through the building. Other than maintaining a steady 72-degree temperature, the system had a second advantage, Hofheinz joked. "If we're behind in the top of the fifth inning," he cracked, "all we have to do is turn off the air conditioning and it will start to rain."

The gigantic arena, occupying 9½ acres seven miles from the middle of the city, had an outside diameter of 710 feet and an inside diameter of 516 feet. A paved parking lot provided accommodations for 500 buses and 30,000 cars.

The peak of the dome rose 208 feet above the playing surface, higher than any batter ever was known to have hit a fly ball. Though no one expressed an interest in such an impracticable endeavor, it was noted the Astrodome was so massive that it would be possible to place the Shamrock Hilton Hotel of Houston or the Atlantic City Convention Center or the Cow Palace of San Francisco entirely within the enclosure with space to spare.

Other distinctions attributed to the revolutionary pleasure palace were:

—Longest major league dugouts, 120 feet, which included the bullpens for pitchers and catchers.

—Longest and largest scoreboard . . . 474 feet . . . with a half-acre of information surface, 50,000 lights, 1,200 miles of wire, standing four stories tall and costing $2 million.

—Brightest major league playing field . . . maximum of 300-foot candles.

—First domed structure of more than 400 feet clear span (it is 642 feet).

—Elimination of irritating fumes in the facility by filtering the air through 10 boxcars of activated charcoal, largest operation of its kind ever attempted.

—Capacity to produce 18 tons of ice daily, the largest installation of machine-made ice in the country.

—The prospect of 40,000 persons washing their hands simultaneously without exhausting the supply of water.

—Closed-circuit television made available in five clubs and restaurants, enabling patrons to watch events in progress while away from their seats.

—First baseball seats (of foam rubber) that could be vacuumed instead of wiped or washed.

—The first "bomb sight" pictures of baseball or football playing fields made possible, thanks to a retractable gondola stationed over the center of the field.

—Because the playing surface was 31 feet below ground level, spectators could walk *down* to 81 percent of the stadium's opera-type seats.

—An employee roster of 2,019 was needed to handle capacity crowds. Included were 70 parking-lot attendants, 10 parking-lot checkers, 15 deputy sheriffs, 15 city policemen, 775 concessions workers, 300 cooks, 35 daytime maintenance men, 100 post-game cleaners, 31 restroom matrons and 22 restroom porters.

The Astros appeared in the Astrodome for the first time in April 1965. It was an intrasquad game in which it became quickly apparent that conditions would not permit normal daytime contests. The glare of the sun made it all but impossible for

APRIL 12, 1965									
Philadelphia	ab	r	h	rbi	Houston	ab	r	h	rbi
Taylor, 2b	5	0	2	0	Lillis, ss	4	0	0	0
Allen, 3b	4	1	2	2	Morgan, 2b	3	0	2	0
Callison, rf	4	0	1	0	Wynn, cf	4	0	0	0
Covington, lf	3	0	0	0	Bond, 1b	4	0	0	0
Herrnstein, lf	0	0	0	0	Aspromonte, 3b	4	0	1	0
Gonzalez, cf	4	0	2	0	Beauchamp, lf	3	0	0	0
Stuart, 1b	3	0	1	0	Gaines, rf	3	0	0	0
Wine, pr-ss	0	0	0	0	Bateman, c	2	0	1	0
Dalrymple, c	4	0	0	0	Bruce, p	2	0	0	0
Amaro, ss-1b	3	1	1	0	White, ph	1	0	0	0
Short, p	3	0	1	0	Woodeshick, p	0	0	0	0
Totals	33	2	10	2	Totals	30	0	4	0

Philadelphia	0	0	2	0	0	0	0	0	0—2
Houston	0	0	0	0	0	0	0	0	0—0

Philadelphia	IP	H	R	ER	BB	SO
Short (W)	9	4	0	0	3	11
Houston	IP	H	R	ER	BB	SO
Bruce (L)	7	9	2	2	1	5
Woodeshick	2	1	0	0	1	1

E—Allen. DP—Philadelphia 1, Houston 2. LOB—Philadelphia 8, Houston 7. 2B—Taylor, Morgan. HR—Allen. SH—Short, Herrnstein, Bateman. T—2:34. A—42,652.

The explosive new scoreboard gave Houston fans a real treat when Leon McFadden homered in a 1965 exhibition game against the Yankees.

outfielders to track fly balls. How could the situation be remedied? The most feasible suggestion, reported Hofheinz, came from operators of greenhouses "throughout the length and breadth of the nation" who had dealt with glare problems.

The solution lay in 700 gallons of acrylic off-white paint approximating the shade of the translucent plastic roof. In three days, 10 paint guns covered the dome and eliminated *that* problem.

However, yet another problem was created in the process. Without sunlight, the grass could not be expected to grow—and it didn't. The Monsanto Co. was consulted and ultimately developed AstroTurf, a synthetic rug that withstood excessive abuse and soon found its way into other major league parks. (Artificial turf was first used at the Astrodome in 1966, with the infield covered from the beginning of the season and the outfield fitted with the synthetic grass later in the year.)

The first exhibition game in the Astrodome was played on April 9, 1965. The night game between the Astros and Yankees attracted 47,876 fans, including President and Mrs. Lyndon Johnson, who saw the Astros register a 12-inning, 2-1 victory when pinch-hitter Nellie Fox singled home Jimmy Wynn. Mickey Mantle was credited with the first hit in the Astrodome, a first-inning single, and also the first homer, a sixth-inning smash that caromed off a railing in right-center field, about 400 feet from the plate. On April 10, an afternoon crowd of 22,457 saw the Astros pound out 17 hits in defeating the Orioles, 11-8. That night, 48,145 were on hand as the Yankees scored a 14-inning, 4-3 decision on Clete Boyer's home run.

Another split doubleheader was booked on Sunday, April 11. In the afternoon, 48,172 looked on as Fox delivered again with a 10th-inning single that defeated the Yankees, 3-2. That night, 22,112 watched as the Orioles scored four unearned runs in a 5-0 triumph.

By the time the Astros were ready to open the National League race, more than $3 million had been added to Hofheinz's till. The five exhibition games that drew more than 188,000 netted $500,000 in ticket revenue. Moreover, 53 luxury boxes encompassing 2,000 seats on the ninth level had been sold for prices topping out at $34,000. Also, Hofheinz sold 5,000 seats in other sections to less-affluent folks at $280 apiece. Another $1.25 million was harvested from the sale of tickets on the lower levels.

Dignitaries of every persuasion were in the

The Astros added a touch of showmanship to their new domed stadium by having astronauts doing pregame and midgame cleanup work.

throng of 42,652 when the Astros ushered in the regular season on April 12. They included Commissioner Ford Frick, National League President Warren Giles and Gov. John Connally of Texas, who threw out the first ball.

Twenty-four of the nation's 28 astronauts were present and received lifetime passes to all major league parks. In the press box, 253 writers from all corners of the country reported the first indoor game in the regular season.

Bob Bruce, who had won 15 games in 1964, drew the starting pitching assignment from Houston Manager Lum Harris. Chris Short, coming off a 17-9 season, was Gene Mauch's selection to start for the Phillies, who still were attempting to forget the nightmarish climax to the 1964 campaign when they squandered a substantial lead and finished in a tie for second place.

Short was masterful in his first outing of the year. The 27-year-old lefthander allowed only four hits, including a single and double by Joe Morgan, in gaining the first of his 18 victories for the season. He won, 2-0, as Richie Allen, N.L. Rookie of the Year in 1964, clouted a two-run homer in the third inning.

Though the Astros finished ninth in their first season in the Astrodome, they drew 2,151,470 paying customers, which stood as a club record until

the West Division champions of 1980 played before 2,278,217.

With an all-weather stadium in which to play, the Astros felt confident that never again would a home game be delayed or postponed for any reason whatsoever. In the main, they were correct.

But on July 24, 1966, a game with the Pirates was interrupted in the eighth inning because 100 lights to the right of home plate went out. Umpires demanded the problem be corrected before resuming action. They relented, however, when engineers explained that a heat buildup on the roof had caused circuit breakers to kick out and the situation could not be remedied until after the game.

On June 15, 1976, a game actually was postponed because of rain. Players arrived at the Astrodome ahead of a torrential downpour, but when umpires, stadium personnel and fans set out for the game, they found the flooded streets impassable. No game!

Otherwise, the Astrodome—later joined in the majors' covered-stadium category by the less-luxuriant Kingdome (Seattle, 1977) and Metrodome (Minnesota, 1982)—was everything that the visionary Judge predicted it would be.

Hofheinz lived until November 21, 1982, when his monument was more than 17 years old. He was 70 when he suffered a fatal heart attack.

Baseball Arrives On West Coast

On April 15, 1958, opening-day ceremonies at San Francisco's Seals Stadium marked the arrival of major league baseball on the West Coast.

Reports of imminent cataclysmic changes in the major league baseball map had circulated for months, depressing thousands of fans in the New York area while exhilarating thousands of others a continent away.

Yet, when the announcements of the two historic franchise shifts were made in 1957—the Giants disclosed their intentions in August, the Dodgers in October—they struck like thunderclaps, shocking and stunning those who, like their sires, had worshiped at the shrines of the New York and Brooklyn baseball teams. The Giants were headed for San Francisco, and the Dodgers were bound for Los Angeles. Clearly, the booming and population-rich West Coast was an untapped treasure chest.

Earlier transfers of the Boston Braves to Milwaukee (1953), the St. Louis Browns to Baltimore (1954) and the Philadelphia A's to Kansas City (1955) were accepted with relative equanimity since those franchises had fallen upon particularly difficult times. But the Giants and the Dodgers were breeds apart. These teams were facing increasing hardships, yes, but the franchises were steeped in tradition and dotted with the names of luminaries.

In New York, the names of Jim Mutrie, Christy Mathewson and John McGraw, of Bill Terry, Mel Ott and Carl Hubbell, were as bright as in the days of their prime.

In Brooklyn, the same could be said of Charles Ebbets, Zack Wheat and Dazzy Vance, of Larry

The 1957 arrival of Dodgers officials in Los Angeles was occasion enough for
a group picture, with team President Walter O'Malley at the top of the steps.

MacPhail, Leo Durocher and "Dem Bums," fabled for their zaniness as well as their brilliance.

To uproot clubs with such character, and with their legions of loyalists, was not only unconscionable, it was downright unpatriotic.

But soul and tradition and heroes failed to influence balance sheets. Dwindling attendance at the Polo Grounds and inadequate facilities that inhibited growth at Ebbets Field foreshadowed dramatic geographic upheaval.

The Giants, in their 52,000-seat Polo Grounds, suffered from twin agonies—an acute shortage of parking space and a steady shift of population to the suburbs. After the club drew 1.15 million fans in its World Series championship season of 1954, attendance skidded to 824,112 in 1955, 629,179 in 1956 and 653,923 in 1957.

Likewise, the Dodgers were gripped by an economic stranglehold in their 44-year-old park with fewer than 32,000 seats. The perennial flag contend-

ers managed to draw one million fans regularly, but might easily have doubled that figure in a more commodious stadium.

Walter O'Malley, president of the Dodgers, made no secret of his dissatisfaction over his cramped quarters. A hint of things to come was dropped in 1956 when O'Malley transferred seven home contests to Roosevelt Stadium in Jersey City. The Dodgers played eight more home games in Jersey City the following year.

O'Malley also transmitted his discontent to civic officials. For a time it appeared likely that the borough would condemn slum housing to make room for a new stadium, but when the estimated cost proved prohibitive, the plans were abandoned.

The first concrete evidence that California was going to inherit major league ball occurred on August 19, 1957, when the directors of the National Exhibition Co., the corporate name of the Giants, voted 8 to 1 to permit President Horace Stoneham

One of the first orders of business after the Dodgers' arrival in Los Angeles was the conversion of the Memorial Coliseum into a baseball field.

to move the club to San Francisco. The only negative vote was cast by M. Donald Grant, later the chief executive officer of the New York Mets.

Commenting on the transcontinental leap, Stoneham said, "It's a tough wrench. We're very sorry we're leaving. I'm very sentimental about the Giants and New York City. But conditions were such we had to accept now or they might not be so favorable again."

Asked what had molded the decision to move, Stoneham repiled, "Lack of attendance. We're sorry to disappoint the kids of New York, but we didn't see many of their parents out there at the Polo Grounds in recent years."

Among the lures extended to Stoneham was the promise of a new stadium, already approved in a voter referendum. Until the park was completed, Stoneham revealed, the team would play in Seals Stadium, a 22,500-seat structure that had served as home for the Pacific Coast League Seals for 27 seasons.

News of the Dodgers' move to Los Angeles was disclosed officially on October 8, while the World Series between the Yankees and Braves was in progress. A bulletin in the press room at the Waldorf Astoria Hotel disclosed ". . . the stockholders and directors of the Brooklyn Baseball Club have today met and unanimously agreed that necessary steps be taken to draft the Los Angeles territory."

Under baseball law, the Dodgers, as well as the Giants in San Francisco, were required to indemnify those who held the rights to professional baseball in those areas.

In anticipation of the Dodgers' move to Los Angeles, O'Malley had acquired the Pacific Coast League's Los Angeles Angels from Philip K. Wrigley, owner of the Chicago Cubs, in February of '57. As part of the transaction, the Cubs acquired the Fort Worth franchise in the Texas League.

Initially, there was considerable speculation over

Comedian Joe E. Brown, flanked by L.A. Manager Walter Alston and Giants coach Herman Franks, was part of the Dodgers' home-opening festivities.

the park to be used by the Dodgers. Wrigley Field, Los Angeles' minor-league facility, accommodated only 25,000 persons. The Rose Bowl in Pasadena was mentioned as a probable site, but eventually the Dodgers settled on the Memorial Coliseum, an enormous amphitheater that could hold 90,000-plus fans.

To the Giants went the distinction of playing host to the first major league contest on the West Coast. The landmark date was April 15, 1958. Before a crowd of 23,448 that included Ty Cobb and Mrs. John McGraw, widow of the late, great New York Giants manager, the San Francisco team marked the occasion in superlative style against its old archrivals from the East, the Dodgers.

The throng that came to admire the consummate skills of Willie Mays and other established stars also found itself cheering the talents of three Giants rookies—first baseman Orlando Cepeda, third baseman Jim Davenport and right fielder Willie Kirkland.

Bearing no resemblance to the team that finished sixth the previous year, the Giants battered Don Drysdale for five hits and six runs before the right-hander retired in the fourth inning. They tagged Drysdale for two runs in the third inning, which started with bases on balls to Danny O'Connell and Valmy Thomas. An infield single by pitcher Ruben Gomez, a sacrifice fly by Davenport and a single by Jim King netted the runs.

Daryl Spencer launched a fourth-inning bombardment against Drysdale with a home run. A walk to Thomas, who advanced on a passed ball, was followed by Gomez's RBI single. Another single by Davenport chased Drysdale and brought on Don Bessent. After King walked, Mays socked a two-run single to complete the uprising.

In the fifth inning, Cepeda sliced a home run over the right-field fence and, in the eighth, a walk to King and singles by Mays and Kirkland produced the final run in the Giants' 8-0 victory.

While the Giants were amassing 11 hits, Gomez

The Dodgers got just what they expected when a baseball-record regular-season crowd of 78,672 showed up at the Coliseum on April 18, 1958.

was checking the Dodgers on six safeties. The right-hander also walked six batters and eluded numerous jams as the Dodgers had 10 baserunners in the first seven innings.

As Lefty O'Doul, former major league outfielder and longtime manager of the San Francisco Seals, strolled from the park, he heard the chant of his favorite newsboy. He stopped short and listened a second time. His ears did not deceive him. The hawker was screaming: "New York Giants win opener."

"Hey, Charlie," O'Doul called, "what team was that?"

Charlie did a double take and forthwith changed his spiel. "Giants win opener," he yelled.

Before the Dodgers could introduce major league ball to Los Angeles, extensive alterations were necessary at Memorial Coliseum. In addition to laying out a diamond, the club constructed dugouts, erected three new light towers, a backstop screen and a five-tier press box.

The most noticeable change took place in left field, where the fence loomed only 251 feet from home plate. To minimize chances for cheap home runs, a 40-foot-high screen was installed, extending for 140 feet from the foul line to the 320-foot marker in left-center field. The project cost the Dodgers an estimated $300,000.

The Coliseum inaugural was played on April 18 and, fittingly, the Giants furnished the opposition. Appropriately, too, for the huge arena, and the city that had hungered for big-league ball for many years, the game was witnessed by the largest single-game, regular-season crowd in the history of the majors, 78,672.

The Giants, who had won two of three games against the Dodgers in the first series at Seals Stadium, grabbed an early lead in the Los Angeles opener. With two out in the third inning, Davenport collected his sixth consecutive hit in two days, a single, and took third on Kirkland's double off Carl Erskine, the Dodgers' veteran righthander.

One of the intriguing features of the Coliseum was a left-field fence only 251 feet from home with a 40-foot screen that discouraged cheap home runs.

Erskine, who won only five games the previous year (a season in which he was hampered by a shoulder ailment), then walked Mays and Spencer, forcing in Davenport.

The Dodgers bounced back in their half of the third, which opened with a walk to Jim Gilliam. An infield out sent Gilliam to second, from where he scored on Duke Snider's single to center. Snider took second when Mays misplayed the ball for an error and scored on Charlie Neal's single.

Hank Sauer's home run enabled the Giants to tie the score in the fourth before the Dodgers broke loose for three runs in the fifth.

After Gil Hodges was retired, Neal coaxed a walk off Al Worthington and took second on Dick Gray's single. When Gino Cimoli singled to right field, Kirkland threw to the plate, but Neal scored on the play and catcher Bob Schmidt mishandled the ball, permitting Gray to cross the plate, too. Cimoli, who went to second on the play, moved to third on a fielder's choice and raced home with the third run of the inning on a wild pitch.

The Dodgers scored their last run in the seventh when Gray homered to the right of the left-field screen.

Schmidt's triple and a passed ball in the sixth inning had accounted for the Giants' third run, and San Francisco added a fourth run in the eighth when Sauer's fly ball arched over the left-field screen.

San Francisco, which outhit the Dodgers, 12 to 8, made its final charge at Erskine in the ninth and, except for a baserunning blunder, might have tied the score.

Davenport opened the inning with a double, his third hit off the screen. The blow knocked out Erskine and brought on Clem Labine, who immediately yielded a 400-foot triple to Kirkland. Davenport raced across the plate with what appeared to be the fifth San Francisco run, but the marker was nullified when the umpires upheld the Dodger appeal that the runner had failed to tag third base. Kirkland eventually scored on a bad throw, but the rally died as Labine retired Spencer on an outfield fly and Cepeda on a pop foul.

The opening series at the Coliseum produced 12 home runs and an ensuing three-game set against the Cubs netted another dozen. For a time, there was speculation that the short porch in left field could produce a record total of home runs and possibly lead to a toppling of Babe Ruth's one-season mark of 60 set in 1927. Fears of such developments evaporated, however, as pitchers adapted to the conditions. At season's end, a total of 193 homers had been clouted at the Coliseum, 101 by the opposition and 92 by the Dodgers. The total was considerably short of the big-league record for homers at one park in one season (219, at Cincinnati's Crosley Field, in 1957).

Although the 1958 Dodgers finished in seventh place, 21 games behind the pennant-winning Braves, they drew 1,845,556 paying customers. The previous year, in Brooklyn, the Dodgers attracted 1,028,258.

The Giants played in Seals Stadium through 1959, drawing 1,272,625 in their first season (almost double their attendance in New York in '57) and 1,422,130 in the second year. Each season, the team finished third under Manager Bill Rigney.

On April 12, 1960, the Giants moved into new Candlestick Park, celebrating the occasion with a 3-1 victory over the Cardinals as Willie Mays tripled home two runs in the first inning and added a run-scoring single in the third.

The Dodgers, meanwhile, played in the Coliseum through 1961. Manager Walt Alston's team played to 2,071,045 fans in 1959 on the way to a World Series title, then drew 2,253,887 as a fourth-place team in 1960 and 1,804,250 as a second-place club in 1961.

The largest crowd during this period was 93,103, which turned out on May 7, 1959, to watch the Dodgers play an exhibition game against the Yankees and, particularly, to honor Roy Campanella, the future Hall of Fame catcher who suffered paralyzing injuries in a car accident during the winter preceding the Dodgers' move to the West Coast. Los Angeles drew a World Series-record crowd of 92,706 in 1959 and also had throngs of 92,650 and 92,394 during that classic.

The Dodgers moved into gleaming Dodger Stadium on April 10, 1962. Cincinnati, outhitting Los Angeles, 14 to 8, and getting a three-run, tiebreaking home run from Wally Post in the seventh inning, spoiled the opening-game festivities with a 6-3 victory.

APRIL 15, 1958

Los Angeles	ab	r	h	rbi	San Francisco	ab	r	h	rbi
Cimoli, cf	5	0	1	0	Davenport, 3b	4	1	2	1
Reese, ss	3	0	0	0	King, lf	3	1	2	1
Snider, lf	2	0	0	0	Mays, cf	5	0	2	2
Hodges, 1b	4	0	0	0	Kirkland, rf	5	0	1	1
Neal, 2b	4	0	2	0	Cepeda, 1b	5	1	1	1
Gray, 3b	4	0	2	0	Spencer, ss	4	1	1	1
Furillo, rf	3	0	0	0	O'Connell, 2b	2	1	0	0
Walker, c	3	0	1	0	Thomas, c	1	2	0	0
Roseboro, pr-c	1	0	0	0	Gomez, p	4	1	2	1
Drysdale, p	1	0	0	0					
Bessent, p	0	0	0	0					
Larker, ph	1	0	0	0					
Negray, p	0	0	0	0					
Gilliam, ph	0	0	0	0					
Totals	31	0	6	0	Totals	33	8	11	8

Los Angeles ....0 0 0   0 0 0   0 0 0—0
San Francisco ....0 0 2   4 1 0   0 1 x—8

Los Angeles	IP	H	R	ER	BB	SO
Drysdale (L)	3⅔	5	6	6	3	1
Bessent	2⅓	4	1	1	1	0
Negray	2	2	1	1	3	1
San Francisco	IP	H	R	ER	BB	SO
Gomez (W)	9	6	0	0	6	6

E—Hodges. DP—San Francisco 1. LOB—Los Angeles 10, San Francisco 9. HR—Spencer, Cepeda. SF—Davenport. Balk—Negray. PB—Walker. T—2:29. A—23,448.

APRIL 18, 1958

San Francisco	ab	r	h	rbi	Los Angeles	ab	r	h	rbi
Davenport, 3b	5	1	3	0	Gilliam, lf	3	1	0	0
Kirkland, rf	5	1	3	0	Reese, ss	4	0	1	0
Mays, cf	4	0	2	0	Snider, rf	5	1	2	1
Spencer, ss-2b	4	0	0	1	Furillo, rf	0	0	0	0
Cepeda, 1b	5	0	0	0	Hodges, 1b	4	0	0	0
Sauer, lf	4	2	2	2	Neal, 2b	3	1	2	1
Schmidt, c	3	1	2	0	Gray, 3b	3	2	2	1
O'Connell, 2b	2	0	0	0	Cimoll, cf	3	1	1	1
King, p	0	0	0	0	Roseboro, c	1	0	0	0
Gomez, pr	0	0	0	0	Jackson, ph	1	0	0	0
Bressoud, 2b	0	0	0	0	Pignatano, c	1	0	0	0
Lockman, ph	1	0	0	0	Erskine, p	4	0	0	0
Worthington, p	2	0	0	0	Labine, p	0	0	0	0
McCormick, p	0	0	0	0					
Speake, ph	1	0	0	0					
Antonelli, p	0	0	0	0					
Jablonski, ph	1	0	0	0					
Grissom, p	0	0	0	0					
Rodgers, ss	0	0	0	0					
Totals	36	5	12	3	Totals	32	6	8	4

San Francisco ....0 0 1   1 0 1   0 1 1—5
Los Angeles ....0 0 2   0 3 0   1 0 x—6

San Francisco	IP	H	R	ER	BB	SO
Worthington (L)	4⅓	7	5	3	5	4
McCormick	⅔	0	0	0	0	0
Antonelli	2	1	1	1	2	0
Grissom	1	0	0	0	0	1
Los Angeles	IP	H	R	ER	BB	SO
Erskine (W)	8	10	4	4	4	6
Labine	1	2	1	1	0	0

E—Mays, Gray, Schmidt, Reese. DP—Los Angeles 2. LOB—San Francisco 7, Los Angeles 9. 2B—Kirkland, Davenport. 3B—Schmidt, Kirkland. HR—Sauer 2, Gray. SB—Neal. SH—Lockman. WP—McCormick, Erskine. T—3:06. A—78,672.

Braves Receive A Warm Welcome

With starting pitcher Warren Spahn warming up on the sideline, the Braves were introduced to their new fans in Milwaukee's 1953 home opener.

Other pregame festivities marked the occasion of major league baseball's return to Milwaukee.

For 50 years, the major league baseball map withstood threats of change as club owners accepted their losses as a natural consequence of an uncertain sport and hoped for brighter days when old-time fans would once more storm the turnstiles.

Not since 1903, when the Baltimore franchise of the American League was shifted to New York, had there been an alteration in the club alignment, with eight teams in each major circuit, divided neatly by geography into eastern and western sections. Five cities accounted for 11 of the 16 big-league clubs—New York (Yankees, Giants and Brooklyn Dodgers), Chicago (White Sox and Cubs), Boston (Red Sox and Braves), St. Louis (Browns and Cardinals) and Philadelphia (Athletics and Phillies).

In the years following World War II, however, conditions underwent marked change. Boston, St. Louis and Philadelphia were no longer capable of supporting two franchises. Dwindling patronage foreshadowed dramatic change.

Nowhere was the economic garrote tighter than in Boston where, in eight years of ownership, Lou Perini, a wealthy road and bridge contractor, had seen attendance soar to a club-record 1,455,439 in the National League pennant-winning season of 1948 and then plummet to 281,278 by 1952. The

gate plunge was accompanied by a $600,000 deficit in '52.

Perini saw no chance to reverse the attendance trend in Boston, where the Red Sox were regular pennant contenders. He determined that his fiscal salvation lay in a franchise shift to a community eager for major league ball.

Fortunately for Perini, such congenial conditions existed in Milwaukee, where the Braves already owned the local American Association franchise and where a new $5 million, 35,000-seat stadium awaited a big-league tenant.

While the baseball community watched and wondered and—to a large degree—doubted that a shift would be approved, The Sporting News, in its issue dated March 18, 1953, reported in a page-1 scoop that Perini very shortly would obtain permission to move his club to Milwaukee. It was written that the team, already in training as the Boston Braves, would depart Florida as the Milwaukee Braves.

The story was soon confirmed when National League executives, meeting in St. Petersburg, Fla., gave Perini the unanimous approval that was necessary for a shift.

Immediately after the sanction, the Braves gave

The occasion was fittingly marked by a group picture, showing the Braves in their Milwaukee inaugural.

the American Association $50,000 as an indemnity for invading the minor league's territory. And in Milwaukee, $500,000 was appropriated for improvements to County Stadium. These included stadium-type seats to replace wooden benches in the upper grandstand, better lights and adequate office space. Eventually, the park capacity was enlarged to 43,000-plus.

The arrival of the Braves in the Wisconsin metropolis proved a love affair at first sight for the citizenry, long starved for big-time baseball. When the train bearing the players arrived at 10:10 a.m. on April 8, an estimated 60,000 persons roared a thunderous greeting. Two brass bands maximized the din as each player detrained at Union Station and was escorted by a white-sweatered model across a red carpet.

Outside, an estimated 10,000 thronged Wisconsin Avenue, renamed "Braves Drive" for the week-long welcoming celebration.

From the railroad station, Manager Charley Grimm and his players were ushered into convertibles, one to a car, and chauffeured through dense lanes of humanity to their downtown hotel. There they were paraded through the lobby to a gaily decorated parlor dominated by a huge Christmas tree festooned with miniature baseballs and bats. A large sign announced: "You Brought Us Christmas in April."

Stacked around the base of the tree were 400 gifts, 10 going to each player. These presents included clocks, billfolds, lighters, golf balls and assorted items of every description, donated by local businessmen.

That night, approximately 6,000 fans braved a chilly rain and endured inadequate parking facilities to attend a rally at the city arena.

Grimm, who earlier had felt the city's warmth when he managed the minor league Brewers, was flabbergasted by the demonstrations.

"I've never seen anything like it," Jolly Cholly beamed. "I was looking at the expressions on some of the players' faces and I could feel the way their emotions were choking up. It's all such a wonderful compliment. How can anyone ever live up to something like this? This is fantastic . . . just out of this world."

After two exhibition games against the Red Sox were canceled because of bad weather (the games were scheduled at County Stadium), the Braves opened the 1953 season on April 13 at Cincinnati, where they further whetted Milwaukee baseball appetites by beating the Reds, 2-0.

In that early inaugural, rookie Bill Bruton dazzled spectators with his bat and speed. He collected the first hit of the season, stole the first base and scored the first run.

In addition, Bruton was positively incandescent while patrolling center field. "Six times," said a wire-service report, "his speed prevented ground-rule doubles from going into temporary seats.

"He collided with (shortstop) Johnny Logan in the eighth," the account added, "and needed first aid before he could continue. But he held the ball and remained in the game to steal a double from Bobby Adams in the ninth with an against-the-wall catch."

As if the Braves did not already possess sufficient crowd appeal, they also could offer a spectacular 23-year-old jackrabbit. Bruton was no stranger to Milwaukee fans, though. He had starred for the city's minor league team the previous year.

Four hours after their victory in Cincinnati, the Braves arrived at Milwaukee's Billy Mitchell Air-

At the conclusion of the 1953 season, Braves Owner Lou Perini stepped to the microphone and thanked Milwaukee fans for their overwhelming support.

port, where an estimated 3,000 loyalists boomed still another stirring salute.

Milwaukee, which had a National League team in 1878 and an American League franchise in 1901 (plus entries in two old-time "major leagues"), played its '53 home opener on April 14, with the St. Louis Cardinals providing the opposition. Perini, caught up in the excitement of the day, arrived at the stadium at 7:30 a.m. And, two hours before the first pitch, at least 5,000 heavily garbed fans sat in 46-degree temperature awaiting the magical moment. At game time, the crowd numbered 34,357, which was larger than the Braves' attendance for any series at Boston in 1952. Among the spectators were city, county and state dignitaries, Commissioner Ford Frick and National League President Warren Giles.

The modern debut of major league ball in Milwaukee reminded those with hoary memories that two of the city's earlier big-time entries had fared

APRIL 14, 1953									
St. Louis	ab	r	h	rbi	Milwaukee	ab	r	h	rbi
Hemus, ss	3	0	0	0	Bruton, cf	5	2	3	1
Schoendienst, 2b	4	0	0	0	Logan, ss	2	0	0	0
Musial, lf-cf	5	0	0	0	Mathews, 3b	3	0	0	0
Bilko, 1b	4	0	0	0	Gordon, lf	4	0	1	1
Slaughter, rf	3	1	0	0	Pafko, rf	4	0	0	0
Jablonski, 3b	4	0	2	1	Adcock, 1b	3	1	1	0
Haddix, pr	0	1	0	0	Crandall, c	3	0	1	0
Johnson, 3b	0	0	0	0	Dittmer, 2b	4	0	0	0
Repulski, cf	3	0	1	0	Spahn, p	4	0	0	0
Lowrey, ph-lf	1	0	1	1					
D. Rice, c	3	0	1	0					
Benson, pr	0	0	0	0					
Fusselman, c	1	0	0	0					
Staley, p	4	0	1	0					
Totals	35	2	6	2	Totals	32	3	6	2

St. Louis ....0 0 0   0 1 0   0 0 1   0—2
Milwaukee....................0 1 0   0 0 0   0 1 0   1—3
One out when winning run scored.

St. Louis	IP	H	R	ER	BB	SO
Staley (L)	9⅓	6	3	2	2	6
Milwaukee	IP	H	R	ER	BB	SO
Spahn (W)......................	10	6	2	2	3	2

E—Dittmer, Spahn, Jablonski. DP—Milwaukee 2. LOB—St. Louis 7, Milwaukee 6. 2B—D. Rice, Lowrey. 3B—Bruton. HR—Bruton. SH—Schoendienst, Crandall, Logan. HBP—By Staley (Logan). T—2:29. A—34,357.

Braves Owner Lou Perini (left) received an
Executive of the Year citation from The Sporting
News after the 1953 campaign.

poorly in their first games. In 1878, Milwaukee lost
its National League inaugural to Cincinnati, 6-4. In
1901, Milwaukee led, 13-4, entering the bottom of
the ninth inning of its first American League game
when Detroit exploded for 10 runs and pulled out a
14-13 triumph.

The opening of the 1953 season, however, provided for no such mischief. First, there was the victory
in Cincinnati. Then came a spine-tingling home
opener, a game during which many shivering partisans fortified themselves with succulent sausage and
overflowing steins of lager. (According to statistics,
Wisconsin had the largest per-capita consumption
of beer of all states in 1952, 26.6 gallons for every
man, woman and child.)

Warren Spahn, who had won only 14 games in
1952 after three straight seasons in the 20-victory
class, gained the honor of starting the Braves' first
home contest. He was opposed by Gerry Staley,
coming off a 17-victory campaign.

The Braves opened the scoring in the second inning, the run crossing the plate on a wild throw by
Cardinals third baseman Ray Jablonski. Spahn protected the slim margin until the fifth when a base
on balls to Enos Slaughter, the pitcher's own wild
pickoff throw and a single by Jablonski produced

the tying run.

Milwaukee went ahead again in the eighth when
Bruton tripled and, after two walks, Sid Gordon
legged out an infield single.

After the first two Cardinals were retired in the
ninth inning, center-field bleacherites started moving toward the exits, thereby forming a shaky background for the batter. At home plate, umpire Jocko
Conlan stopped play until park police could correct
the situation, whereupon Jablonski singled and Pea-
nuts Lowrey rapped a pinch double to knot the
score.

Through the first nine innings, Staley had been
the more effective pitcher, allowing only five hits to
six for his rival. Twice Spahn had wriggled out of
tight spots. In the sixth inning, a bizarre double
play bailed the lefthander out of a jam. With Solly
Hemus on second base, Stan Musial grounded to
Logan. The shortstop trapped Hemus between second and third base, and Hemus was tagged out. Musial was retired sliding into second base.

Spahn also dodged misfortune in the eighth. Del
Rice opened the inning with a double and gave way
to pinch-runner Vern Benson. Staley tapped in
front of the plate, but Spahn slipped and fell on the
wet turf and both runners were safe.

When Hemus grounded to first baseman Joe Adcock, Benson was run down between third and
home. An infield out and Bruton's spectacular
catch of Musial's long fly doused the uprising.

The teams dueled into the last of the 10th when
Bruton sent the multitude on its way in unbridled
delirium. With one out, the rookie sent a long drive
to right field. Slaughter made a valiant effort to
catch the ball, but it spurted out of his glove and
over the low fence.

Umpire Lon Warneke at first ruled it a ground-
rule double, but after a howl of protest from the
Milwaukee bench, the umpires conferred and decided that, after all, it was a legitimate home run,
giving the Braves a 3-2 triumph.

Bruton, the catcher on a softball team only four
years earlier, held an enraptured state in the hollow
of his hands. In two games, he had five hits, one-
third of the team total of 15, had scored three of the
Braves' five runs and was batting .556. The freshman completed the season with a .250 batting average—and exactly one home run.

The romance between the Braves and Milwaukee
flourished for a number of years. As never before
in any city, players were overwhelmed with sweet
charity. They were lionized wherever they went.
Cab drivers and bellhops refused their tips simply
because they were associating with major leaguers
or with persons connected to a big-time team in
even a small capacity.

One month into the 1953 season, Coach Johnny
Cooney told a visiting writer, "I have new shirts,

By 1966, the Braves had moved to Atlanta and once-devoted employees and fans were forced to listen to opening-day games played in other cities.

new ties, $100 for endorsing a cookie, a weekly order on a food market, free gasoline, cases of beer, and I'm only a coach."

In 20 years as a player, coach and interim manager for the Boston Braves, Cooney added, he had not received a solitary gift.

Eddie Mathews was a particular darling of the populace. The handsome, 21-year-old third baseman, who socked a league-high 47 homers and drove in 135 runs in '53, seldom was permitted to open his wallet.

Once, early in the year, he walked into a haberdashery and bought a suit of clothes. When he attempted to pay for it, the proprietor told him, "No, Mr. Mathews, we'd consider it an honor. Just let us have your picture."

In a similar manner, Bruton benefited from fan largesse. Admirers helped him find a three-room apartment, and a store granted him free use of furniture until his own arrived after the season. When Bill went house-hunting, fans gave him $1,500 as a down payment.

Ethnic groups idolized their own representatives. Jewish fans honored Sid Gordon, Germans paid tribute to Spahn (he received a tractor for his Oklahoma farm) and Poles tossed a gigantic birthday party for pitcher Max Surkont. Among Surkont's gifts was a year's supply of Polish sausage, which Max apparently devoured none too wisely. The next year, badly overweight, he was pitching for the lowly Pittsburgh Pirates.

Throughout the state, the Braves virus raged unchecked. The town of Cedarburg (population 2,500) purchased 3,000 tickets. A railroad line built a passenger platform outside County Stadium and ran 26 specials into the city in 1953. The line rejected 23 other applications for specials because of a shortage of rolling stock.

One-man business establishments caught the fever, too. In Portage, Wis., a barber locked up his shop and hung a sign on the door reading, "I can't stand it any longer. Closed for two days. Gone to see the Braves."

One of the most rabid fans was Lou Perini, wallowing in wealth after years of red ink. After sitting bareheaded through a game-long drizzle, the club owner observed, "Anywhere else the umpires would have called the game, but what could they do when 35,000 fans sat in the rain and wouldn't go home? And I couldn't leave either."

The Braves played to an N.L.-record 1,826,397 hysterical fans during their first season in Milwaukee. And their success opened the relocation floodgates. In 1954, the Browns moved to Baltimore, and in 1955 the A's transferred to Kansas City. The unthinkable then occurred in 1958: The Dodgers bolted Brooklyn for Los Angeles, and the Giants shifted to San Francisco. The baseball map would never be the same.

Milwaukee topped the two-million mark in attendance from 1954 through 1957 (its World Series championship season). The Braves drew 1.97 million in 1958, about 1.75 million in 1959 and almost 1.5 million in 1960. Then came a plunge to just over one million in 1961, followed by yearly turnouts of 766,921, 773,018 and 910,911. With the promise of new riches in the Deep South, the Braves were committed to a move to Atlanta when, as a lame-duck team, they drew 555,584 fans to County Stadium in 1965, their final season in Milwaukee.

A relationship that promised eternal love and prosperity only 12 years before had ended.

Frank Robinson's Debut a Big Hit

The television cameras were primed and so was Frank Robinson as he made
his Cleveland managerial debut.

Racial integration in the major leagues, which struck with blockbuster impact in 1947, was no longer the great sociological phenomenon in the mid-1970s.

Jackie Robinson, who carried the torch in Branch Rickey's liberation movement, had come and gone. On the trail that he blazed at the cost of cruel personal abuse were countless black superstars, all blending beautifully into the baseball panorama.

Spectators were no longer walled off in ball parks like first- and second-class citizens. Skin pigmentation on the field and in the stands was of no apparent concern, and fans cheered as lustily for the other race as they did for their own.

Discrimination in the major leagues—at least in terms of the players—was virtually extinct. Blacks enjoyed the same courtesies and privileges as their white colleagues. Hotels and restaurants eagerly solicited their patronage. Salaries were negotiated and contracts signed irrespective of color. Talent within the white lines was all that seemed to concern an employer or the ticket-buying public.

For all the advancements, however, questions remained about managerial and front-office breakthroughs. And perhaps the biggest question of all was: Who would be the big leagues' first black manager?

It was not that candidates were in short supply. Anytime the subject came under discussion, names certain to emerge were Willie Mays, Henry Aaron, Maury Wills, Elston Howard, Larry Doby and Jim Gilliam. All were preeminent as players, all knew the game, yet when a managerial vacancy occurred, for one reason or another, the position was filled by a Caucasian.

While the baseball community watched and speculated, a well-proportioned outfielder, a native of Beaumont, Tex., but raised in Oakland, was building a strong case for himself as the precedent-setting black pilot.

At age 21, Frank Robinson was named Rookie of the Year in the National League after hitting 38 home runs, batting .290 and scoring a league-high 122 runs for Cincinnati.

In nine subsequent seasons with the Reds, he ranked consistently among the hitting heavyweights

Frank Robinson, the first black manager, was a big hit at Cleveland's 1975 opening-day ceremonies.

and, in 1961, when he paced the Reds to a pennant with 37 homers, 124 RBIs and a .323 batting average, he was named the Most Valuable Player in the N.L.

Traded to Baltimore after the 1965 season, Frank continued to make life unbearable for opposing

Player-Manager Frank Robinson watches his first-inning drive head for the fence.

pitchers. In 1966, he won the Triple Crown and earned a second MVP award, the only player ever to win such honors in each league. Moreover, he paced the Orioles to four pennants and two World Series titles in six years, including the stunning four-game upset of the Dodgers in 1966.

While his career still was in its zenith, Robinson determined that someday he would be a manager, although not necessarily the first black pilot. Toward that end, he spent several months each winter as a skipper in the Puerto Rican League. And he laid the groundwork well. Winter-league players were lavish in their praise of the slugger. He knew how to handle men, they reported, he knew the game, he was ripe for a managerial portfolio in baseball's most elite circle.

Robinson was 36 when, in December 1971, he was traded to the Dodgers.

After one unhappy season under Walter Alston, Robinson moved on to the California Angels, for whom he socked 30 homers and drove in 97 runs in 1973. The time for Frank Robinson to become a major league manager, the savants argued, was in late June of 1974. Bobby Winkles was under fire as the Angels' pilot; California's general manager was Harry Dalton, who had served Baltimore in a similar capacity when Robinson was battering fences for the Orioles.

It didn't happen. Winkles was fired, all right, but the job went to Dick Williams. Frank remained with the Angels until September 12, 1974, when he was sold to the Indians on waivers.

This was the time, the cognoscenti insisted, for the breakthrough. "I'm here only as a player, because the Indians accepted the terms of my contract," Robinson said.

"We got him," General Manager Phil Seghi said, "because we feel he can help us win the division title."

One day following the close of the '74 season, a year in which the Tribe finished in fourth place under Manager Ken Aspromonte, Seghi called a news conference. It was not a run-of-the-mill meeting, as evidenced by the presence of Commissioner Bowie Kuhn and American League President Lee MacPhail.

To the great astonishment of nobody, shortly after 10 a.m. on October 3, 1974, Seghi informed the 100 assembled media persons, "We're pleased to make this very formal announcement of the selection of Frank Robinson as manager of the Indians." Robinson would continue to play for the American League team, primarily as a designated hitter.

Robinson's appointment, MacPhail said, was "second in importance only to Jackie Robinson's entry into (major league) baseball in 1947."

Kuhn added, "Now that it has happened, I'm not going to shout that this is something for baseball to be proud of, because it is too long overdue."

Despite the unfamiliar environment, Robinson was poised and comfortable. "I'm the first black manager only because I was born black," he noted with conviction.

Asked by a black reporter how he would have handled a young Frank Robinson—fiery, outspoken and combative—the new manager replied, "I'd have been fatherly toward him, tried to reason with him. I think that's the way young players should be handled."

As for his managerial philosophies, Robbie de-

claimed, "I'm not a miracle worker. Judge me only by our play on the field. I may be able to influence some of the players, but if we win don't make me a genius. If we lose . . . if things go wrong, look to me,

Robinson is greeted at home plate by teammate John Lowenstein after his dramatic homer.

One of Frank Robinson's toughest problems as new Cleveland manager was dealing with veteran pitcher Gaylord Perry.

not to the players.

"I plan to adjust myself to the players we have, not vice versa. I think my biggest problem will be to get to know my players, what makes them tick, what makes them sneeze. I'm not a believer in a lot of rules, but the basic rules I lay down will have to be obeyed.

"In 19 years in the big leagues, I can't say that I never missed a curfew—but I was never caught. I believe men are men, no matter what their age, and they should be treated like men. I'm not going to be a baby sitter. I've got to play myself."

After almost five months at his home in California, Robinson greeted the Cleveland players in Tucson, Ariz., on February 24, 1975. Not unexpectedly, a horde of newsmen was on hand for first-day ceremonies and, again, Frank fielded a torrent of questions with aplomb.

Robinson's chief source of irritation was pitcher Gaylord Perry, the 21-game winner of the previous year. The righthander grumbled about Robinson's training program. He preferred his own system, honed through many major league springtimes.

Nor did Perry endorse the selection of George Hendrick, a black, and Frank Duffy, a white, as cocaptains. "The honor should be earned," Gaylord said, "and neither did anything to deserve it."

Eventually, Seghi stepped into the ring and achieved a degree of harmony for a day or so. Then Seghi read a newspaper story in which Kuhn expressed regret that Seghi had arbitrated the dispute. The two should have been permitted to work out their differences, said Kuhn, which led Seghi to the telephone and a blistering denunciation of the commissioner.

The first exhibition game for the 1975 Indians was played on March 13, and a major television network was fully prepared for the event. Robbie was wired for sound two hours before the game; cameras whirred from every conceivable angle. Hollywood had come to Tucson.

Every syllable that escaped Robinson's lips was preserved for posterity, every chuckle, every grunt. Yet he never faltered for a second. The freshman pilot comported himself like an old pro.

Asked for his thoughts on the historic occasion, Robinson replied, "This is the end of a long road, but the sacrifices were worthwhile. I have a feeling of gratefulness to all the players, black and white, who made this possible, especially Jackie Robinson, who is in my thoughts almost every time I put on a uniform."

A young Frank Robinson (right) met with the great Jackie Robinson in 1957 in a prophetic picture with landmark significance.

Pregame ceremonies at Hi Corbett Field consisted of a handshake with each of the umpires and with Wes Westrum, the Giants' manager who, Robbie said, "congratulated me and wished me luck."

The game went into the 10th inning with the score tied, 4-4, when the Giants placed two runners on base. Ed Goodson, a lefthanded hitter in other years, was up next. Playing the percentages, Robinson summoned lefthander Dave LaRoche. Too late, Frank learned that Goodson had been practicing to become a switch-hitter and, batting righthanded, he belted a two-run double, giving the Giants a 6-4 victory.

The Tribe played only 17 exhibition games, winning nine and losing eight. Frank played sparingly and garnered three hits in nine trips to the plate.

On the flight to Cleveland for opening day of the American League season, the rookie manager reported that, on the whole, he was pleased with the results of training camp. His only wish was that the relief pitchers had progressed as rapidly at the finish as the starters had done. He predicted a .500 season for the club and added, "I'll be disappointed if we don't do better."

On Tuesday, April 8, Frank arose at 6 a.m. and puttered around his hotel suite until departing for Municipal Stadium at 9 o'clock. At the park, he donned the team's new-style uniform, a fire-engine red that, according to Cleveland first baseman Boog Powell, made an Indians player feel "like a massive blood clot."

Rachel Robinson, widow of Jackie, was accorded the honor of throwing out the ceremonial first pitch and took the occasion to tell the 56,204 fans, "I'm proud to be here and I want to congratulate you for honoring yourselves by being the first to take this historic step . . . I've wished, since I was asked to do this, that Jackie could be here, and I'm sure in many ways he is."

The lineup card that Robinson presented to umpire Nestor Chylak showed the Indians' player-manager batting second as the designated hitter. Doc Medich was the starting pitcher for the Yankees, Perry for the Indians.

After the New Yorkers failed to score in the first inning and Oscar Gamble was retired as the Tribe's leadoff batter, Robinson stepped into the batter's box. A stirring ovation told Frank the crowd was with him.

The first two pitches from Medich were called

strikes. Robbie fouled off the next two, watched two sail wide of the plate and then stroked another foul. Crowding the plate, as was his custom, he awaited the eighth delivery from the righthander.

Robinson swung at the ball and, as he had done on 574 previous at-bats in the majors, he made solid contact, driving the ball beyond the fence in left-center field.

He circled the bases as an ear-splitting roar tumbled out of the stands. As he approached the plate, the 39-year-old manager/slugger tipped his hat to his wife, sitting in a loge box. At the plate, he was welcomed by a swarm of players, led by Perry. They embraced.

The home run had been ordered by Phil Seghi earlier in the day, Robinson revealed later. Feigning forgetfulness, the general manager conceded, "I might have suggested he hit a homer, but I never dared dream he'd do it. But knowing Frank (they were contemporaries in the Cincinnati organization), I shouldn't be surprised by anything about the man's ability to rise to an occasion. Frank Robinson doing the unusual is usual for him."

The Yankees scored three runs in the second inning, two riding home on a double by Chris Chambliss and the other on a single by Thurman Munson.

The Indians retrieved one of the runs in their half of the second on singles by Powell and John Ellis and a sacrifice fly by Jack Brohamer.

A fourth-inning homer by Powell, Robinson's former slugging mate at Baltimore, knotted the score. The Indians scored their last two runs in the sixth when Hendrick walked and stole second, Powell doubled and Brohamer singled.

As Perry retired the last Yankee in the ninth inning, wrapping up a 5-3 victory, Robinson raced from the dugout. He headed for Perry. Again, the adversaries of a few weeks earlier fell into a bear hug.

Robinson confessed that he was nervous only twice on opening day, once when the band played the national anthem and again when the crowd unleashed its game-ending roar.

He made no monumental decisions during the game, Robinson said, but he revealed he was on the brink of removing Perry at two critical junctures. "If the Yanks had scored a fourth run in the second inning, I would have had to get Gaylord out of there," he said.

In the ninth, after Ed Herrmann laced a single, Frank walked to the mound and told Perry, "Don't give Chambliss a ball he can pull. If he hits it, don't let him pull it."

The skipper was barely seated on the bench when Chambliss drove a pitch to deep right-center field. "Holy smokes," Robinson told himself, "it's out." He was greatly relieved when Charlie Spikes backed against the fence and made the catch.

Though not a collector of baseball memorabilia, Robinson took two souvenirs from the opening-day victory—his home run ball and the ball that Perry threw to start the game. "I thought he'd appreciate it," Gaylord commented.

The Indians did not perform as well as Robinson had hoped in 1975. They finished one game under .500 (79-80) and in fourth place, 15½ games behind the East Division-winning Boston Red Sox. Robbie appeared in 49 games and batted .237 with nine homers and 24 RBIs.

The team topped the .500 mark in 1976, winning 81 games and losing 78, but again finished fourth, 16 games behind the first-place Yankees. Playing only 36 games, Robinson batted .224 with three homers and 10 RBIs.

The 1977 Indians were in sixth place with a 26-31 record when, on June 19, Robinson was fired. His successor, bullpen coach Jeff Torborg, led the team to seven consecutive victories, but the improvement was illusory. The team finished fifth, 28½ games back.

Robinson went on to serve as a coach for the California Angels and the Orioles and managed in the International League. The man who in 1975 made history as the majors' first black manager became a trailblazer again in 1981 when he became the first black to manage a National League team. Robbie was called upon to direct the San Francisco Giants, and he managed the club for more than 3½ years.

During his second season at the Giants' helm, Frank Robinson was inducted into the Hall of Fame.

APRIL 8, 1975

New York	ab	r	h	rbi		Cleveland	ab	r	h	rbi
Alomar, 2b	2	0	0	0		Gamble, lf	5	0	1	0
Johnson, ph	1	0	0	0		Robinson, dh	3	1	1	1
Stanley, 2b	0	0	0	0		Hendrick, cf	3	1	0	0
Piniella, lf	4	0	0	0		Spikes, rf	4	0	0	0
Bonds, cf	4	0	0	0		Powell, 1b	3	3	3	2
Blomberg, rf	4	1	2	0		Ellis, c	3	0	2	0
Nettles, 3b	4	1	1	0		Bell, 3b	4	0	0	0
Herrmann, dh	4	0	1	0		Brohamer, 2b	3	0	2	2
White, pr	0	0	0	0		Crosby, ss	4	0	1	0
Chambliss, 1b	4	1	3	2		G. Perry, p	0	0	0	0
Munson, c	4	0	2	1						
Mason, ss	3	0	0	0						
Medich, p	0	0	0	0						
May, p	0	0	0	0						
Lyle, p	0	0	0	0						
Totals	34	3	9	3		Totals	32	5	10	5

```
New York ..........................0  3  0    0  0  0    0  0  0—3
Cleveland .........................1  1  0    1  0  2    0  0  x—5
```

New York	IP	H	R	ER	BB	SO
Medich (L)	5⅔	8	5	5	2	2
May	1⅓	0	0	0	1	1
Lyle	1	2	0	0	1	0
Cleveland	IP	H	R	ER	BB	SO
G. Perry (W)	9	9	3	3	1	6

E—Lyle. DP—Cleveland 1. LOB—New York 5, Cleveland 8. 2B—Chambliss, Powell. HR—Robinson, Powell. SB—Hendrick. SF—Brohamer. PB—Munson. T—2:43. A—56,204.

Major League Baseball Is on the Air

Red Barber interviews Dodgers Manager Leo Durocher (center) after W2XBS presented the first telecast of a big-league game in 1939.

Across the nation, newspapers and radios spouted alarming news from Europe, where a former paperhanger from Austria was threatening to kindle a worldwide conflagration barely 20 years after Americans had fought the "war to end all wars."

In Germany, Adolf Hitler screamed imprecations at the Allies and talked menacingly of moving his Panzer units into Poland. In England, Prime Minister Neville Chamberlain warned his constituents of an impending global conflict, and in France the government advised Parisians to evacuate their city.

While the world tottered over the abyss, an experiment of little immediate import but loaded with vast potential took place at Baker Field in New

Red Barber is shown in the 1940s with a board that coordinated his commentary with the cameras, a problem in baseball's first telecast.

York City. The date was May 17, 1939, and the experiment involved the baseball teams from Columbia and Princeton universities.

Aside from the fact that visiting Princeton swept a doubleheader, thereby eliminating the Lions from contention for Eastern Intercollegiate honors, the day was made memorable by the presence of a television camera for the second game. The photographic device was owned by W2XBS, an experimental NBC-TV station, and was on the premises to help telecast a sporting event for the first time in history.

The distinction of providing the voice for the notable event went to Bill Stern, the dominant member of NBC's staff. Stern began the broadcast after the Tigers won the first game, 8-6, by interviewing the rival coaches, Andy Coakley of Columbia and Bill Clarke of Princeton. The players, including Sid Luckman, the Columbia football great, were so enthralled with the historic moment that the TV director was forced to wave them into position so that they would be in place when the camera panned the field.

The second game, won by Princeton, 2-1, in 10 innings, taught NBC a valuable lesson in TV technique. "We learned a complete lesson on how not to televise a sports event," Stern recalled. "For one thing, we learned that you cannot televise a baseball game with one camera."

NBC personnel also learned that a monitor was a necessary component of a successful telecast. "I never knew at any time what the camera was shooting," Stern said. "Half the time I was talking about things that weren't even within camera range."

The single camera was mounted along the third-base line on a 12-foot-high wooden pedestal 19 feet from the diamond. From that position it covered only 50 feet of the playing field. When it focused on the pitcher, the batter and catcher could not be seen. Infield plays and outfield catches were not shown.

Rarely were as many as three players pictured at one time. In the words of one reporter, players resembled "little white flies" flitting across the screen. Another reported that the ball looked like "a phantom aspirin tablet."

Though the "only people who saw the game (on TV), I think, were back at Radio City," Stern said, the significance of the telecast was not entirely lost on writers from the major New York dailies. The New York Herald Tribune's correspondent wrote that the second game was more interesting than the first "perhaps because it was being televised, the first regularly scheduled contest accorded this distinction." Other scribes, however, mentioned the telecast only in passing.

It was a modest beginning, but the potential of using TV in the coverage of sports was readily apparent to many. Mike Jacobs, the foremost boxing

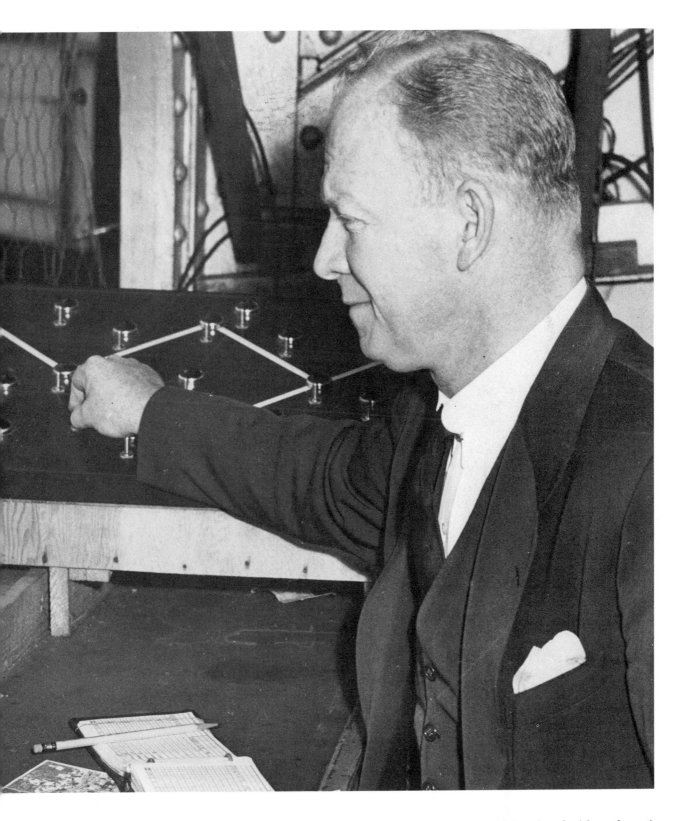

promoter of the day, predicted that "someday I'll sell television rights for a championship bout for as much as 1 million dollars." Before too many years, even that fancy figure was dwarfed in the mushrooming industry.

Life magazine noted that "reception was fuzzy . . . but no fuzziness can hide what it (the telecast) means to American sports. Within 10 years, an audience of 10 million sitting at home will see World Series and Rose Bowl games." Like Jacobs' figure, Life's projection also would prove quite modest.

Shortly after the Baker Field experiment, Doc

Morton conceived a more ambitious venture. The TV director for NBC laid his scheme before Walter Lanier (Red) Barber, a former Cincinnati Reds broadcaster who had followed Larry MacPhail to Brooklyn after the baseball executive moved east in search of larger worlds to conquer.

Reminding Barber of the collegiate telecast, Morton said: "Now I want very much to do a major league game. The Giants and Yankees do not like broadcasting, and I'm sure they would turn me down. But from what I hear, MacPhail might go for it. Would you approach him and try to get permission for us to put one of his games on our television station?"

Barber promised to try. He was aware that Mac-Phail, the Dodgers' executive vice president and general manager, had a keen perception of history and relished his reputation as an innovator. Upon arriving in Cincinnati in 1933 after a spectacular stint as president of the Columbus (American Association) club, MacPhail attacked the National League establishment. He asked the club owners for permission to play night ball at Crosley Field. Grudgingly, the owners agreed to let the Reds play each of their seven opponents in one night game in 1935. In time the same reactionaries recognized the huge profits to be realized from night games and fell into line, raising hosannas to the vision of their young compatriot. MacPhail also pioneered the sale of season tickets and broadcast all Cincinnati games on radio at a time when rival clubs were reducing or eliminating their broadcasts.

When he took over the reins of the Dodgers, MacPhail informed the Yankees and Giants that he would not enter into a renewal of the three-club agreement not to broadcast games. Radio, he insisted, was an ideal medium for popularizing the game. It worked in Cincinnati, he maintained, and there was no reason why even greater success should not attend daily broadcasts in Brooklyn.

Following up on his promise to Morton, Barber approached MacPhail with a proposition that he was certain the executive would like. The dialogue, as related by the Old Redhead, went thusly:

MacPhail: "What did you come here for?"

Barber: "I wanted to know if you wanted something."

MacPhail: "What are you talking about?"

Barber: "Larry, would you like to be the first man ever—ever in history—to put on a television broadcast of a major league baseball game?"

MacPhail: "Yes."

And the matter was settled. While MacPhail asked no fee for the TV rights, he did exact one small favor. He requested that a TV set be installed in the press room so that he could witness the electronic marvel along with reporters, team officials and special guests.

Having learned a lesson at Baker Field three months earlier, W2XBS installed two cameras at Ebbets Field for the first game of an August 26 doubleheader with league-leading Cincinnati. One was located at ground level near home plate, the other in the upper deck near third base, where space had been cleared for the equipment, a technician and Barber.

The Saturday afternoon game attracted 33,535 fans to Ebbets Field. The turnout created the unique situation that, for one of the few times in history, more people saw a sporting event in person than watched it on TV. That's because there were no more than 400 TV sets in all of New York in 1939.

Barber would have been elated, and eternally grateful, if the producers could have found one more set to serve as a monitor because, like Stern, he was sorely handicapped without one.

"I had to watch both cameras carefully to see which one's red light was on," he explained. "And then, of course, I could only guess what it was pointed at—especially when my telephone link to the TV truck went on the blink. We were making video history—and all of us were flying blind."

The Dodgers had three sponsors for their radio broadcasts—Wheaties, Ivory Soap and Mobil Oil—each of which was given one free commercial during the telecast. None had prepared advertisements, so Barber had to improvise. For one, Red opened a box of Wheaties, poured the contents into a bowl, added sliced bananas and milk and proclaimed the product the "Breakfast of Champions." He held up a bar of Ivory Soap while rhapsodizing over its cleansing power and, for Mobil Oil, donned a service station attendant's hat to lend a degree of authenticity to his ad-libbed spiel.

Bucky Walters, who was on his way to a 27-victory season and N.L. Most Valuable Player honors, started the televised game for the Reds. He was opposed by fellow righthander Luke (Hot Potato) Hamlin, who appeared well on his way to his 16th win when he took a 2-0 Brooklyn lead into the eighth inning.

The Dodgers had scored both of their runs in the second, thanks largely to a pair of bungles by Ernie Lombardi, the hulking Cincinnati catcher. After Leo Durocher, the Dodgers' manager and shortstop, hit into a bases-loaded double play via home plate that left Babe Phelps on third base and Gene Moore on second, Lombardi let a pitch to Hamlin get away from him for a passed ball. The catcher retrieved the ball and fired to the plate in a bid to nail Phelps, but the ball struck the runner in the chest as he started to slide. Both Phelps and Moore crossed home plate as the ball bounced toward the

Brooklyn dugout.

But Walters, the victim of two unearned runs, did not allow a hit the rest of the game, thus keeping the Reds within striking distance. And when Phelps, the Dodgers' catcher, reciprocated with a pair of blunders of his own in the eighth, Cincinnati struck.

With one out, Phelps muffed left fielder Nino Bongiovanni's pop fly in front of the plate. A walk to shortstop Billy Myers and Walters' single loaded the bases. When third baseman Bill Werber bounced a single off Hamlin's shin, Bongiovanni scored. Hamlin, visibly upset, walked second baseman Eddie Joost on four pitches to force home the tying run and was replaced by Vito Tamulis.

The lefthanded reliever induced Ival Goodman to lift a fly to Moore in short right field. Moore's throw home appeared to beat Walters, but Bucky slammed into Phelps, who dropped the ball, and the Reds led, 3-2. First baseman Frank McCormick's rap to center went for a double when Dixie Walker fell flat while pursuing the ball. Two more runners romped home to give the visitors a 5-2 victory, Walters' 21st of the year.

As the game ended, Barber left his upper-deck perch and hastened down to the field to conduct a few interviews. While he was in transit, the producer showed random shots of the field without benefit of commentary.

Barber chose the rival managers, Cincinnati's Bill McKechnie and Brooklyn's Durocher, as guests on TV's first postgame show. Like hundreds who came after him, Barber asked the skippers for their views on the pennant race. He also asked Walters to demonstrate his grip on his various pitches and chatted at length with Dolph Camilli about the Brooklyn first baseman's large, strong hands, which had long fascinated the veteran broadcaster.

The Reds, who went on to win their first N.L. flag since 1919, suffered a 6-1 defeat in the second game of the doubleheader, which was not televised. In reporting the activities at Ebbets Field, however, the New York Times published an August 27 article under the somewhat inaccurate headline: "Games Are Televised / Major League Baseball Makes Its Radio Camera Debut."

The three-paragraph account said in part: "Over the video-sound channels of the station, television set owners as far away as 50 miles viewed the action and heard the roar of the crowd. . . . To those who, over the television, saw last May's contest (between Columbia and Princeton) . . . it was apparent that considerable progress has been made in the technical requirements and apparatus for this sort of outdoor pickup, where the action is fast. At times it was possible to catch a fleeting glimpse of the ball as it sped from the pitcher's hand toward home plate."

MacPhail was highly pleased with baseball's first venture into television. When the 1940 season rolled around, cameras were at Ebbets Field to cover the Dodgers' home opener against the Giants. About one game per week was telecast from Brooklyn through the seasons of 1940 and '41.

American involvement in World War II curtailed baseball telecasts for a while, but the return of the soldiers in 1945 signaled the return of baseball to the tube. MacPhail, who had moved to the Bronx as president of the New York Yankees, negotiated the first commercial television baseball package, receiving $75,000 from the Dumont Network in 1946. A year later, the World Series was televised for the first time, and in 1951, CBS-TV telecast the first major league game in color.

"The reproduction was excellent, striking and only faintly phony," sports columnist Red Smith wrote about that contest between Brooklyn and Boston. "The Dodgers and Boston Braves all came out as beauteous critters, except for Roy Campanella, who had neglected to shave. . . .

"If you watched intently while a batsman swung in a close-up, you saw a regular rainbow of bats of varying colors. For a fraction of an instant the moving bat became a big Japanese fan."

The origins of television were humble and unpretentious. Even by 1951, most U.S. homes did not have a TV set. But as broadcast technology improved, TV manufacturers produced sets at an ever greater speed and TV antennae sprouted on rooftops near and far. No household could afford to be without a receiver, often in duplicate and triplicate, as Americans succumbed to the lure of the electronic gadget. Before long, television was the most influential communications medium known to man —and baseball was being watched by more people than ever before.

AUGUST 26, 1939								
Cincinnati	ab	r	h	rbi	Brooklyn	ab	r	h	rbi
Werber, 3b	4	1	1	1	Coscarart, 2b	3	0	0	0
Joost, 2b	3	1	1	1	Lavagetto, 3b	2	0	0	0
Goodman, rf	3	0	0	1	Walker, cf	4	0	1	0
McCormick, 1b	4	0	2	2	Parks, lf	4	0	0	0
Lombardi, c	4	0	0	0	Camilli, 1b	3	0	0	0
Craft, cf	4	0	0	0	Phelps, c	3	1	1	0
Bongiovanni, lf	3	1	0	0	Moore, rf	2	1	0	0
Bordagaray, lf	1	0	0	0	Durocher, ss	3	0	0	0
Myers, ss	3	1	0	0	Hamlin, p	2	0	0	0
Walters, p	3	1	1	0	Tamulis, p	1	0	0	0
Totals	32	5	5	5	Totals	27	2	2	0

```
Cincinnati ..............................0  0  0   0  0  0   0  5  0—5
Brooklyn ................................0  2  0   0  0  0   0  0  0—2
```

Cincinnati	IP	H	R	ER	BB	SO
Walters (W)	9	2	2	0	5	1
Brooklyn	IP	H	R	ER	BB	SO
Hamlin (L)	7 1/3	4	5	4	2	2
Tamulis	1 2/3	1	0	0	0	1

E—Lombardi, Phelps 2. DP—Cincinnati 1. LOB—Cincinnati 3, Brooklyn 3. 2B—McCormick. SB—Joost. SH—Goodman. PB—Lombardi. T—1:46. A—33,535.

The End
Of an Era

Ebbets Field, home of Dem Bums from Brooklyn, was in all its glory in the
early 1950s as players and fans enjoyed opening-day festivities.

The Dodgers Sym-Phony Band was part of the enjoyable wackiness that made Ebbets Field one of the most unusual parks in baseball history.

Ebbets Field in Brooklyn was a shrine to baseball eccentricities and frequently the site of superior achievements as performed by the Brooklyn Dodgers.

This ball park, situated on a 5½-acre tract and able to accommodate about 35,000 fans for most of its existence, was where:

—The club owner was apprehended on a chilly World Series afternoon in 1920 for distributing alcoholic stimulants to sportswriters.

—Three Brooklyn runners occupied the same base simultaneously.

—Mickey Owen committed his soul-wrenching muff during a World Series, and where Cookie Lavagetto bashed a pinch double in the ninth inning to wreck a no-hit bid, also in the World Series.

—Casey Stengel, responding to a strident chorus of boos, made a sweeping bow, doffed his cap and released a bird which had been secreted there for whatever purpose.

—A prison parolee attacked umpire George Magerkurth on the field and pummeled him unmercifully until restrained by gendarmes.

—The indefatigable Hilda Chester clanged her cowbell and shouted kudos to her idols.

—Larry MacPhail ranted and raved ad infinitum until silenced by Bill Klem, the flinty "Old Arbitrator," who informed him, "You, sir, are an applehead. I repeat, sir, an applehead."

—Johnny Vander Meer pitched the second of his two consecutive no-hitters.

—Names like Leo, Zack, Dazzy, Dixie, Campy, Jackie, Pee Wee and Duke remained eternally green.

When it was dedicated in 1913, Ebbets Field was a monument to elegance. Its handsome rotunda with tile floor remained its most distinguishing feature for nearly half a century. It cost Charles Ebbets $750,000 to build the park. Not all of the money was his. When funds ran low in the middle of construction, Ebbets acquired a partner, Steve McKeever, a member of a building firm who supplied the necessary capital to complete the project.

Until construction was in its final stages, Ebbets

An Ebbets Field regular and contributor to the Brooklyn Dodgers mystique
was Hilda Chester, who always came armed with her trusty cowbell.

gave no thought to a name for the park. When he
was queried on the matter, he said he thought he'd
call it Washington Park, the name of his team's former playground in the Washington Heights district.

"Why don't you call it Ebbets Field?" a sportswriter asked. "The park was your idea." The owner
adopted the suggestion.

As the finishing touches were being applied to the
park, baseball writers who had examined and approved the plans were horrified to discover that no
provision had been made for a press box. Ebbets
remedied the oversight by removing several rows of
seats on the second deck. Newsman operated in this
area until a permanent facility was built.

On the day of the first game at the new park, an
exhibition against the Yankees, fans milled outside,
clamoring for admittance. Eventually, the caretaker
belatedly unlocked the gates.

Several days later, when dignitaries and players
marched to center field for flag-raising ceremonies
on opening day, it was discovered that nobody had
remembered to bring "Old Glory." While the band
played another patriotic air, a courier was dispatched to the club office to fetch the flag.

Though the park, bounded by Sullivan Street,
Bedford Avenue, Montgomery Street and Cedar
Place, was born in less than auspicious circum-
stances, it matured quickly. Before long it was rec-

It was a sad day in 1960 when Brooklyn witnessed the destruction of an old
friend and Ebbets Field was reduced to a fond footnote in baseball history.

ognized as a citadel of wackiness inhabited—according to columnist Westbrook Pegler—by "The Daffiness Boys."

The reputation for zaniness was well earned. It didn't, however, preclude extraordinary performances at other times and it was this unlikely mixture that helped create the remarkable Brooklyn fan, the loud and boisterous loyalist who could heap praise on an idol one instant and, a moment later, scream invective at the same performer who suddenly was transformed into a miscreant because of a misplay.

This was Ebbets Field, site of World Series combat in 1916, 1920, 1941, 1947, 1949, 1952, 1953, 1955 and 1956; where Uncle Wilbert Robinson sat imperturabably—when not enjoying an afternoon nap—and directed the fortunes of the Dodgers; where firebrand Leo Durocher inflamed friend and foe alike, and where Walter Alston reigned with a firm but gentle hand.

Ebbets Field was 44 years old and in the prime of life when its tenant stole away like a faithless spouse. The ball park had its blemishes, though, and they eventually overshadowed its charm. Foremost among the flaws were the lack of seating capacity and cramped conditions overall.

For 13 consecutive years, 1945 through 1957, the Flatbush faithful had twirled the turnstiles more

As Ebbets Field was being demolished, home plate and other mementos from
her storied past were auctioned off.

than one million times annually. They had be-
stowed their unrivaled support in good times and
bad. And for this sort of devotion, what was their
reward? It was a divorce, final and uncontested, obtained by Dodgers President Walter O'Malley, who
found a new love and the promise of much greater
riches in California.

Rumors of desertion surfaced months before the
actual walkout. Then, an August announcement
that the Giants were to forsake New York in favor
of San Francisco sent shudders through Brooklyn.
Even the most obtuse fan realized that if one team
leaped to the West Coast, a second was sure to follow. The Dodgers were that team, even though the
official announcement would not be made until October, during the World Series between the Yankees and Braves.

The last rites for what had once been Charles

Ebbets' palace of pleasure were performed on September 24, 1957. There was little to attract customers to the night game between the Dodgers and Pirates. Brooklyn was in third place, 10½ games out
of first; Pittsburgh was lodged in seventh place,
more than 30 games back. Moreover, a chilly autumn breeze whipped through the borough. Who
needed a funeral under those conditions?

Still, 6,702 intrepid souls showed up to bid old
friends goodbye, to wave one last farewell to those
who had given the borough and its wild-eyed citizens a national identity.

But names that had made the Dodgers great were
scarce on this dolorous occasion. There was Jim Gilliam at second base, Roy Campanella behind the
plate and Gil Hodges, normally the first baseman,
at third. Before the night was over, a fourth storied
Brooklyn figure appeared on the field. He was Pee

Former Dodgers great Roy Campanella, now confined to a wheelchair, was on hand as Ebbets Field and its glorious heritage was laid to rest.

Wee Reese, the team captain whose sparkling play at shortstop for many years would land him in the Hall of Fame. On this night, the Little Colonel played third base briefly. Also, Sandy Amoros, who starred in Brooklyn's 1955 World Series clincher, was in left field.

Walter Alston's choice to pitch the mournful finale was Danny McDevitt, a rookie lefthander seeking his seventh victory. Danny Murtaugh's selection to hurl for the Pirates was righthander Benny Daniels, who was making his major league debut.

McDevitt, a native of New York, was never in trouble during the 2-hour, 3-minute game. He allowed only five scratch hits, struck out nine and walked one.

The game was decided in the first inning when Gilliam walked, went to second on Daniels' errant pickoff throw and scampered home on Elmer Valo's double off the right-field wall.

The Brooks added a second run in the third when Hodges' single drove in Gino Cimoli, who had singled and moved to second on an infield out. And that was how it ended, a 2-0 Brooklyn victory.

The game was handled by five umpires—Augie Donatelli, Vic Delmore, Vinnie Smith, Jocko Conlan and Ed Sudol. That fact, in itself, tended to support the universal contention that "everything different happens in Brooklyn," even a five-man umpiring crew.

On the contrary, the five had been working together for several weeks. When veteran umpire Dusty Boggess was incapacitated by illness in midseason, Sudol was acquired from the International League. On Dusty's return to duty, Sudol expected to be returned to the minors. Instead, National League President Warren Giles, impressed with the newcomer's work, assigned him to the Conlan crew. Sudol was stationed on the foul lines, alternating by games between the left- and right-field lines. On September 24, 1957, he was in right field.

Between innings on the lugubrious night, veteran organist Gladys Goodding kept reminding the fans of their impending loss. She exhausted her supply of appropriate tunes, including, "Thanks for the Memories," "After You're Gone," "What Can I Say, Dear, After I Say I'm Sorry," "Say It Ain't So,"

"Memories," "Am I Blue" and "Whatever Will Be, Will Be."

As the game ended, she pounded out "Auld Lang Syne." When she started to play it a second time, however, Tex Rickard, the indomitable public-address announcer, slipped a rock 'n' roll record into the P.A. system.

The players shuffled off the field and the ground crew, faithful to its duties, rolled the tarpaulin over the field. A caretaker dimmed the lights, which had illuminated the field for the first time 19 years earlier, when Larry MacPhail was Brooklyn's major-domo.

Spectators appeared reluctant to leave the tradition-filled ball park. They stayed around, many with moist eyes, just looking and reminiscing. An era was ended. Never again would the community with its peculiar mores rally behind Dem Bums. Without the Dodgers, the borough would become just another segment of the world's foremost megalopolis.

For more than two years, Ebbets Field stood as a silent sentinel for past glories. Occasionally, it was reopened for a soccer match, or a second-class baseball or football game, or a fraternal rally.

On a cold February morning in 1960, a small group gathered at home plate to pay its final respects. A brief program was planned, started by Lucy Monroe, who sang the national anthem.

Al Helfer, former Dodger broadcaster, served as master of ceremonies and introduced the guests, including Lee Allen, the Hall of Fame historian who was given the Ebbets Field key, mounted on red velvet, for display in the Cooperstown, N.Y., shrine.

Nearby stood 70-year-old Otto (Moonie) Miller, who caught for Brooklyn in the first game at Ebbets Field. "You know, Moonie said, "some guys are ashamed to cry at times like these. Not me." And, as he spoke, Otto fought back the tears.

Also on hand was Roy Campanella, the Dodgers' starting catcher in the last game at the park. Campy, confined to a wheelchair because of a 1958 auto accident, was given three treasures from his illustrious career—his uniform with the number 39 across the broad back; his old locker with his name scribbled on a piece of tape at the top, and a chunk of sod from the area where he had crouched in more good times then bad.

Others who acknowledged introductions were Carl Erskine and Ralph Branca, Campy's Brooklyn batterymates in brighter days.

After the ceremonies, the group retired to the park rotunda, where a caterer dispensed grub and gruel to thwart the winter's chill. At a table sat Mrs. James A. Mulvey, daughter of Steve McKeever, former co-owner of the club. Mrs. Mulvey, who still held a 25 percent interest in the Dodgers, was asked about her sentiments.

"When Lou Perini moved the Boston Braves to Milwaukee (in 1953), everybody thought he was a genius," replied Mrs. Mulvey, who was Branca's mother-in-law. "But when Walter O'Malley moves to Los Angeles, everybody jumps on him."

As she expressed her views, a wrecking ball, painted white with stitches to resemble a baseball, was starting its work just a fungo fly away. Workmen on the demolition crew were attired in blue windbreakers, not unlike those worn by the Dodgers. The first objective of the wrecking ball was the visitors' dugout, which yielded without a whimper.

By late April, the double-decked stands were reduced to rubble and it was time to examine the cornerstone that Charles Ebbets had laid in 1912.

To some, the contents of the cornerstone's copper box proved a disappointment. They consisted of personal cards, some coins and baseball publications. Newspapers chronicled the activities of President William Howard Taft, state and city officials, but were soggy from moisture that formed inside the container and fell apart at the touch.

The cornerstone was bought for $600 by a representative of N.L. President Giles, who bequeathed it to the Hall of Fame.

Between 11 a.m. and 1 p.m. on April 24, an auction was conducted for memorabilia from the old park. Bricks, pictures, bases, bats and baseballs, some of them autographed, were sold to the highest bidders. Most items went for less than $5. So that nobody would go home empty-handed, sponsors of the auction gave everyone a flower pot filled with infield soil.

On the site where Charles Ebbets had erected his $750,000 monument, and which was purchased for a fancy seven-digit figure, the Kratter Corp. erected a 1,317-family housing complex for $22.3 million. It was named the Ebbets Field Apartments.

SEPTEMBER 24, 1957								
Pittsburgh	ab	r	h	rbi	Brooklyn	ab	r	h	rbi
Baker, 3b	4	0	0	0	Gilliam, 2b	3	1	0	0
Mejias, rf	4	0	0	0	Cimoli, cf	4	1	1	0
Groat, ss	3	0	1	0	Valo, rf	4	0	1	1
Skinner, lf	4	0	1	0	Hodges, 3b-1b	4	0	1	1
Fondy, 1b	4	0	0	0	Amoros, lf	3	0	0	0
Mazeroski, 2b	3	0	1	0	Gentile, 1b	2	0	0	0
Clemente, cf	3	0	1	0	Reese, 3b	1	0	0	0
Peterson, c	3	0	1	0	Campanella, c	2	0	0	0
Daniels, p	2	0	0	0	Pignatano, c	1	0	0	0
Freese, ph	1	0	0	0	Zimmer, ss	2	0	2	0
Face, p	0	0	0	0	McDevitt, p	1	0	0	0
Totals	31	0	5	0	Totals	27	2	5	2

```
Pittsburgh ............................0  0  0   0  0  0   0  0  0—0
Brooklyn ..............................1  0  1   0  0  0   0  0  x—2
```

Pittsburgh	IP	H	R	ER	BB	SO
Daniels (L)	7	5	2	2	3	2
Face	1	0	0	0	0	2
Brooklyn	IP	H	R	ER	BB	SO
McDevitt (W)	9	5	0	0	1	9

E—Daniels, Reese. DP—Pittsburgh 1, Brooklyn 2. LOB—Pittsburgh 5, Brooklyn 5. 2B—Valo, Zimmer. SH—McDevitt. T—2:03. A—6,702.